"This is an exploration of deviar[...] edge of academic reflexive ethno[...] [...] that would have made Kinsey proud. A Henry Miller-esque porn-memoir. This inquiry treads where most qualitative researchers fear to gaze."
Michael Hemmingson,
Author: Zona Norte: An Auto/ethnography of Desire and Addiction.
Screenwriter: Watermelons

"As the litany of sex 'scandals' to befall political and religious leaders reminds us, there remains a major gulf between how sexual desire is socially regulated and how it animates individual fantasies and practices. Bryan is one of the few who is prepared to both act on his strongest sexual inclinations while having the courage to lay those impulses bare for others to interrogate. Whether titillated or revulsed, all readers must agree that such an exercise is a major contribution to a more honest and reflexive relationship to sexual desire in general."
Jamie Paquin
PhD Candidate, Global Studies
Sophia University
Tokyo

"Guns, sex and racial suicide. And that's just chapter one."
Alon Ziv, Author: Breeding Between the Lines.

"This work is important, revealing and took a lot of courage to write."
Lawrence J. Goss, Amazon Kindle reader.

"This book is worth reading if one would like to understand the psyche of the third world. Maybe one has to have seen where the likes of Bryan grew up and understand the incredible, sheer luck it took to crawl out of such a hole and be able to write a memoir of his experiences. That this author could still access his feelings, write about them and eventually overcome his sex addiction is laudable. As an example of overcoming obstacles in a way that most people in the first world can't even begin to comprehend, it is a shining hope for others. The sexual experiences in the book are simply examples of his addiction, but if one read through that to the sensitivity he shows in understanding the abuses the women went through to be so available to him and other western men, that's what makes it interesting. Much more of the world has these underlying abuses as part of their culture. The first world would be smart to pay more attention to what is being said in this book and others like it, which unwrap the brain and emotions of foreign cultures. Then maybe there would be a little understanding and less bumbling in their foreign relations. Don't read this book for the sexual content, read it for the sensitivity it exhibits to two cultures not your own, but cultures that are valid nonetheless and reflect a large part of the population of the globe."
Carolyn Barrett, Amazon Kindle reader

"Revolutionary!"
Cabel: Myspace reader

BLACK Passenger
YELLOW Cabs:
Of Exile and Excess in Japan

STEFHEN FD BRYAN

KIMAMAPRESS

FIRST KIMAMA PRESS EDITION, JANUARY 2009

© Copyright 2007 by Stefhen fd Bryan

Published in the United States by Kimama Press. Originally published on the Amazon Kindle in the United States, August 2008.

This is a work of NON-fiction. All persons' names and those of some locations have been changed for obvious reasons.

ISBN 978-0-615-26810-1

There is something awe-inspiring in one who has lost all inhibitions, and who exhibits first rate intelligence in the ability to hold two opposing ideas in the mind at the same time and still retain the ability to function. — F. SCOTT FITZGERALD

To Xyon Yasunami

TABLE OF CONTENTS

PREFACE

The body of work now known as *Black Passenger Yellow Cabs* began simply as musings about Japan. Immediately upon my arrival here I was flabbergasted by the paradoxes of the society, and the discrepancy between the West's perception and the actual Japan was blatantly obvious to me. Just two months into my residency on the island my friend Bahar sent me a New York Times article about parasite singles in Japan: the social phenomenon of unmarried women who continue living with their parents, some well into their 40s. "What's up with this?" she titled her e-mail. And indeed such was my initial response upon observing that the overwhelming majority of unmarried women I had encountered in those initial 2 months, were still living with their parents. So after obtaining a used PC some 2 years later, I simply began documenting my observations. However, when I began writing about my own hedonistic experiences and those of my friends, I found it curious that I had not read about the sexual state of affairs which I was experiencing. That was the point at which my musings adopted an erotic tone.

After sending the first 25 pages to a friend in Australia, she strongly advised that I could not possibly write about my sexual predacious behavior in Japan without informing the reader about my history and socialization. Hence the work took on memoir characteristics. Responding to the first 100 pages, another dear friend of mine, a Professor of English at the University of Denver, impressed by the work thus far informed me that I was writing an ethnography with sex. Prior to her ravings about the pages she had read, I was not familiar with the term 'ethnography.' And behold a new genre: the erotic ethnographic memoir was created.

Before sending those pages to my friend at the University of Denver, I had made the first 50 pages available to my mentor, an internationally renowned Author, Japanologist, Futurist and Policy Consultant, just for his personal perusal. It was horrifying to learn that he had forwarded it to his Agent in New York. However to my pleasant surprise a Junior Agent responded positively but shared my mentor's concern that erotica, ethnography and a memoir could not peacefully co-exist in the same body of literature, and suggested that I wrote 3 separate books. ADHD adult that I am, I accepted the compliments but resisted the suggestion to make the genres exclusive of each other, as I thought all three were perfectly harmonious in my work. That's how I conceived it, that's how it flowed organically and that's how I documented it.

— Stefhen Fitzgerald DeCorcia Bryan, Kobe Japan 2008

MAKING OF A RICE KING

Way back in 1989 my then girlfriend was reading Paul Theroux's *My Secret History*, a novel about a man who engaged in unbridled sex with teenaged natives for a few years during his time as a Peace Corps volunteer in various African villages. "Oh my God! You should SO read this book," she screamed. "You're so much like this guy!"

What you are about to read is my own predacious history, a history which is by no means a secret, since I wear my secrets like I do my skeletons: on my sleeves. Kathy knew of my childhood fantasies and the daydreams of unending sexual rampage that consumed my boyhood, and as she told me of the character's exploits my envy of him swelled. *That is exactly what I want to do*, I fantasized.

At the tender age of 8, my little teapot, as it was often referred to in my native Jamaica, would stand at full attention at the sight of those beautiful bare-breasted African women, who periodically adorned the covers of *National Geographic* magazines. Most unfathomable to me – even at that age – was the calmness with which the men appeared to interact with them, the women and their breasts, as though the breasts were invisible. No one was even slightly aroused and the tribesmen all seemed so capable of restraint from attacking those perfectly shaped mammaries 24 hours a day. It's not normal for 8-year-olds to harbor such thoughts, and indeed a normal 8-year-old I was not, as my first sexual experience had been only a year earlier. Technically it was molestation, but not until initiating therapy at 23 was I made to interpret it as such. Such experiences were the norm in the East Kingston Dunkirk ghetto, and all my friends had been *initiated* from their eyes were at knee level. This was simply breaking in the boy child, an encouraged implicit rite of passage into manhood, which in uber-homophobic/machismo Jamaica, at least proved I wasn't gay.

The perpetrators of what many today would consider child sexual abuse were 16 and 17-year-old girls whom I had been fondling as far back as I could recall. Putting my hands up theirs and other girls' and women's skirts was my greeting, a constant embarrassment to both my mother and the unwitting victims. The two girls, the daughter and granddaughter of church sisters, grew tired of my constant sexual harassment since I was about five or six and eventually acquiesced. Upon seeing me bursting through my pants, they were shocked at my unusual size for a 7-year-old and wanted to further investigate what strange equipment this *pickney* (little child) was packing.

After negotiating with them, we came to an agreement.
"Mi wi show oonu it if oonu show mi fi oonu own fus," (I'll show you if you both show me yours first.) I said in an aggressive whisper.
But there was only one problem: the constant presence of adults.

One afternoon we found ourselves in my mother's one room dwelling atop the church on the commune where we resided. There the younger of the two lifted her skirt, exposed her torn baby blue panties as the other watched out for the big people. My 7-year-old anatomy lost control and her 16-year-old eyes widened in disbelief. As I reached to touch her pubic area, she dropped her skirt, slapping my hand away.
"Weh your own deh?" (Where is yours?) she insisted.
So I dropped my pants, exposing my white y-fronts.   Just then, the girl on look-out whispered, "smaddy a come." Quickly pulling up my pants, I began to pretend they were helping me with schoolwork, as they sometimes did. It was a false alarm and when we resumed I renegotiated with her to not only lift her skirt, but to also drop her panties before I fulfilled my end of the deal.

She started by pulling down her underwear, then lifted her skirt as I proceeded to pull down my shorts and fruit of the looms. Their jaws hit the floor as my early childhood teapot enlarged. Touching her transferred her pungent woman's smell onto my little fingers.
"Jezas chrise! A weh a likkle pickney lacka yu get dat deh supm deh from?"
"Mi wouldn' wau meet you when you tun big man, a kill you aggu kill ooman wid dat deh weapon deh." (Jesus Christ! Where did a little child like you get that thing from? I wouldn't want to meet you when you become an adult, you will be killing women with that weapon.)
But I was not oblivious to my apparent anomaly, for as far back as I could recall, around 3 or 4 years old, my mother often lamented on my size as she bathed me.
"I don't know how you are going to find a wife with this teapot," she often worried. "Where did you get this?"

After that day, I stepped up my harassment of both girls and soon they began allowing me further exploration for extended periods, even directing my actions. As I explored their bodies with my little hands, from the looks on their faces, it put them in a whole new universe, as if they were having out of body experiences. It was then that I became utterly fascinated by the act of giving pleasure to women. For days I would refrain from washing my hands, as I savoured that *fragrador*, finding it simultaneously pleasant and repulsive. To this day I still savour the scent of a woman on my fingers. Hence, if ever I am spotted on the train with my fingers in my nostrils, rest assured I'm not digging for gold.

After sustained pestering, I and Madge, the younger of the two, ventured under the house where we would do *the thing*, she had been promising me we'd do.

The houses in our East Kingston ghetto were raised and the space between the floor and the dirt was dark, usually harboring many treacherous insects and sharp debris. Normally, the cellar - home to scorpions and centipedes - was a most terrifying environment, but as the blood rushed from the young upper head to the lower, fear was no longer an issue. I was just too aroused to be scared.

It was there in the dark cellar, upon my baptism in that sea of warm Jell-O, that an addict was born.

It was a most unforgettable and infinitely euphoric experience, especially because prior to that moment my very short existence was consumed with severe daily depression and an overpowering desire to end my life from as early as four years old. Depression and suicidal urges persisted well into adulthood and so did my newfound addiction.

Soon after my debut, I began to lust after my friends' mothers and couldn't stop commenting to my friends, how sexy their mothers were and what I'd like to do with them. But to my surprise, they were interested in my mother – a sure sign that they too had been initiated - which I found utterly repulsive. Invasive thoughts of sex with my own mother would bring me close to vomiting. Typical of our dire socioeconomic conditions, we shared a bed 'til just past my tenth birthday, and when those deviant thoughts invaded my mind, I was repulsed. My mother had no other children, but I always wanted a sister, who I thought would have been my sex toy. And why my friends weren't giving their sisters a regular rogering was a mystery to me. As a young child, I was of course unaware of the possible biological and or sociocultural mechanisms which prevents one from being sexually attracted to immediate family members, thus could not understand why they didn't want to ravage their sisters, when I so desperately did.

After my sexual inauguration my cravings knew no bounds – nor end, which drove me at eight years old to make an attempt with a cat. However, tabby was having none of it and clawed her way out of my grasp.

Marjorie and I had infrequent meetings under the cellar, which started what would turn into a love for sex in risky places. Frightened in ecstasy, we were only too aware of the consequence if caught by the adults: a beating to within seconds of our lives. Among my most memorable sexual experiences was one many years later in a boardroom of an internationally renowned company, on the twenty-sixth floor of their San Francisco headquarters. She, a young Asian-American with her palms against the big glass window overlooking the San Francisco bay, her skirt hiked above her posterior, panty and nylons at her ankles as she pushed her round bottom outward in reception. I can still see my life making fluids dripping from her onto the carpet. Instant termination, a permanently charred reputation and perhaps even minor criminal charges would have been the consequences had we been caught.

My Jamaica was not the Jamaica that beckoned from travel brochures around the world, enticing you to frolic on horseback along heavenly white sand beaches. It was not a place to "come back to," as one of the ad campaigns by the Jamaica Tourist Board inveigled. Instead for me, from my earliest memories at three years old, it was a wretched environment from which to flee, a place of incomprehensible barbarianism, senseless murders and grinding wretched poverty.

The hundred and eighty degree opposite of its tropical nirvana image, my Jamaica was and still is anarchic, peaceless and hopelessly mired in ruthless violence, much of which make the international news only during election time when the violence takes on an added brutality.

The bombarding, omnipresent signs of neglect and decay - burnt out buildings, splintered rooves - wreaked havoc on my delicate sensibilities since I was a toddler. In MY Jamaica it was normal for raw sewage to stagnate or flow through the streets, daily life was a perpetual struggle and just simply getting out of bed was a perilous act, accompanied by a high risk of a fatal encounter with a bullet. Death and symbols thereof decorated the neighborhood. From the frequent funeral excursions, which were among my few enjoyable events, the nightly hails of gunfire, the 'black heart men' who preyed on children, to the daily maggot infested road kills from speeding cars, I had seen more death in the first ten years of my life than I would witness in the next thirty. In this dark, dilapidated, crime-plagued hood, brutal murders, wife beatings and police shootings were regular occurrences, generating in me at an early age, a strong fascination with death. In my neighborhood, the stench of dog carcasses and, tyres set alight to incinerate them were the neighborhood air fresheners. Yet even so, unlike the shanties of West Kingston, my eastern slum was the Beverly Hills of ghettos.

Among my most vivid memories was one night at 9 years old being accosted at gunpoint with a request to
"Identify yuself"! "Woo a yu bloodclaut madda?!"(Who's your fucking mother?)
"Yeow, Yeow Yeow," someone shouted from across the street.
"A sista Andisn yout." (That's sister Anderson's kid.)
"Awoah! Bloodcleet, a sista Adisn yout dis?" (Au fuck, this is sister Anderson's kid?) Turning to me he advised,
"likkle yout, yu fi identify yuself quick y nuh, cau it dread out ya." (You should identify yourself faster, because it's dangerous out here.)

Another indelible memory is that of my friends and I being accompanied to Franklin Town Primary School by Jamaica Defense Force amphibian tanks. By ten years old I had witnessed countless beatings, killings, acid attacks, wife beatings with machetes and two fatal torchings: one simply because he was a supporter of the wrong political party in the wrong neighbourhood, the other because he was alleged to be gay.

Contributing to the already curious state of affairs, my formative years were spent on an all-women church commune, some 50 or 60 of them with whom I shared living quarters, undoing their bras for them and peeping through tiny holes to watch them in the nude.   As a boy, one of only two males and the only male child socialized in this otherwise female environment, I grew to become a lesbian happily trapped in a man's body and from my first sexual experience until recently, sex was the first thing I thought of upon meeting every woman.

In an attempt to protect me from the perils of my surroundings, venturing even to the gate for a glimpse of the outside world was strictly forbidden with severe penal consequences.   Isolated from the community at large and left only to entertain myself with my obsessions in thought, I was far less assertive and street smart than the other boys. Resultantly, I was often the football for the neighborhood bullies, young murderers in the making, who were armed with mini ratchet knives, roaming the streets on their noisy home made wooden skates (scooters) with ball bearings for wheels. Their other pass times included rolling old tyres with sticks and guiding wheels made from garden hoses with hooked, wire clothes hangers. Especially on rainy days, their favourite by far was the game of buode aus (wooden horse), in which pieces of carved fudge sticks were placed in the sewage infested gutters, to simulate horse racing. In my childhood, news to my mother that I was even a spectator of these activities, would have her sending me to the tamarind tree to select the most suitable branches, which she would then promptly introduce to my bare naked bottom.

The first school I attended, the First Holiness Basic School was also on the commune, just 30 seconds' walk from the matchbox mother and I shared. However, my second school, Elletson All Age School, where I skipped the first and second grade, on account of being an advance reader, was located a fifteen minute walk away. Again, in the interest of protecting me from my surroundings, one of the quickest ways to ensure a meeting between the tamarind tree switches and my bare black bumbo, was to exceed the allotted 20 minutes for my return home from school.

Also beginning quite early was my yellow preference. In that impoverished and homicide ravaged cesspool of a neighborhood, there were three Chinese shops which sowed the seeds of my yellow fever, earlier than my first sexual experience. One at the corner of Windward Road and Brays Street, another next door to my tenement and the Ho's shop on Telephone St and Elletson Road. Ho is not a pseudonym, it was their actual name. They drove a brown 1973 Buick Skylark, one of four American cars in my neighborhood. The others, one a 1973 Chevrolet Chevelle which belonged to the bishop who presided over my mother's church and the other two were '69 Pontiac Bonnevilles, both belonging to the near white pastor of an adjacent Pentecostal church.

The Chinese, not even those who lived atop their shops, never ever associated with anyone in the neighborhood. For sure they had good reasons not to. With their straight jet-black hair and upward slanted, hardly opened eyes, they were enigmatic and I frequently anticipated being sent on errands in order to admire and lust after the women. Absent was that round, big bottom and big shapely legs which I was socialized to find sexy. However, developing a love for their long waists and short legs,

I began to entertain a strong desire to introduce them to my boyhood. But that would've been impossible. Never had I even seen one walking in our decrepit neighborhood, let alone talking to a person of African decent, other than their employees during work hours.

"How did they – many of whom who had only marginal command of English – get here, to this neighborhood from China?" I often pondered. Those who did not live atop their shops, perhaps resided in some faraway gated, uptown community, to which they fled at the end of the workday. They did not hang around. To this day, while making the beast with two backs with yellow women, I sometimes imagine myself with one of the shopkeeper's daughters. Apart from wanting to give their daughters a proper introduction at that tender age, the Chinese shop owners quickly became my economic role models.

My enigmatic personality as a child manifested itself in ways other than sexually, and so the pronounced disparity between the races were quite clear to me from as early as five years old. But no one, not the least my mother, who didn't even make it beyond the ninth grade, could provide me with an explanation as to why these outsiders were so economically well endowed. Most people of African decent in Jamaica, including my own family, subsisted then and now in abject poverty, daily *praising the Lord*, for what I was never sure. It was simply beyond my comprehension, why it was necessary to incessantly praise the Lord for "sparing us another day" in that living hell. Meanwhile the yellows were shop owners, driving big American cars and all without ever setting foot in a church.

With no one to answer my early questions on race and those curious socioeconomic arrangements, I was left on my own to develop massive inferiority complexes, believing that African people indeed were cursed, exactly as indoctrination from bible stories about the so called descendants of Cain had taught. That along with my yellow obsession resulted in total and absolute resolve to abandon any idea of perpetuating my race, while at the same time making me resolute and definite about procreating only with yellows. This decision, made by a young child, was later given its proper label of *racial suicide* by Michael Pariser, my best therapist ever.

Parallel to the aforementioned decision was my observation that children of black/yellow or any mixed race combination seemed to show a higher frequency of attractiveness than their pure race counterparts and in my childish view during the early days of my self-hatred, they were especially more attractive than their Negroe parents. Later in my adulthood I discovered that scientist had labeled my early childhood observation as the *hybrid vigor* phenomenon. And though years of therapy, education and travel have evicted my self-hate, the drive to act on the hybrid vigor phenomenon still persists.

SIMONE CHANG

Eleven-year-old Simone Chang was my closest encounter with my yennings at nine. An anomaly in my neighborhood, she suddenly began to appear on my street, walking past my tenement once in the morning, on her way to school and again in the evening. Petite with a wide long braid down the middle of her back to her buttocks, she wore a white skirt, white blouse and a red and white plaid tie, the uniform of the downtown school Holy Trinity.

"But what would this Chinese girl be doing in my cesspit of a neighborhood, attending a public junior secondary school?"
"Did her Beverly Hills or Cherry Gardens parents go bankrupt and if so, why would she end up here in Dunkirk, in the ghetto?"

Everyday at around three o' clock, countenance of trauma, fear and wretched despondence, eyes fixated on the pothole infested road beneath her, braving an onslaught of harassment from the local ragamuffins from number 4 Wild Street, she meandered past my yard. And everyday, whenever I could, I ran to my wall to watch the girl of my fantasies go by. Ugly, was among the many renowned neighborhood terrorists from the aforementioned thug house diagonally across from me. A troglodyte with tribal mark-like telephone slashes adorning his face, his was a character crass and uncouth enough to curdle stone. Scarcely was there a day when Simone could walk by on her way home without the assault of his rough, coarse drawl.

"Pssssssttt, aaay Chinie girl, Ms Chin, come 'ear nuh."
To which Ms Icy, pot black, loud, lewd and quarrelsome would intervene on Simone's behalf.
"Weh yu nu lef di likkle girl alone? Yu nuh si se shi a likkle pickney a guh a school? "Yu tink shi cyan tek big man hood?" (Why don't you leave the little girl be? Can't you see she's a child going to school?)
To which Ugly would respond expressing intentions, not quite suitable for print.
"MI SE FI LEF HAR!" (I SAID TO LEAVE HER BE.)

Subsisting among the rats and cockroaches, my and my mother's hand me down shoes - which we were lucky to have - were in constant need of repairs. On one occasion my mother instructed me to go to the cobbler up the street, as opposed to our usual cobbler around Bryden street, as there had been some fatal shootings in the aqueduct near there. Upon entering the new cobbler's yard, lo and behold, there was my fantasy girl hanging her laundry on the line.

"Is in 'ere suh yu live," (So this is where you live.) I said to her, as though solving the puzzle of a lifetime.

"Why?" she asked, with the same melancholic face, focused on the bed spread she was hanging on the line.

"Jus' choo mi always si yu a walk dung a Wild Street," (Just because I always saw you walking down Wild Street.) I responded with the confidence of an amoeba. On my return home, floating several feet off the ground, I lighted up on a scheme to run errands to the cobbler for all the church sisters on the commune.

As it turned out, Simone was only half-Chinese, which answered my question about why she had ended up amongst us in the war zone. Whichever way I tried to imagine it, in my conclusion her ending up on Wild Street could have been attributed only to her *cursed* half. No full-blooded Chinese would be living in this hell hole without some connection to business. In the ensuing months we got to know each other and discovered our shared commonalities. Like me, she was ruled by a punitive, Christian zealot for a guardian, difference being mine was my mother whereas hers, her *aunt* wasn't even related to her. After being abandoned by her Taiwanese father, her mother sent her and her younger sister from the countryside to live with *Aunt*, an over bearing Seventh-day Adventist. We were both miserable and depressed about our plight in that wretched environment, but as if that weren't enough, she later revealed to me during our adult years that among her routine chores, were unspeakable *manual labor* to her father's brother since she was about nine years old.

Once while talking to her on her verandah, on a rare occasion with no adults around, the chance to play doctor arose. Reminiscing about that day some fifteen years later, she tried to describe the euphoria of that utterly novel experience when she was 12 and I 10 years old.

"I had never ever felt anything like that," she said.

"I just can't explain how good it felt, it was like heaven. I remembered that more than my first sexual experience."

That rare chance to make mischief never again availed itself, as we were constantly surrounded by adults and she was always under house arrest. But nine years later, four years after I had emigrated from the island, I returned for a visit and accidentally ran into her as she turned from Wild Street to Little Telephone Street, wearing oversized curlers in her hair and a gleaming ear to ear smile. Two days later, like wild animals on Wild Street, we shredded the fitted sheet on what was my bed in my mother's two room dwelling. With ten years of pent up desire, I unleashed in her miles and litres in an orgas-ma-fest, hoping to leave her pregnant, so that I could have gained *respect* among my peers upon returning to the States, by claiming to have sired a child. Only four years removed from Jamaica, I had not been rid of the socialization which taught me that real men made children and abandoned them, while weak men took care of the children that real men made. But as probability would have it, no sperm met her egg, at least not until she later emigrated to America, after I embarked upon a business arrangement to get her there. Unfortunately in the end she was only half Chinese, not enough to satisfy my preference and our relationship became mired in ensuing baby mama drama.

PRELUDE TO JAPAN

After a heart wrenching separation from Korean-American Anne Moo Young, I arrived in Japan in April of 2001 for a fresh new start, a rebirth of unimaginable proportions. Anne and I had been dating for about a year, three months of which were spent in cohabitation. Overdosed on sex appeal, she was a sexual inferno, with freak oozing from every pore. Inseparable, we did almost every thing in tandem, even commuted to and from work together. Anne, a short, nubile 24-year-old with a captivatingly pretty face had breasts that were abnormally sized for a woman of her height, and race. They were like two watermelons on a slight downhill race. Upon meeting her for the first time in a shopping mall in Orange County, I stood at full attention throughout our entire conversation and fortunately upon my first visit to her apartment, she was quite permissive. Had she not been, I would have been rotting in a penitentiary as we speak, as I pounced on her like a desperate crack fiend the minute she opened the door. Throughout our relationship she would always refer to the pouncing in jest. From the first hit it was clear that addiction was inevitable. Hence, with inexplicable, out of this world chemistry, I fell hard and we moved in together shortly after meeting.

Fruit fairy living with a gay roommate, with whom she partied heavily in West Hollywood, Anne loved ecstasy and cocaine. Hailing from the typically oppressive Korean-American family, she was unceasingly insecure about her physical appearance and extremely uncomfortable around straight men, a clear signal of fire in the hole. All indicators pointed to a high probability of some sexual trauma during her childhood. On the surface she appeared to relish in her ability to bring men to their knees, but in private, twice the victim of date rape drugs at parties at her alma mater USC, Anne confided in me that she hated that the only thing men saw in, on, around or about her was sex.

"I'm short, pretty and all tits. The only thing men wanna do is fuck me. I hate that," she said, sometimes tears streaming down her burgundy cheeks.

The cocaine and ecstasy consumption, the heavy drinking and partying, *"she's masking something,"* I thought. Fruit fairy, no straight male friends, short, self-perceived overweight with humongous breasts, especially for a Korean woman, *"she hates herself,"* I concluded. *"Something definitely happened to her in her childhood, she might even be borderline,"* I analyzed. After all, I knew her type very well. They are the most exciting women on the planet. Those borderline personality disordered women are without question the pinnacle of sexual nirvana. Normal women fail to deliver the kind of sexual excitement that borderline women can, who until recently, were the only women to whom I was attracted.

Getting to know her, she revealed to me that indeed - like all freaks, all the sex addicts with whom I have been - she too had been constantly molested by a family friend since five.   Since that revelation I had begun to encourage her to seek therapy and after convincing her of my unconditional and unending support, she had finally heeded my advice. But for the first time, Anne and I would have to separate. Charged with domestic abuse and vandalism for destroying (Simone Chang's) my daughter's mother's cell phone in post OJ Simpson California, I was sentenced to participate in a month long work furlough program in San Francisco. In her emotional amnesia Anne freaked out, convinced that I had abandoned her. Though only thirty days, the separation was unbearable for her and during that time she met someone else at the supermarket, abruptly ended the relationship and I became an instant enemy. It was as though we had never even known each other, let alone made plans for a future together. Our previous Siamese-like state, attached especially at the lips and genitalia, was a fugitive from her memory.

"You just up and left me," she kept repeating. "What was I supposed to do?"

In the first week of our separation I shed ten pounds, wept like Jesus for three months, and was forced to visit the cardiologist for crippling and debilitating chest pains. Making matters worse, it was the Christmas season and I was a mess. I made the bold move of unloading even on total strangers, sometimes comically. And thanks to their support and that of a few friends, the pain became manageable.

Aware that my yellow desire was now carved in diamond and that it would be impossible for me to become interested in anyone non yellow, I packed up and moved to Japan, where I could act on my extreme preference and get over my lost love, especially our   plans to get married and move to

Monterey. I couldn't have made a better move. This complete change of environment and what was to follow, was the perfect prescription.

JAPAN: YEAR ONE

Wednesday, April 18th 2001. Unlike many of my Western contemporaries in Japan, I conducted no research about my future home prior to my arrival and engaged in no preparations. However, upon arrival, I soon discovered that nothing could have prepared me for this Fantasy Island. Immediately besotted by its physical beauty, Japan struck me as an infinitely more beautiful version of my native Jamaica, meets England where I had spent some time.

My introduction to the lay of the land occurred in a very small rural town in the Kansai region, about a hundred miles from Osaka. Immediately I was surrounded by the women of my extreme preference, surreal to say the least. That unforgettable Wednesday of my arrival coincided with a weekly house party held by one of the teachers from the school where I was to commence teaching. In attendance were many of the local students, mostly women who numbered about fifteen, in the presence of about five or six men. I was the first person of African decent to descend on this small town and the very first that many of the natives were beholding in the flesh. Months later one of the girls told me in glee, she was beside herself when I walked in the room, as she had been a hip hop fan in this Hicksville for many years, constantly wondering what it would be like to meet an African-American. She later became my first stalker in Japan.

Ayumi was what I later came to label an *untouchable* in Japan; 26, about a hundred and twenty pounds, overweight by Japanese standards and divorced with two children. Though we had not been intimate, not even a kiss, many mornings found her in her car, dictionary in hand waiting for me to emerge from my apartment in order to negotiate with me to be her boyfriend, occasionally even soliciting the assistance of perhaps her only friend with marginal English skills.

Before long I realized that being African-American or Jamaican in these parts was akin to being some kind of film star, and having been born in Jamaica and lived in America, I had a double advantage, which I milked to the hilt. For the Japanese girls who idolized and fetishized Beenie Man and Bob Marley, I was Jamaican and for those who worshipped JZ, I was an African-American, though the latter sometimes created discomfort as hip hopper I was not. And when told by Japanese girls that I bore a strong resemblance to Jo, they were dismayed at my ignorance about the artist. The only Jo(e) I knew was my favourite uncle Joe who died when I was ten.

Present at the party was one of the managers of the language school which had sponsored me to Japan. With her otherworldly beauty, barely opened upturned eyes, small dainty concave nose and creamy tofu skin, she was unerringly my type. It was love and lust at first sight and unbeknownst to silly me, the feeling was mutual. I came to learn that my specialized attraction is to Manchurian women. Small concave noses with a low nose bridge, small upturned eyes with the epicanthic fold and milky skin. That really rang my bell, ever since I was a child. Her general responsibilities were to ensure my smooth transition to this small town, so we spent much time together as she introduced me to Japanese culture.

In addition to her Louis Vuitton handbag and other name brand items, she wore me like jewelry, flaunting me to everyone. Though 23 years old, Miyuki bubbled with the innocence of a juvenile, a trait which, having been new to Japan, I found quite sexy and arousing. Little did I know that in a few short years, I would become sickened by that general characteristic among Japanese women. Within two weeks we were all over each other, necking and fondling her baldness in her Honda Life and when she finally visited my apartment, her milky shaven beauty was a sight to behold. Her shoulders were ever so slightly wider than her hips but, her petite frame and shaven heaven mesmerized me. As to her shaven venus mound, that I found a bit uncomfortable, as it reminded me of my prepubescent days when I would try it on with little prepubescent girls. Their baldness and absence of breasts disgusted me and since my introduction to sex at seven, until my mid-twenties, I had always preferred older women. However things changed and I found myself, not only being attracted to younger women, but also attracting them the older I got.

Miyuki reminded me of school girls, the kinds I frequently saw riding their bicycles in their ultra-mini uniforms upon my arrival in Japan. And as I tasted her and fondled her small but perfectly shaped breasts, my imagination would momentarily place her on a bicycle in school uniform.

"I don't want to have sex as yet. I want to get to know you first," she said, to which I was respectful. After releasing my tension all over her pearly skin, she would shower me with profuse apologies for having caused me to resort to what she thought was such a shameful act. Instantly madly in love, I refrained from consummating the relationship and suspended my usual predatory tendencies, which I later lived to regret. This sudden immersion in Eden was unbelievable, making out and receiving fellatio from my superior, the manager of the school where I would be teaching was nothing short of fantasy. But my roommate who had arrived a year earlier, assured me, "You ain't seen nothing yet, in Japan, nothing is off limits."

Shortly after, another manager from a different location was introduced to me, butt ugly with apple catchers for teeth, which were the norm in the countryside. However, hers was a curvaceous physique of amazement and within only a month after my arrival she introduced me to the love hotel scene and gave me my first piece along with my first venereal disease in Japan: the ubiquitous Chlamydia. One thing I quickly realized in that rural town, was that my limitation to women who spoke only English, was a fairly small pool, but no hindrance to regular action. However, more disturbing than that was my observation that it was the less attractive women who spoke English. The super babes, my type, couldn't even recite the alphabet. Especially in the countryside, there was an inverse relation between their English abilities and their level of unattractiveness.

This second manager was near fluent, with teeth of varying shades of yellow-brown, which seemed like rusted barbed wire protruding from her crooked, asymmetrical face. But man, that bod! Later I discovered that she had given my roommate, other teachers and at least one American manager the same welcoming treatment, minus the Chlamydia because they went in strapped. Three or four times a week as soon as the last student vacated, she and I transformed the school she managed into our own love ho, going buck wild leaving body fluids everywhere, like dogs urinating to mark territory. I couldn't help but pity her, as it was clear her self-confidence was on the soles of her feet, a trait of promiscuous women in the West and indeed a common trait of many Japanese women.
"I was born in a car," she revealed. "My mother was on the way to the hospital," solving the mystery to why her face was so asymmetrical and twisted.

Shortly after my arrival, the weekly school party was relocated to my apartment owing to the departure of the previous host, and every

Wednesday night an onslaught of beautiful, eligible female students descended on my living room.

Rapidly the collection of sex partners grew and soon it became impossible to conceal my whoring character in this small town. Inevitably, the first manager discovered this and decided that she wanted nothing more to do with me intimately, a painful decision magnified by conflicting forces within. On one hand I loved her though on the other, I was a sex addict with uncontrollable yellow cravings in yellow candy land with a bottomless supply of yellow pleasure. Especially difficult was the fact that we had to continue working together for a year, which required daily preparedness for pain.

Though my whoring soared to new heights, she was one who got away, the one I really wanted. My fragile male ego was trampled and I to this day regret not introducing her to the dark side. She would've been hooked, unable to let go, like the mass of fans which were accumulating. They say once you go black, you never go back. But more accurately, once you go black, you always, go back.....for more.   But I was new to Japan, not knowing then what I now know about the psyche of Japanese women. Word got around fast in that small town and pretty soon it was clear that I had to expand beyond the immediate community. The community harem was growing and within three months, I had a steady rotation of seven women, a predictable attrition rate, most of them my students, each with their allotted time.   I was living my fantasy, I was living everyman's fantasy, at least every sex addicted, yellow fever afflicted man's fantasy, totally immersed in a limitless sea of yellow women.

MOTHER AND AI

Among my roomie's many private students, were a royally attractive 50-year-old woman and her 22-year-old daughter, who graced our apartment twice a week for one-hour lessons. Planning a trip to Kyushu he requested my substitution, which I initially resisted, possessing no interest in teaching outside of the language school. My personal time was for rampant sex and naught else. But the mother was a very nubile and beautiful woman, for whom I had been lusting at the gym since my arrival. I had been drooling at her in her swim suit some four times a week, befuddled at how delicious she looked, especially for fifty. Frequently she invited me to join her in the pool which I always declined, as there would have been no way to conceal my leftward pointing excitement. Intent on focusing my attention on her daughter, to whom I had no attraction, I agreed to teach them. But to my dismay, upon Peter's return from his trip they decided that they had no desire to return to him and insisted that I continued being their teacher. Again I protested, but upon making the acquaintance of her older daughter, my protest was transformed to retarded, slobbering, speechless babble.

Ai was stunning, a younger version of her mother, nubile, wide child-bearing hips, small waist and extremely steatopygic. Spontaneously I stood at full attention upon seeing her, especially in my favourite bob hairstyle. Upturned and unusually big, her almond eyes glistened and unlike many girls in the countryside, her snow-white teeth were perfectly aligned. Though she spoke as much English as a dolphin, we quickly became acquainted using whatever means of communication possible, including her amazing drawing skills which came in handy, as she expressed most of her ideas in detailed pictures.   During her debut at my apartment, I attempted to cook for her, but she insisted on helping and I acquiesced so that I could lust after her while she stood in front of the stove. Giggling in shyness, she tried to turn my head away from staring at her, as never before had she been admired or more accurately, visually defrocked in such a manner. With my tongue on the saliva drenched floor, I strolled over to her and held her from behind, turned her around and began kissing her, sometimes polishing her pearl white teeth with my tongue. I begged her

27

to remove her pants and after moments of shy resistance, she allowed me. Then I requested that she simply stand away from me so I could engage in a visual feast. But again, in her chronic shyness she wanted to dim the lights, but I pleaded with her to keep them on as I removed my stretched, starched limb, stroking it as I admired her.

This was her first experience with a foreigner. She wanted to touch it, but I refused her and insisted that she stand in position, as I watered the floor. Almost instantly I blew off and she was taken aback by the large quantity, as she dashed for some tissues. Even after arrival, I remained in active mode with no refractory period. So I lead her into my room and immediately removed her bikini. Her overgrowth, through which I waded, concealed surprisingly black lips which I began to devour whilst playing with her breasts. For a full hour I feasted on her. Though her overgrowth was well deserving of a trim, I was preoccupied with introducing her to the foreign object for an entirely new cultural experience, even if it meant ingesting a few strands of hair. After driving her crazy with my mouth, I entered and as with most Japanese women thus far it was like a camel passing through a needle's eye.

"Mecha dekaii," (very big,) she responded. But she was a trooper, receiving me with minimum protest. I asked her in my prehistoric Japanese and sign language what she liked in bed and what would stimulate her arrival, but to my disappointment, at 26 years old, she had never experienced an orgasm but said she liked everything, especially if I were enjoying it. My hardened negritude was up to her belly button where she pointed, indicating that's where it felt like it was. Turning her around exposing her dark lips further heightened my arousal, but again like most Japanese women, she was unable to engage in proper dorsal reception. So I retreated and relieved myself, while planting my lips on her jet black lower lips.

Weeks later, Ai's mother proposed the unthinkable; that I marry Ai and give her three grandchildren. I was beside myself and found her request impossible to grasp. After many years living in the States, a far more liberal society, it was unfathomable that some white woman in Walnut Creek, California would literally offer me her lily-white daughter and request three mulatto (I know it's politically incorrect) grandchildren. But here I was in Japan, in xenophobic, conservative and racist Japan, where a mother is encouraging me, not just to marry her daughter, but to produce children with her. Japan is all of the aforementioned, and a country of astounding paradoxes. Not just normal oxymorons, but contradictions which will cause one to do triple and quadruple takes.

In Japan, one is bombarded everyday with hyper-etiquette, but in contrast, especially recently it seems that every week or so, one hears about heinous crimes committed on 7-year-olds, sometimes by 11-year-olds. Reports of matricide frequent the newspapers in this tranquil country. Nippon is the land of the bullet train, but no central heating in one's home. Here in Kobe, an international port city which was hit by a devastating earthquake in 1995, I heat my modern apartment with kerosene heaters, which every winter pins me between two choices: death from hypothermia or asphyxiation. There are hi-tech 3G cell phones with global positioning navigation systems, but classrooms in elementary schools use the same nauseating kerosene heaters I use in my apartment and there were no heaters or air conditioners in the junior high and high schools where I taught. And these are but a few of the numerous paradoxes.

As marriage was on my mind upon initially arriving, Ai quickly became a potential candidate. My objective was for her to attend a university, a move discouraged by her parents before my arrival, as even in these modern times in Japan, though many women are indeed attending universities, it is more likely that parents will encourage their sons to obtain a tertiary education, while encouraging their daughters to stop at two years. Such is the case especially in the countryside. She had already attended a two-year college and was now working in retail but - even whore that I am - a paradox in my character is that I'm also a feminist. And as such I firmly believe women should be educated to the highest possible level, especially one who I would make a life partner. However, neither Ai nor her mother could understand my alien ideology. Her mother thought me loftily ambitious and that I should not worry about money, as they had had enough, just as long as we produced her three grandchildren.

While waiting for Ai at her home one afternoon, the strangest thing occurred. She had gone to work unexpectedly but was due home in a couple hours. Having no intention of waiting for her I began to bid my good-byes, but her mother in typical Japanese hospitality insisted on preparing me a meal at least. While we sat at the kotatsu - a small low table with an electric heater mounted on the underside - she placed her hand on me.
"Okii desu ne?" (It's big isn't it?)
"Well," I thought, *"if it weren't big before, it's definitely big now."*
But I couldn't say that in Japanese. Instead, I immediately unzipped my pants and allowed her to touch it as it grew before her very eyes.
"It's too big," she said.
Then I placed my palms to her breasts, caressing them beneath her

blouse, while kissing her lips. Nervous, lips quivering, she reciprocated awkwardly by slightly opening her mouth, then as she started trembling, I expertly undid her bra and raised her blouse to reveal her still perfect, beautifully shaped mount Fujis, hardly a wrinkle in sight. Like many Japanese women her age, she was well preserved and when I placed my mouth on her nipple she gasped, grew more nervous and began to tell me in her skeletal English that, she had not had sex in twenty years. Hadn't even been touched, not even a hug since 1982.

In the West, no sex is grounds for divorce and the only time I had heard any such tale of a sexless marriage, was from a 53-year-old African-American woman in Southern California. Sexy and vivacious like Ai's mother, Dorothy looked about forty, with a most beautiful crown of silver hair. Difference being, her husband had been ill for fifteen years, but we met and on a few occasions fulfilled her needs. However, shortly thereafter, having been a Christian and very active in the church, she was eventually consumed by guilt and overpowered by the shame she thought would have followed had her 30-year-old daughter discovered her affair, especially with a man her daughter's age.

In Dorothy's case, sexless for fifteen years but maintaining the marriage was quite understandable. But in Ai's mother's case no sex for twenty years while still married to a physically functional man was beyond my grasp especially with her being so show stoppingly libidinous. New to Japan, I had not yet learned of the tendency in marriages here to be sexless, an incredible state of affairs that sets in usually after the obligation of producing the first or second offspring had been fulfilled.

Ai's mother told me her husband for the last umpteen years returned home drunk in the wee hours of the morning from work, only to be up at six to do it all over again. Indeed this experience was echoed by most of my married female students. Japanese society, consequently most Japanese men unfortunately, still subscribe to the notion that the corporation is family, benevolent in nature and therefore of greater significance than real family. The motto might as well be: Until death do we work. The Japanese, whose workforce consists overwhelmingly of men, toil inefficiently long hours. Thirteen hours a day, six days a week is the norm and 16-hour days, seven days a week is not uncommon. In addition, the amount of unpaid overtime is criminal. So prevalent is death from overwork in Japan, *karoshi* is a dedicated word in the language to describe death through that medium. Until recently, Japanese was the only language with a word specifically for dieing of overwork. However, the Koreans, with a workforce even more inefficient and grueling than that of the Japanese, have since adopted the word to their vernacular. A group of attorneys organized in 1990 to monitor karoshi in Japan, concluded that up to 2004, karoshi annually takes the lives of over ten thousand people, many literally at their desks clutching their keyboards.

Among those startling statistics is a former student of mine who worked for a firm where I taught. Only 27 years old at expiration, he had started his death career as company slave at 22, where since his debut there, he had worked 16-hour days until his exit by heart attack. A prime example of Japan's many paradoxes is a 2004 Office of Economic Development report that Japan had the eleventh most efficient workforce in the world, behind Thailand and Italy. Italy! Who could have a more inefficient workforce than Italy? In Italy, if you mailed a letter to your neighbour just one floor below you, it may take two weeks to arrive, maybe even longer if it's being mailed to an upstairs neighbor. More recently, according to a 2006 Japan productivity centre's report, after adjustments for price differences, among the 30 member OECD countries, Japan ranked 19th in labor productivity in 2004. Contrary to the West's perception of Japan as a high-tech haven, is the fact that Japan's IT investment grew only 90% between 1995 and 2004, in comparison to over 300% respectively in Britain and the United States during the same period.

In stark opposition to the West's image of Japan, corporations the likes of Toyota and Canon represent a precious small percentage of Japanese firms which are operated efficiently. Westerners arriving here are easily bedazzled by advanced cell phones and heated toilets with built-in bidets, and presume that all of Japan is more technologically advanced than the West. However the fact is much of Japan's application of technology appears to be for gadgetry as opposed to creating significant improvements in quality of life, or bringing efficiency to the workplace. In the words of Darren Huston, president of Microsoft Japan, "There is a tremendous opportunity to increase worker productivity in Japan with Information Technology." Huston noted in July 2007 that many Japanese companies "rely on piecemeal collections of personal computers and often have only one or no central server." Weeks later the Japanese government was moved to launch a task force to boost labor productivity, focusing on efficiency through Information Technology.

Which begs the question, why do the Japanese work themselves to the grave, or more accurately, to the crematorium? The answer lies in their socialization. Whereas organisms, especially humans and especially

Western humans seek to maximize pleasure and minimize pain, the Japanese from thousands of years of programming seek to do the opposite, cultural tendencies on which businesses and political leaders capitalize.

During the Manchurian war in the 1930s, the government embarked on a campaign to gain the support of the masses, purporting benevolent family status. Corporations seized on this ideology after the war and the absurd idea of lifetime employment was born. Japanese leaders after World War II, set annual GDP goals and implored the nationals to persevere at all costs to meet these goals. Among the many casualties of this policy was sex within matrimony.

A study by the United Nations in 2002 found that Japanese couples had sex an average of 36 times per year, while the American average was a hundred and ten times per year. More recently, the 2005 Durex Sexual Wellbeing Global survey revealed that the Japanese were the world's least amorous, coming, pun intended, dead last at an average 45 times a year. Greece was the busiest, at 138 times a year. And when they do get *busy*, a June 2008 Durex survey which questioned 26,000 participants in 26 countries, revealed that the average Japanese was among the least likely to achieve orgasm. When it comes to the ultra-euphoric act of *arrival*, only 27% of Japanese experience such fortune. This compared dismally to 66% of the Spanish, Mexicans and South Africans, who were most likely to climax during every sexual act. Only the Chinese and Hong Kongese – both at 24% - had a lower propensity for orgasms than the Japanese. The survey continues, while 43% of Japan's males almost always achieve orgasm, only 11% of females do.

Japan is an island of sexually frustrated women, especially those in middle-age, waiting to be pleasured by foreigners the likes of present company. Fact is that the institution of marriage equals gross neglect for women in general in Japan, whether young, old or middle-aged. Common knowledge in the West is that women are in their sexual peak toward middle-age, as opposed to men, who peak in our late teens to twenties. However, in Japan, sex starved middle-aged women are neglected in vast numbers, the wealthier the more neglected, as their husbands are more dedicated to their companies. The Japanese male is defenseless against his company's demands to separate him from his family, by relocating him domesticly or overseas.

Tanshinfuni, the practice of companies relocating the husband from his family, though unimaginable in the West is a Japanese norm. In many cases such arrangement can continue for years or indefinitely, though in less painful cases the man returns home only on weekends but stays in the company dormitory during the week. Which of course leaves their wives wide open – pardon the pun - to foreign men. Again, present company included. On many occasions the socially castrated Japanese husband knows his wife is getting pleasured by an outsider, but chooses to ignore it, in some cases supporting it. In the West this would be perceived as ceding one's manhood, but here in Japan many of the perceptions of manhood and masculinity runs counter to the Western notion of what it is to be a man.

Western men equate manliness with the ability to please one's wife and indeed, Western women expect to be pleasured. In fact, less than stellar performance on the man's part, especially if he is Jamaican or African-American would result in ridicule and serious bad mouthing within the community. On the other hand, it seems manliness is defined in Japan by the ability to neglect one's wife, which leaves a staggering amount of women starving for attention. According to an article entitled, The spawning grounds of the Japanese Rapists of Nanking, written by Stanley Rosenman, which appeared in the Journal of Psychohistory, among all civilized countries, Japan has the highest rate of mother son incest, a further testament to the widespread and sheer sexual frustration of many married Japanese women.

During their sons' periods of stress, especially during Japan's examination hell, it is documented that some mothers are even known to stimulate their sons to orgasm, or engage in sexual activities with them under the pretense of easing their sons' tension.   As a result, *mazacom* or mother complex, where a man is excessively attached to his mother - even during marriage - is a staple in the Japanese vernacular.   This is one of the many gross dysfunctions in Japanese society packaged under the auspices of culture.   Of course, being the equal-opportunity-yellow-worshipping sex addict that I was, I was only too happy to do my duty and come to the rescue of as many of these young and middle-aged women as I could.

MOTHER'S ARRIVAL

I had quickly brought Ai's mother to orgasm twice with my fingers and it seemed she came in litres, releasing twenty years of pent up frustration. But her shrubbery, like that of a great majority of Japanese women with whom I've been, was unkept and over grown. Requesting the scissors, I assumed the position of forest ranger, clearing the jungle till I could see the valley in which I would descend. Japanese women, at least the ones with whom I've had biblical encounters, just simply allow the hedge to grow uncontrollably, which never failed to force my hand at gardening. After trimming her, she remained in the bathroom to wash off the clippings and I returned to the living room waiting for her to emerge. Sparsely clad in white high-waist panties with red flower prints, the same kind the church sisters wore during my childhood, a minimal amount of cellulite dimpled her otherwise firm athletic thighs. Some cellulite arouses me, no doubt the result of peeking at the church sisters in the nude. My growth mesmerized her and she explored my anatomy in disbelief.

"Muri it won't fit," she exclaimed, so I invited her instead to insert me orally. After some coaxing, she succeeded in accepting this completely new and frightening experience, a rebirth of sorts at fifty. Sucking on her index finger, I began to demonstrate to her how I wanted it done, but she choked on her first attempt with only half the foreign object in her mouth hitting her throat. Raising her head, I interrupted her. I don't like fellatio anyway, much prefer cunnilingus and once I partook of her southern cuisine while fondling her at the same time, her levies broke again almost immediately.

Viscous in lipless beauty, though lubricious, entrance required gentleness and numerous attempts, at times feeling as though my foreskin was being pulled back to my belly button. As she grimaced and spoke in unrecognizable Japanese, I expanded and liberated her for full accommodation.
"Itakimochii." (Hurts but it feels good.)
"Inside dame desu, don't come inside."

And for a moment I imagined the catastrophe of this woman in this small rural town, whose daughter with whom I am intimately involved, being pregnant with my child. As usual, before arrival, I withdrew the vehicle, stimulated it manually to release its contents on her. Not trusting myself to withdraw in time, that was a common practice of mine. Her chest and face covered with me, "It looks like natto," she responded, a popular Japanese health food of fermented soy beans, with the appearance of crunchy peanut butter, slimy and with the odor of dirty socks. After seven years in Japan, I have yet to muster the courage required to even bring it within a mile of my face, let alone ingest it.

Suddenly aware of the insanity with which she was just afflicted, she sprang from her momentary lapse of reason and hastened me to get dress, as Ai would be returning soon. Though initially her movements were restricted, in the ensuing months she gradually learned to relax and enjoy her new found freedom, by far surpassing her daughter's pleasure giving. Twice Ai's age, she was immeasurably more enjoyable, especially being orgasmic, both internally and externally, which lead to our continued covert intimate escapades even after I had moved from the countryside, where upon periodic returns to visit Ai, I had to also perform my expected duties to her mother.

MEGU

Megu a farmer's wife, was my second married woman in Japan. Baring a strong resemblance to Meg Ryan, mother of two she was already neglected at the tender age of 32. I relished in the fact that she was the first manager's best friend, the same manager who had sworn left and right that her friend Meg had no interest in me, as she was not the kind of girl to cheat on her husband. So I turned her out not only for my own enjoyment, but also to make a point to the first manager that, it matters not what kind of girl you are if your needs are not being met at home, then they will be met abroad. Miyuki was devastated and my objective was met, which gave me relief in some sick immature fashion.

A regular at our weekly parties, one Wednesday night Megu vacated the premises with everyone, but soon called me to ask if everyone had left and if she could return. Upon returning, she made it clear that she couldn't stay for long, as her husband would get angry if she returned home too late. So we went to my room for a quick introduction. She was a smoker which ensured brevity in our encounter. Upon removing her jeans, the crotch of her panties was already soaked in anticipation. I wanted to wrap my mouth around her breasts but she just wanted my invasion, so rolling on the magnum 500 I proceeded without further hesitation. With every inch, she gasped with mouth wide open, but she managed a full reception as I gyrated, sometimes imagining she was her friend the manager, as that was the closest I would get to the one that slipped away. Blast off was delayed on account of my being strapped, so I positioned her on top so she could ride to her destination. Gently I caressed her nipples but she demanded harsher, rougher treatment, as she rode into a trance. For a moment I thought her nipples would fall off in my hands, as she gyrated violently attempting to sever me inside her.

"Iku, iku!" Japanese women say they are going instead of coming, cultural difference I guess. In that small town, Meg and I never had seconds and she grieved every time we saw each other, lamenting over being married with two children and unable to pursue anything further with me.

MAYUMI

Miki Ando look-alike, Mayumi's dilemma was typical among many Japanese women: Having been in a fruitless seven-year relationship from 23 years old, she was devastated by the heart wrenching separation at 30. For women in the West, that is nothing over which to lose sleep. However, for Japanese women, such an event is a catastrophe. In fact, three years later Mayumi had a nervous breakdown obsessing over the reality of being unmarried without prospects at 33 and was admitted to hospital for six months. Our meeting was accidental. Her teacher for her dyadic class, for which I substituted, was ill and though it was a class setting, it was pretty much a preliminary interview before a first date. Being very sensitive to sexual harassment issues and not wanting to overstep any boundaries, I made no advances to her after the class and showed no interest. After all, I was coming from America where at least trying to procure sexual favours from students and especially on the premises of the school, could land you a prime position in the unemployment line and maybe even in court. But while we were bidding our good-byes, the manager loudly suggested that we should go out on a date. And so Mayuchan was introduced to the dark side.

Mayumi was beautiful with perfect curvature and proportions, though had she not inherited her father's slightly convex nose, which made her face less ravaging than her mother's, we would most certainly have been married.   Like her mother, Mayu was covered with the porcelain complexion I fetishize. Like many Japanese women she too was a walking department store mannequin, wearing every name brand possible and like most women in that small town – and all throughout Japan - her teeth were a repulsive sight to behold. One of the very first things I brought to her attention was the paradox between wearing every piece of garment from Vogue magazine, while having a crocodile smile. My Western mind could not grasp the incompatibility of a Prada handbag accessorized by rusted barbed wire teeth. And much to my surprise, she quickly withdrew 600,000 yen ($5,500) from the bank and embarked on a journey to improved dental care through orthodontics.

Initially there was protest from her friends and parents, telling her there was no need and that it's a waste of money. However, after two years and beautifully aligned teeth, they understood the objective. Just three weeks after we met, perhaps feeling the pressure of being unmarried at 30, Mayu took me house hunting and hinted that her parents would be happy to make the purchase if we got married. She wanted to lock me down, put some definitions on our relationship, as she was becoming attached, given our frequent jaunts and overnight stays in her parents' penthouse condo by the beach. Mayu was the first unmarried woman I met in Japan who did not live with her parents, at least not directly. Instead she lived alone in their beach front high-rise, which afforded me unlimited visitations and overnight stays. Before her, all the unmarried women I had met, even the ones in their thirties had a parental curfew, usually at ten o clock, which I found most odd. Adult women having curfews is normal practice in Japan, especially in the countryside where women must return home sometimes by nine at night. Frequently, their mothers would call whilst we were in the midst of the act.

"Ima kuji han yo. Ima doko?" (Its now nine thirty. Where are you?)

WOMEN'S SOCIAL CONDITIONS

Most women in Japan live at home until they are married, in some cases forever. And after divorce, many, especially in rural areas must return to their parents, unable to support themselves and their children. Close to 90% of Japanese women in their late 20s and 60% in their late 30s exist at home as *parasite singles*. In a Health Ministry's estimate, 2.5 million women between 25 and 39 years old live with their parents. This constitutes nearly 20% of all women in that age group. With low enforcement of child support payments, dismally low wages for women, and insufficient social services, many divorced women with children have no alternative but to return to their parents' home. In response to attempts at implanting some much needed teeth into child support collections, sexist male lawmakers - the chauvinistic gatekeepers - claimed that making men responsible to pay for the welfare of their children after a divorce would run counter to so-called "Japanese traditions," misogynistic, oppressive traditions which work so well in favour of men. It must be noted that Japanese men are relieved of their child support responsibilities, once their ex-wives remarry.

According to a published Japanese government survey in 2005, In fiscal 2003, the Number of fatherless families had reached an astonishing 1.22 million, representing the largest number documented and a whopping 28 percent increase from a survey in 1998. Further highlighted was that, a significant majority of children in these households subsisted well below the poverty level. Given the stretched work hours of men, Japan was already a de facto society of absent fathers. But at least in the Japanese rendition of absentee paternalism, fathers in general, contribute financially to their children's welfare. In a stark change in contemporary Japanese society, single mother families now comprise the majority of its poor, a dramatic shift from the elderly households of yesteryears. Much to the bullet train nation's chagrin, in February 2005 a 27-year-old mother and her 3-year-old son were found dead of starvation in their Saitama apartment near Tokyo. Police stated that there was no food in the apartment and only 80 yen, less than a dollar was found in the woman's purse.

Further cementing their place in poverty, the ruling Liberal Democratic Party is reducing public assistance to single moms. In addition to welfare payments unemployed single mothers now receive a mother-child supplement, or a boshi kasan. However, the Health Labor and Welfare Ministry began reducing the supplement in 2005 and in 2007 plans to terminate payments to mothers with children over 15 years old, with an eye on eventually axing the supplement completely. Single mothers also cannot escape the wrath of the tax man. The Japanese tax code includes a "widow deduction" established in 1951 for war widows, but is now inclusive of single mothers. The widow deduction consists of four categories where deductions are reduced in the following order; widow, divorcee, single father and never married mother.

A widow can deduct up to 350,000 yen from her annual income for her entire life, even if she is childless, while a never-married mother gets no deductions unless her income is dismally low. The tax code provides a larger deduction for single fathers – a rarity in Japan - than it does for never-married mothers. As the Finance Ministry explains it, the tax code is based on the principle of legal wedlock, which means that a never-married mother qualifies for less government assistance than a divorced or widowed parent. The state finds little or no importance in securing the welfare of single mothers' children, which shines a floodlight on why only 1-2% of Japan's children are born out of wedlock.

These deplorable conditions are the result of ultra-low wages for women, hostile social and working environments and equally impacting, spineless child support payment enforcement. In male chauvinist Japan, after divorce a woman must wait six months before re-marrying and if she falls pregnant within 300 days of her divorce, her ex-husband, whether he likes it or not, will be the legal father of the child even if DNA tests prove otherwise. According to government figures, only about 20 percent of divorced single mothers receive child support from their ex-husbands. The late great, Godfather of soul, James Brown once acknowledged, it's a man's world, but it means diddly without a woman or a little girl. But In Japan it's a man's world, full stop, period. And it's been that way, with marginal signs of abatement since the shoguns took over in the 1100s.

Japanese women are among those who suffer the lowest economic and political status around the world. According to a May 2005 World Economic Forum study of 58 developed, developing and underdeveloped countries, Japanese women were placed 52nd in economic empowerment and 54th in political empowerment.

But a more current report in November 2007 by the same organization validated my conclusion from two years earlier that, indeed, Japan's gender gap is the worst among the Group of 8 major industrialized nations. In this new report of 128 countries, Japan placed 91st in gender equality - an 11 point descent from only a year prior – and 97th in economic participation and opportunity for women.

In the 2005 World Economic Forum survey, 1/3 of working women in Japan were in part-time dead end jobs, but according to a more recent March 2006 Internal Affairs and Communications Ministry report, in 2005, 52.5% of Japan's 21.4 million female workforce labored part-time. This was compared to 17.7 percent of the nation's 28.6 million working men. The Internal Affairs and Communications Ministry reported that in 2006 women accounted for 42 percent of the workforce, 40 percent of whom labored in part-time jobs of less than 35 hours a week. On the other side of the coin, only 10 percent of working men are part-time employees.

Japan is without question, the most male chauvinistic of all industrialized countries and among the most sexist, female unfriendly societies in the world. These are characteristics of which the men are quite proud and having internalized their status, the women simply *gaman* or endure. Though the geriatric patriarchs refuse to admit it, this system, second to industrialization, may well be the most profound contributor to Japan's plummeting birth rate. In this day and age when brainpower is more important than arm power, Japan's misogyny deprives itself en masse of the superior cognitive skills of women, refusing to recognize their benefits to society in any capacity beyond that of sperm receptors. Political leaders openly and candidly express their convictions in this regard. Observing these social conditions, it's quite clear why Japanese women walk on their self-esteem.

In one of several examples, Lower House LDP lawmaker Seiichi Ota at a panel discussion in June 2003 addressing a gang rape of young women by male Waseda University students, said he could see no problem with the *train*. Asserting his approval, he stated that it simply demonstrated the "virility" of the men. Though many found his statements shocking, indeed they were quite apt in a nation where gang rape was not even recognized as a crime. Fact is, it was only since January 1, 2005, following a revision to the criminal law, that gang rape became a criminal offense. Around the same time as Mr. Ota's comments, former Prime Minister

Yoshiro Mori commented during a debate, "It's peculiar that any woman who's never given birth to even a single child, but enjoys her freedom and has fun, should demand taxpayer support when she gets old."

The Japanese patriarchy creates a hostile and unattractive environment for women in the institution of marriage. There is a well known saying in Japanese: Kekon wa jinsei no hakko (marriage is life's grave.) and many women in contemporary Japan who observe through the media and travel, the liberties of women in the West and especially in the United States, are opting to remain unmarried. Hence, given the current state of connubial affairs in this country, women faced with the choice between living at home and holding all that disposable income, traveling overseas, clad in every name brand item known to people kind or, subsisting in the proverbial grave, opt for remaining unmarried and existing parasitically on their parents. The decision to delay marriage inadvertently puts many in the unmarriageable category, as the immature men in the patriarchy, have a penchant for extremely young women. Make no mistake, men around the world have a tendency toward younger women, recently myself included. But given Japan's pronounced male dominance and the unempowered status of women, in Japan those tendencies are even more pronounced and indeed more accepted.

Among my neighbors is a divorced, pudgy, beer bellied, balding, unattractive, 54-year-old, white-Canadian English teacher and *fake* pastor. Taking full advantage of these dynamics, he is married to a strikingly beautiful 26-year-old woman. The tendency of men to desire women no older than 25, results in many of these women becoming victims of the *Christmas cake* phenomenon, from which Mayu was suffering and from which foreigners like me benefit tremendously.

The poster child victim of Japan's primitive patriarchy is poor Princess Masako. Her frustrating existence in the imperial palace highlights the general plight of women in Japan even if they are educated. For here is a woman who graduated from Harvard and Oxford universities, not Todai or Kyodai, whose names I'd never heard before moving to Japan. And what is she doing? Probably what amounts to gardening in the imperial palace, deprived of a stimulating existence and the ability to engage in fulfilling activities. Having grown up in an international environment, she anticipated a life representing Japan diplomatically, perhaps even picking up where Princess Diana left off. So it was only natural that she has developed *adjustment personality disorder* and other psychological illnesses. When lions and tigers are encaged they pace around aimlessly in circles under the weight of insanity and caged parrots mutilate themselves by plucking their own feathers as they lose it. So then it's only natural that an advanced mind, the likes of Princess Masako's, whose sole role is limited to just perpetuating imperial bloodlines - as was articulated by one of those old geezers who control the Imperial household - would be suffering mental illnesses.

Had the Japanese been astute, they most certainly would have seized on the opportunity to use *brain* – as she was referred to by her peers – to bring about the recognition in world affairs which they so desperately crave. Worsening matters and further highlighting the sheer stupidity of the Japanese patriarchy is the pressure levied on her to deliver a boy child who would be heir to the throne. Weren't the members of the imperial palace in the equivalent to my Miss Thompson's seventh grade general science class in third world Jamaica, when she taught us that it is the sperm, not the egg, stupid, which determines the sex of the child? Lets see, seventh grade, I was 11 my first year in high school. If I knew from the tender age of eleven, that it's the man who determines the sex of the baby, then why don't those octogenarians in the imperial palace?

MAYUMI: THE PARTY CONTINUES

Mayumi's independence from her parents, at least not living with them or having a curfew, afforded us limitless nights together in *cultural exchange*. Initially she couldn't handle full penetration, always going to the doctor for bladder infections. But in eventual expansion, she quickly grew to appreciate the ride. Her favourite was the mounting position, where she drenched me in litres, earning her the nickname Biwachan, after Biwa, Japan's largest lake. Perfect could not adequately describe Biwachan's body. From the size and shape of her porcelain breasts and phallus-hardening cello-esque dimensions, to her circular rump from which her almost too long legs jettisoned, she was faultless. Her pigeon toed walk, so ubiquitous among Japanese women, kept the scud in a constantly activated state. For some odd reason, this deformity – the result of sitting in the seiza position since toddler hood - always brought on the uncontrollable urge to bend them forward and make a full delivery, until I emerged through other orifices. This is exactly what I attempted outside the Westside Mall in Osaka.

My condition had become unbearable, for not only Biwa was taunting the anaconda, but all those other pigeon toed honeys were wreaking havoc on my manhood. Unable to exert further restraint, I grabbed her under a bridge, hoisted the back of her long brown pleated skirt, tore off her lacy panties and rammed her violently against me from behind. Still irriguous from my thrice fondling her to orgasm during the drive to the mall - a regular practice on our road trips in her small Honda Life - I slid in with ease. By passers sneaking a peek through the corners of their eyes, pretended to be oblivious to our suspicious dance. Yellow-fevered sex addict that I was, condoms were the least of my concern. Strung out sex junkie, unprotected sex was my hobby and the only consequence which concerned me was paying for an abortion, which in Japan is at least a thousand dollars.

Unfortunately, I transmitted to Mayumi the school manager's Chlamydia, which I thought, coming from the West, would be the end of our relationship. However, to my surprise she expressed no anger and I accompanied her to the ladies clinic, as it's so endearingly called in Japan. There were no consequences whatsoever, no anger, fighting, rage, name calling, or any other show of emotions. And we simply continued our fiesta after her medication was completed. Mayu was the first woman of whom I began to take erotic pictures in Japan, but we were unable to develop the more pornographic ones - the ones with her smoking the cigar, or with it embedded in her tofu - because in conservative Japan such photos are confiscated. However, thanks to phone cams, digicams and camcorders, we circumvented that problem and began to make quadruple X rated movies shortly thereafter. Although very shy initially, like all my subsequent Nippon conquests with the exception of one, she really got into it and started opening up on camera, and letting me record us in full action, performances to which I still pleasure myself.

COREAN CHRISTMAS

My first Christmas on *Fantasy Island* was not spent there after all, but instead in Itaewon South Korea, a very sleazy city with uninhabitable hotels. It was a spontaneous low budget trip where, to my grave disappointment, foreigners especially Negroes were not given deity status as in Japan. It was a white man's paradise, which gutted me because, compared to Japanese women, I found Koreans to be hyper-super-babes, thicker, more curvaceous, prettier and possessing a more international fashion sense. So inhospitable was Korea, I was blatantly prohibited entrance to night clubs.

"You can't come in, no brack people," like a chapter from fifties Americana, though it was December 2001. Whiplashed and frustrated from viewing all the unattainable candy, for the first time ever, the decision to buy pleasure began to occupy my thoughts. But even that met with rejection. "No brack man, dick too big," was often the response. Later that evening I beheld a hostess, exactly my type, outside a brothel and approached her. Nubile, thick with big legs, a round protruding posterior and my Manchurian face, she lead me inside for a drink.

"I don't drink, I just want you."
"No English. You army?"
"No, I live in Japan."
"Nihongo wa?" (Do you speak Japanese?") And it was then that I realized that my Japanese language skills had evolved to the point where, upon returning to Japan, I could step to any woman I wanted to.
"Sake nomanai. anata dake hoshi." (I don't drink, I only want you.")
"But I'm just the hostess, I don't do that," she protested in basic Japanese. After insisting, she acquiesced, ridding me of ten thousand yen and led me to an apartment.   Far from being a chopstick, up until then she may well had been the thickest yellow woman I had undressed.   Only 22 years old, she owned a derriere as erect and circular as that of any African woman's. But I was nervous, it was my first time with a prostitute and all I could think about was the incurable AIDS, as I didn't have my own condoms and damn sure was not about to use the condomettes she provided.

Such was the magnitude of my nervousness my anatomy failed, creating a potentially embarrassing situation, until it dawned on me that the best way to recover from this and save face, was just to be a nice, caring human being. This led to my holding her in bed for an hour, making deep and personal inquiries. Showing compassion and affection I wanted to know everything, her entire biography, why she was hooking. Moved to tears by my kindness, she began to express guilt for my having paid the equivalent of a hundred dollars just to listen to her woes. Later when I relayed the incident to my friend, he thought I was the dumbest man on the planet, but at the end of the hour, she had given me her phone number and we spent the remainder of my holiday together when she was not working.

Seven days of sexless bliss were spent with her preparing me delicious meals and treating me to the best massages. We took long showers together and I would allow her to leave the shower before me so I could acquaint myself with, well, myself. Repeatedly, oftimes in tears, she begged for us to have sex, and without my mentioning reasons for my hesitations, she would insist,
"I'm clean! Why don't you believe me? I just went to the hospital last week and everything was ok."

"I just want to hold you and get to know you," a partly true statement, as I was falling in love and so was she. At the end of my stay, it was a difficult and emotionally teary departure for both of us and in my knight in shining armor sickness, I even proposed that she moved to Japan the following April so we could live together. But she had owed her pimp some $5,000 and homie, though kind hearted, wasn't willing to carry that piece of baggage. Initially it seemed unwise to pay for services that I didn't receive, but the hundred bucks I lost, saved me 600 in hotel costs.

Upon arriving in Korea, it was clear that there would be no red carpet welcome like there was in Japan and I was immediately greeted with hostility and general unfriendliness. Korea, an extremely foreigner unfriendly society, is even more blatantly and overtly unwelcoming to Africans, or to be specific and use a most politically incorrect term: Negroes. It is and always has been my preference to use this supposedly outdated, offensive and politically incorrect term, as it defines clearly the phenotype of the individuals to whom I am referring. There are no ambiguities in Negroe. But on the other hand, there are people in India who are black but not Negroes. Like the Jamaican philosopher Mutabaruka, I despise being referred to by one of my phenotypical characteristics, completely ignoring that I have an origin. The biggest piss take of all is that those of European decent in South Africa are referred to as Afrikaners whereas the authentic Africans are diminutively referred to as blacks. Besides, black does not require capitalization in print, to which I take great offense.

Speaking to the many African immigrants residing there, confirmed what I had suspected. Korea is hostile and exploitative to Negroes, especially those from the continent. This was an astoundingly painful hostility, especially because, in contrast, hip hop and R&B music are salient in Korean pop culture, where young people were seemingly always in hip hop attire, emulating African-American culture. Then it all started to come back to me, the schism between Koreans and African-Americans throughout the United States and especially in Los Angeles where I had lived for a decade

Since the eighties, a great divide had emerged between the two groups and there had been accusations of mistreatment on both sides. African-Americans often claimed the Korean shopkeepers were condescending and disrespectful, unable to communicate in English, often watching them suspiciously, ignoring their inquiries and insultingly tossing their change at them. On their part, the Koreans claimed the African-Americans too were disrespectful, loud, vulgar, often using foul language, proned to shoplifting and too unapologetic.

AfriKo relations took a precipitous nosedive after the fatal shooting of Latisha Harlins, who on March 16th in 1991, entered a Korean owned shop to purchase a bottle of orange juice. According to reports and video footage, the 15-year-old African-American girl put the bottle of juice in her backpack while approaching the Korean shopkeeper with the $1.79 she owed for the drink. However, the shopkeeper, a Korean-American accused her of trying to steal the beverage. The shopkeeper grabbed Latisha's backpack and she responded with two punches to Soon's face. Upon turning to exit the store, Soon Ja Du shot her fatally in the back of the head. But what really riled African-Americans was, though Latisha's killer was found guilty of voluntary manslaughter, she was given only a suspended sentence, placed on five years probation and given 400 hours of community service.

Within that same year, another African-American was gunned down by another Korean shopkeeper, further destroying any potential for peace, and the Rodney King uprising a year and a month later was the stake in the coffin. African-Americans and Latinos targeted Korean owned businesses for a looting and burning spree, to the tune of an estimated $400 million.

This violent state of affairs was fodder for hair-raising and passionate debate between my then Korean-American girlfriend and me. Anne would repeat all the perceptions that I thought Koreans held of Africans in America, arguing emotionally that we are lazy, stuck on welfare and crack and that the general negative socioeconomic plight of African-Americans should by no means be of any concern to Koreans. "Koreans are simply doing a job." Her arguments would confirm to me what I had known all along; Koreans were oblivious, unempathetic and unsympathetic to the social dynamics in the environment where they chose to do business and arrived in America with negative preconceived ideas about Africans and Africans in America. I firmly believed that many Koreans and indeed other Asians and Europeans, arrived in the land of opportunity with unsavoury images of African-Americans as lazy, criminals, alcoholics, drug addict and irresponsible fathers on welfare. In fact, even I, a Negroe, and many others from the African Diaspora, held those perceptions of African-Americans upon first arriving in the United States.

The Koreans especially, arrive in the States with archaic Confucian values, attaching one's social ranking to one's educational background, hence their condescension toward African-Americans. Moreover, most Koreans went to the United States after the civil rights movement in the sixties and thus were completely unaware of the racial discrimination that African-Americans had endured at the hands of white America. They were also ignorant about African-Americans' struggle for freedom and equality of which they the Koreans are beneficiaries, only too eager to exploit their racial and social advantage.

Anne and I frequently engaged in volcanic exchanges which often culminated in my ripping off her clothes, tearing off her G-string, (T-back in Japan, thong in Australia) thrusting my tongue down her throat and ramming my hardened timber inside her as she screamed. Anne was always *ready* or she got *ready* very quickly.
"What do you think your father would say if he knew his beautiful little girl was taking it like this?" Then I would hoist and curl her onto me while standing up.
"He would be so pissed off," she'd groan, biting her bottom lip in ecstasy.
"Do you wanna call him and tell him that his daughter is about to have the black elephant flood inside her?" Our volcanic arguments about African-

American/Korean relations always ended with bonobus like sex, as I sometimes imagined she was one of the Chinese-Jamaicans shopkeeper's daughters, about whom I had avid and vivid fantasies as a child.

Though I had firm convictions about Korean-Americans animosity toward us, perhaps because of my relationship with Anne, I was inclined to give them the benefit of the doubt. But deep inside I knew that the Koreans bore the brunt of responsibility for the problem. Shopkeepers of other ethnicities or nationalities; Indians, Syrians, Iranians, to name a few, had been present in African-American ghettos, not without drama, but not to the Korean extent. My trip to Korea was motivated by sex, but what I found instead was the absolute and resounding answer to my longtime burning question. African-Americans will be happy to know that they are absolved of most, if not all the blame for fierce Korean, African-American relations in America.

In one week in Korea, more people refused to sit by me or moved from beside me on the trains, than has been the case to date in Japan. In Itaewon, groups of Korean men attacked foreign men for even thinking about approaching Korean women. In blatant offense to Negroes, in 2003 the immensely popular Bubble Sisters, a hip hop R & B group consisting of four girls, performed in black face and donned hair curlers, in what they thought was a tribute to African-Americans. Contemporary Korea is a society awash in advertising featuring caricatures of loin cloth clad Africans, bone in nose and spear in hand. As suspected, the images of Negroes as pimps, hustlers drug dealers and murderers abound in the Korean media and given their homogenous nature and the absence of analyses, they readily accept these images as facts. Reinforcing this was a personal experience after impregnating and planning to marry one of my students who was third generation Korean in Japan.

A curious social observer, I set out to inquire about the current state of affairs, to any Korean who would speak about it and who had some command of English. "Why do Koreans hate Africans and African-Americans with such vehemence," I asked two elderly English speaking men. To my surprise the two war veterans began to profess their adoration for African-Americans.
"They fought on the frontline with us, they saved our lives." But a group of young female university students cited interesting contributing factors.
"Here in Korea we are all homogenous. We learned in school from day one that racial purity is the most important thing." As a result they said, inter-racial unions involving Koreans were extremely rare, especially 50

years ago. An exception to this, were the prostitutes and they occupied the lowest rung on the social ladder in Korea. Therefore upon seeing a biracial child, or "tugi" as they are derogatorily referred to, Koreans would first conclude that the mother of the child was a hooker and especially of the most stigmatized and lowest class of whores: the "yan kal bo" or, hookers for Westerners.

The "tugis" or "half-breeds" are often ostracized with yellow-white children carrying a lesser stigma, perhaps because they stood a better chance of assimilating in society, given the closeness of Caucasoid and Mongoloid phenotypes, relative to those of Negroid and Mongoloid and or, because the white man is held in higher esteem than the black man. For whatever reason, yellow-black children bore the brunt of immense social ostracism. She continued by saying that a larger percentage of white American soldiers either stayed with the children they created or took them and the mothers back to the States. Black American soldiers on the other hand, had neglected with greater frequency, the offsprings they had created with prostitutes in Korea. This I found credible. It is possible that given the higher socioeconomic status that white soldiers enjoyed, they would definitely be more able to support and or return home with their children. And as a Jamaican native, I am only too aware of the proclivity of us descendants of slaves to neglect our off-springs.

There is no official data on the number of mixed raced people fathered by American servicemen, as their existence is rarely acknowledged let alone debated by a nationalist government far more interested in indoctrinating the masses with pure-blood dogma. What is known is, except for the few who excel as singers and athletes, most exist in sheer misery and despondency, being members of the most disparaged group in Korea. And up until 2005 mixed race people were banned from the military, ineligible for government jobs and benefits. According to a 2006 survey by Pearl S. Buck International Korea, an organization supporting mixed heritage youths, more than one in four Amerasian youths abandoned by their American fathers, are drop outs before or during middle school.

The young ladies also pointed out that, for many Koreans, these mixed raced people are a "strong" reminder of the war. However, in a stark display of hypocrisy, after Hines Ward of the Pittsburgh Steelers was named the Super Bowl's most valuable player in 2006, South Korea embarked upon a fervent public embrace of this "tugi." Ward who is half Korean and half African-American, scored the touch down which took the Steelers to victory in the super bowl of that year. Photos of his touchdown pass were emblazoned on the front page of every newspaper in South Korea and bloggers began to express pride in his achievements, even demanding honorary citizenship and a parade if he were to visit.

Not since the national outpouring of pride for the now notoriously discredited scientist Hwang Woo Suk had South Koreans been so proud of someone, even referring to Ward, a member of the most denigrated class in South Korea, as "one of us." Indeed Hines Ward and his former nightclub waitress mother were among the lucky ones, having been taken by his father - an American soldier - to the States when he was 2. Upon continuing our discussion, the students also cited the 1992 Los Angeles riots as an exacerbant to the schism, noting that news of African-Americans looting Korean owned stores created even more disdain for Negroes in South Korea.

Whatever the reasons, Korea's extreme inhospitability to Africans was a great disappointment. Moreover, being 25% Christian, the society places a high value on virginity, a factor making it less receptive to promiscuity than Japan. So important is virginity in Korea, hymen replacement surgery, like cosmetic surgery to toddlers, is widely administered. After just one week there I was only too eager to return home to my hedonistic lifestyle in Japan.

RETREAT TO KANSAI

Back home in Japan, Chef, a recent arrival from Jamaica had been working for a company, whose Japanese owner, Toshige had been communicating online with a woman from Chiba. After learning that she had *chocolate eyes*, especially for Jamaicans, Toshige told her he was a Yaudie, (slang for native Jamaican) born and raised. This hurled Chef into the position of Yaudie Persona Consultant, advising him what to say to her, which singers and DJs to mention, and where in Jamaica he should tell her he's from.

"Tell her your favourite artistes are Elephant Man and Vibes Cartel," he advised.
"Really?! They're my favourites too," she typed in response. As expected, in every sentence, she began to reveal to him her excited condition and when he hinted at his resemblance to Beenie man and what he would do to her upon meeting, the inevitable dilemma came to pass. So they embarked on a plan whereby Chef would be his surrogate and report his activities back to Toshige along with graphic cell phone images. Indeed, these are the things that friends do for friends. That's what friends are for. And actually, this was almost like the Japanese tradition of two friends bedding the same woman, though not in a threesome, symbolizing the closeness of their friendship.

Tosh gave her Chef's cell phone e-mail address and they made plans to meet in Kobe. He was armed and ready with protection. There was no way he would've entertained the thought of riding saddleless with some reggae groupie, from cyberspace, who had spent a great deal of time backstage with various reggae artists. On the day of their scheduled meeting, at the designated location in front of the Sogo department store in Sannomiya, he arrived about twenty minutes early for a preliminary look see. There he observed a young girl rubbing her palms together in the crisp Kobe cold. The first thing which struck him was her juvenile features, far from the 25-year-old he was expecting, a clear case of internet misrepresentation.

"Why di raus people cyau jus' be 'onness?" (why the fuck can't people just be honest?) he said he thought. But she was cute and reminded him of those

high schoolgirls in their micro-minis on their bicycles, after whom he too had been salivating since his arrival in Japan. They had big strong athletic legs from riding their bikes everyday and it was a favourite past time of ours to conspicuously peer between them as they rode. We saw no reason to be covert and discreet about our voyeuristic tendencies. After all, it was they who converted their otherwise below-knee length skirts after school. What could they possibly be seeking if not erotic attention? But that's as far as we went, we looked and fantasized.

Cyber-girl was about 5'2" and though he couldn't conduct a thorough assessment, she was more on the thick side. Beholding the impression of an onion protruding from her tight, long coat, especially relieved him.

"You're waiting for me right?" he interrupted. To which she greeted him with the typical shy Japanese grin, unlike, he relayed, "a girl who was used to getting hosed down by reggae super stars." Her personality then was 180 degree different from her cyber-personality, not as extroverted as had been expected and she seemed to know her way around Kobe very well, leading him to a love hotel. Their conversation was sparse on the way and though she was shy, she appeared to be on a mission: to enter the dark side. Upon arrival at the hotel she whipped out her cartoon character infested purse and inserted a 5,000 yen note in the slot, standing with her legs spread slightly apart and her toes turned inward. Immediately upon entering, he attached his lips to hers and commenced peeling away her layers until she stood only in her panties.

In Chef words, "the sight of her tofu complected, perfectly proportioned, five foot two frame sent the fire hose into a frenzy. "I was right about the bumpa," which he said, appeared to have been carved with a compass. Her legs were the schoolgirl legs after which he had been yearning since arriving on the island: perfectly toned.

"Are these peach johns?" he asked, pulling her panties down to her ankles, revealing her beautiful hairless and lipless majesty, a vertical line with a pin head sized clitoris peeking out. "Why do you know about Peach John? No I didn't wear PJ today."

"Whoever designed her glory must've laboured on it painstakingly," he thought, as he picked her up, legs wrapped around him and placed her on the bed. Yearning to stare and admire this creation, he lay on his back and asked her to stand over his face, which provide this unbelievable sensation. "Brejrin, mi cyau explain it." (I can't explain it bro) I understood, it must

have been tantamount to the feeling you get at the edge of the Grand Canyon. "Looking at her was almost more rewarding than going in," he said, and slowly he began to pull her down, until she was resting it on his mouth. Understandably his long standing rule was never to go south on a first encounter and definitely not on a cyber-babe, but amnesia kicked in, he forgot about the rule and his tongue began to explore her as if it were seismic equipment checking for oil. She was odorless and tasted like spring water from the Blue Mountains. He couldn't stop drinking or eating, as she crept up to the top of the bed and whined in that high pitch voice in which most Japanese girls whined on reception. In a momentary lapse of reason, he attempted to enter unstrapped, but his senses returned prompting him to roll on a raincoat before her introduction to darkness.

On the verge of emptying his vas deferens, he accelerated his ride and prayed to the condom god for no failures.
"Come?" she asked.
"Oh yeh," withdrawing and holding the rubber on to his pulsating instrument.
"Kimochiokata." (it felt good.) Chef's next move was to the bathroom, where whilst there he received an e-mail.
"What's taking you so long?" It read.
"Chotto matte ne. soo come."
"Couldn't you wait?" he joked, after reuniting with her in bed. But she had no clue as to what he was referring.
"Your e-mail while I was in the bathroom."
"My e-mail? I don't have a phone."

Chef said he couldn't believe what he had heard but immediately understood what had just transpired. Brain racing at light speed, he began to get dressed as neither of them had enough command of each other's language to iron out this case of mistaken 'cyber-identity.' Best case scenario, in this police state Japan, as a foreigner, he most certainly would have done time for statutory rape, then get deported. Worse case, rape, as it would've been easy to tell the police that she didn't know who he was, which was true. They didn't even know each other's names. Panic set in.

"Where are you? It's cold out here," read the second e-mail, in response to which he abruptly got dressed and fled the room.
"Chotto matte ne," (Wait here a bit.) he requested of cyber-girl one. "I'll be right back." Cyber-girl two was almost exactly what he had expected; dyed blond hair, overdone make up and gaudy nails. A *yanki* as they're called here, who are to Japan what white trash is to America. So it seemed

that he had literally abandoned Grade A Kobe beef, or veal, to be more exact, to engage in some charity copulatory activities with a girl from the Special Olympics. Chef was not happy, but she had traveled three hours by train. During the mercy lay, Chef said his mind wandered frequently to the young dame he had just abandoned. Who was she and what was her name? Who was she awaiting? We both imagined their e-mail conversation to go something like:

"What happened? Why the fuck did you make me wait for three hours?"

"What are you talking about? It was you who made me wait at the hotel. You said you would've been right back."

"What?! What hotel? What do you mean I made you wait at the hotel? I was waiting for you on the street, near Sogo like we agreed." We both would've loved to have been a fly on the wall, the moment they realized what actually transpired.

Only in Japan.

TOMOKO

New year's eve 2001 caught me at Murphy's, a smoke engulfed, Irish pub in Osaka, where upon emerging from the lavatory I made eye contact with a petite, more attractive Rosie Perez, making her way to the ladies' room.

"Are you going to buy me a drink?" She jokingly demanded.

"If your ass is big enough," I thought to myself, offended by her presumptuous attitude and turning her around to assess her buttocks.

She knew what time it was. After spending seven years in England, she knew that the posterior was of utmost importance to the Negroe male.

"Don't worry, you'll love my ass," she retorted, disappearing to powder her nose. Finding the pollution unbearable, my friends and I stepped and landed at Bar Isn't It in Shinsaibashi. "Bar" was a well known gaijin spot and as the night was still early, it was relatively smoke free and sparsely populated.

"Are you stalking me?" Shouted a familiar voice over driving house music. "You definitely have to buy me a drink now."

It is said that freaks come in small packages and as I would later discover, Tomoko was no exception. Since she was so readily available, this being one of my rare nights out in Osaka, I stayed with the *bird in hand*. Typical Japanese beauty she was not, her features were more rounded and gave her the appearance of a Southeast Asian, more Negroid with beautiful upturned eyes. Her English was near perfect, but contrary to my theory, she was quite an attractive, sexy, petite 34-year-old with enticing dimples below the edges of her mouth and like most Japanese women, she looked ten years younger than her age, especially standing at five feet tall.

Tomi, as she liked to be called, was experiencing the double edged effects of spending so much time in the West and returning to Japan. On one hand, seven years in England were very good for her English, however it exposed her to the freedom of foreign men, which rendered her incapable of any readjustment to the primitive and oppressive mentality of Japanese men. Especially those like her father, who perpetually beat her and her mother into several galaxies. So upon returning to Japan some three years prior, she dated white Western men exclusively. However, as a significant percentage of Western men in Japan are fully aware of our erotic capital and the high frequency of gullible Japanese women, this posed a dilemma in her quest for love. Predictably she always fell prey to them, giving it up immediately upon meeting them, while naively expecting a relationship of substance. Aggravating her state of affairs was her age. Having been nine years past her *sell by date*, according to the standards of Japanese men, she was a victim of the Christmas cake phenomenon. Hence, since her return from England she had been desperately seeking love but instead, always predictably being turned out in love hotels by gaijins. Such is the quagmire in which many Japanese women dwell.

Within a few hours she was plastered and our tongues began to do the tango on the dark dance floor, with my fingers exploring her. It was impossible to ignore my left pointing, boulder rubbing against her, which she grabbed.
"Why don't you reach inside and hold it?" I invited.
After unzipping my pants, I felt her small palm around me.
"This is not Japanese," she responded humorously.
"Of course not, I'm Jamaican," continuing to devour each other's face.

Toward the end of the night as she became more inebriated and less attractive, the predator in me hesitantly suggested that we find a place for the night. However, to my surprise and relief, even in her drunken stupor, she objected. It was a new year and she was ardent about her resolution to cease her loose behaviour of opening her legs in sleazy love hotels, to foreign men she met the same night. Her rejection was a relief.

There is nothing more repulsive to me than a drunken woman and or, the smell of alcohol on a woman. While many men, in persistent insecurity, strive to intoxicate women in order to take advantage of them sexually, women who drink like lushes repulse me. They are anti-Viagra. Besides, a biblical encounter with me is a life changing experience, an obsessive, addiction which I have been honing since seven. Providing pleasure to women is an art form about which I do not jest, hence she must be wide awake, with unimpaired faculties during the ride.

At about 5:00 AM, Tomoko and I kissed our good-byes at the JR Umeda station and arranged to meet at two o' clock the same day at JR Sannomiya's central exit, the same time and place where I was scheduled to meet Ai, who was traveling from her home in the countryside. In my aversion to details and inferior executive functioning, my plans to meet Ai at the same time and location had completely slipped my mind as I boarded the train, fingers up my nose savouring Tomoko's smell.

At a quarter past two that afternoon, my friend's home phone jarred me from deep slumber, with Tomoko on the line.
"You're late!"
"I'll be there in three minutes," nervously, heart racing at the quandary awaiting me at the station, I dragged on some clothes, covered it with a coat and scurried out the door, wiping the sleep from my eyes. Upon my arrival, she was easily noticeable, wearing a pink sweater and a jacket with a fur edged hood and was more beautiful than the night before. Immediately I took her by the hand and began to hastily escort her away from the station, back to my friend's apartment. "Why are you late?"
"Can we talk about this at Rambo's place? I'm freezing," as we hurriedly made our way up to Yamamoto Dori.
"I'm sorry babe, I overslept," entering the safety of the apartment.

What followed was a fairly exciting date around Kobe, including a 1 1/2hour voyage to and from the Akashi bridge, but nothing compared to the icing on the date. Only a block away from where Chef had been with mistaken cyber-girl, this hotel room had a toilet theme, the bed was shaped like a toilette bowl with the lid down and the head of the bed shaped like the tank. On the tank there was a lever simulating the flush lever, which controlled the lights in the room and all the walls and ceiling were covered with mirrors. I had already sprung to attention. In fact, I was at attention since the night before, sleeping with my right hand near my nostrils. I began to kiss her full Southeast Asian-like lips as I unhooked her skirt, which fell to her feet revealing her black tights hugging the lower half of her guitar figure, her curvy buttocks and her short, shapely legs.

She undid my pants, eager for a glimpse of the limb, which would soon be planted inside her. Unlocking her bra I then removed her sweater. This was her debut on the dark side and she was flabbergasted by my size.
"I wont be able to take all of this," she exclaimed.
"Yes you can." On her chest was a pair of perfectly formed 36 Bs with dark nipples, on which I feasted before saddling up, throwing her on the bed and ravishing her, slowly sinking inside her. Ambrosia greeted nirvana, as I docked in her bay with euphoric precision. In the mirrors on the walls, I could see the bulbous posterior of this black beast, gyrating to and

fro, sometimes arching his back as he buried himself deep inside a little yellow girl. *"If she felt this good strapped up,"* I thought, *"I can't even begin to comprehend how she would feel if I were riding sadleless."* In less than two minutes she began to contort her face as though she were in excruciating pain, her eyes squeezed shut and in slow motion, a fierce grimace engulfed her.

Tomi metamorphisized into the ugliest woman I had ever seen, as I held her tightly, restraining her, slowly grinding on her with nowhere to go. Uglier and uglier, mouth twisted, lips crooked, in what seemed like an eternal orgasm. Exploding every three to five minutes until she was supersaturated, lying in a pool of her own body fluids, by her twelfth orgasm I had lost traction, withdrew, removed the rubber and jumped back in barefooted.

Given Japanese women's unempowered social status, they rarely protested when I desired to enter without protection. In this profoundly male dominated society, women are not even in control of their reproductive rights. As condoms are the most popular form of birth control, it is the man who always determines when the women will get pregnant. Abortion, the fourth most popular form of birth control in Japan, after withdrawal and the rhythm method, is a multi-trillion yen industry also controlled by men. Even as we speak, in 2007, women are still being misinformed about oral contraceptives in order to protect the extremely lucrative abortion industry.

I had all intentions of keeping on the magnum 500, but you know the saying about great intentions. Tomi became my hell and in her fiery cave, I became her cave dweller. I tried to hold out until the last nanosecond before withdrawing, but failed miserably and soon the Jamaican fire brigade was dousing her infernal cave with litres of high viscosity flame retardant.
"You came inside me?" she yelled.

"Yeh," I answered nonchalantly. Like many descendants of slaves from similar socioeconomic and cultural backgrounds, I too possessed the proclivity to unabashedly and irresponsibly sire countless children. Within me raged an incessant battle between reason and the forces of addiction, awareness and the effects of maladaptive socialization, glorifying stud psychology. A war which escalated in vehemence ten fold in Japan, where society keeps women on sperm receptor status, wide open beaver for men like me. And there are many, I meet them everyday. But unlike many of my contemporaries, I had harboured fantasies since five or six years old of being the outstanding father, unlike my own. I took no pride in, and found nothing to be proud of, actually siring countless offsprings for whom I wouldn't care.

Such was my argument for the abortions I funded, some 13 or 14 of them. In my dissocial state, I lacked the ability to empathize or sympathize with the physical and emotional trauma those women experienced, as I was more concerned with feeding my addiction and terminating the consequences when they arose. But on the other hand, I was well aware of the need to be a good father to my children. And given awareness of my own paternal unpreparedness, I thought it better to abort than to sire some 14 children. In my thinking, quality of life is of far greater importance than absolute life.

"I can't get pregnant anyway," a proclamation I had heard at least eight times before, each time succeeded by a pregnancy. So I began to prepare psychologically and in Japan, financially.
"No really, I've never been pregnant. I think there's something wrong with me." "Well' I don't fire blanks." And on that note we fell into a coma-like slumber in the spoon position, with her petite body fitting perfectly in my arms. Though just a week prior in Korea I was in love, cupid had struck again and I was head over heels.

Immediately I began to consider her for a life partner, as she possessed many of the qualities I sought; We were close in age, she was an adult, beautiful, well traveled, entrepreneurial and most importantly, off the charts sexual compatibility. The next morning when we woke, upon switching on my phone, there were countless voice and e-mails from AI's sister Rie, saying that Ai had waited for three hours after the three-hour train ride to Kobe and in acquiescence, took the three hour journey back home.

"*This calls for serious damage control,*" I thought. Had I done this to a woman in the West, she would have most certainly relieved me of my testicles. Tomoko and I agreed that she would visit me in the countryside every two weeks, and after brunch at the Jamaican restaurant in Sannomiya, we bade our good-byes. Initially, I protested the long intervals between visits, but before long I began to appreciate them, as it became clear that our arrangement was without question to my benefit. Unlike women to whom I was accustomed in the West, Japanese women for the most part, are far less independently mobile, relying mostly on public transportation.

In fact most people in Japan rely much more on its hyper-efficient public transportation system than on cars.

During my time in San Francisco, I frequently dated women who lived as far as San Jose, a distance of 80 kilometers, equal to the distance between Osaka and this rural town. And in those relationships it wasn't uncommon for us to meet at least every other day, as sometimes she would drive down or I would take the one-hour drive up. In Japan such frequent visits are impossible even if both parties have access to private transportation. The exorbitant highway tolls make it cost prohibitive and the train fare is similar in cost to the tolls. From Osaka where Tomoko lived to my apartment among the rice fields and expansive terraced landscapes requires the equivalent of twenty dollars in tolls round trip and the same price in train fares. So seeing each other daily would cost almost $300 a week. As a result, prevalent in Japan are very long distance relationships where the parties see each other once or twice a month. This I found ludicrous and was more than eager to exploit the opportunities the situation availed me.

"Rie, what happened to Ai yesterday?" I asked Ai's sister on the phone.
"She waited at the west exit for about two hours," exactly where I had instructed her to. Jack Frost had exceptionally jagged, razor-sharp canines that day and I was overcome by a great sense of ill worth, at the thought that Ai waited in Siberian temperatures for three hours while I pranced off with another woman. Reduced to nano dimensions, I felt as though I could have sat on a dime and swing my legs.
"She came back crying yo."

"Let me talk to her. Aichan, gomenne. I'm so so so so sorry. I waited at wrong exit," I lied in vocal intonations used when speaking to 2-year-olds.
"Watashi wa waruii desu, it's my fault. I made a mistake. machigaimashita" finally finding the word for mistake in Japanese. Before returning, in appeasement I bought her a hundred dollar fossil watch. But what started as a superficial gesture of empty apology for a cold-hearted act, ended up being sincere, as I saw the delight on her face while she opened her gift.
"Phew, that was close."

As probability would have it, Tomoko's first visit was met with yet another close encounter with Ai. Had I subscribed to the concept of destiny, I would have thought that those two women were destined to meet.

As Tomoko's train screeched to a measured halt, I sat waiting in the company car outside the station, only to have a surprise greeting by Ai and her sister entering a cab. "Stechaaaan" Ai screamed, waving her palms frantically like Japanese people do.

"Udetokei arigatou" she yelled from the back of the cab, left rear door ajar, as the train expelled a rush of air locking the brakes.
"She said thanks for the watch," her sister translated. "What are you doing?"
"Oh I'm just waiting on a friend" I said, stealing a line from the Rolling Stones. To my left, from the corner of my eye I could see Tomoko emerging through the wickets and a warm sensation appeared in my underwear.
"He's coming from Osaka," I continued.
"We have to go, okaasan no tanjoubi" (mom's birthday) they yelled, frenetically wagging their palms good-bye.

As the cab door closed and the car drove away, Tomoko exited the station, hair bouncing as though she were in a television commercial for Pert shampoo. Her fashion was big city and she strode as if on a Paris runway, flashing her cosmopolitan smile.
"What's wrong?!" she enquired in concern, entering the Daihatsu Mira. It was obvious I was having a near death experience.
"Ate some bad salmon," I retorted.

After recovery from my *food poisoning*, she and I embarked upon a weekend of wild, unfettered hedonism. Tomoko was the most orgasmic woman I have met to date. When her levies broke, her river flowed down the insides of her legs and we frequently needed towels between her and the futon. Before the weekend was over, her face appeared permanently stuck in the ugly position, especially after her record 26 orgasms in one hour. That Sunday saw me venture on my maiden drive outside the countryside, taking her home to Osaka. By the time we arrived in Osaka, I had turned her into the ugly duckling six times and it was during that hour and a half drive that my post countryside plans were formulated and solidified: I would move to Kobe where we would live together in hyper-copulatory bliss.

After that virgin long distance drive, Tomo and I took many trips by car where we measured distance not in kilometers but in the frequency of her orgasms before arriving at our destination. From my home to Shirahama, about 200 kilometers, was ten; to Kobe, 100 kilometers, was a five or six and Osaka to Kobe, 24 kilometers, a three. Our bliss began to unravel when Tomo started to sometimes bleed during intercourse, at times just spotting and at other times in hemorrhages, dyeing my sheets crimson. Adding to the disappointment, I began experiencing some discomfort in the tool, upon which we both went to the doctor where we discovered that she had shot me with another dose of Chlamydia. Just 2 months after my arrival, my first visit to the doctor, where I was prescribed a 30 day dosage of new quinolones for the school manager's infection, had clued me in on the state of medical delivery on the island. "What about Azythromiacin?" I inquired to the doctor. "We need only one dosage of 1000 milligrams," I informed him. But he had never heard of that medication and insisted that I take his prescribed tablets, three times a day for thirty days.

This new contraction posed a dilemma, having to inform Biwachan for a second time of transmitting the same disease to her and having to relay the same news to Ai, with her sister as interpreter. In retrospect, luckily Ai's mother was spared, as our encounters were post diseases. In some disturbed way probability had finally gotten its wish to connect Ai and Tomoko. A few days after going to the hospital with Tomoko, Ai's sister Rie summoned me for a talk and of course, I was only too aware of the topic of this future conversation. Already accepting guilt, I began to apologize to Rie on the phone, but she had no idea why I was expressing such remorse and to my bewilderment, she began to apologize on behalf of Ai.

"What are you doing now? Can you come to our house?" I speculated on the possibilities of the crisis, recognizing that once again there was a chance that probability might just be siding with me. After a long period of silence around their dining table, equipped with an electronic dictionary, pen and paper for drawing, Rie started on the task of relaying to me that her sister may have given me some hechi no byouki, sexual sickness she had recently contracted. However, the illness with which we were both concerned respectively was different.

My concern was transmitting Chlamydia to her and from her explanation, Ai was worried about having giving me the crabs. She apologized profusely for her phantom disease while I begged her forgiveness for my real disease and made arrangements to accompany her to the ladies clinic and we were even. Not being one to harbor double standards in male female sexual behavior, her admission was a relief, as now we were both aware of other sex partners in the equation. Sex junkie that I was, for me that was to be expected and once again, just as before, when I had stood her up for three hours for the woman from whom she indirectly contracted the disease, things were resolved perfectly. As to Mayu, thanks to Asano San - a student of mine who was a doctor - I secured a dosage of new quinolones and explained to her that it was possible all the bacteria had not been killed, being that we never went in for a follow up but should, after completing this new dose of antibiotics.

After extinguishing those fires, it was back to the business of grand pleasure and discovering new experiences in and outdoors with Tomoko, Mayu, Ai and occasionally her mom. Deep In the woods of a local natural park, I bent Mayu over by a stream for some quick outdoor exploration, her first experience out in the open. Being in nature, the hypnosis of a flowing river and birds singing in the crisp, fresh air was a backdrop for what seemed like a National Geographic special, where we went at it like animals in the wild. As I withdrew to unload on the ground, from atop the hill came a cheerful family of three with a little boy of about five, taking what they thought was a pleasant, wholesome stroll in a breathtakingly beautiful park on a perfect day. The parents' eyes pulped and their mouth gaped in fright and distress to see what perhaps appeared to be this Jamaican beast punishing an innocent Japanese woman.

Immediately they covered their little boy's eyes and whipped a U-turn, almost dislocating his arm and neck.
"Now, that is an image indelibly etched in that little tyke's memory," I thought. He may well need therapy. The next week I took Ai to a picnic at the same park, where I sat on a log beneath a tree, rocket pointing skyward, inviting her to ride in the pouring rain. As she mounted me, mouth open to take in raindrops falling among the leaves, I raised my pelvis for maximum penetration, as we got soaked to the bones. By then, Ai was able to take me with less pain, bouncing on her toy until I stopped her, indicating to quickly dismount lest I release inside her.

Tomoko and I had a penchant for public men's rooms. Or more accurately, I had a penchant for dragging Tomoko into men's toilets. We sneaked in male lavatories for her regular uglification and took delight in seeing men's expressions as we emerged from the small hole in the ground benki room together. One of Japan's vastly underutilized treasures is the ever vacant, spacious toilets for the handicap. They seemed larger than most Japanese apartments and we visited them as though we were just going to Starbucks, but in actuality, like jonesing heroine addicts, we were sneaking in these public love hotels for a fix. It was as though they had made those bright and spacious areas especially for us. Those three women became the core of my collection in the countryside, with a string of revolving peripherals, satellite honeys as I called them, whom I had met at various places in Osaka and Kobe.

CHIKAKO

Satellite honeys were not granted more than three or four encounters. Not because of a lack of desire to, but they were too numerous and time consuming. So abundant were they that usually by the fourth encounter I had met their replacements, or in some cases perhaps, they had met mine. The only satellite honey with semi core status was a 28- year-old store clerk, who lived and worked in the area.

Since my arrival there, Chikako had caught my attention from the nearby jewelry store where she worked. Not the normally petite Japanese woman, her facial features were more like those of a *Gonzales* instead of a *Tanaka* and her body type was like that of a more curvaceous Carmela Soprano, which meant she was much too big for Japanese men. This also meant that she was without question single and perhaps had been single and sexless for ages, waiting for the first Negroe ever to grace the town. After all, only a *yaudie* would appreciate her big legs and round posterior bursting through her tight black pants, and Japanese men would be clueless about what to do with those C cups. What's more, I was confident her non-Japanese, Latina face would most certainly be a repellent to them.

I was right. It had been five years since her last boyfriend or intimate experience. Chikako spoke absolutely "Japanese only" and that literally was the extent of her English. We spoke only the language of sex. Upon gradually stripping her I revealed a beautiful healthy, curvaceous body, thick and toned even in the absence of much exercise. Her big legs reminded me of the heat which greeted my tiny hands when I precociously stuck them between the legs of women her size, during my childhood. Bursting through my pants, I fervently anticipated that heat as I placed my hand in her furnace to pull aside the crotch of her panties in order to get her on my fingers. Having been neglected for so long, she melted to the couch like an ice cube in a volcano and her lava engulfed my fingers as I wrapped my mouth around her dime sized nipples. I was anticipating easy entry, but unlike the skinnier women, she squealed in pain. I never could understand why it was so much easier for thinner women to receive me. After a very slow dive, I was able to penetrate deep insider her and she gasped in ecstasy, predictably uttering, "okii desu ne."

With 12-hour work days and only two days off a month, Chikako's schedule ensured that her demands on my time would have been limited. Like other untouchables in Japan: divorced, single parents, thick, late twenties and up, or all of the aforementioned, she was only too eager to settle for the one or two days of pleasure I made available to her every month. It was better than nothing, which was what she had grown accustomed to during the preceding five years of drought.

NEGLECTED WOMEN

Japan, the island of perpetual or prolonged singleness, is littered with these lonely souls – many having to resort to dance lessons with their dogs - only too eager to be penned in my schedule and that of my Western friends for a day or two a month. Western men place ads with great success, specifically targeting these women and opening any popular local English magazine will reveal ads placed by these desperate women for 'discrete' relationships with Western men. Within eight months in Japan, feeding my addiction had become the only stressor, as I manipulated my schedule to accommodate the harem. Another source of anxiety was the worry about an abortion, for it wasn't a matter of if, but when. My existence was tantamount to that of a crack fiend locked up in a crack house, an alcoholic living in a brewery with endless supplies of free crack and booze.

Far from what I had imagined prior to my arrival, it was like fishing with a wok in a Japanese bathtub. And this was only the introduction. Yes, there were rejections. Not all Japanese women are attracted to foreign men and not all Japanese women who like foreign men like Negroe men. In fact, as is the social norm internationally, most Japanese women are with Japanese men. Simply put, most people will choose to be with someone of their own race, ethnicity, religion or any other social demographic. Such is the socialization of humans that only three to five percent of us will choose someone dissimilar to ourselves. But so few and far between were rebuffs, they served as respite from the onslaught of acceptances. Absolutely implausible were the state of affairs. By no means did I attribute my successes to anything special about my person, as this phenomenon was not limited to my own experiences. Upon meeting fellow African-Americans, Africans and Jamaicans and other Western foreigners in general, our first topic of discussion was always the effortlessness required to bed the native women.

Contrarily, foreign women do not enjoy similar status and generally their experiences are the exact opposite, especially for women of African descent. Some, like a dark skinned Jamaican-Canadian acquaintance of mine have reported frequent acts of contempt by the Japanese, including being spat on twice in Osaka. Almost immediately after arriving here, it became my passion to unravel the mysteries shielding the apparent ease with which Japanese women "put out" to Western men.

I wanted to know what was behind this *yellow cab* phenomenon as never before, not even in my days of whoring at university – which was the zenith of my promiscuity prior to being in Japan – had I been able to score so frequently and easily, many times not even knowing their names. Among the contributing factors to this phenomenon are; curiosity, fetishism, inferiority complexes, lack of female empowerment, male dominance, a socialization as pleasure givers, the gross ineptitude of Japanese men, in general absent fathers and a society devoid of sexually restrictive Christian doctrine, all of which I will later explore.

Among Japanese women who date inter-racially, there are those who prefer black or white men exclusively and others who swing either way. Some even migrate from black to white, or vice versa. Inferiority complexes are behind their blond blue eyes passion, as Japan is a society twisted by collective inferiority complexes, placing the white man among the clouds while berating themselves in intense self-hate. This self-deprecation became even more pronounced after their stunning defeat by the white man during the Second World War. The Japanese thought they were Gods, but upon this startling injection of reality, they relinquished their God-like status and transferred it to white Americans. Hence, for Japanese women who are inclined to engage in intimate inter-racial relations, the white male is most desirable. However, thanks to the media, with the advent of hip hop and reggae, black men are fetishized and objectified, resulting in magazines- yes this is true - dedicated to teaching those Japanese women so inclined, how to simulate being black. Articles include instructions on hair weave extensions, skin dye and the latest hip hop fashion imitating Li'l Kim. Recently I was asked whether or not I took offense to this objectification of Negroes, especially African-Americans in Japan.

"*How odd a question,*" I thought. It was my own fetishism and objectification of yellow women, which brought me thousands of miles across the Pacific in the first place and moreover, objectification in Japan is by far a more palatable option to racial profiling in Europe and America. The overwhelming contributing factor to the yellow cab phenomenon is a male chauvinist society, which produces blatant and unequivocal sexual retardation in Japanese men, while socializing women to be givers of pleasure. Japan's male dominance is severe, a society where men treat their dogs better than they do their wives. This being the year of the dog will only further ensure that the animals meet with better care than female spouses.

Recently I observed a woman waiting in a car at the train station in my suburban neighborhood, which was not an uncommon occurrence, as many women delivered and collected their husbands to and from the station on a daily basis. Patiently she sat waiting in the driver's seat, when suddenly her face gleamed as the object of her patience emerged in view. Shortly thereafter, a man appeared and entered the vehicle through the rear door, as many Japanese husbands do and to my surprise, blissfully greeted a dog with a hug and kiss as the woman longingly looked on, envious of the canine. Moments later her countenance changed in acquiescence as if coming to her senses, realizing she yearned for the impossible. She quickly engaged the car and departed the curb.

Upon relaying this to many of my female students, especially an astute socially aware nurse in her mid forties, they assured me that such was the norm among Japanese men. In another incident I observed, an exquisitely dressed woman standing in the rain beneath an umbrella outside a Family Mart convenience store. Moments later a poorly attired man in his mid thirties emerged, took the umbrella for himself as they walked along each other, with her out in the rain hanging on his upper arm.

In the spirit of bushido, Japanese men are oblivious to women's needs, and for them it is most unmanly to strive to give pleasure to their partners. No true samurai would be concerned about whether he brought his wife to orgasm. The entire society is structured around women humbly serving men and not surprisingly, the bedroom is no exception. Enter exhibit A: Japanese porn, where the man fondles the clitoris mechanically for a predetermined amount of strokes, twists the woman's nipples as if trying to find his favourite radio station, then inserting, thereafter quickly releasing. A significant majority of Japanese women to whom I've posed the question and or, whom I've known biblically, have not had a satisfying sexual experience with a Japanese man and a hundred percent of them who had had no prior experiences with foreigners, exclaimed that they had no idea that sex could be as enjoyable as our sex.

As only a small percentage of Japanese women date inter-racially or inter-nationally, this island of extremely sexually frustrated and neglected women, is paradise for the Western sex addict, especially one with a yellow preference. Further evidence of this deprivation is the presence of host clubs for women. These are clubs patronized by women, beautiful, young and middle-aged, in order to receive attention and engage in conversation and intimacy all for a price. Only in Japan! In an interview with one of the hosts in Tokyo, he admitted that such clubs could exist only in Japan, because the men here are so excruciatingly unkind to women.

Excessive imbibitions are cultural rites for Japanese men. In a society of institutionalized alcoholics and heavy smokers, there is a marked increase in the erectile dysfunction probability, ensuring non-performance among a great many men. According to an annual nationwide survey conducted in May 2007 by Japan Tobacco Inc. - a company in which the Finance Ministry has a near 50% interest, and indeed Japan's largest tobacco maker – the smoking rate among Japanese men had declined to 40.2%, still among the highest in the world. The survey by mail questioned 32,000 adults from twenty years old and was responded to by 19,205 people.

Japan's male chauvinist society, the most pronounced in the industrial world and among the most female oppressive in the industrialized world, is directly responsible for socializing the most diffident and unempowered women in the developed and some of the developing world. Brow beaten for hundreds of years, they are generally naïve, unaware of their potential and possess negative self-worth, instilled in them by their fathers' and society's expectations of them, only to be "baby-making machines," as stated by one of the country's top politicians in early 2007. His comments caused an uproar among women, who maybe are slowly starting to revolt against their subservient role in society.

With precious little expectations from Japanese men, many Japanese women find being used by Western men – to which they are sometimes unmindful – a far more fulfilling experience. This I found quite troubling albeit an open invitation to wantonly plough through them. Also present is what I call, the trophy effect. Many of my Japanese encounters wore me like the latest accessory in this internationally acknowledged brand name-obsessed land, rebelliously thumbing their noses at their society as if to say,
"hey, look at me, I broke away from your oppression and I'm free. See? I can even kiss my kokujin (black) boyfriend right here on this train."
Not minding accessorization, I was only too eager to oblige, completely relishing in it. After all, it was Pareto efficiency for both parties, she got her accessory and I received pleasure from her and from providing her pleasure.

FAREWELL RICE FIELDS

Finally a year passed and my planned departure from the countryside was met with a barrage of love letters, extending gratitude for the experiences and some imploring me to stay. But that was impossible. Fueled by stories from veteran foreign residents, and the possibility of close proximity to a vibrant nightlife, I eagerly anticipated prospects in the big city.

By then Tomoko's bleeding had increased which became the source of enormous frustration on my part and I began to seriously reconsider my plans to cohabitate, marry and eventually start a family with her in Kobe. After visiting the doctor, we learned that her bleeding was related to several years of untreated Chlamydia, which may have caused damage to her reproductive system and could result in an ectopic pregnancy. This in my mind, was the nail in the coffin and dashed any hopes of a long term relationship between us, as I was not willing to risk the possibility of marrying someone infertile, especially if this infertility was the result of carelessness with her own health.

Callous as it sounds, it was not my problem that Japanese women in general were still in the dark ages and didn't make it a common practice to get an annual pap smear. It was not my problem that women, people in general are uninformed in this backward traditional society and are unaware that Chlamydia is asymptomatic in 80% of women.

Though she was quite disappointed, in my transition from the countryside she seized the opportunity to be supportive, introducing me to her parents, telling her mother we had met in England, sometimes even allowing me to stay at their home, harboring hopes of my changing my mind and reverting to plans of our sharing a life. However, though I appreciated her endeavor, staying with her and her family solidified my decision indelibly, after being exposed to her less than healthy family dynamics. Tomoko's mother was one of the many elderly women in Japan, who end up abusing their bed-ridden husbands in retribution for abuse those husbands had inflicted on the family when they ran the show.

A former construction company executive and daily imbiber, he would repeatedly open several cans of whoop ass on her, her sister and her mother from as far back as she could recall. Now immobile from a stroke some five years prior, her mother being the only caregiver, felt angst and bitterness at having to care for her former abuser. Adding to her aguish was the fact that his illness had been rapidly depleting the family's funds, driving them hastily to bankruptcy. Shortly after, I began to read with frequency about this phenomenon throughout Japan and as barbaric as it was, I clearly understood the women's motivations and could not help commending them on their acts of vengeance.

For these women, years of enduring in quiet desperation finally came to a hilt. Pay back is a bitch. Indeed, as Japan becomes the most aged society in the world, according to the National Police Agency, in 2005, over ten percent of crimes committed in Japan, excluding traffic violations, were by the elderly. In the same year, 141 seniors were arrested for murder, which was 3.1 times the 1990 level. In many cases the victims were spouses. The agency also states that in the year 2005, 17.9 percent of all murders were of spouses, compared with 31.9 percent among the elderly. I envisioned Tomoko's mother's future among those statistics. However, it's rather ironic how the guards and enforcers of the patriarchy during their silver years are reduced to having to hold onto their wives for support when while during their youth, the wives were relegated to trailing humbly behind them, taking the utmost care not to step in their shadows.

Historically in Japan, it was customary for women to walk behind their husbands and it was forbidden for her to even step in his shadow, as that was a sign of gross disrespect. Still today at some weddings, that tradition is observed as the woman trails the man.

This is diametrically opposite to my practice, where if we are not walking hand in hand, I insist on her taking the lead so that I can savour the view from behind, which is why it's important that there BE a *view* from behind. Nevertheless, Tomi's mother treated me with great hospitality, especially after presuming her daughter, who was well beyond the Christmas cake age, had finally found a marriage candidate, never mind that he was not Japanese.

On the way back from our final trip to Kobe Kaisei hospital, regarding her bleeding, in a café at Rokkomichi, a tearful Tomoko presented me a touching letter and dived into what appeared to be a well thought out marriage plea. But given her affliction and my addiction, there would be no connubial arrangements between us. Still, in the ensuing weeks, she helped me to find an apartment in a Kobe suburb and our meetings withered to rare booty calls, as she began dating online.

My back up plan was to groom Ai for marriage and in so doing, tried to instill in her the value of higher education. Given her artistic talent, I tried to get her to continue her education in graphic art or design at a university in Osaka, but neither she nor her mother saw the importance of an education. To them, it was much better for her, like a significant percentage of Japanese women, to continue working at some dead end retail job. But homie wasn't having any of it. In the event I returned to the States, which was most likely, I was not open to my wife slaving away at K-mart and moreover, in my omnipresent daydreams during my childhood, my imagined wife was more educated than I was. After realizing that Ai and her parents could not appreciate my values, Ai, like the others in the countryside, was demoted to a "satellite honey," guaranteeing me pleasure whenever I visited.

KAORI

Kobe Sannomiya, the city with the most genitalia baring public art was a starkly different place from the countryside in my rearview mirror. On almost every corner one would be assaulted by sculptural montes veneris or phalli. The women, waxed, over-polished apples, were clad, or more accurately unclad in sexualizing attire: knee-high boots, fishnets, micro-minis even in the dead of winter and adorned in every name brand fashion and accessory. It was an effortless thrill to sneak a peak at their panties, a favourite past time of mine since my childhood. Women in Sannomiya were dressed for action. Similar to my first impression of Japan, they were too beautiful and I instantly recalled the first rule of economics, taught to me in my weeder econ 101 class: If it looks and sounds too good to be true, it probably is too good to be true. Though they all appeared to have stepped from the same pages of CanCam magazine – the fashion bible for Japanese women - nonetheless, they were most delectable and I stood whiplashed in awe at the sea of choices.

Kaori had *cakes* the likes of a *sister*. At first I spotted her from behind walking in the muggy Kobe summer, *onion* quaking north and south on gyrating hips, cloaked in skintight back pocketless jeans. Her small waist accentuated the curvature of her stunningly beautiful childbearing hips. Not much on the anterior, but that was ok.

"Breasts are for white guys, prematurely weaned after six months of breast feeding," I opined.

I on the other hand, suckled my mother until I was five years old and can even remember my grandmother offering her bosom to pacify me at the ripe old age of eight. So for me, breasts are over-rated. My only requirements are; they must be teardrop shaped, big enough to fit in my grasp and be live not Memorex. Homie simply cannot live in silicone valley. Posterior, cakes, glutes, onions, on the other hand, to which any normal, sane Negroe man can attest, is indispensable and the sight of a wicked rump on a woman makes me hyperventilate. Kaori had one of those, her cheeks were illegal, shuddering like two leaves caught in a gentle breeze as she walked. I just wanted to just, reach out, grab them, sink my teeth in them and bury my face deep between her cheeks. For several blocks I stalked her in hypnotized concupiscence, my tongue cleaning the Kobe sidewalks. Her stride was powerful and resolute, with her feet cradled in black square-toed heels, as opposed to those pointy toed, roach killers that other Japanese girls wore. She had no choice but to walk in such a bold manner, her load was weighty and though she was not well endowed in the anterior, so determined was her ambulation that her little mounds jumped like the fishes in the summer time song.

Collapsing madly in love, all before even seeing her magnificent face and lighthouse smile, I knew I was a goner, because my usual confidence did a disappearing act, with verbal paralysis emerging in its stead. Judging from her disposition, she was not the typical diffident Japanese woman and I was fully aware of the monumental social taboo of *nampa*, or picking or chatting up Japanese women, especially on the streets in public.

To a great extent, human relations here are based on the Buddhist/ Confucianist approach, which makes things unnecessarily difficult and complex and usurps fluidity from otherwise normal human social interaction. The *Buddfucianist* system generated many requirements in order for relationships to be established, hence from the traditional Japanese perspective, a relationship cannot be initiated because there was no relationship before it. Therefore a middle person is necessary in bringing parties together. Keeping with the rigid over stylizations of their society, they still rely on structured, organized arrangements for people of the opposite sex to meet, so strangers speaking to each other at random - as is common in the West - is out of the question. Instead, the kompa, - a variant of the English word companion - where an intermediary organizes a meeting between an equal number of men and women, in most cases over drinks, is widely utilized.

An ironic exception to this stylization is the netto shinjou, or internet suicide phenomenon, which emerged in October 2001. In this trend, the suicide minded can efficiently meet on the web, decide on a time, location and an automobile in which to conduct their group exit. A lit charcoal burning stove is placed inside the vehicle, followed by their peaceful farewell as a group. To date the largest group has been nine members.

The kompa, or omiai parties are big business in Japan, with men being charged around 4,500 yen, about $US45 and women, around $25 to enter. There are even special kompas for women whose sights are set for example, on doctors and lawyers. Exposing the darker side of these parties, the National Consumer Affairs Center of Japan recently reported that there were 3,197 complaints from patrons of these events in fiscal 2005, three times the amount a decade ago. In August 2006 a 42-year-old man from Osaka was arrested for confining, starving and beating a 24-year-old woman whom he had met at an omiai party and according to the police, he had targeted these parties, abusing several women he had met at the events, including a woman found collapsed and emaciated at his apartment in 2004.

Marginally recovering from my regression to elementary school days, I managed to muster some courage, as time was of the essence. I could have stalked her only for so long without being discovered.

"You look like you speak English," an opener with a high success rate in the big city. They all wanted to be cosmopolitan and that line complimented them on their alleged international appearance, without clueing them in on my real objectives. "Yeh, a little," flashing her white picket fences. And my cocky arrogant confidence from my Jamaican socialization resuscitated with furor. Ching ching! It was in the bag. In no time I had her phone number and as I watched her disappear in the crowd to meet her friends, I decided yes, "*there is a God*." My new found deity was Kaori's glutusmaximus and she became my first stated, officially acknowledged girlfriend in Japan.

Love was blissful and I relished in nightly insomniac obsession about her, sometimes even calling her as early as five o'clock in the morning, only to hang up before the phone started ringing. On one particular morning, after a night of complete sleep deprivation, I inline skated down to Harborland to kill time before calling her at seven o'clock sharp, when I knew she would be up.

"Are you up?" I asked like an elementary school pupil. "I'm sorry to call so early, but I've been thinking about you." And like a 12-year-old, at the ripe old age of thirty-seven I mustered up the courage to propose to this 24-year-old.

"I think I want you to be my girlfriend." Her response was not exactly what I wanted to hear.

"I will have to think about it." I couldn't believe I was having this juvenile exchange at my age.

"Take your time, whenever you're ready. It's OK." And after many dates, including one paragliding in Kanabe it just gradually happened. On our first kiss, in the stairwell of her parents' government subsidized apartment building – a nice name for the projects - she was awkward and trembling and at 24, a grown adult. "*Such behavior implied trauma*," I thought. Like many other women and especially in Japan, after much coaxing she recounted to me her molestation at five years old, by two high schoolboys, in that very stairwell. Tears rolling down her cheeks, this was her first time to reveal to anyone how they pulled her pants down, held her against the wall and began to probe her genitalia. As usual upon hearing stories like this, I immediately began to fantasize about finding them and bashing their heads erratically and incessantly against the ground. Again like most women, she had internalized this for all this time, before her revelation to me after much probing and persuasion.

Socially primitive Japan is void of any support mechanism for victims of child molestation and in this archaic, folk society, no one even dares to talk about these experiences, but they are rampant. Such is the retarded patriarchy that, often whenever a teacher molests a student, the authorities are far more concerned about the reputation of the school, than the rights of the students. In their warped sense of reason, or a lack thereof, the teacher is not dismissed because "he has a family to feed" and "we simply can't allow this incident to tarnish our image, so it must be concealed." In this day and age, this the year of the dog, such is still the dark thinking of the Japanese.

Kaori was adventurous, played saxophone and loved jazz, but up until then, had been exposed only to mediocre or flat out bad Japanese jazz. Hence it was my duty as a Negroe male to school her on the music of my people, which the Japanese so frequently butchered. An introduction to John Coltrane was a must, but like many other Japanese who claimed to be into jazz, Coltrane was too fukuzatsu (complicated). They all seemed to think that jazz was Kenny G's elevator music or some song by Frank Sinatra. Indeed, the Japanese, owing to their low emotional quotient and perpetually childish socialization, have a strong aversion to the complicated. They have a low threshold for difficulties and bothersome issues, and an extremely high tolerance for the monotonous.

Kaori soon began to appreciate the exposure to the real deal and I grew more attracted to her avante garde personality. The pusillanimous demeanor which was the embodiment of the average Japanese woman, was nowhere to be found in her and like I did with the manager with whom I was in love in the countryside, I suspended my predatory behavior, delaying her introduction to the beast, though I wanted to ravage her daily. But, there was always Tomoko, the women in the countryside and many more

I would meet in the big city, including Kyoung, who I had met at the
Kobe International Community Center.

KYOUNG

Kyoung was a Korean immigrant, who had left home about four months prior to our meeting. An Asian Audrey Hepburn, she was drop dead gorgeous and classy. No Japanese woman then matched her warmth, spunk and outgoing personality, but there was one major flaw: her shoulders were wider than her hips. Though a major turn off for me, the imbalance was not so much as to be a complete repellent. I could've lived with it, given her train stopping beauty and could hardly wait to be on display with her in public. What rendered her proportions unacceptable was my suspicion that the mounds on her chest were Memorex and not live. Ten years in Hollywood had honed my skills in detecting silicone implants even if hidden under a nuclear bunker. It would be easier for me to be aroused by a utility pole in fishnets than for breast implants to stimulate me. And as such, I pursued only a friendship with her savouring the radiance of her presence. This backfired as she fell madly in love, thinking I was a "nice guy," as no other man had been around her without crumbling to his knees in lust, wanting to connive his way into her panties. Such was her experience since forever, always the object of every man's desire back in Korea. But little did she know, as stated earlier, silicone valley is not even on my list of places to visit. There's nothing more horrendous than the taste of plastic covered wood.

REIKO

After three long months of homelessness and a few nights sleeping in the outdoors on a bench at Harborland, I joined the ranks of the employed, teaching at an Osaka based firm, where Reiko was a student. A veteran employee of 25 years, she was 45, divorced fifteen years before we met and the single parent of a 23-year-old daughter. Except for slightly drooping cheeks and being a bit on the svelte side having been a vegetarian, she was breathtakingly beautiful and well preserved. An older Tia Carrerra, her fashion was extremely feminine, but more girlie with lots of pinks, light greens and frills. Nothing about her said she was 45 except for the smell of fermenting gums which is common among people, especially her age in Japan. The dental hygiene of the Japanese is worse than that of the British in the 1980s. But I am happy to report that, in my 7 years here it has improved.

Susceptible to gum disease, I make it a routine to visit the dentist four times a year for scaling and polishing, but whenever I visit the dentist here, they'd tell me that the plaque on my teeth is not enough about which to be concerned and that my teeth are still beautiful even with the small amount of tartar. To that I would respond by imploring them to clean my teeth anyway and on two occasions, I was forced to give them a mini lesson on scaling and relaying to them the importance of scaling all teeth. Though the Japanese are advance in dental research, paradoxically, preventive dental care is foreign to most Japanese.

Given Reiko's current state of affairs, she was prime target for a take over, as not only was she among the demographics of neglected women in Japan, but she was also among what I call the untouchables: divorced with a child. Small wonder her sex life had been a desert for some fifteen years. But help was on the way, I would soon be her oasis. As the divorce rate rises in Japan, so does the number of these women.

About three weeks after the beginning of the semester, Reiko invited me to a performance of the company's choir and symphony, where I seized the opportunity to exchange phone numbers and e-mail addresses. In fact, that was my sole motive for accepting her offer, as for me any Japanese reproduction of Western music was likely to be excruciatingly intolerable. And as I had anticipated, the experience was tantamount to being stuck on an elevator with muzak torturing my tympanic membrane. Among the repertoire was the song 'The Happy Wanderer,' a song I tired of in the fourth grade. But the two-hour persecution was a means to an end and my mission was accomplished.

It was through our telephone conversations that I learned of her divorce, the fifteen year celibacy - albeit not self-imposed - and her love for the gym, something we shared in common. This resulted in my proposing to train her after class on Thursdays, which would give me a chance to see her in gym attire and assess her physique. Thinking this could be another mother daughter arrangement, I wanted to meet her daughter, but was terribly disappointed and relieved at the same time, to find that Reiko was more beautiful than her offspring.

"So how do you live without sex for fifteen years?" I asked on the phone.
"Muzukashi, its difficult" she sighed.
"I try not to think about it."
And from those responses, it was clear that she was game.
"Then we should just go to a love hotel after class" I suggested jokingly, but serious as my erection. And I could hear the rapids of Niagara falls in her panties. "Really?"
"Yeh, It'll be our secret. I don't wanna get fired."

The next Thursday after class, Reiko bade me good-bye and boarded the Keihan train with her friends as usual and I waited in the plaza at Kyobashi between the JR and Keihan lines as planned. About thirty minutes later she emerged from the station with a mile wide grin, like a kid who had been promised a trip to Disneyland and lead me to a nearby hotel. There I began to defrock this grinning 45-year-old little girl, as the beast rose. Leisurely I removed her jacket, then unhooked her skirt allowing it to fall to her ankles as she stood there like a blissful fruit being peeled. I unbuttoned her blouse to reveal her frilly, lacy bra and began to gently bite on her cups before unhooking it. Her breathing became heavy as I stuck my hand inside her nylons, expecting to meet a forest, but to my surprise she was well groomed.

"Did you shave because we were meeting today?"
"No, I always do." And with that I peeled off her nylons and panties, all the while throbbing in my pants.

"Touch my cock," I requested.

"What is cock?"

I unbuckled my pants, stepped out of them to show her the bulge through my undies.

"Chotto doki doki. I am a little nervous."

"I know," I said comfortingly. "It's been a long time for you."

Speechlessly she placed her hand on me and I began sucking on her teardrop shaped breast as I eased her on the bed. Avoiding her mouth, I went straight to tenderly feasting in the southern hemisphere, which sent her head flying backward and caused her to release loud grunts. My lips met with an avalanche of pent up fluids and I feasted on her for about twenty minutes, torturing her with pleasure. Then I stopped to remove my shirt and freed myself from the confines of my underwear as she removed her slip and bra.

Upon seeing the patriot with her name carved on it, she blurted out the predictable

"okii desu ne. Ita so."

"It won't hurt," I tried to assure her. "And if it does, it'll only be in the beginning." Having been fifteen years since her last act of intimacy, the sight of any phallus would've spell bounded her, let alone a charcoal one. She watched me roll on the magnum 500.

"I can't imagine that inside me," she whispered, as I spread her legs and slowly eased inside her invulnerable pseudo virginity.

"Dame, dame dame!"

"I'm almost in," as she squealed and inched her way up the bed before I was parked deep inside.

"Sugoii! Kakuii! You're so muscular," exploring my body with her hands as I re-devirginised her. Soon her squeals turned to groans, as I watched myself in the oversized mirror at the head of the bed. Once again, the devil was coming to the rescue of some poor Japanese soul, bringing her life's pleasures, of which she had been deprived for so long. After a few minutes she began grunting like an animal in the wild and this once passive and gentle lady was transformed to a breathless, railing ape as she climaxed.

"Iku, iku, iku, iiiiiikuuu," eyes pressed shut, squeezing every drop from her orgasm.

"Kimochii, Kimochiokatta," trying to catch her breath.

"Sugoii, sensei."

"*Today is the first in a long weekly series of 'dinglish' classes for you*," I thought to myself, turning her around to face the mirror at the head of the bed.

I wanted her to see herself being pounded by her English teacher from behind. Fondling her while pounding her doggie style drove her crazy and in no time flat, the ape was back and her once neatly styled hair was now all over the place. After her fourth orgasm she was exhausted.

"Shindoii, mo dekinai." "Sensei ikanai?" "Nande?" (I'm tired, I can't go anymore. Teacher, aren't you going to come? Why not?)

"Because I want you to come and enjoy yourself."

"Sugoii, you have good technique."

"Here, put it in your mouth."

"I'm hetta desu yo, I'm no good."

"That's ok, let's do a level check." Removing the condom, she accompanied me to the bathroom to wash the latex off, and even after a mini bath in the face basin, I was still as hard as steel, desperately wanting to release, preferably in her mouth. This desire was not driven by chauvinism and having power over women, but by the need to ejaculate in an orifice, any orifice.

As she knelt and placed me in her mouth in the bathroom, it was clear she was right. She was no expert. So I instructed her to hold her mouth in position around me as I pleasured myself to release the rapids. In no time it was high tide as I grabbed her by her ruffled locks and pulled her head toward me. My white syrup, enough to populate the universe, or certainly Japan, filled her mouth as she looked up at me, then rose to her feet to spit in the face basin.

"Ipaii." "Sugoii desu ne?" "Hajimete kono keiken. I never experience like this before. I almost didn't take your class."

"Why was that?" I queried.

"Kowaii kara." "I was afraid, kokujin kowaii. (Negroes are scary) I never saw a black person before, telebi to, eiga dake. (Only on TV and in movies.) Sometimes around Osaka, but we never had kokujin sensei before, so I almost cancel."

"So, are black people still scary?"

"No, no. subarashii (wonderful)."

This was not the first time that I had assumed the role of ambassador for my race in Japan. Since my arrival I had changed for the better, many Japanese people's perception of Negroes, at least the male of the race anyway. It was not a responsibility of which I made light. Even when I was *getting busy*, I thought myself an ambassador for Negroes in this country and while teaching I was always a teacher with great impact on students, whether in the class or bedroom. Teaching was my passion and it came in all forms.

"No, I'm glad I didn't cancel."

Our weekly *dinglish* classes continued for nine months, even after introducing her to my girlfriend Kaori and when she experienced withdrawals, she would take the long drive to my apartment for a fix. As I predicted, she became exceedingly attached, desperately requesting love and companionship from me, of which I could give her neither. All that was available from me were multiple orgasms and English classes until the following spring. But of course I was not so harsh to reveal this to her. Instead I told her of my desire to start and raise a big family and without telling her directly, she understood that her age was a deterrent. Especially since my then girlfriend shared the same age – and name - as her daughter. Every week in class I got a rush maintaining our little secret and remembering the wild ape to which I could transform her. Sometimes memories of me deep inside her, or of the charcoal in her mouth excited me in front of the class, which I had to conceal by placing my hand in my pocket.

"You're a good actor," she always said. "Nobody can know about us, from how you act in class."

In the end her rotting gums and more so, incurable naiveté and infantilism lead me to abandon her. Like all Japanese women I'd met thus far, except Kaori, Rieko's emotional development lagged far behind her chronological age. She might have been 45, but emotionally, my then 14-year-old daughter in California was her emotional senior. This created deep frustration toward Japanese women and to Japanese society at large. Indeed, many Western men, after extensive residency here find themselves becoming angry for reasons unexplainable to them. However, from my far from professional analysis, the constant existence in Disneyland, the sheer childishness of this society is a major contributing factor to that phenomenon.

Curing Reiko's gingivitis or periodontitis was a simple matter of introducing her to the idea of biannual dental visits, but at 45, curing her toddler-like behaviour - the constant giggling and unstimulating conversations - would prove impossible. So I introduced her to a Jamaican friend of mine in Kobe. Having been turned out by a foreigner and now addicted, she wanted to expand her circle of foreign friends, especially when I informed her that most Western men wouldn't care that she is a divorced single parent. Foreign men and especially black men – the very men of whom she was afraid only some months prior – offered some semblance of hope to quench her human desires. Reiko thought it a simple introduction, but little did she know I was passing her on, like hand me downs from relatives when I was child. Coincidentally, some two years later Reiko bought a condo five minutes away from my apartment and invited me to participate in a threesome with her and a Canadian man she had met and bedded the same day in Kyoto. However, recalling those festering gums, I declined.

KAORI CONTINUED

Kaori was the second woman after Tomoko, who visited my apartment, where instead of consuming the concoction I had intended serving her, she prepared me a tasty treat of rolled cabbage stuffed with beef. Little did I know that what I started with her, inviting her over to engage in some culinary experiments, cooking the only meal I could prepare – chicken – would come to be the sex ritual. In all cases, having been accustomed to so little from Japanese men, the women were excited at being waited on, even if the food was insufferably bad.

After ingesting my culinary experiments, they'd insist on doing their programmed womanly duties, washing the dishes and cleaning up, but I would insist on doing it myself, a situation they had never before beheld, reinforcing their perception of the kind foreigner.

Before we could clear the dishes from the floor of my tableless kitchen, Kaori's lips and mine were glued, as I pried her out of her skintight jeans. Her round cheeks hung out of her pink lacy low cut panties and Charlie was like an out of control fire hose upon seeing the object of his lust in the nude. After two months of salivating in anticipation, that afternoon I grew to an unusual size and knew I wouldn't have lasted more than two seconds after entry, magnum 500 covered and all. Immediately I did what I had been fantasizing about for the past two month: knelt down slowly in front of my deity to lick then suck and massage her cakes, while nibbling at her lilac-fragranced crotch through her panties. Wanting desperately to gawk at her, I removed her top and bra, revealing her champagne glass sized breasts and made her stand only in her panties, in the middle of my bare tatami room. Looking more Latina than Japanese, her skin was a mocha brown and I began to conclude that my fetishized face with upturned slitty eyes, a concave nose and tofu skin, did not come with a posterior of such curvature. That was until I met Shoko some seven months later.

Though Kaori was not what my extreme preference required, her beauty was astonishing, and that rump, it inflicted pain throughout my body.

While looking at her, imagining she was an inaccessible magazine girl, I began to pleasure myself, predictably firing off on my tatami in two seconds flat. Kaori was conservative, one of those serious types and this was her first gaijin experience. My fascination with her rump was befuddling to her, as she held a massive complex about her atypically Japanese *bumpa*. Also astounding to her was my uninhibited self-pleasure in front of her, which to her had been a whole new experience.

"Hazukashikunai? (Aren't you self-conscious?)

"Hell no!"

"Why did you do that?" she asked. And with that I removed her panties, waded through her bush and began to dine. Self-pleasure before entrance was a good move, as unlike other Japanese girls up until then, she required work in order to climax.

Within the succeeding three months interpersonal problems arose and the marathons she required for just one orgasm soon became torturous. This is purely anecdotal, but there seems to be a high correlation between hypo-orgasmic tendencies and a protruding rump, just as there's an apparent correlation with hyper-orgasm and a protruding pubic mound. It may well be that steatopygia and a protruding pubic mound are mutually exclusive. Stamina on my part was no problem, I'm a cardio freak. But as an attention deficit hyperactive adult, it simply became boring and I soon derived more pleasure in reciting in my head during our sex, the names of the train stations between Osaka and Kobe on the JR line.

Although sporting this new *kakoii kokujin* (cool Negroe) boyfriend was very impressive to her friends, she found it most frustrating having to communicate, her feelings.

"I didn't have to do that with my ex-boyfriends," she frequently complained. "They always knew what I was thinking."

"That's because they were Japanese! I am not."

The Japanese are proud of the apparent missing need to communicate verbally in their intimate and other relations. They claim to just know about each other's thoughts and needs without words. However, this is less attributable to some innate ability and more to do with their over-stylised, homogeneous socialization. Given a certain context, the Japanese have been all programmed to think and act in the same way.

There is a Japanese way for everything including a prescribed way to pack the kids' obento (lunch) for school. Parents rely on books to explain to them in great details, how to pack their children's lunch. Any deviation may result in bullying and or teasing, and the impression that the mothers don't love their children. As a result, the victim may stay home and become a hikikomori (recluse) sometimes never again setting foot in school. Many schools prohibit the purchase of lunches at convenience stores, as that would supposedly cause the child to feel unloved. Daily existence for the Japanese is steeped in a dazzling myriad of rituals. From the proper degree of a bow (15 to 45 degrees depending on the occasion) to how a lady eats a rice cracker (a handkerchief should be placed on her lap and the cracker must be broken by hand into bite sized pieces), these over-stylised practices are the main source of stress for the Japanese.

On the subject of chopstick use, there are over 30 faux paus maneuvers. Collectively, the Japanese are androids with the same operating system, coded to respond to various situations and stimuli in the exact fashion. This conditioning begins in infancy and has continued for hundreds, if not thousands of years. It covers every aspect of their lives, from how to hand someone a business card to what to say before and after a meal or upon entering a house, even if the house is empty. Whereas this communication style, or lack thereof, might be effective if all the parties involved are Japanese, it usually proves disastrous in intimate relations between a Japanese and a foreigner, especially a Westerner.

In fact, as any thinking person can conclude, this non-communication pattern has only a limited positive effect. It may have worked for the Japanese for many hundreds of years, but in these modern times it only highlights the communicational retardation in which the Japanese are socialized. Among contemporary Japanese, employing this non-verbal communication usually exacerbates the problems and leads to extensive periods of silence and misery between spouses. Many of the married women with whom I have been intimately involved, have expressed to me the absence of verbal communication with their husbands, except to talk about the day's meal, sometimes lasting up to fifteen years.

Our second problem was Kaouri's housing projects-dwelling-uneducated-redneck parents who, previously not having interacted with any foreigners, displayed immeasurable ignorance. Her mother, who may have never left Hyogo Prefecture, thought it would have been an embarrassment to her if her friends knew her daughter was dating a Negroe and adamantly opposed Kaori's continuing her education from the equivalent of community college. Her sentiments made me livid and I decided immediately upon hearing them, to have no part of her family. After all, this is Japan and I'm a novelty in this big sea of choice, which I was devouring, unbeknownst to her and her mother.

ANITA MCKENZIE

Among my choices was Anita McKenzie, an unusually, strikingly stunning young woman of 19 years old. Half-Canadian and half-Japanese, she was the poster child for the advantages of hybrid vigor, the result of heterozygousity, or race or species mixing, bearing a strong resemblance to an infinitely more attractive Gina Davis. She was all that and much more and having been raised partly in the West, she was fully aware of it, standing near the cinema at Hankyu Sannomiya train station waiting for her friend.

"You definitely ain't Japanese," to which she responded like I was the biggest piece of excrement she had ever smelled.
"I'm half," snarling scornfully.
"Yo, it ain't gotta be like dat, I'm just happy to see someone who look like they can speak English. What's the other half?"
"My dad's Canadian," she said with much attitude. Only thing missing was her head moving back and forth on her neck like an African-American woman, or a dancing Indian woman, or even one of those figurines with a spring for a neck. Now, most women are beautiful, but Anita fell under the extreme far right of the bell curve, the hyper-babe area, and experience taught me that hyper-beauts required an even more indirect approach, as they are always being bombarded and accosted by unwanted advances, especially by what they considered to be undesirable men.

One of my hyper-beaut exes, told me she was shocked I had the confidence to speak to her, as she was always being approached by unsavoury characters who had nothing to lose by chatting her up. My sensitivity to women's issues never failed to get me laid and this was no devious scheme I concocted to get them in bed. In fact, having been socialized by some 60 women on a church commune until I was 14, I am fully in tuned with women's psyche and am genuinely concerned about women's issues. Still to this day, I am far more comfortable in the presence of women. Indeed a perfect description of myself, as I once told a woman in Los Angeles, and as I've stated earlier, is that of a lesbian happily stuck in a man's body. Having such early sexualization in this all female environment, made me

– as one Japanese woman told me – a woman's worst nightmare and up until my recent recovery, nothing could be closer to the truth. Another lesson I had learned from my experiences is that, hyper-babes appear to have more and bigger emotional suitcases than the DSMR-5 could list. Unscientific research from my personal encounters showed a high rate of childhood sexual abuse, warping or destroying their perception of self. It was overly clear to me that Anita's attitude was a defense mechanism to protect herself, having possibly encountered some trauma.

"Why the hell would you, as beautiful as you are, having spent ten years in Canada and nine years in Japan, a native speaker of Japanese and English, why would you wanna come back to Japan? I'd think that for a person like you, there'd be more opportunities in the West. Except if you wanna be an office lady or a hostess."

And with that question and statement, I broke down the wall, softened her attitude and revealed a major vulnerability: her identity crisis being biracial and living in both countries for almost the same duration.
"Yeh, I totally hear you on that one, but I don' know. Sometimes I feel like Canada is home and sometimes I feel like Japan is." However, knowing what I knew about the social retardation of Japan, I still found it extremely curious that her family returned here after living in Canada for ten years.

Shortly there after her friend arrived, sporting an even nastier attitude than Anita's, but the reason behind her funky disposition was easier to recognize. Hers was the angst of the less attractive friend, or more accurately, the unattractive friend, always in Anita's shadow and getting far less attention. Anita then introduced me to the Japanese wannabe flygirl, who thought a bit much of herself.
"Hiiiiiiii! Anita let's go."
And on that note they started to leave. "Hey wait, you ain't even gonna leave me with an e-mail address, or supm?" A request for an e-mail address is less imposing for hyper–babes and women in general in Japan.
"Daaaam, feel like I'm in Siberia, it's so cold," bringing a smile to her face as she rattled off her AOL address.
"I'm going back to Canada indefinitely next month."
"I'll e-mail you," I responded, hiding my gargantuan disappointment as I rode off on my mountain bike to meet Kyoung, whom I had kept waiting for about an hour.

KYOUNG CONTINUED

Kyoung and I had been locking lips for several months at my shared apartment in Motomachi. While Kaori slaved away at two jobs, Kyoung and I were getting to know each other very well, during which time I confirm my suspicions sucking on her wooden textured breasts. One evening during one of our sessions I asked directly and perhaps insensitively,

"uso no mune, itsu kara desu ka?" (how long have you had those fake breasts?) "Sona koto nai yo, uso ja nai," (That's not the case, they're not fake.) denying it even after I questioned her about the scar beneath her right breast. She said she had some kind of heart related surgery. *"Yeh right! I was born on a night, but not last night,"* I thought to myself. And we continued our necking with the instrument only at half mast. Soon thereafter she ventured to my new apartment for our first night together and to test my level of repulsion for breast implants. Immediately upon entering my empty apartment she abruptly asked,

"Nande shiteru?" "Darimo shiranai." "Nande shiteru?" (How did you know? Nobody knows. How did you know?) I explained to her that my ten years in Hollywood had perfected my silicone radar.

"Is that why you can't be with me?" she asked with tears welling. *"That and your shoulders being wider than your hips,"* I thought to myself.

"There are many guys who like them," I tried to reassure her. "I au, I just don't." Her countenance was consumed by disenchantment and regret and I empathized. Here's a woman who only four months prior, underwent surgery for what she thought would have enhanced her attractiveness – and to some it did - but has discovered that this expensive surgery was working against her as a repellent to the man of her desire. But even if I could've gotten past the taste of plastic covered wood, the emotional drama of which implants are indicative is beyond my level of tolerance.

"Kedo watashi tachi naka yoku yo," (we get along so well) tears streaming down her face. This dilemma was one of my most painful ever. Kyoung and I with perfectly matched personalities got on like a house on fire, even with our language difficulties. Everywhere we went there were daily compliments on our compatibility. She was striking, educated with an Audrey Hepburn kind of sophistication, traveled and of the least importance, from a very well to do family.

Being that she was a Korean woman and considering their propensity for cosmetic surgery, I enquired of other *enhanced* body parts. I began to suspect her perfectly beautiful nose, even began to suspect that the woman sitting in front of me crying, may at one time been a man. But that thought was fleeting, some women's shoulders are naturally wider than their hips, especially among Asians, and I had been around enough transsexuals to detect the nuances even if the outward appearance was perfect. Over eagerly, she tried to assure me that her nose was in its natural state and nowhere else on her body had gone under the knife.

"Mune dake." (Only my breasts) Unable to find some flexibility in my preferences, I sat there staring at the ceiling in silence.

"Anata no kangai kata kaeru koto ga dekinai no?" (Can't you change your thinking?) Unfortunately, that was something on which I could not compromise after which she suggested the unthinkable.

"Ja, toru." (I'll remove them). This sat very uncomfortably with me.

If there's one thing I have learned from the many years of torture I have inflicted on countless women in my past is, it's not good to try to or participate in changing physical features of one's partner. One must always accept the other person as he or she is: fat, slim, zaftig, flat-chested, protruding pubic mound, inadequately endowed, you name it.

So I objected to her proposal, expressing my appreciation, but objecting on the grounds that there are men who like fake breast and I was not worth her going through that pain. "But we can become good friends," I continued, knowing full well that after this rejection, that would be impossible for her.

"Kaeru." (I'm leaving.) And with that she picked up her handbag and headed for the door. Before putting on her shoes she turned to me and asked,

"Yate miru?" (Can you try?)

"I can't change my thinking, gomme ne (I'm sorry)

"I don't mean that," she responded. "Hechi." (sex).

I thought myself odd, putting this stunningly beautiful woman in a position where she saw it necessary to ask me if I could try to have sex with her. So I gently pulled down her jeans with her panties, bent her against the wall, with her handbag still around her arm, eased inside and unloaded irresponsibly inside her in seconds flat. This mercy lay was a cheerless sight as she pulled up her underwear sobbing, with my semen dripping from her.

"Don't worry about baby," she said. "Dai jyobu." (It's ok). The brief ten minute walk together to Koyoen station from my apartment seemed endless as we perambulated in silence. As she boarded the burgundy Disneylandesque Hankyu train, the imaginary violins played. It was a heartbreaking moment, especially because I was too inflexible to keep her fake breast from eroding our otherwise wonderful friendship. Not even as a satellite honey could I have kept her around, less because I hate silicone but more out of respecting her too much. And she couldn't have kept me around as a friend because her attraction for me was too strong. So as the violins played, the train departed and we waved solemnly to each other until out of sight.

For more than a year thereafter, Kyoung and I had random uncomfortable encounters on the streets of Kobe, where after the third such encounter, we endeavored to maintain contact by phone. But over the next year or so, the awkwardness got the better of us and our contact faded.

With Kyoung out the way, I could now focus on my futile relationship with Kaori, who had been telling me about her consultations with her Buddhist priest, for advice about our relationship. His advice was for her to bail. "Gaijins and Japanese are a mismatch, they can't understand each other," he recommended. And from the looks of things, she had begun to heed his guidance. One good thing was, her independent minded personality, more so than most Japanese women I met. As a result, I was able to convince her that at 24, it was high time to move away from her oppressive redneck parents and into a place of her own. A month later, against her parents' protest she found a quaint studio apartment in Kitano.

HENNI

That summer of 2002 I spotted the profile of bleach blond locks on the platform at JR Sannomiya station. Her hypnotic derriere was visible from miles away but her chest protruded even more.

"Where are you from?" I inquired, walking up to her, getting my mack on, as she looked me over with big, piercing, blue grey Betty Boop eyes.

"Romania."

"You know where is Romania?" pores drooling attitude.

Since my departure from the West, I had not paid attention to white women but, she, was, fine. In fact the only white women who attracted me, even before my arrival here, were Eastern, Central European and Nordic women, specifically Danish women.

Like most Eastern and Central European women I met here and in Korea, Henrietta was a hostess, in great demand by Japanese men, especially with her peroxide hair. She made bank from middle-aged Japanese men who paid her large sums to pour their drinks and stroke their egos along with the added privilege of conversing with her. Humility was not in her vocabulary and even as she rejected me, as though she was flicking a bug off her arm, it was somewhat refreshing to finally meet a woman with an edge and an air of confidence.

"I would love to take you back to California with me," I jested.

"Is that what you tell all the Japanese girls?" You tink I'm yellow cab?"

"Anyway, I'm getting married," showing me her rock. "So you're late."

"Is he from Romania too?"

"NO, of course not! I live in Japan, he's Japanese."

"He's a very lucky guy," I amused, seething with envy.

"*No Japanese dude can handle that!*" thinking to myself. And with a cockiness alien to Japanese women she blurted,

"I know he's lucky and I'm gonna make him know too."

"Does he treat you well?"

"He is very kind and considerate. He is soooooo different from other Japanese men."

"Well just gimme your number anyway and we'll go to Starbucks or supm.

Maybe you can invite me to the wedding. I've never been to a Japanese wedding before."

Reluctantly she gave up the digits, not knowing that I had sussed her out and accurately presaged her future in my bed with her lips, southern and northern sets, caressing me. In my prediction her insecure Japanese husband would insist that she ceases all hostessing activities and employment for that matter and become fully dependent on him. After which he would neglect her, opting for fifteen hour work days over fulfilling her needs. He would then impregnate her, escalating his neglect after the birth of the child and definitely leaving her saddled with all the child care and household duties. All this of course would take some time, maybe a couple of years but, not wanting to be the fox crying sour grapes, I kept my prophecies to myself. Moreover, as my days of dating white women were now behind me, I was afflicted with acute and incurable yellow fever which rendered me otherwise occupied, so I could've waited. Time was on my side.

Henni perhaps had not heard of the common Japanese saying relating to men, particularly Japanese men: Tsuta sakana ni wa esa o yaranai (You never feed a fish you've already caught.) It is often reported by many Western women who marry Japanese men, that once they are married, the exceptional, kind, loving open minded Japanese males they once knew, cease to exist and regress to the average uncaring, cold and inconsiderate economic animal which is the archetype of the Japanese male.

From online chat rooms to interviews I have conducted with strangers, most Western women who were married to Japanese men, reported stark frustration with their husbands after marriage. Japanese men with a preference for foreign women are fully aware that Western women would not tolerate their chauvinism, at least not initially. Resultantly, they modify their personalities to attract the apples of their eyes. In fact this is by no means limited to Japanese men, as men in general use all manner of devices to attract women and Japanese men also utilize these tactics to attract Japanese women.

However, this phenomenon appears to be more prevalent among Japanese men than among men in the West. And if it is not so, most certainly, more women − Japanese and otherwise − voice their discontent about this actuality in Japan than do women in the West. Among the couples who met in the West, the women recalled how compassionate and egalitarian their Japanese men were, but all that changed drastically when they moved to Japan and the males were reintroduced to their society of origin. They were blind to the pressure that their husbands or boyfriends would experience, to reconform to their social norms and, incognizant of the impact it would have on their relationships, many times ending in divorce. Certainly there are happy unions between Japanese men and Western women, but most such women to whom I spoke, four out of five expressed unhappiness and frustration.

In all fairness, this frustration is by no means limited to the Japanese male Western female union, as frustrations abound in unions between Japanese women and Western men. It is widely known that differences in culture, religion and intellect between two parties can be deleterious to marital longevity. It is also commonly known that Japan is a society averse to critical thinking, where interpersonal problems are solved predominantly through underdeveloped emotions, as opposed to through effective discussions. But more impacting than actual cultural differences of the parties involved, is the types of culture from which the parties originate.

Intercultural relationships are less problematic if both parties hail from cultures which place a high value on tradition and conformity, or are both from non-traditional cultures. Japan, a country the size of California, is an antediluvian, feudal, folk society, hidden under the façade of modernism. Still in this day and age intellectual thought (rikutsupoi) is near sinful and conformity is venerated. Therefore intimate unions between Japanese and Westerners from traditionally nonconformist societies, contain innate elements of hardship, even before the parties meet. In the West it is widely known that similarities in educational levels are key determinants of longevity in intimate relationships. If one party holds a tertiary education, while the other only a high school education, the relationship is more likely to fail. This disequilibrium in education between parties and the consequential likelihood of failure is tantamount to the intellectual imbalance in relationships between feudal, traditional, conformist Japanese parties and nontraditional Westerners.

Peace in this union requires that either the nonconformist party conforms, or vice versa. If both parties live in Japan, transformation pressure bares greater on the nontraditional party to at least appreciate popular village psyche though inversely, adjustment to folk society is far more difficult for the nontraditionalist than the other way around. From my unscientific finding, most white Western men express discontent with their Japanese wives, especially after the birth of their children. Citing her 180 degree change after childbirth, rants about wives withholding sex are especially rampant. However, a common religion serves to ameliorate the innate potential discord in the *NippoWestern* union and functions well as an intercultural lubricant. Evidence of this was found among the Western Christian men I have met in Japan, many of whom arrived as missionaries and none of whom had any complaints about their Japanese spouses, who were also followers of Christ.

Starbucks in Sannomiya was where Henni and I first agreed to meet, where I hustled in cold, pouring rain to make it at 11, fully anticipating her flaking. At Starbucks I waited 45 minutes before giving up to wander in the library for a browse through the classifieds for a second job. As probability would have it, I found an ad requesting a teacher for junior high schools throughout Kobe and Osaka, which had to be filled in two days. After rapidly firing off a resume to them, I dashed home to change into my suit and flashed back to Sannomiya where I rang the company from their lobby, to verify the receipt of my resume.
"When are you available for an interview," queried the voice at the other end. "What floor are you on?" I investigated.
"We are on the second floor."
"I can be there in thirty seconds."
During the interview, after a very quick analysis of the company, I told them of fabricated plans to get married and raise children in Japan, because I knew that's what they had wanted to hear. It gave the impression of stability, certainly masking my whoring tendencies. It worked and three days later I began employment.

Henrietta was by no means apologetic for standing me up in the rain and or not calling.
"Hey, it was raining," she reasoned, justifying her dis. But that was okay, I had found the perfect job teaching at junior high schools. Specifically I sought to avoid high schools as I knew it wouldn't have been long before I ended up like my buddy Big T, a dried out player from the 5 boroughs who had come to Japan in the good old bubble days. T impregnated one of his high school students during his tenure as an Assistant Language Teacher. Indeed, it was the potential for exactly that kind of drama which kept me away from Japanese high schools. Sex junkie that I was, that would have unquestionably been my destiny. However, escaping a life of drama in the States, I had decided that drama should be limited to the stage or in front of a movie camera, but certainly not in my life. And to that end, I chose to teach at junior high schools. With the students being 12 to 15 years old, I saw my daughter – who was then 14 when I left her in the States - in many of my female students and found nothing sexual

about them. Moreover, the trains, in particularly Japan Rail, provided an endless supply of beautiful and available women on tap.

Months passed when Henni and I bumped into each other, she on her way from school, I on my way to work. After all, to her surprise, I was now working for the school she attended. The shock on her face when she first saw me, the absolute last person she'd wanted to behold.
"What are you doing here?!" she screamed.
"You did me a favour. Remember when you stood me up in the rain? I found a job where you're studying Japanese."
"See, aren't you glad you met me? You can't be mad at me anymore." Relieved that something positive accidentally resulted from her standing me up in the freezing rain.

Frequent random encounters became the norm and on every occasion I mentioned Starbucks in sarcasm.
"I'm so busy, but I am gonna make it up to you."
After a year I began to notice a bulge in her clothes, which became more visible, along with a marked change in countenance as months passed. The once boisterous and cocky Romanian had wilted to a depressed Bo Peep, seeming to be in a deep funk every time we met. The more her belly protruded, the fatter she thought she was and the more her husband neglected her.
"How's married life?" I asked her once.
"I hate him! Do you see what he did to me? Pointing to her rotund abdomen.
"He doesn't even look at me now."

Some months later I saw Henni pushing a stroller with her son, by then reporting that she was completely neglected by her husband and now existing in the typical sexless Japanese marriage. Her son was then nine months old with her existing in a sexless marriage since shortly after the child was conceived. It was then that we finally made it to Starbucks as we had planned some eons back. During our conversations, or more accurately, her venting, I struggled not to say, "I told you so," and in the pursuing year I supported her in friendship as best as I could, mostly facilitating her venting about her inconsiderate husband and how he no longer returns home until the wee hours of the morning. In her native Romania she was a law student who had experienced severe physical abuse at the hands of her alcoholic father, who finally left when she was a teenager. Her mother followed suit, abandoning her to her grandmother.

"I made the biggest mistake of my fucking life."

"No you haven't, he is going to change." Knowing full well that yes, she had made a grave mistake and no, he wasn't going to change.

"If I had known you were so kind, I would've married you instead."

"And moved to California," I interrupted, though that would've never happened. I would not have been returning to Cali with any color other than yellow.

"So desu ne." (That's right, isn't it?)

"And this would have been your son," looking at me as though she had missed the chance of several lifetimes.

"Hey don't worry," I comforted.

"He can still be my son and though you're already married, I can still be your husband."

After a few more dates accompanied by her son at Starbucks in Sannomiya, I informed her of my plans to travel to Jamaica for an extended period, struggling with the reality that we could do nothing about my two and a half year old desire to at least bury my head in her voluptuous bosom before I left.

"Don't forget about me and your son in Jamaica, okay."

"Don't worry, I won't. I'll e-mail you."

KARIN

Among other fringe benefits, the dispatching language school offered steeply discounted Japanese language classes, of which I took full advantage. By then it was my birthday in mid November and Kaori, in the twilight of our relationship, had arranged a birthday dinner for me at Jamaicana, the Jamaican restaurant in Sannomiaya. Present were a few of her friends and my new Japanese language teacher, Hirota sensei. Karin Hirota could have been Bjork's beautiful sister. Her feline face was the epitome of the face I idolized and her hardly opened upwardly angled eyes disappeared to two lines when she flashed her heart melting, but sinister smile. Her perfectly concave nose - the nose Michael Jackson tried so arduously and with great futility to achieve - pointed slightly skyward at the ideal angle.

She had skin of porcelain and a tiny mole strategically placed on the outside of her upper left eyelid. Her face, though young in appearance, to me spoke of unspeakable trauma and freakiness, evil meets sexy and standing at 161 centimeters, her 59 kilograms was definitely over-weight by Japanese standards. Random old women frequently stopped her, telling her of the evil that she exuded and at least once every few months, she was the victim of stalkers - some mysteriously phoning her apartment - a phenomenon I loathed and enjoyed at the same time.

Even my grandmother in Jamaica commented on her sick appearance. "A weh yu get dat de gyal de fram? Yu nuh si se supm du har?" (Where'd you get this girl? Can't you see there's something wrong with her?) She confided to me during a trip to Jamaica with Karin. The evil those elderly ladies observed was perhaps some kind of Autistic Spectrum Disorder and further signs of fire in the hole was her Jaja Binks like gait, slightly slouching as she perambulated tiptoed, always seeming to be on the verge of falling on her face. These characteristics could have easily been invisible to most, but to me they were quite salient. It was as though she never quite recovered from the weight of her oppressive parents and the backpacks that she and other Japanese children were made to lug around in their elementary school years.

In deed among my earliest observations in Japan was its seemingly high rate of Autistic Spectrum Disorder, only to be validated by scientific data stating that Japan has the highest frequency of autism in the developed world. According to a March 2005 report by Hideo Honda of the Yokohama Rehabilitation Centre, even after Japan banned Measles Mumps Rubella (MMR) vaccines in 1993, autism shot up from 48-86 cases per 10,000 to 97-161 cases per 10,000. This is in comparison to a Center for Disease Control report in the same year, of 40 people per 10,000 in the United States. Experts disagree on the causes of the increased frequency in Japan, with some attributing it to contaminants in the environment and others, to changing diagnostic criteria and rising profile of the disorder. Those subscribing to the later, claim that Japan is more thorough in its analysis of the disease and includes conditions ignored by experts in the United States.

However, as a person acutely aware of this disorder since my childhood in my native Jamaica, the Autistic Spectrum Disordered were far more visible in Japan during my first few months, than they were during my 20 years in the United States, which has over two and a half times Japan's population. Individuals with this illness in Japan were surprisingly quite visible, though not as much so as the afflicted in Jamaica with a rate of 1000 per 10,000 people.

Environmental and genetic factors seem to be the most viable explanation for the higher frequency in Japan. One theory is, since a significant portion of the Japanese diet consists of fish, consumers thereof are affected by traces of mercury therein. Add to that the fact that in this vastly homogenous society, a significant majority hail from the same homozygous gene pool, which increases their genetic propensity for the disease. Upon setting foot on this island, I often lamented the frequent sightings on the train, of well suited men with attaché cases, engaging in extended intrusive exploration of their nostrils, sometimes playing with their findings between their fingers. Coincidentally, Japan shares some commonalities with Jamaica in this sense. Jamaica, an underdeveloped economy implements substandard ecological conservation measures, hence pollutants may well be a contributing factor to the ASD rate and almost like Japan, Jamaica is a near monoracial society. Some 95% of Jamaicans are of Negroe African decent.

At times Karin's arms seemed suspended motionless by her side as she walked, and other times they *pendulumed* ever so subtly out of sync with the rest of her body. Ever since nine or ten years old, I had observed a correlation between arm movements like hers, and some emotional or psychological disorder. Again, her abstract symptoms might have been invisible to the average person, but commingling with her exotic beauty, they were clearly discernible to me. As to her generally manly fashion sense, a corduroy blazer with masculine trousers gathered at the waist was her uniform. Uniquely attractive, along with elderly ladies who reproached her about her devilish aura, other random women showered her with compliments, and commended me on my taste. Bilingual, educated, well traveled, hailing from a well to do, notwithstanding, high pressure invalidating family, ten days after my birthday dinner, on November 25, she made her debut at my apartment for *dinner*.

On that Wednesday evening my Japanese language teacher arrived promptly, revealing a whole new Hirota Sensei right on my kitchen floor. After the meal and stimulating conversation on a wide variety of topics, I gambled and kissed her lips.
"Why'd you do that?"
"Because I couldn't resist."
"But I'm your teacher."
"Which makes me wanna kiss you even more," kissing her a second time, locking our mouths together. In no time I was at full attention just at the thought of invading my teacher, gradually stripping her down to her boring, anti-Viagra, slightly over-sized skin-toned panties. A former swimmer, her legs were thick and I began to cup her overly protruding mons veneris and explore her bush.
"Dame, we shouldn't be doing this, I'm your teacher," as she jerked abruptly to my touch and collapsed on the kitchen floor. With my hand still in her panties playing with her, I followed her to the ground where she wiggled, panted and began to flail and kick aggressively on the floor.
"IKU IKU IKU IKU IIIIIKU!"
"*Impossible*," I thought, as I had been touching her for less than two minutes. "*Was that fake?*" I investigated to myself as she tried to catch her breath post touchdown.

From my experiences, I discovered a correlation between a protruding pubic mound and the ease with which women achieve orgasm. Though I have not read anything scientific on the matter, all the women whom I had known biblically and who possessed this anomaly, climaxed with great ease. This condition in women for me made for a most unpleasant sexual experience, as they were often too large and at an odd angle with the protruding bone always painfully hitting against my pubic area. However, it may well be conducive to effortless delivery during childbirth, I surmised.

Karin had the most protruding mons pubis I had ever encountered.

Shortly after, I began to lead her to my bedroom.

"No, no dame, I should go. I shouldn't be doing this." But it was too late, her Achilles heel was already revealed and with that I merged my lips with hers again in perfect union and ventured between her creamy sallow thighs. Almost immediately she lost control and once again collapsed on the floor between my bedroom and the kitchen as my fingers worked their magic.

"I know you have to go, but I want you to come for me one more time before you go."

"DAME! DAME! IKU! DAME!"

"Don't fight it," I said calmly. "It's ok, just let it out and enjoy it. There's nothing to feel bad about," I whispered to her, sensing that she may have had some kind of complex about her ultra-frequent and violently animated orgasms. Again, she began to flail, rail and kick, but with far greater intensity than before. She became increasingly belligerent and destructively animated, even hitting her limbs and head against the wall, as if being tickled to death. Amazed at her goliath strength, I straddled her while fondling her, taking care not to rest my weight on her as she lay on her back. Bucking like a bronco, she yelled at the top of her voice,

"SHINU! SHINU! (I'm dying, I'm dying.)DAME! (STOP!) IKU! IKU IKU, ita, ita." (I came, I came.) Hyperventilating, "I thought I was gonna die." Picking her up off the ground again, I finally lead her to my bedroom where I stripped, rolled on protection in preparation for the descent. Though she was like a well deep and wide, penetration was unpleasant for her, something to do with the angle of her heaven. She hated penetration. So I withdrew and settled for torturing her orgasmicly with my fingers and mouth. Before leaving my apartment 45 minutes later, I had released twice on her pearl skin and she had achieved some 17 orgasms.

"I could get addicted to this," I thought. *"Pleasuring a woman so effortlessly would work wonders for my already inflated ego."* But I caught myself in mid thought and recalled that the ease with which she arrives, had more to do with her anatomy and less to do with me. The hope also crossed my mind that if we did this on a regular basis, in no time with the release of large amounts of oxytocin she too would become hopelessly attached to me. However, contrarily the hunter was captured by the prey, developing an irreversible addiction to her, even to the point where I became one of her many stalkers.

KAORI CONCLUSION

Later that night my girlfriend Kaori came over and after telling me about how well she was getting on with the guy at her temple, I depth charged inside her in jealousy, released the life cream after her climax, and went to bed. The next day, while walking her to the station, in a preemptive move to being dumped, I suggested to her that maybe,

"We should just break up so you can be with him. You guys are both Japanese and you understand each other, wouldn't have to do all this communicating. Maybe that's the best way."
"I didn't say I wanted to be with him." But with the rejection of her redneck, uneducated parents in mind and my Japanese language teacher on the scene, I insisted, "really, you'd be better off with him." And with those words she waved good-bye boarding the train - the same train which Kyoung had boarded - with unspoken plans to finalize our separation at a later date. On Christmas day, Japan's most romantic holiday, we met at the Sannomiya subway under the peering eyes of the public, to talk about our end. Under the influence of my blood thirsty rod, I suggested that we should stay together.

"No, you said it was better for us to break up, so that's what we're doing. I didn't want to do that, I was just telling you about him because he's my friend and we grew up together."
"Ok, maybe I was wrong," I interrupted. "Why don't we talk about this at your place?" "We're loud and people are staring."
"I don't want to go home, I'm meeting him here soon."
"*Ouch, that hurt.*" But with a bit of begging and beseeching she acquiesced and we bussed it to her matchbox studio apartment in Kitano.

Still under the influence, I begged her to stay, knowing full well that this was just my ego and the little head talking, the fragile male ego that doesn't like to be left or rejected.
"NO!" She insisted. "He's already my boyfriend."
"That was fast. Then can we just do it one last time?"
I began to kiss her on the cheeks as I grabbed her round cakes and in

no time evacuated her out of her skin-tight denim. Lowering her to the futon I awkwardly and hurriedly unbuckled my pants freeing my jealousy enraged member. Pulling aside the crotch of her panties, I slipped inside her with my pants at my knees. *"DAAAM!"* Palming her cakes.

"Imo have ta give this up?"

The thought crossed my mind to squeeze off inside her irresponsibly, but I regained my senses and withdrew in time. After all, she didn't seem happy to be doing this, she was just mercy laying me, which showed in her tears on her dark, somber countenance. Given her disposition, and my paranoia, I thought she could've even gone to the police to report a rape and being a foreigner in this country, I was only too aware of the consequences.

"Are you done?" "Lets go, I have to go meet Yusuke."

"Yeh, I gotta meet Karin too."

"You're taking Japanese class on Christmas day?"

"Of course not, she's my girlfriend," I blurted in childish vindication hoping for some kind of jealous reaction. But as was typical for a Japanese woman, though she may have been burning up inside, there were no external signs, only a long silence on the bus back to Sannomiya. After introducing me to Yusuke, she handed me the keys to my apartment before entering his Accord.

"Keyotsukete ne," (take care) flashing that trillion yen smile. And with a slight hint of jealousy, "Nihongo no benkyou ganbatte ne." (Good luck studying Japanese.) Walking into JR Sannomiya to board the train, it was perfectly clear to me that, propelled by the unstoppable force of fetishism I had just traded in a well adjusted, perhaps the most well adjusted girl I had met in Japan, for one who was dramatic, unstable, damaged and obviously unwell.

KARIN CONTINUED

Like Tomoko before her, Karin had been extensively exposed to the world and men outside Japan. Traveling since her early years at a prestigious all girl school in Kansai, she even spent three years on a Japanese government program teaching Japanese at high schools in Illinois. The last thing she wanted to do was return to oppressive Japan, she said. But it was impossible to remain in the States with the love of her life – an African-American Architect – as it was forbidden under the restrictions of the program, which stipulated that no participant therein could have his or her visa status modified to permanent resident without first returning to Japan for some years. Bitter and heartbroken, after experiencing the freedom of the United States, she, like countless other Japanese women in her shoes reluctantly returned home to confront the daunting feat of readjusting to her strangulating society and trying to find a suitable man as her thirties encroached. Like Tomoko, she was in her early mid thirties and intolerant of Japanese men, but was fully aware of the ease with which many Japanese women hurled themselves at Western men and the tendencies for these men to eagerly oblige. The all too familiar catch 22 for these women exposed to the world outside Japan.

"I hate Japanese men, but you guys are such whores. Doshio?" (What should I do?") Along with Japanese men, she had a profound disdain for, in her words, those baka (stupid) Japanese women who open their legs to every Western man. Mukatsuku!" (FUCK!) Oblivious to her was the fact that going to my apartment and opening up her legs to me had placed her in the same category.
"What are you talking about? You raped me."
"I raped you?"
"Yes, I told you to stop. I went to your apartment for dinner, you are my student and you invited me to dinner."
"You're perfectly right, I am your student and I did invite you to my apartment for dinner but I didn't rape you."
"You did!"
"Why didn't you call the police and why did you come back to my

apartment and why did you continue to be my Japanese teacher if I were your rapist?"

"You were a private student and I couldn't change because it would look bad."

"So, I raped you, but you were more concerned with how things would look if you stopped being my teacher or reported me? That's a dumb argument, that's just stupid. If I raped you, if I violated you I'm very sorry, but why are you here now, in my bed, did you fall in love with your rapist?"

"Maybe I'm lonely," she sheepishly replied after giving some thought to my queries.

"Yeh, you and most Japanese women."

"Well, maybe you were lonely then too."

Had I not extensive experience with her kind in the West, those borderline types, Karin and Japanese society in general would have posed a mystery. But it was through her that I observed that the enigma and perplexing behaviour which surrounds the Japanese, bares some resemblance to those surrounding people with personality disorders in the West. After all, hers was a typical Japanese existence, from a typical invalidating and oppressive Japanese family, with the typical pressure cooker upbringing. And then like a bullet train it hit me: Understanding the Japanese requires a firm grasp of abnormal and child psychology. Truth be told, a thorough understanding of abnormal child psychology would be more applicable.

PRESURE COOKER SOCIETY

After over two decades of wanderlust I have come to understand that no society is perfect. Instead, each displays varying levels of imperfection and dysfunctions. In order to garner a clear understanding of Japanese women and the Japanese in general, it is necessary to comprehend the environment in which they are socialized. Not just kimonos, tea ceremonies and Shrines, but the negative externalities and dysfunctions resulting from their over-stylized society. The Japanese socialization generates profound sociogenic psychological disorders in its subjects, all under the auspices of culture. In fact, Japanese society is in part a collection of psychological pathology.

Think of contemporary Japan as one big Jackson family, and the leaders thereof as Mr. And Mrs. Jackson, especially Mr. Jackson. Japanese society is lead by the likes of the Jackson patriarch with striking similarities. Just as Mr. Jackson's objective was to create famous pop star offsprings by hook or crook, Japan's leaders were hell bent on transforming the country from a nation of economic cave dwellers after the Second World War, to the privileged league of industrialized nations, by any means necessary. Perhaps Mr. Jackson himself wanted to be a pop star but instead was stuck in a factory unable to realize his dream and decided to live vicariously through his children. Japan on the other hand, propelled by collective inferiority complexes, by which it is still plagued, set annual targets to increase GNP after the Second World War, targets which were met even if it meant having to die trying. But Japan's *Jacksonization* began well before the end of the Second World War, hundreds of years ago when harsh and rigid Confucian ideologies were brought here from China.

Therefore, like the Jackson children, Japan underwent a heavily regimented and abusive molding process to achieve its end. There is a high probability, given human nature, that no Jackson child emerged unscathed, but it was Michael, whether for genetic and or probability reasons, who bore the most salient symptoms of abuse from his oppressive parents. Similarly, it's possible that all Japanese are emotionally scarred by their collective oppressive socialization, but not all develop personality disorders, leading them to act out. However, Japanese culture is in part defined by this resultant behaviour.

If twelve percent of the United States population has some kind of personality disorder, then given Japan's choking social structure, the number of such people here must be double or triple that of the US.' In each case the objective was met: the Jackson family produced several internationally famous pop stars and Japan, second largest economy in the world, became an economic pop star, albeit at a high cost to the individual, as the natives suffered and are still suffering dearly. But we dare not mention the mental state of Japan, as they are economic rock stars with grand international economic influence. Besides, that would be most politically incorrect.

Likewise as with Michael, any acknowledgement of his warped mental state would be blasphemous. However, the harsh reality is, the existence of such a highly structured society is impossible without at least some frequency of socially induced pathology, conditions hinted at by Japanese psychiatrist Rieko Shiba, in a report in the Asahi Shinbun.

"We Japanese are brought up in ways that leaves us with very low self-esteem," stated the psychiatrist, in a gross understatement. But what she failed to address in her vagueness, I will expand on in detail. According to a 2002 survey by the Ministry of Health Labor and Welfare, one in fifteen Japanese suffer debilitating depression, much like I suffered from birth to my mid thirties. However, those figures were challenged by another renowned Japanese psychiatrist, Dr. Kazuo Sakai, who states that a 1:5 ratio more accurately portrays chronic depression among the Japanese. Dr. Shiba thinks that the Japanese are especially susceptible to depression owing to their diligent nature. But contrarily, the Japanese diligence is derived less from any self proclaimed innate factors and more from a brow beaten socialization process, itself conducive to immobilizing depression.

Beginning from the days of feudal Japan, there were designated ways for performing every action in life. There was a designated way for speaking depending on your rung on the social ladder, an exact way of entering and leaving a room, when to change from spring to summer wear and back, just to cite a few examples. These social mores were heavily and stringently enforced by the samurais, the Mr. Jacksons of the day, for hundreds of years. The samurais didn't play. Any minor infractions, and as Richard Pryor said, you could cancel Christmas. In fact, this is a major contributing factor to Japan's emergence as a hyper-polite society, as back in the day the consequence of disrespecting the wrong person was fatal. Hell, the samurais were even known to just randomly test their swords on people. Feudal Japan was no joke. If the samurai didn't whack you, you had to off yourself, and there was even a prescribed form to commit suicide, that too contingent upon one's social status.

Among the many aspects of her culture about which Karin complained, was the absurd concept of giri, or the incessant unending obligation to which the Japanese are bound from birth. They are obligated to their parents, teachers, siblings, doctors and in particular to anyone who provided a favour. Obligations extend to returning favours and presents, hence the Valentines Day, white day phenomenon. On Valentines Day in Japan, thanks to the brainchild of genius marketers, women give chocolates, not just to guys in whom they have a romantic interest, but also to their bosses, co-workers and other men in their periphery, as a token of their kindness and consideration. These obligatory chocolates, or giri choko, as they are loathingly referred to, are permanent fixtures in the seasonal consumption landscape. Again, extending a similar gratitude to these same marketeers, the opportunity to prey on Japan's obligatory mandates was seized upon when one or more of the big three chocolate makers designated March 14th *White Day* the day for men to obligatorily reciprocate confectioneries, and confectionery makers laugh their way to the bank to the tune of 30 billion yen annually.

Karin constantly bemoaned her parents' constant indebtedness to the neighbors for enduring just a few months of commotion when their Ashiya house was being remodeled. "My mom was always thanking them and taking them gifts even twenty years later."

Western ideology is anti-giri, we loathe the idea of anything obligatory. Yeh, we think it would be great to reciprocate directly, but if we cant we are quite content with doing good for someone else. Another of their many sources of pathology is the concept of tatemae and honne. Tatemae, tate meaning building or creating and mae meaning in front, is in essence culturally sanctioned hypocrisy. In the interest of maintaining wa or harmony, the most important tenet of Japanese society. The Japanese are socialized to refrain from expressing any ill feelings during their interactions with each other, even in the presence of abuse, always maintaining a facade of good naturedness. Imagine having to internalize ones feelings, especially ill feelings for all one's life, a feat Karin often protested. Honne on the other hand, are the true feelings of the individual and are most likely to be expressed only when inebriated.

Codependent behaviour in the form of amae, is an intricate part of the Japanese social fabric. Where as in the West we promote independence and self-sufficiency, a constant state of dependence and the inhibition of personal growth are virtues in Japan. Identity integration, separating ones identity and becoming independent from one's parents, are alien concepts to the Japanese, as they exist in a perpetual state of arrested childhood, quite frequently even in their forties. Amae, the concept of absolute dependence and trust in all human interactions permeates all aspects of this society, contributing to their obliviousness to their surroundings, in some cases darting out in on coming traffic, amaeing on approaching traffic to yield. Employees amae on their employers to find them marriage partners. In theory the idea of amaeing, repressing selfish tendencies and putting the welfare of others before ones own, should work very well. But while this process is learned, its opposite, self-preservation is innate, hence amae, like the tenets of many popular religions – to which Japanese society bares a striking resemblance – discounts and suppresses normal human tendencies. As a result, having to rely completely on others for their happiness, they are forever being disappointed, eternally crying woe is me.

According to the media and government surveys, 60% of contemporary Japanese, experience abnormally high stress on a daily basis, kindergartners included. Sushi and stress are inalienable elements of Japanese society. Beginning in elementary school, students are required to absorb a startling amount of kanji and must lug around heavy school materials, contained in three or four bags. In the winter boys are compelled to wear micro-mini pants in order to toughen them up. Many junior high and high school students do not have the luxury of heaters in their classrooms and when they do, they are usually inadequate, nausea and headache inducing kerosene heaters. The mercury in the classroom descends to arctic levels in the winter and reaches volcanic temperatures in the summer with not even a fan in some schools.

In the winter of 2005, the coldest and longest since my arrival in Japan, classroom temperatures dipped to minus two celsius in the Kobe area, with my students too cold to even think about learning English. The Japanese are simply unaware that in order for learning to take place, basic human needs, like heat in the dead of winter must be met. It is these harsh conditions for students and lack of students' rights in general which vastly contribute to the hikikumori phenomenon.

In over 400,000 families nationwide, students including the brother of one of my marriage candidates and the sister of one my subjects, refuse to even leave their rooms, sometimes for several years. Aided and abetted by overindulgent Japanese parenting, coupled with an unsupportive educational system ignoring students' needs especially as it relates to bullying, many do not even leave their rooms for meals. For adults the stressors are the demands of working excruciatingly long hours, living under Lilliputian and densely populated conditions, while paying dearly for the lowest standard of living of all G8 countries. A person earning US$50,000 a year in Jamaica enjoys a standard of living much higher than that of someone on a similar salary in Japan, albeit with a higher probability of getting murdered.

According to a March 4, 2004 Bloomberg News article, financial socialism, a mind bogglingly, hyper-inefficient multi-layered distribution system and mammoth ongoing efforts to protect domestic producers from foreign competition make this country exceedingly more expensive than it should be. As an example, the average miles per year driven in Japan is approximately 7,000, compared to 15,000 per annum in the US, but the cost to operate a car here is triple that of the US, creating an inverse relation between cost and utility.

Highway tolls, averaging a dollar a mile, are inescapable even if just traveling to the next exit. From my home in Kobe to Tokyo by car, a distance roughly equal to that between Los Angeles and San Francisco requires the yen equivalent of a hundred and twenty dollars in tolls, one way, which is equivalent to the cost by train to the same destination from the same point of origin. The same maintenance free Japanese cars driven in North America for up to 200,000 miles and beyond, are subject to unnecessary and costly inspections every two or three years depending on the age of the car, and at an average of 4,000 kilometers per year, a 3-year-old vehicle is still relatively new when it must undergo its first inspection at 200,000 yen, or about $1,800.

In Japan, a drivers' license, which many do not utilize after obtaining - often deprecatingly referring to themselves as paper drivers - cost 300,000 yen, half the cost of obtaining a private pilots license in North America. There is simply only one way to obtain driving privileges in Japan: through nose bleedingly high cost driving schools. Drivers' ed in the twelfth grade? Forget it and neither can your big brother or a good neighbor teach you to drive. Not that driving here is anymore difficult than anywhere else. Except for the confusing traffic signals which show a solid red but green arrows pointing up, left and right, driving here is quite uneventful. The drivers license issuing agencies, along with vehicle inspection are vibrant industries like the industry providing abortions. A pregnancy termination is 120,000 yen (about $1,200) and during the bubble era was 250,000 yen.

The overwhelming majority of stress experienced by the Japanese is a result of the exhausting demands of their social rituals and traditions and given the lethal enforcement of these mores in feudal times, over centuries the Japanese have been socialized with a compulsive attention to detail in every aspect of their existence, which we in the West refer to as anal retentive. This is a key factor in their dominance in the international marketplace, in some, especially the automotive sector.

Not even pets can escape the high stress of daily life in Japan. A series of attacks on children by small dogs has prompted the authorities to caution pet owners to ensure that their pets are kept stress free. In April 2006, a Fukuokan 3 month old was mauled to death by three miniature dachshunds, as the parents slept. The parents awoke to the horror of bits of their baby's bones and flesh strewn around the apartment. Bites to the child's head had even pierced the brain. In the same city a few months earlier, another dachshund chewed off a child's testicle. According to experts, these cuddly creatures become vicious if confined to a small apartment everyday without proper exercise. If stress can convert these huggable creatures into murderers, imagine its effects on people.

Failing or coming second is unacceptable in Japan, conditioned from feudal times when even slight mistakes would be an invitation for ones neck to form an intimate relationship with samurai Jackson's sword. Under these conditions it's only natural that imbibing is the most common pastime for the Japanese. From a Western standpoint, Japan is a society of functioning alcoholics, where alcoholism, like depression, is institutionalized, again, all under the auspices of culture.   Similar to the social scene on college and university campuses throughout the United States, much of Japan's social activity is centered on consuming large quantities of alcohol.   As an anxiety reducer, alcohol demands no social skills, which are already in short supply in Japan.

So embedded is alcoholism in the society, one of my students at a large electronics firm where I taught, assured me that alcohol tolerance was one criterion for choosing his wife.   If she could hold her alcohol he reasoned, there would be an increased chance that their children would have a high tolerance for liquor. In another example of institutionalized alcoholism, a friend who had reluctantly returned from spending her high school and university years in the States, upon applying for a job in Kyoto, was shocked and insulted by a question on the application regarding her alcohol tolerance level. Unbeknownst to the Japanese, this culturally sanctioned chugalug may well be, according to research, a pathway to Japan's tradition of depression.

Centuries of fear of decapitation has ensured the absence of critical thinking and independent action from the Japanese individual. To demonstrate this frustrating void, I always take my visiting Western friends to Mr. Donuts, where I would order a honey-glazed and milk with ice to go. At various Mr. Donuts the response is the same: the honey-glazed can be had to go, but the milk, DAME DESU. You can't have the milk to go.
"Observe carefully," I would tell my friends.
"What are those paper cups for?" I would enquire to the clerk. "Why can't you just put the ice in the paper cup and pour the milk in the cup?" "Taihen moushiwakegozaimasen kedo, sore wa dame desu." (I'm so very sorry but that's strictly forbidden). When I asked why, I was always told that while the donuts can be ordered for a take out, the milk can't, company policy. One hundred percent of the time, neither the clerks nor the managers could explain the reason for that policy, but being the foreigner that I am, I would insist in some flexibility, which always resulted in a 30 minute summit, not unlike six party talks to denuclearize North Korea, or to discuss global warming. Employees and managers would be huddled and telephone calls would be made to other authorities enquiring about the feasibility of pouring some milk in a paper cup, all the while with my encouraging and coaxing them.

Daijoubu, ikeru, dekiru. (It's ok, you can do it) Usually after some thirty or forty minutes of deliberation, my honey-glazed and milk is presented to me. If it takes 40 minutes to pour some milk in a small paper cup, imagine how long it will take for Japan to, for example, fully integrate women in its society.

Up until 2006, the only way to get an extra packet of ketchup at Kentucky Fried Chicken was to purchase a separate meal.

Like all other societies either occupied or colonized by Anglo-Saxons, collectively the Japanese possess deep seated inferiority complexes and self-hate. Though some fifty years have elapsed since the stunning defeat in the Second World War and even after a flabbergasting ascent to the position of world's second largest economy next to the United States, Japan is wrought with insecurities and diffidence. It's ever clear, regardless of how fast their trains are, or however much Toyota is poised to take over the world market for automobiles, they haven't quite recovered from the impact of that stunning defeat.

While the white male is looked upon as an ideal candidate for a life partner, the black male is perceived as a transitional partner, someone with whom to *floss* and prance around, but not with whom to create a child or to take home to the parents. A quick glance through the dating section in the Metropolis, a popular English language magazine in Tokyo, will reveal a disproportionate number of Japanese women seeking white men, versus those seeking black men. Of course, our reputation for abandoning our offsprings only reinforces their sentiments. Among single Japanese mothers I have met, who were parents of mixed children, a significant majority of the children's fathers were of African extraction. In fact, in my seven years of being in Japan I have only met one Japanese single mother of a half-white child, and there are far more white men than black in Japan.

Further evidence of their complexes is common in the media where for example, in the majority of ads featuring foreigners, whites are ubiquitous as the principals. This is especially prevalent in advertisements for automobiles, where the foreign actors are almost always Europeans. Indians, whose presence here has spanned some three generations, are absent from commercial advertisements and the African face is almost always relegated to poverty alleviation campaigns or events relating to entertainment, sports in particular.

October 2005 saw the launch of a national print campaign promoting the census, with posters reminding us that, "everyone must be counted." Featured on these omnipresent prints were a middle-aged yellow male perhaps in his fifties, a young yellow female appearing to be in her twenties and a white male in his forties, all clad in traditional Japanese attire. The statement was unquestionably clear. It was a pathetic and patronizing attempt at portraying the image of an inclusionary society, which instead illuminated their ideal of - in Mr. Ishihara's words - the "good foreigner" and the fact that Japanese society, hence Japanese men, still perceive their counterparts as disposable toys and ephemeral accessories of beauty.

For if they wanted to convey some semblance of *everyoneness* then at least one more woman - ideally an elderly woman, given that Japan is the most aged society in the world – and another ethnic minority would have been featured. Ravaged by inferiority complexes, the Japanese depend on the validation of whites when marketing their products, especially big ticket items associated with status and class. It's just not a cool car unless the ads feature a European at the wheel. On a somewhat amusing note, recently print ads for erectile dysfunction have been popping up on the trains. Featuring drawings of Caucasian looking men, with Japanese dialogue bubbles, it could be interpreted that the Japanese are so embarrassed they couldn't stand their own image being associated with erectile dysfunction or, Caucasian are afflicted too, so its okay to talk about it, or both.

At least one Japanese male in his drunken stupor, unaware of my command of the language, in my presence confided in one of my Australian friends that, "We Japanese think that you white people are above us, we cannot measure up. But we are definitely above black people." Abandoning tatemae, that culturally sanctioned hypocrisy so integral to Japanese society; he was able to speak honestly and candidly in his inebriated state. And it is without a doubt, that given the homogeneity and uniformed character of the Japanese, I'm confident his statements would be echoed by the society in general.

A quick scan of Japanese manga will reveal that all the Japanese characters therein are drawn with oversized eyes. Sometimes green or blue, but always disproportionately oversized, further evidence of their complexes, a projection of how they see themselves and of the features they covet. This is especially patent in the emerging fad of xenophobic manga, where the Japanese characters are drawn with big eyes, blond hair and Caucasian features, while the *inferior* characters, the Koreans and Chinese are depicted with black hair, narrow upwardly slanted eyes and mongoloid phenotype. It can be said quite accurately that the Japanese perceive themselves as the white people, the Caucasians of Asia, mired in longstanding inferiority toward the West but engaging in scapegoatist superiority complexes toward their fellow Asian brethrens.

High self-monitoring is a staple in the Japanese psyche. They are bound by the circular insanity of severe self-consciousness and obsession with their perceptions of other people's perceptions of them. The all-pervading hi-tech toilettes in Japan, the ones equipped with power windows, two-way electric moon roofs, dish washing capabilities, a cuisanart function and of course heated seats, are also outfitted with a flushing sound effect in order to mask the sound of women passing their urine, or God forbid, the sound of their splashing turds.

Long ago, suffering similar conditions of unremitting inferiority complexes, diffidence, extreme shyness and pathological self-consciousness, I would induce a cough to coincide with my feces hitting the water below. However, frequent mini-vacations at county jails for traffic violations as a teenager in Colorado and as an adult in California, purged me of such self-obsessions and paved the way for my exhibitionist and voyeuristic penchant. Those incarcerations, which made the weekends longer than usual whenever I was arrested on a Friday, forced me to either die holding my bowel movements, or lose my inhibitions and just pass my feces in a tiny room with a few other inmates.

Retrospectively, those experiences were therapeutic, freeing me of the bondage of high self-monitoring and taught me to accept the human being and bodily functions for what they are: a necessary part of the human existence which required no shame. By no means am I advocating delinquency in paying for traffic violations or ensnarement in baby mama or daddy drama in order to obtain therapy, but it's my understanding that as we progress in age and grow toward Maslow's self-actualization, we should be able to free ourselves from the shackles of being overly self-conscious. Not so in Japan, where the perpetually juvenile state is considered virtuous.

The tradition of women's obsession with perfect attire can be viewed both from a historical and contemporary perspective. In feudal Japan, the Shogunate dictated what clothes to wear based on one's social standing, an arrangement designed to prevent incorrect etiquette to members of different social classes. Taking it an extra mile however, the government later established dates on which people were obligated to change from winter to summer wear and visa versa. Observed in context, it is clear how contemporary Japanese women plagued by deep seated collective inferiority complexes, were so easily manipulated and molded into fanatic fashionistas. Painfully lost and consumed by a mad, frantic and futile dash to discover their identities, product image is an indispensable crutch for the masses of insecure Japanese women.

In the words of the late Japanese psychiatrist and author Masao Miyamoto, validating my conclusion months after my arrival here, "comforting as a child's security blanket, high status brands like Gucci and Vuitton serve as soporifics to ease and calm a vacuous national psyche. And the more insecure the Japanese feel in their volatile and unstable world, the more they'll seek such fetishlike goods to make themselves feel better. This profound Japanese hunger to attain some superficial forms of status, some display of self-worth, also suggests collective inferiority, since the purveyor, not the customer, establishes the fashion, designs the "look," and gets to decide one's "worth." He continued by saying, "people think that by buying up designer purses they are somehow asserting their own style, but if you slavishly buy a brand product, you can deny your personality and take on someone else's. Eventually it's not any reflection of your own personality, but of the brand's."

This brand fanaticism, kin to my mother's God-freak behavior, was observed in September 2002 at a Vuitton store's grand opening in Omotesando, Tokyo where a growing mob camped out on sidewalks for up to three days, waiting for the doors to open. Overseeing the cattle, Yves Carcelle, Vuitton's then chief executive opined, "conspicuous consumption is supposed to signal the extravagance of the very wealthy and subtly advertise their status. But no French heiress or Italian baroness would deign to stand in the street for hours just to buy an expensive handbag. It would be downright undignified. This kind of scene could only happen in Japan."

Indeed I had observed a similar dynamic of conspicuous consumption, among the rich but lonely Beverly Hills types, during my ten years in Los Angeles. Some who like many Japanese dressed their Chihuahuas to the teeth, even applying nail polish on the canines' claws. While this abnormality was regional and limited to the rich in the US, most would consider it decadent, pitiful rich people having nothing better to do with their time and money. However, in Japan this human vacancy is widespread, as even the lower middle class masses, on marginal incomes, emulate their wealthy counterparts in the West in consumption of these high-end brands. One Vuitton handbag could cost the entire monthly salary of the average *Office Lady*. And in an even more horribly prevalent trend in Japan, young high school and junior high school girls sell sexual services to middle-aged *salarymen*, in order to afford these over priced accoutrements.

More than a few Western women, especially those on the heavy side have expressed to me their envy of these Japanese Barbies, some even lamented on the inferiority complexes they themselves have developed since arriving in Japan.

"They just always look so fucking perfect," exclaimed an Aussie friend of mine. Making matters worse, Japanese men's inattention or lack of positive attention causes many white women to feel invisible or nauseous. By no means is this inattention attributable to a lack of desire on the part of some Japanese men to explore intimate relations with a foreign woman. But if Japanese men are too diffident and insecure to approach their own women, then they are absolutely terrified of Caucasian or Negroe women. After all, what would they do with those breasts? And indeed, as reported to me by many white women here, it is their breasts which are major sources of perverted attention.

On the other hand - though this does not create chances for heterosexual white women to engage in intimate relations – many Japanese women look upon Blonde blue-eyed women in envy and as someone to whose likeness they aspire. Though ironically, blondes and other white women who were the center of attention in their home countries, arrive here only to discover that Japanese men are simply too socially inept and or intimidated to approach them, except to grope their breasts and masturbate in front of them in public, a disturbingly common encounter.

One such victim was my friend and downstairs neighbor, a buxom Canadian blonde. On her way home to our upper middle class neighborhood one evening, sitting directly across from her was a suited *salaryman*, appearing to be in his fifties, holding a briefcase in front of his crotch, discreetly getting off while looking at her. Well prepared with tissue in hand, he wiped himself after climax and replaced his penis in his pants. Infrequently but often enough, these socially retarded males even resort to murdering the unattainable apples of their eyes.

As Japanese men are too intimidated to approach them and Western men are here for yellow, many Western women, black and white, return home after nun-like celibacy, missing the crass cat calls of men on construction sites in the West. But what these Western women fail to realize - not that it would make them feel any better - is that, these otherwise spotless fashionista victims exist beneath a façade of name brands, masking deep seated, crippling and disabling insecurities, inhibiting them from even venturing to the toilette without perfect make up. Invariably, like many aspects of Japanese society, the beautifully manicured exterior conceals puss and infestation, just beneath the surface.

In this misogynistic society, where women and little girls are perpetually sexualized, females' only values are their physical beauty, sex appeal and childbearing capabilities. Though in exaggerated form, the award winning film 'Babel' demonstrated this clearly. It is to their peril that women in Japan exert intelligence. Collectively, women are not seen as persons capable of independence and any decision making process, but instead for men's sexual use – or abuse in many cases.

In 2005 the Japanese government approved some 48,000 'entertainment' visas for Filipinas to work in the 'water trade' – a euphemism for prostitution - but failed to grant visas to the few hundred who sought to enter as nurses, which are in short supply in Japan. Sexualization of girls and women is endemic in the West, especially in the United States. However, in Japan, female sexualization is socially and nationally sanctioned with women having internalized this objectification for nearly a thousand years, again all under the auspices of culture.

Sexualization occurs when one's value is derived from one's sexual appeal or behavior, much to the exclusion of other characteristics. Other criteria include, sexual objectification, inappropriate imposition of sexuality, especially on children and finally, holding a person to a narrowly defined standard equating physical attractiveness with being sexy. The existence of only one of the four criteria is necessary for sexualization, however, here in Japan, all four coexist in wa, embedded deep in the national psyche.

Cognitive and emotional consequences of hyper-sexualization run rampant among Japanese women, who as it is, hail from a high self-monitoring society. This marriage between high self-monitoring and hyper-sexualization ensure en masse, undermined confidence, discomfort with their bodies resulting in shame, self-disgust, eating disorders, low self-esteem, depression or depressed mood and profound appearance anxiety. Women in contemporary Japan, having long since learned to think of and treat their bodies as objects for men's desire, unwittingly sexualize themselves as they parade in sexually available attire perennially.

In studies, self-objectification has repeatedly demonstrated erosive effects on cognitive functions and the ability to concentrate and focus one's attention, thus leading to impaired performance on mental activities such as mathematical computations or logical reasoning. This *fragmenting* was vividly demonstrated by a study (Fredrickson et al) in 1998. While alone in a dressing room, college students were asked to try on and evaluate either a swimsuit or a sweater. While they waited for 10 minutes wearing the garment, they completed a math test. The results revealed that young women in swimsuits performed significantly worse on the math problems than did those wearing sweaters. No differences were found for young men. "Thinking about the body and comparing it to sexualized cultural ideals," the study reports, disrupted mental capacity. This may well explain why seven years in Japan, among the deluge of eye candy, I could encounter only a precious few specimens of brain candy.

Like many of Japan's other social ills, sexualization of women is institutional, as self-sexualized mothers engage in *transfer objectification*, by dressing their little girls in sexually provocative attire, from early childhood. Schools contribute by turning a blind eye to students who, by rolling up the waists, elevate the hemlines of their otherwise below knee length skirts. In my five years of teaching elementary through high school in Japan, never have I witnessed any substantial reprimanding of students who engaged in this practice on campus. Occasionally, in a whiny high pitched 8-year-old voice, a teacher would tell a student, "your skirt is too short yo," which almost always fell on deaf ears. Japanese culture dictates that women should never be seen outside without the full armor of make-up, as that would be most disrespectful to the public. Most Japanese mothers are incognizant of transfer or self-objectification's detriment to women, men, girls and society in general. They are unaware for example, of their contribution to the increase in demand for child pornography. Mothers' support of their daughters' T-back junior idol careers shines a flood light on the parents' naiveté.

Japan's institutionalized objectification of women is among the contributing factors to the national enjo kosai phenomenon. Euphemistically translated as compensated dating, enjo kosai is the practice of female students selling sex to middle-aged men, in order to obtain the name brand objects required for sustained self-sexualization. Though most of the victims are junior high and high schoolgirls, it is by no means unheard of for elementary school girls to prostitute themselves. Recently, one of my company class students, told me of a group of 11-year-olds from his daughter's elementary school, who sold sexual services in order to acquire Nintendo DS gear.

From the Japanese's perspective, this schoolgirl prostitution is nothing over which to raise a furor, and many Japanese sociologists purport that it's simply a right of passage from adolescent to adulthood. By interacting with older men, it is reasoned that enjo kosai supposedly teaches girls proper behavior with the opposite sex and protocol for engaging in mature relationships, lessons which should have been taught by generally absent fathers. Since the interaction between Japanese girls and boys are limited to school or club activities, it is believed that enjo kosai provides a medium through which girls can view themselves in a romantic situation, in essence reinforcing the fruits of self-objectification. More often than not, the media and society place blame squarely on these 'errant' teenagers and preteens, while absolving the adult paedophiles, sometimes thrice their age, of any moral responsibilities. But such is male chauvinist Japan, where the mostly absent fathers fail to see the importance of engaging and empowering their daughters.

BABY MAKING MACHINES.

Women's only other values outside the realm of pleasure and social adornment, are their childbearing attributes. This was reconfirmed as recently as January 27th 2007, by Health Minister Hakuo Yanagisawa. Addressing prefectural assembly members of the Liberal Democratic Party, Yanagisawa expressed how he and other members of the gerontocracy truly felt about women. "The number of women aged between 15 and 50 is fixed. Because the number of birth-giving machines and devices is fixed, all we can ask for is for them to do their best per head." A month later on Feb 24, Kochi City assembly member Toshiyuki Shimazaki of the ruling Liberal Democratic Party, referred to women as rusted machines, after Social Democratic Party leader Mizuho Fukushima and other women politicians had criticized Yanagisawa, demanding his resignation after his uncouth and insensitive remarks.

"The SDP's (Social Democratic Partly) Ms. Fukushima and those old women whose machines are rusted are making a fuss, septuagenarian Shimazaki was reported as saying at a party of three hundred. Showcasing the errant ineptitude and insensitivity of the misogyny, Shimazaki was happy to state that, at a previous gathering, he had passed a similar remark, which drew protests from women in the audience but, applause from men.

Though currently and rightfully on reproductive go-slow, or womb strike, most women continue to internalize the aesthetic expectation from centuries past. Consequently, in this nation of acutely insecure women, it is impossible for them to even venture to collect the mail without make up and their armor of Gucci, Prada, Salvatore Ferragamo, or other name brands about which I knew nothing before arriving in Japan. Collectively timorous and self-effacing, Japanese women rely on these brands as a source of identity. In fact wearing make up and being well dressed is an obligatory display of courtesy to strangers, a cultural tenet which all but ensures abiding self-hate and the inability for them to accept themselves for who they are. Among those who go to the gym, especially in the countryside, many women do so in full regalia, and some, again especially in the country side, even wear nylons to do aerobics, for reasons still a mystery to me.

Hence, Japanese society sees it as a woman's duty to look as beautiful as possible at all times, while continually concealing any speckle of intelligence. Women are objects to be exhibited, which explains why on any given day in Sannomiya one will often see an impeccably clad woman on the arms of a shabby hoodlum attired man. The spotlessly dressed fashion models can be observed on a daily basis on the trains, peering at themselves in hand held mirrors in their ritual primping and preening, applying full make-up, even using eyelash curlers, engaged in what seems to be an endless futile battle to secure that unruly lock in place. Like prepubescent or teenage girls in the West, they suffer chronic appearance anxiety, constantly relying on the mirror for reassurance, checking every few minutes in utter disbelief at the discrepancy between their real and ideal perception of self.

Further reinforcing this behaviour is the fact that praises and compliments are not customary in the cultural terrain. In fact, Japan customarily relies more on negative than on positive reinforcement, so that it is the norm to be derided by family members, in hopes that one will become thicker skinned, stronger and a better person. But in achieving just the opposite effect, many of the chided and derided grow up with a strong hate for self and the inability to accept themselves for whom and how they are. One of my girlfriends, Azusa, among the most beautiful women I have met ever, who grew up in an extended family, was always told since childhood that she looked too Asian, especially her eyes. So at nineteen she went under the knife to remove her epicanthic fold, in the hopes of making her eyes more Western looking. Fortunately the operation was somewhat of a failure and after spending some $2,000, to my delight her epicanthic fold was still present.

I am all too familiar with such insecurities. As a child, I too checked the mirror obsessively in hopes for a metamorphosis of my then perceived ugly black face. Akin to repeatedly opening the door of one's bare refrigerator, hoping that some food would mysteriously appear between viewing intervals, I too was compelled to constantly comb my hair, hoping that the kinks would straighten. Like many empty women in the West, the Japanese female's tenebrously low self-esteem propels rabid consumerism in desperate attempts to fill the void created by their oppressive socialization. Japanese men too can be observed in this public preening ritual, tirelessly fixing their hair and on occasion the string in their eyelids to give their eyes that *Western* look.

As a voyeur the unhealthily high level of self-consciousness and insecurities possessed by Japanese women were exceptionally frustrating. Frequently they wanted to have sex in the dark, while I wanted the flood lights on. But a few showers together did the trick of deleting their inhibitions and self-obsessions. In fact no Japanese woman without prior contact with foreign men, with whom I have *had dinner* had ever been bathed by a man except her father in her childhood. Programmed to be givers of pleasure, they had never experienced the ecstasy of a lover giving them a bath, which I always did, in complete role reversal. Possessing a full understanding of the power of the sheer heavenly nature of receiving a bath, it was my ritual to impart this watery pleasure to all my Japanese *dinner guests*. For if there is one thing at which I excel, that is giving a woman the most sensuous and sapid ablution of her life. My memories of my mother washing me in that yellow plastic tub are as vivid as if they were this morning. Her fifteen minute washes were brief escapes from my wretched environment and I would cry, plead and beg her to continue when she was done. In giving those affection deprived Japanese women the unspeakable pleasure of a proper cleansing, I always applied my mother's technique.

If they didn't return for the sex – in cases where it was too painful - they would most certainly return for the shower, about which many said they'd often read in Japanese romance novels, but never actually experienced.

Soon thereafter, they all lost their pre-occupation with their bodies and began to allow me to shoot cell phone photos and videos. In no time these insecure overly self-obsessed women became porn stars in my apartment. Having shed the burden of unhealthy self-consciousness, they gained self-confidence and lost their make up dependence, which had been plaguing them for years. Many expressed to me that my having complimented and approved of them even without make up, gave them the confidence to accept themselves. By no means am I some kind of Amish or member of some other fundamentalist group who, like my mother, thinks that wearing make up ensures a one-way ticket on the bullet train straight to hell. On the contrary, I quite like make up. What I hate is make up dependence, an affliction of most Japanese women and of many insecure women in the West.

Unlike in the West - especially in the United States - the pursuit of individual happiness is not a right and is a relatively recent foreign concept in the Japanese psyche. During feudal times the masses held no rights, only obligations, an arrangement still present in contemporary Japan, though hidden under the pretense of a democracy. However, in February 2007, the education minister Mr. Bummei Ibuki gave us a glimpse of Japan's elite's sentiments regarding basic human rights, when he stated that too much respect for human rights would give Japan "human rights metabolic syndrome." In a comment igniting fierce attacks from Amnesty International, Ibuki in a statement comparing human rights to butter said, "No matter how nutritious it is, if one ate only butter every single day, one would get metabolic syndrome. Human rights are important, but if we respect them too much, Japanese society will end up having Human Rights Metabolic Syndrome."

In this hierarchal Confucian society, human rights abuse is the norm. Workers have the right to paid overtime, but a hundred hours per week of unpaid overtime is common in Japan. Running counter to natural human thinking, the Japanese appear in general to minimize pleasure and maximize pain. All of life is an unending, character building shugyou (endurance course) to develop one's strength, one of the reasons promoting the absence of central heating in Japanese homes. Only after arriving in Japan did I become cognizant of how much I had taken for granted the constitutional right in the United States, to the pursuit of happiness, a pursuit which in Japan is likely to invite the term wagamama (selfish). It is this socialization to view life as mostly painful, which causes them to cling so desperately to their hobbies, that one thing in which they bury themselves obsessively. The hobby is of utmost importance to the Japanese and when I tell them that my hobby is life itself, their faces are usually consumed by a discombobulated countenance.

KARIN: THE HEAD GAME CONTINUES

Karin was constantly aloof with no display of affection, private or public and though I didn't know her father, she reminded me of him, who she said was the typical Japanese male. In public she was especially cold, according to her, out of fear of our being discovered by our co-workers. Months after we had been intimate, I still had not been to her place, the result of some traumatic experiences a few months before we met which added to her girl school derived paranoia of men. Three months before we had met, a Japanese ex-boyfriend of hers had severed a dog's head and placed it in front of her apartment door. Initially, passing judgment on the guy, I thought he was crazy, and indeed, he had to have been. But placed in proper perspective, I understood why he resorted to such a heinous act. Perhaps his Japanese socialization had deprived him of necessary communication skills and in his anger, resorted to this unspeakable act of cruelty. On the other hand, I pondered deeply, what she could have done to evoke even a fraction of rage, which would cause someone to behave in such horror. I would soon find out.

For three days from New Year's Eve 2002, Karin and I spent 72 hours cemented in bed in orgasmic bliss, connected like Siamese twins at the lips and at the genitalia, and other times genitalia to lips. We separated only for toilet breaks and when we were not conjoined, we peered deep in each other's eyes incessantly. Eating only whenever we remembered to, we simply engaged in an *orgasm - a - thon*. Surprisingly, even though like all Japanese she was anal about time and appointments, during her sojourn on my futon, she ignored telephone calls from friends wanting to know where she was and why she hadn't shown up for their engagements. This I interpreted as sure attachment on her part and it seemed like my plans for roping her in were coming to fruition. But all this backfired as her arctic personality only intensified, converting me to a stalker, whipped and obsessed. After those three days of paradise she disappeared, ignoring my countless e-mails and phone calls.

By then my schedule had changed and was unable to accommodate Japanese lessons, but as we worked for the same company, I ventured upstairs to the teachers' offices to find out what was up and why she was dissin' me like that. The other teachers knew me as an employee of the company and her former student, and as such, were unsuspecting of our relationship.

"Oh hiiiiiiii," greeting me with pretend sincerity as she stepped outside the office and in a harsh angry whisper she blurted, "What are you doing here?"

"I work here. Remember? What, is, up? Why are you ignoring me? It's been three weeks since you left my apartment."

"I'm busy."

"Oh and you can't e-mail me at least to tell me you're busy?"

"I wanna see you," I commanded.

"Can't, I'm teaching in ten minutes."

Sensing the fragility and the potential catastrophic scene outside her office, she agreed to go to my apartment that night. "Matta ne (see you later) and thanks for visiting," waving mendaciously, flashing that perfidious smile.

Karin and I embarked upon a volatile, tumultuous relationship, with her ripping my heart from my chest, hurling it in an Osterizer, whipping it up and feeding it to me. Possessed and helpless like a rag doll in the jaws of the fiercest Pitbull, after a discombobulating two days of dissociation, I began plans to abandon Japan, for a retreat back to California. No plethora of sex could help me recover from that state and it then became crystal clear, how someone would be motivated to sever a dogs head and place it in her doorway. For six months we separated almost every Saturday, succeeded by my trudging up to her office on successive Tuesdays to beg for reconciliation. Frequently she flipped and went into volcanic rages, quarrelling about things of little or no significance.

Our first such experience came after one of our frequent episodes of pure animal sex. We had started a conversation where I stated that if I were to be caught driving without a license by the Japanese police, I would fake an inability to understand Japanese. "YOU WOULD DO THAT?" She yelled. "I can't believe I am with someone who would do that." And in no time it escalated to her shouting, "GET THE FUCK OUT OF MY APARTMENT," threatening to call the police and immigration, which of course led to one of the many separations. Sometime later she lamented about paying too much taxes and needing to find ways to deceive the taxman.

"Wait a minute," I interrupted. "You kicked me out of your apartment because I would deceive a cop about not understanding Japanese, but you think it's ok to cheat on your taxes?"

"Yes," she answered. "You were going to lie to a person. I am not lying to anyone?" Sensing the futility of arguing and knowing full well that it would have lead only to another rupture, a crash from our intermittently euphoric relationship, I acquiesced. For it was then that I was introduced firsthand to the red herrings of Japanese reasoning, a form of inference generally awash in illogical constructs and extremely loose associations.

Outdoor smoking ban has been spreading slowly, very slowly throughout Japan, enforced by a 2,000 yen fine and posted signs informing us of the reasons for the ban; cigarettes are held at the level of a child's eyes, the butts generate litter and last but not least, we should be mindful of those with respiratory infections. However, given the overmuch of information on the dangers of second hand smoke – including research in June 2002 by an Osaka medical institution that second hand smoke can affect the heart in just thirty minutes – authorities are lethargic about limiting second hand smoke indoors.

In a perfect example of red herring reasoning similar to that of Karin's, popular author Masako Bando in August 2006, addressing Japan's problem of over-populous stray cats, advocated murdering kittens over spaying and neutering cats. Bando wrote that as soon as her cats gave birth, she murdered them by tossing them off a cliff near her house. Sterilizing cats for human convenience is no better than killing newborn kittens, she reasoned. Opting to allow her cats to live to the full, in her words, "despite the huge pain and grief in doing so, I kill their kittens as my social responsibility." In other words, it was wrong to take away the cats reproductive rights, but its right to take the life of the cats' offsprings. This famous author must have been a close relative of Karin's, putting a morbid twist on Jean Piaget's object permanence. Perhaps it could be called *pain permanence*: if the cats are in her presence and are adults, the pain of spaying and neutering them is unbearable for her. But if they are kittens, it's alright to toss them over a cliff, because after all, they are no longer in her sight so they can't be in pain. And besides, it's ok to kill kittens, they are not adult cats. It is my strong belief that Masako Bando should have been arrested for cruelty to animals.

In other ass backward logic, it used to be that milk was not sold with happy meals to go at McDonalds, but coffee was. Thanks to Karin, the mystery surrounding that and why Mr. Donuts doesn't serve milk to go was cleared up. According to her big time lawyer dad, this was out of concern that people, retards and incompetents that we all are, may consume the milk after the expiration date.

After her explanation why one form of deception was acceptable and the other not, I looked at her as though she had lost her mind. But it was a rhetorical look, if there is such a thing, because in fact, she had lost her mind long before we had met.

Around 7 years old, under the pressure of archetypically overbearing Japanese parents, and perhaps genetically predisposed, she began to experience illusions. On the train while traveling with her family, she reported seeing hands emerging from rivers.
"I always tried to show my mom the hands as the train passed the rivers, but she couldn't see them."
"*I wonder why she couldn't?*" I thought sarcastically. People around her - parents included - labeled her *talent*, sixth sense. I on the other hand, having spent most of my life in a non-folk society, thought *sick sense* was more appropriate. Karin's parents, mother especially, hammered and berated her for anything less than stellar performance in everything. The constant recounting of her mother's torture was enough to cause me to develop a strong disdain for the woman, having never even met her.

Obsessed with familial honor and saving face, her mother was always showing her off to the neighbours and comparing her with her peers.
"You are so worthless," her mother would say, sometimes in tears.
"You have shamed me, you've let our neighbor's child take home a better score than yours. After all we do for you!"

As I concluded, given the high self-monitoring tendencies of the Japanese, Karin was extremely self-conscious about her hyper-orgasmic condition, especially with Japanese men.
"I just couldn't allow myself to come so much with Japanese men, 'cause they would think I'm some kind of slut. So when I was with Japanese guys I always had to pretend I wasn't enjoying it too much. But with foreigners, I don't have to hide." In fact she frequently complained about not being able to be herself to her parents or to anyone, bounded by the custom of *tatemae* and was always expected to be this *goody two shoes*. But in reality she was a licensed buck wild freak. And it only made sense. Japan is equivalent to one enormous Catholic School and to exacerbate things, she had attended an all-girl Catholic School.

NATSUKO

While strolling through my local supermarket one afternoon, I came across Natsuko in the meat section.

"Is this beef or pork?" I asked, not caring whether or not she understood. "Oh that's pork," as though she had been anticipating this moment her whole life. Then she quickly seized the opportunity to display her English skills by taking me on this drawn out journey about her blood type, family, ("My husband is a heart surgeon,") her English school and her ski trip to Breckenridge, Colorado in a week. Like a CD box set from the carpenters, she went on and on, blah blah blah blah blah! And as if that did not suffice, she broke out her cell phone to display photos.

"This is my cat, my dog, my two daughters and oh, this is the car my husband bought me for my birthday last month."

"Well enjoy your trip to Colorado and here's my number. Call me when you get back."

Two weeks passed and Natsuko called the day after her return, to arrange a date within a couple of days. Clad in the most hideous, bright pink dress, a pink feather scarf, a multi-coloured coat only Joseph would wear, some baby blue K-mart shoes and gaudy jewelry from a Cracker Jack box, she appeared at my door, gleaming from ear to ear, bearing gifts from Colorado. It was as though she had consumed every fashion advice from Tammy Fae Baker and Cza Cza Gabore. Had I been the fashion police she would've been arrested and given the electric chair.

"Let's go find something to eat." And I shuddered to think I could be seen in public, walking with this mascot.

"It would have to be local," I thought.

"Definitely not in Osaka or Sannomiya, heaven forbid, one of my homies would see me traipsing with this spectacle," I scolded myself.

In our Palo Alto, California-like suburb just three minutes' drive from my apartment, there was a bar, Steelers, owned by an American. It was there that I suggested we take cover, but to my disheartenment she insisted on walking - a cringe inducing proposal. Along the way she insisted on holding hands and snuggling up against me while I tried to conceal my disdain for her actions. But recognizing her meal ticket to getting her pent up needs met, she took charge and continued by breaking it down to me in Japanese English and a whiny elementary school voice, as if laying out the terms for a hostile take over.

"I want you to be my boy*fliend*. I want us to go movies, dinner and to symphony. I like music, I like go to concerts. And oh, I really like to dancing. I want you to take me to dancing. You don't have car, so you can drive me in my car. I'm not safety driver anyway and if you drive, I'll really feel like I'm in date."

"What about your husband?"

"He hates all those things, he just likes work."

"Shiiiiii,' if a nigga go get paid," I entertained myself in caricature African-American pimp vernacular.

"I damn sho wouldn' go, perambulatin' with Tami Fae fo' free." The performance on my futon would also be a determining factor. "If Tammi Fae wuddn go kick down no chedda, she bedda be packin' some good heaven between her legs. After all, she ain't dat bad. She jus' needs a little consultation, you know, a work in progress, a neglected diamond in the rough, but doable. She just needs a little TLC," I was no Versace, but the second thing after her performance assessment would be to get her to buy herself some new clothes and get the hell out of those granny glasses.

At 39 years old, Natsuko epitomized the desperate subsistence of a great many, if not the overwhelming majority of married, especially middle-aged women in Japan. Theirs is a perdurable existence completely devoid of love, affection, orgasm, sex or most other elements listed in Maslow's hierarchy of needs. Many self-opiated with magic mushrooms, legal in Japan up until 2003, but most endure in quiet desperation, developing or exacerbating personality disorders and or psychoses, while others substitute hobbies for fulfillment of vital needs and or, begrudgingly live vicariously through Korean dramas of love on television.

A low percentage, among which Natsuko was included, develop the courage to get pleasured by foreign men. Like most her peers trudging through a loveless arranged marriage of 25 years, she idolized Bae Yong-Joon, the male lead in "Winter Sonata," the most popular television romance series from Korea. For her and those other pitiful women like her, he was exemplary of the soft, gentle, sensitive, caring, kind, attentive and affectionate man they wish they had for a life partner. But instead, are cursed with the chauvinistic, mechanical, frigid, cold, workaholic, android economic animal of a specimen, which is the Japanese male. Also, the relationships portrayed in his television series exemplified nurturing, supportive and compromising unions, which for them were unattainable fantasies, far beyond the dark realities of their oppressive and sexless dyads.

During his public appearances in Japan, Mr. Sama, as I like to call him, would be ambushed by an onslaught of pathetic, emotionally challenged, obstreperous women, ranging from their mid-thirties to well into their sixties. They braced the elements, weeping and wailing, just to get a glimpse of their idol, some even sustaining injuries when his car, attempting to flee the chaos, crushed their feet. Nachan was one of those kawai sou (pitiful) women existing vicariously through her 17 and 18-year-old daughters, often boasting about adopting their musical tastes and wearing their clothes. With Britney Spears, Back Street Boys and Ninety-Six Degrees in permanent rotation in her Benz and her singing along to every song, time spent out with her was a teeth-extractingly painful undertaking.

Huddled over lumber flavored French fries and concerned by the possibility of being spotted by an acquaintance on the way back to my apartment, I ate hastily as we engaged in perfunctory conversation. Returning to my apartment, I wasted no more time to rid her of her Tammy Fae fascia. Once at the doorway inside my apartment, I began by unwrapping the hideous blue feathers from around her neck, then undid the hook at the back of her dress. With the shyness of an elementary schoolgirl, she squealed and franticly attempted to cover her perky-round-bra enclosed mammaries, as her dress fell to her ankles.
"No, no, hazukashii, I'm shy."
But as I cupped her globose C cups, she melted like butter touched by a hot knife.

It had been five years for her and though she had just returned from a family vacation in Breckenridge, Colorado where she made several advances at her husband, he didn't even as much as look her way. But it was by no means because she was undesirable. Daily swimming made her toned, nothing hung out of place. With all my might I tried to devour her 36Cs, through her lacy bra. Savagely I removed the shoulder straps to get a proper mouthful, and as I tried my utmost to swallow her melons, I was transformed into a snake on the discovery channel trying to swallow a tiger whole. She had perfect gravity defiant mountains and was shocked by my instant affinity toward them.

"You like them?! My husband hates them."

"Put them away!" She said he chided deploringly.

"And cover yourself," referring to her phallus petrifying cleavage. He was especially embarrassed around his friends and found her frequent request for sex taxing and taihen, (distressing) so he sanctioned her extra-marital affairs.

To say she was sexually frustrated would have been an understatement.

"My husband doesn't even give me ude makura (arm pillow).

"Sometimes I just ask him to let me rest my head on his arm, and he can't even allow me to do that."

The first thing that came to my mind was that he was gay, but concealing it in heterosexual marriage. Some kind of Brokeback Syndrome.

"No, that's just Japanese men. All my friends' husbands are like that."

"But he's a very good provider," a mantra recited by all middle-aged married women and many other married women I had bedded in Japan.

"What red blooded male, with a functioning penis would reject his come hither wife for so long?" I asked myself, prying off her girdle. The girdle, the same kind my grandmother wears, is a common accessory among some Japanese women obsessed with being, or appearing to be thin. Even 21-year-old women here sport them.

But in answering my own question, I recalled, this is Japan, where according to a 2005 Ministry of Health, Labour and Welfare survey, fully one third of married couples under age 50 are sexless.

SEXLESS IN JAPAN

The Ministry defines sexless as having sex less that once a month. The result also revealed that a fifth of all couples surveyed had no sex in the past year and a third of the respondents found sex tiresome, some even citing timidity as a major contributor to asexual behaviour. Natsuko and many of my other subjects in Japan were among those statistics.

On the other side of the Atlantic, psychiatrist believe that a sixth of all American couples are sexless, but it is without question that timidity is not one of the contributing factors. American sexlessness can be attributed more to stress, overwork – especially with both parents working – an overflowing family schedule and sleep deprivation. In Japan on the other hand, there are two prominent causes of sexlessness among married couples; the ubiquitous mother complex, known here as the mazaakon and, what I have coined the baby mama complex. Perhaps in Japanese that term would be something like, *bebimazaakon* or *bebimamakon*.

The *mazaakon* is a commonly reported psychological phenomenon where the man sees his wife more as a mother figure and loses all sexual interest in her. These men hail from overbearing and overindulgent mothers - the norm in Japan - some reportedly manually stimulating them to ejaculation and others even engaging in full blown sex during their upbringing. It is reported that Japan has the highest rate of mother son incest in the industrialized world. These officious mothers multiplied after the Second World War, as Japanese women – the de facto head of household – were relentless in their actions to leave their mark on Japan's economic growth, by directing their families.

It is necessary to point out that this power that the Japanese woman wields in the home is not the result of some mutual agreement between her and her husband, but like many social movements here, is reactionary. In this case a default arrangement to men working fifteen hours or more a day. In the grand scheme of things, Japanese women's domestic power is academic and does not transfer to the society in general. Also pervasive is successive sexlessness or, baby mama complex. This occurs when a couple who once enjoyed a healthy sex life, desists from sexual activities after the birth of their children. Again the main culprit is usually the man, who after childbirth no longer sees his wife as a woman, but like his mazaakon peer, sees her only as a mother. In their eyes, mother and lover status are mutually exclusive. In some cases it is the women who neglect their husbands, directing all their attention and energy to the children and it must be stated that the tendency of Japanese parents to share their futons with their children, sometimes to elementary school age, doesn't exactly promote a rabbit-like sex life.

There are four main types of sexlessness in Japan; Sometimes partners are mutually content with their asexual behaviour and require a great deal of space from each other. Hence sleeping in different beds, oftentimes even in different rooms, in essence existing as flat mates. In a recent 2006 survey of childless couples, only a third of the couples slept together, while the remainder slept separately. Then there is the scenario of couples agreeing to keep sex away from the home, supposedly in the best interest of the kids, and as a result find some out side location, like a love hotel, to get busy. Also often in this arrangement, are affairs and brothel patronage.

To the euphoria of the Western male, these extra-marital activities are usually consented to, provided they are done discretely. Such is the arrangement of a significant number of my white Western acquaintances married to Japanese women. In the third type, one party simply cannot perform physically and given the high rate of alcohol and tobacco consumption among Japanese men – two things renowned to cause erectile dysfunction – the blame lies again more frequently on the men. In the fourth case, one partner wanting a physical relationship is simply refused by the other. Like many of Japan's social ills, sexlessness is wedded to a hyper-conservative social structure lethargic in its change and being fully cognizant of these social dynamics, I and many other Westerners, my Australian friend Roger McQueen included, see it as our natural duty and obligation to rescue excitement deprived Japanese women, one orgasm at a time.

I sank my hands inside Natsuko's panties and waded through the predictably unmanicured Japanese forestry.
"There should be a law against such over growth," I thought, sinking my finger into her soaked virgin-like well, leading her to my futon, with my finger in her from behind, as she tried bashfully to cover her chest. Though not the max, I was aroused enough to rock her into a different time zone. Natsuko was Ainu looking, not the Manchurian type of my preference.

She had Caucasian features, a slightly convex nose, which I despise and atypically big eyes for a Japanese woman. Hers was a slender cello-shaped body, with no evidence of having given birth once, let alone twice. But her hands, course from household detergents, showed signs of housework.

Except for the hands and the gingivitis, she was a sexy middle-aged woman of above average beauty, who would have been well sought after in the West. I just had to avoid kissing her. The few times I mustered the courage to try, it was like kissing an inflatable doll. Rigid and stiff, she had no idea what to do with her mouth. On my futon, I dined on her breast while slowly occupying her and as expected, she commented on my size, as I was her debut on the dark side.

"Yeah, yeah, yeah, been hearing that since four years old, just shut up and take it," I said to her imaginarily. After a few painful moments she loosened up and flung her long legs in the air, receiving all of me. I fed it to her, gyrating until I was at her belly button. In her thirty nine years she had never had an orgasm and I didn't care enough to try to give her one, she was happy enough just simply being occupied.

The thought crossed my mind to release irresponsibly inside her because, like all Japanese women I had been with thus far, defeated and unempowered, she never requested my wearing a condom. In the West a woman, at least a sensible one will tell you, "no glove, no love." However, Japanese women, having long since lost control of even their own fertility, submit to patriarchal abuse without resistance. In essence, in Japan, the male subtext of those dynamics is, "I don't wanna use a condom, just get an abortion." The women's only response is, "don't come inside me ok?" I am absolutely guilty of taking full advantage of these dynamics, to feed my addiction. But in Natsuko's case I reconsidered and gave some thought to the tailspin, the drama in which her upper middle class suburban existence would descend, if I impregnated her.

"Naka ni dasanaide ne!" (don't come inside me) And with that I yanked out at the final second and splattered all over the futon. Natsuko showed up for regular servicing for a year, many times discreetly leaving her house while preparing the family meal, after telling her husband she's just "running down to the supermarket." Things got a bit out of hand when she began to live on my door bell sometimes at three in the morning when my futon was otherwise occupied. On occasions, if I had no work the next morning and or, my futon was unoccupied, I would let her in for a quickie, for which she was always grateful. But her beggarly demands did my head in. She didn't know what time it was, always demanding girlfriend status and that I held her hands, drive her around in the E class her husband gave her and, take her out dancing and to the movies. All this and, get this, I had to pay. On two occasions where she met Karin at local festivals to which she invited us, Natsuko had the effrontery to speak ill of me to Karin, attempting to discourage her from moving in with me.

"He's a bad person, you shouldn't live with him," she advised in Japanese, unaware that I understood every word.

Once I accompanied her to the Ashiya mall to select some new glasses. Upon arriving at the cash register to pay for the specs I chose, she stood in position looking at me, under the misguided impression that I, on an English teacher's salary, was going to pay the equivalent of $400 for some new glasses for her, the kept wife of a medical professor. Genuinely disappointed, she embarrassingly explained to the sales person that she would not be getting the glasses at that time. That's when I had to break it down to her in the car.

"Natsuko," I said fuming, "You're are married, You're married to a surgeon. You need a boyfriend. I don't need a girlfriend, I got enough. I am a black male in Japan. You should be buying shit for me. If you want to date me because of some fantasy and because you missed out on being courted as a result of your arranged marriage, if anyone's gonna pay, its gonna be you. Not me!" It was gut wrenchingly sad to watch this poor woman hanker and yearn for chivalry, romance, affection, humanness and sexual fulfillment, which were all starkly absent in her loveless, sexless omiai (arranged marriage) of so long.

"I'm not gonna date you, I reiterated, "but you can come over sometimes if I have the time."

"Well, I want more than that, I want boy*fliend* who is loving and kind, who treats me like lady and….." A fantasy she had developed from extensive travels and interaction with the West and Western couples. But the harsh reality was that, she, like legions of Japanese wives in her shoes, was hopelessly bound to a marriage as stimulating as watching sand in an hourglass. My explanation of *protocol* was futile and she just could not understand why she was at a disadvantage.

Natsuko and I continued for years, after which I stopped responding to her e-mails and telephone calls and to her incessant bangings on my door, especially at odd hours in the mornings.

Now 43 years old, periodically we'd bump into each other in the neighborhood at which time she was always available for a quickie. On our final encounter in January 2008, to my surprise she had heeded my advice from years earlier and made a 180 degree change in her appearance. Her wardrobe was now regal, contemporary and stylish and she had begun visiting the dentist on a trimonthly basis.

"I learned many things from you and now, I have many men, young men in their 20s after me."

FU

January 2003 heralded the beginning of a new semester teaching at this Osaka based company, where the first thing I did upon entering each of my four classes, was to survey the terrain for prey. All male classes were always an inexplicable disappointment, especially when they wanted to bond over alcohol or other typical male activities. On the first day of one my classes in Kyobashi, one student caught my interest in electromagnetic style. There was radiance and spunk about her, atypical of Japanese women and her brown slacks were like Saran Wrap around her thick athletic legs and bulbous posterior. Unlike other Japanese women, she was vocal and expressive, never covering her mouth during her hearty laughter. Even her face was different. She shared the same pearl white complexion as many other Japanese, but her other features were not archetypically Japanese. Though not as beautiful as many others, she was well above average and the S curves on her body, her moxie and her outstanding intelligence, surely compensated for the minor shortfall on her facial beauty.

"Yeh," I thought, *"I could definitely live with that."*
It's impossible to have it all; super-fine, super-intelligent with a super-sexy physique, something's gotta give. Super-fine women aren't usually socialized to exert their intelligence, but instead to rely on their beauty, which works quite well for them. Highly academic and scientific women aren't usually drop-dead gorgeous, as they didn't have the beauty to rely on. Fu was a 27-year-old scientist at this company and her position there made me even more attracted to her, as I have always found brainy women and women in power suits - Hillary Clinton types - extremely arousing. Like her peers, Fu slaved diligently for the good of the company, working long 14 hour days five or six days a week, with bags beneath her eyes as proof.

Since shortly after the beginning of the semester, she had been rejecting my advances and innuendos to play tennis or to be shown around her hometown Kyoto, which at least in the US could have been interpreted as sexual harassment.
"C'mon, you can show your teacher around Kyoto. I want to see the

temples," my eyes watering from staring at her onion and knowing full well that I had not even a gram of interest in temples.

"I don't have time. I'm very very busy on weekends."

Fortunately at this corporation, one class within the first month was held outside as an icebreaker, with the location and activity democratically decided. Annoyingly, most times the students elected to patronize drinking establishments and even though I am not an imbiber, always I was obligated to share the cost. This time I deprived them of their democratic process and informed them of plans to go dancing. Most of these economic animals had never even heard the word dancing, let alone to venture to a nightclub. However, Fu on the other hand, a sax player and lover of jazz, frequented nightclubs during her university years. So I wanted to assess her behaviour in a social environment and get the digits discreetly.

Secondarily and of less urgency, I also wanted to break the others out of their rigid existences, have them feel the pounding and thumping of deep driving house music in their veins, as they had never before had such experiences. At the Underlounge in Shinsaibashi I gyrated and pranced erotically with my students, taking care not to give any special attention to Fu, who was limber and flexible like a human rubber band on the dance floor. While the other students, men and women moved awkwardly, some under the influence, her movements were fluid, like that of an Alvin Haley dancer. It was as though I had provided an environment for which she had been yearning, an environment where she could be free to express herself outside the confines of her cubicle or lab, and at the end of the night we exchanged e-mail addresses and telephone numbers.

Mission accomplished. Though I detest nightclubs in Japan, given my strong allergies to smoke, I survived by actually spending most of the time outside the club and upon my returns inside, I had to constantly remind myself of the objective: her telephone number. Fu, short for tofu - a name I gave her after we became intimate. She in turn called me Choco, short for chocolate – told me of her boyfriend with whom she had been for the past two years. Upon hearing this expected news, my heart sank to my toes in disappointment, but when she revealed that he lived in Tokyo and worse, that their visits were limited to only once a month, my heart returned to its proper place of joy.

Like so many women in Japan, Fu was involved in one of those senseless, unfulfilling long distance relationships, getting only a minute fraction of her needs met. Given the choice, women here will always choose to be in these vacuous relationships, over being single. This is perhaps attributable to the rigidity derived from the Confucian influenced interaction between the sexes. In the West, we are fully aware that humans are social animals and we are able to meet each other anywhere and develop Intimate relations.

While living in the States, it was not unusual to meet women while we both waited in our cars for the signal to change. Usually by the third or fourth signal we were exchanging numbers, which sometimes led to intimacy and or friendship. It is true that in the US, especially California and especially Los Angeles, the car is an integral part of one's identity and people are usually judged by the kinds of cars they drive. Therefore the nicer your car, the higher the probability for success at say, meeting women at traffic signals. But in my social experiments, I've even rolled up on beautiful women, while on my Honda 150 scooter, which resulted in a fair success rate of intimacy and or friendship and besides, my cars were normal nondescript cars; Golf, Audi 100, Peugeot 405mi16, to name a few.

I refer to these experiences not to brag about my prowess, but to illustrate the fluidity, ceteris paribus, with which humans can initiate relationships wherever we are, the ease with which boy meets girl. Even under high pressure circumstances such as at a traffic signal, where a man has only seconds to make a good first impression to cause a woman to lower her window, engage in conversation, anticipate meeting at the next signal and eventually giving him a means to contact her. In one vivid case during my university days, a woman and I flirted on the interstate 5 for about fifteen miles before I signaled for her to pull over. Lisa and I remained friends until we lost contact after I moved to Japan.

Laden with Confucian rigidities, the human as social animal is an alien concept to the Japanese, hence it's better to trudge through a grossly unsatisfying relationship, as in their perception it is infinitely more difficult to initiate a new one. Of course, working 14 hours a day, sometimes six days a week ensured diminished possibilities of her finding a new boyfriend. In fact, most of my students at this titanic corporation were in their twenties, prime age for reproduction. However, they complained incessantly about not having any leisure time to socialize and having to work up to 100 hours or more in over-time without pay. As I have previously mentioned, it was at this mammoth company that one of my students died after working 16 hours a day 6-7 days a week, from age 22 until his expiration at 27.

Exacerbating Fu's dilemma and making her even more of an untouchable, was the fact that she was a career woman. On occasions she attended the aforementioned kompas, sometimes arranged by her company, where all the men presumed she was simply an Office Lady at this renowned company. Fu told me that when she revealed her position and gave them examples of products in the marketplace she had either invented or designed, in their gross intimidation, they would have no further conversations with her. As a result, she began to conceal her duties from men at future kompas, leading them to believe that yes, like most women in the Japanese workforce, she too was a lowly Office Lady. And as if matters weren't bad enough for her, Fu revealed she was third generation Korean Japanese, which explained her enigmatic character among Japanese women, a feature which was a liability for Japanese men, who think that Korean women are atsusugiru (too heated and passionate), but in fact, it's the Japanese men who are just too lily-livered and caitiff for Korean women. Like me, though she and her grandparents were born in Japan, she held a resident alien card, which meant she was ineligible for a Japanese passport.

Among other things, Fu's long distance relationship illuminated clearly the crumbs that Japanese women are socialized to expect and accept from Japanese men. Recently I initiated an infrequent encounter with a "*chocolate eyed*" Japanese woman, whom I had met a week earlier, who found it exciting that I had taken her to the supermarket with me on the way to my apartment. The reality was that I had needed some soy milk for breakfast the next morning.

"Let's run to the supermarket real quick," I suggested.
The following week during a conversation on the phone, she told me how delighted she was that we went to the supermarket together before heading for my apartment, as it convinced her that I wasn't just after sex.

Having a firm understanding of Fu's situation and of the social dynamics affecting her, I presaged that soon I, her English teacher will be fulfilling her intimate needs, showing her what she was missing, which would result in her putting an end to her fruitless long distance relationship. A woman as advanced, artistic and passionate as she surely could not have been satisfied with a sorry excuse for a boyfriend, whom she met once a month. In the ensuing weeks we spent every Thursday after class in stimulating conversation over dinner, getting to know each other and it so happened that one of her sisters resided one stop away from me on the JR line.

"The next time I visit my sister and her family, do you wanna go?"

At her sister's house I was an instant hit especially with her 4-year-old nephew and 2-year-old niece and as the day progressed, her sister and brother-in-law encouraged us to go to the movies, forcing the bird in the lion's mouth, so to speak. As the evening was still early, I convinced her to accompany me to my apartment.

"I live very close to here. Let me show you where I live before we go to the cinema." And after a few more hours at her sister's we set out to my apartment. The moment I had been anticipating for some five months had finally arrived. After countless dinners after class, our lips had finally met during a trip to Nagoya and since then my fantasy of inviting her for *dinner* had heightened.

From the time we set foot on the train, my expansion began and upon our arrival at my place I was fully engorged. Fu's exceptionally hard Alps were sturdy but delicate, requiring extra-ordinary gentleness, which I found frustrating. In my eagerness, I just wanted to swallow them whole as I ventured down south with my fingers. Grabbing her bikini trapped, athletic rump with one hand, I licked her from my fingers on the other. Voraciously ridding her of her last garment, my timber hardened to a level seen only by women of her china complexion. There is something infinitely erotic about my midnight hued negritude invading and enveloping their ivory. Fu's southern hemisphere was the most ravishing of all I had seen. Lipless and smooth, it appeared to have been cast with great precision and she became my diet for the ensuing thirty minutes. My tongue glided all over her glossy hairless dessert, causing her to rail in ecstasy and when I finally began the slow and gentle decent, main vein bursting, she gasped breathlessly, mouth agape, "it's too big, stop." Once again, a strong athletic woman the likes of Fu, received me with protest but slim, svelte women had no problems. Finally after gaining complete entry she struggled to make guttural utterances,

"Itakimochii ("it hurts but it feels so good.") "Iku."

In the muggy Japanese summer's night, Fu and I continued in a sweaty *orgas-ma-thon*, futon drenched in mucilage, until well into the night. To my delight she had missed her last train, hence leaving us no choice but to continue the *climax-a-thon* on my soggy futon. The next morning she could hardly walk and experienced some southern bleeding, as well as from her nipples.

"Sugoii, I never knew sex could be like this," I over-heard her telling her sister on the phone. Shortly after she began sojourning regularly at my apartment and mornings would see her setting off to work with the widest grin on her face.

Co-workers found her new found morning chirpiness quite curious. "Recently you've been in such a good mood in the mornings, what happened?" they inquired. And we joked about how lucky she was, as most Japanese women never experience the luxury of a few orgasms before work. In a cry for help, I told her of my demons, hoping she could have saved me from myself.

"But if you moved in with me, I'd be able to stop," I reasoned, absolutely convinced, or at least trying to convince myself that I had wanted to stop my infinite philandering, which Japan made so effortless.

"I don't know, I'd have to think about it, my parents wa dame kamo." (I don't think my parents would agree.) Disappointment and relief became one emotion. Disappointed that we couldn't cohabitate and relieved that I could still continue my whoring of which she was now fully aware, all a part of my buyer beware policy.

Fu and I made full use of Japan's spacious toilettes for the handicapped. Frequently in Kyoto, when her athletic legs jettisoned and taunted me from her miniskirts, I'd pull her into the nearest *hotelette* or *toihotel*, remove her panties and curl her onto the warhead for a quickie.

In the late summer 2003, while returning home from a trip to Shirahama with Anita, I received an e-mail from Fu.

"Where are you?" It read. Our five o'clock plans to meet by the water fountain at JR Umeda had completely slipped my memory.

"I've been at the fountain now for an hour," read her second e-mail.

"Oh my God! I'm so sorry babe, I went to visit some friends in Fukushima," I typed as Anita slept in my arms on the train.

"I can't wait another hour, I have to go home. I really wanted to meet you today yo Chocotan. I went to the doctor today for my polyps and found out I'm pregnant."

A sudden darkness engulfed me as I saw her tears in her words. I had failed her at the worst time.

"But how the hell could that be?" I pondered. I was always sure to withdraw the warhead before releasing the *lifemakers*, but the highly improbable had occurred. Anita awoke to find me in deep narcosis, as if I had just been hit by a train driven by a ghost.

"Dou shitan no? What's wrong?"

"Just thinking about work stuff."

Fu's pregnancy was not my first, second, third or even fourth, but it would be the first ever that I wanted to keep. It was the first time ever that I was fearless, or at least exerted some control over the fear, by focusing on acceptance of my new role of fatherhood. This would be fatherhood, as opposed to absentee fatherhood. We began talk about getting married and moving back to California where our wages, especially hers would be higher. Given the slavery in Japan, as an engineer at this large firm her monthly salary was significantly less than mine. And even with a biannual bonus of some 400,000 yen, my annual income was still greater than hers though I worked less than half the hours she did. Furthermore I argued, we could further our education in the States, where her patents would belong to her, as opposed to being owned by the company. Overall, the task of raising the child just seemed less daunting in the States, given easy access to childcare and the general openness of the society. After all, the harsh reality was that Japan is inconducive to raising children.

NO COUNTRY FOR CHILDREN

According to a Cabinet Office survey conducted from October to December of 2003 in five countries, more than half of Japanese and South Koreans are reluctant to procreate, citing exorbitantly high costs and "unsuitable" conditions contemptible to child raring in their respective countries. Other participating countries included France, Sweden and the United States, where attitudes were in sharp contrast with those in Japan and South Korea. One thousand people between the ages of 20 and 49 were interviewed from each country. Among Japanese who wanted to have more children, 53.1% said that they wouldn't, while more than half of South Korean respondents had a similar response. In Sweden and the United States a large number of respondents said they planned on having as many children as they wanted. When the question was posed about the suitability of their respective countries to child raring, 50.3% of Japanese respondents completely or somewhat disagreed and 79.8% of South Koreans said that their country was unsuitable for raising children. On the other hand, 97.7% of Swedes said their country was suitable, followed by 78.2% in the US and 68% in France. Fertility rates in these five countries reflect the sentiments of the survey. While Japan's fertility rate at 1.25 is not as low as South Korea's 1.16, it pales in comparison to America's 2.04.

A pregnant woman's death in August 2006 sent even greater jitters to would be parents, as it revealed gross inadequacies in health care in Japan. After the 32-year-old woman lost consciousness from convulsions during delivery, doctors at a hospital in Nara contacted 18 other hospitals, as they were ill-equipped to treat the patient. Unfortunately, all 18 hospitals refused her on account that their beds were full. Finally after being accepted by a hospital in Osaka where birth was successful through cesarean section she died during child birth. According to the Nara Prefectural government, about 30% of pregnant women who need emergency or high-quality treatment must be transferred to hospitals outside the prefecture.

More recently in a 2007 survey of the nation's 47 prefectures, 192 cases were revealed where five or more hospitals refused to admit a pregnant woman transported by ambulance, between 2004 and 2006. From 2004 to 2007 the number of such cases stood at 2,939.

Research from Osaka Pediatrician Masatetsu Fujimura confirmed my suspicions of Japan's hostility to children. Obtaining records from the Health Labor and Welfare Ministry, Fujimura San revealed in August 2008 that among the world's 13 most developed countries, Japan held the second highest mortality rate for children aged 1-4-years-old. At 33.03 deaths per 10,000 in that age group, Japan was surpassed only by the United States' 34.71 per 10,000. Sweden's 14.32 deaths per 10,000, was the lowest among the 13 countries, followed by Italy (18.9), Austria (22.65), France (24.72) and Canada (25.33).

There were three reported causes of death among the aforementioned age group; accident, not surprising given my observation of Japanese parents' propensity to allow their toddlers to dash about unattended - among other dangerous places - on the platform of Sannomiya station. Recently while at Starbucks near the Kansai International Community Center (KICC), I observed a toddler gallivanting around the café as his mother – eight months pregnant - chatted with her friends, oblivious to her son's mistaking the café for a thoroughfare. Predictably, at least to me, he activated the sensors to the automatic sliding doors and after pausing in awe at this sudden chance to explore the deadly intersection ahead, he, again predictably, wobbled out into the street, predictably ignored by passersby. After the sound of screeching tires, realizing the absence of her son, the mother rushed outside to greet a stranger holding her child. "*Only in Japan,*" I thought. Only in Japan would adults on the street ignore a wandering toddler.

Accidents were succeeded by various illnesses, followed by foul play, a euphemism for escalating heinous child abuse in Japan. As to various illnesses, of the 636 small children in the report, 399 or 60% died within six hours of falling prey to the cause in question. Mr. Fujimura states that, sadly many of the children were not taken to the hospital in time and or did not receive adequate care upon arrival, for which he blamed a gross shortage of pediatricians and hospitals with pediatric intensive care units or PICUs. Low birthrate and hellish working conditions are repellents to potential pediatricians, and PICUs are present only in a handful of hospitals throughout the nation. Of Japan's 42 prefectures, PICUs can be found only in Tokyo, Nagoya, Kanagawa, Fukuoka and Hyogo. What's more, according to the Yomiuri Weekly, "because children are administered smaller drug doses, treating them is not as remunerative as treating adults." Kickbacks from Pharmaceutical companies are a significant portion of doctors' salaries in Japan.

PRELUDE TO HANSHIN

Our pregnancy was untimely for Fu, who had just received a promotion a month earlier, one that accompanied stellar recommendations from her superiors. Hence a pregnancy, especially one out of wedlock, would be a monumental embarrassment and after discussing the matter with her two sisters, the decision was to save face and terminate.

"I would be disappointing the people who recommended me for this promotion. We will always have another chance, the timing is bad Chocotan."

Though I disagreed with her decision, I supported her.

"But you're gonna pay half," I acquiesced.

"Why?! I'm going through it, so you should pay the whole thing."

"But I don't want you to do this. Why should I pay for something I don't want?"

"Choco, I told you. It's bad timing. We will have another chance."

In an odd reversal, Fu had assumed the role which I had had with my over ten or so pregnancies prior to hers. She was more matter-of-fact about the process than I was. It was as though I had become the emotional female and she the rational male. Perhaps that's why she was the scientist and I the adult ADHD wanderlust. But it was indeed a relief to learn of my new found ability to become emotionally attached in such situations, a sign that my dissocial personality disorder was finally waning in midlife. I also took comfort in knowing that I was not firing blanks, still firing live rounds.

"Well, we should definitely move in together after the abortion, and get married at the end of the year."

And to that she agreed.

On that fateful morning I made the most painful withdrawal from my account, at an ATM near Hankyu Okamoto station: One hundred thousand yen, the equivalent of a thousand dollars. After which we made our way by taxi to the clinic, where I had signed consent to perform the operation. In Japan the husband's signature is required if the woman is married, the partner's signature is required if she is unmarried and the parent's signature is required if she is under 20 years old. We spent two mostly silent hours in the morning, on the second floor of a dark nearby diner, where Fu grudgingly watched me eat breakfast while she starved from having eaten nothing for twelve hours. Soon the bell tolled the hour of reckoning and we set out on the long five minute trek back to the clinic, where after twenty minutes' wait we were lead to the fourth floor, where she disappeared into the chamber.

As a testament to the grossly insensitive, callous and uncaring Japanese patriarchy, the layout of the clinic was of such that women must walk by a display of beautiful, smiling newborn babies, on their way to and from the abortion chamber. This arrangement epitomizes the cluelessness of the Japanese male and was observed at a different clinic at my second termination in Japan.

ABORTION IN JAPAN

Abortion in Japan is an industry, which like all industries here is run by men. According to the Health Labor and Welfare Ministry 289,127 abortions were performed in 2005, the lowest since compiling data began in 1955. This number represents a first for pregnancy terminations to fall below the 300,000 mark since 1955. However, experts agree that the actual number may even be three times that amount, given structural incentives for doctors to under-report. Abortion and contraceptives are not covered by insurance, hence doctors are at liberty to set the price. As most – including three for which I paid – are paid for in cash, doctors are able to manipulate the numbers in order to dodge taxes and what's more, the penalty for total under-reporting is less than the cost of one abortion. Since my arrival here in 2001, there have been at least two reports of authorities finding illegally and improperly discarded fetuses in dumpsters near abortion clinics.

Japan dwells in the dark ages in countless respects and the subject of contraceptives is one such area. Though birth control pills have been made available since 1999, after condoms, the withdrawal and rhythm methods, abortion is the fourth most popular form of birth control in a society where women are oblivious to their rights to control their own reproduction. Several factors hinder the pill from gaining wide spread acceptance in Japan, among them; hesitation for women to seek gynecological care, which is required to obtain the pill. Unlike in the West, except during pregnancy, women here are loathed to pay an annual visit to the gynecologist for a pap smear. This inaction, I am convinced, is a major contributing factor to the spread of Chlamydia in epidemic proportions among young women on the island. Inadvertently, it even contributes to the low fertility rate of Japanese women, as Chlamydia is asymptomatic in 80% of women, who may well become infertile as a result of carrying the disease untreated. Two of my students, both OB_GYNs at a hospital where I taught, validated my convictions.

If Japan as a society is outright hateful to women, then it stands to reason that OB_GYN, male dominated like most of Japan, is not exactly women-friendly. I have read and heard several reports of female patients complaining about doctors making lewd and crude remarks about their genitalia. In fact, during visits to the OB_GYN, two of my partners reported to me that the doctors commented on their apparently frequent sexual activities, on account of the darkness on their labia.

Cost is another contributor to the gross unpopularity of the pill. Before prescription, gynecological exams, blood and STD tests are required, all at a cost of the equivalent of $27-$100, as prices vary among doctors. None of these services is covered by insurance and subsequent STD tests are required every six months, with the cost to fill the prescription around 3500 yen ($32).

But the number one reason why the pill is still lagging behind after being approved since 1999, is the grand effort to maintain the vibrancy of the $400 million a year abortion industry. In the event I am beginning to sound as though I am against abortions, let me make it absolutely and unequivocally clear that I am a pro-abortionist. Japan was the first country to make it available as a form of birth control after the Second World War and for that I fully commend them. One of the most refreshing aspects of Japanese society is the near absence of Christianity (0.08% of the population) and the absence of the ludicrous abortion controversy so interminable in the West, especially in the United States. Here there are no protesters brutally murdering doctors outside abortion clinics in order to get their point across. Japan as religion is plenty oppressive without the presence of other dogmatic organized religions. My objection lies in the *industry* status of abortion provision. Aerospace and industry are words that match very well, so are electronics and industry. But abortion as an industry? Somehow that makes me queasy.

HANSHIN

During the three-hour wait, I passed the time reading in the waiting area and at times venturing outside where I found amusement in observing a Chihuahua left inside a Brabbus S600 Mercedes, with the engine running to keep the air conditioner operating, for some four hours. Though this was a common sight in Japan, I couldn't help pondering, *"which moron, would leave a car like this – or any car, for that matter – running for three hours for a dog, especially one which looks like a cross between a rat and a bat?"*
"I'm sure he paid more attention to the ratbat than he did his wife or girlfriend."

Upon re-entering the clinic, I was summoned to the abortion chamber by a doctor. "She wants to see you," which started me ambulating toward the room, passing a group of newborns on my left. Fu's legs were still suspended at her ankles, by stirrups pendent from the ceiling and the freshly used utensils were still in the aluminum tray above her right leg. As I have stated earlier, I was no rookie to abortions. Truth be told, since the age of 19 this was my fourteenth, but the first I truly felt, the first in which I was a participant, her legs in the stirrup were also mine and for the first time I could be empathetic about the agony of the process. Not that I have become sentimental about pregnancy terminations, for I haven't. However, in this case, for the first time I became intimate with the process and tears flooded my face in that bleary room, as I stood next to her.

Fu, this strong, athletic, vibrant and spunky woman that I had met only six months prior, had been hit by a roller traveling at bullet train speeds. She had been reduced to a listless, lethargic and barely coherent cadaver, lying with eyes shut as I caressed her haggard ashen face. Shortly after, the doctor reappeared to instruct me to wait outside the room while she recuperated.

The ten minute taxi ride to her sister's home was eternally surreal, seeming as though that Friday was not a day of the week but some existence in a sphere never before experienced. Buildings, bridges and trees meandered by as the taxi traveled into outer space before arriving at her sister's, where we slept spooning for some twelve hours.

In the succeeding days, we made extensive plans to move in together. It would have been easier to console each other under the same roof and we would marry in December of that year. There was no reason for me to believe that, given the fact that she was an adult of 27 years old and that we as two adults had just made one of the biggest decisions in our lives, that she would not be able to leave her family's home for us to begin our lives together. In fact, she assured me that her family would have been no problem. "I am an adult," she stressed.

MEET THE PARENTS

And so it came to pass that after an exquisite day together at Karuma, taking in speechlessly beautiful scenery in the bliss of each other's arms, it was time to meet the parents. During her childhood, Fu's father was a successful businessman, trading in goods from Korea. But at the time we met he had been driven to insolvency, thanks to his deceased brother for whose debts he had been a guarantor. Still he was confident in his attempts to launch various ventures even in his sixties, as Fu, I found out, was saddled with the responsibility of sole provider for her parents. Missing from her parent's personality was the self-deprecating and perpetually apologetic characteristics of the Japanese of Japanese ancestry. Instead her father exuded the kind of arrogance akin to that of Jamaicans, an arrogance I knew quite well and with which I was much more at home. And her mother, an extension of her father, while less loquacious, it was obvious she had her husband's back all the way. It was most refreshing to meet people who weren't constantly berating themselves.

Her father was most direct in his speech, none of this beating around the bush like other Japanese.
"Nande watashi no musume to kekonshitai no?" ("Why do you want to marry my daughter?")
"She's a beautiful, intelligent, confident woman," I responded in Japanese.
"Of course, that's how I raised all my daughters, to be confident."
"I really like this guy, he is well chill," I thought. He then went on to explain to me how initially he was extremely worried when Fu told him she was dating a Negroe. Not having ever laid eyes on someone like me, he thought we were all thieves, pimps, murderers and other villains, like the characters we over represented in programs he had consumed regularly in the media. On the other hand, my teaching at this well reputed company was a source of great relief for him. I wasn't that bad after all, he might have thought. As we got to know each other, he expressed empathy and drew some parallels between my being a Negroe in the US and his being Korean in Japan.
"This dude is way chill, he gets it." And I was suddenly overcome by the

urge to hug him and to let him know that yo, "I feel your pain." "Yo" by the way, is part of Japanese vernacular and used in the same context as in African-American vernacular.

As Fu helped her mom prepare a feast, her dad and I rapped easily with occasional interjections by her mom. It wasn't long before the barriers began to fade and I was made to feel completely welcomed in the family, partaking in the Korean cuisine which mom had painstakingly made for the occasion.

However, with weather-like abruptness, dark clouds rolled into the apartment after Fu's dad shot us down point blank upon hearing our plans.

"No! You have to date for one more year and then get married," he ordered. This was even after she explained to him that it was her deep desire and that our cohabitating would bring her great joy.
"Don't you want me to be happy?" She asked her dad.
What's more, they insisted on my parents flying to meet them before any connubial arrangements. But my mother had died six months earlier and my father? Who knows where THAT Negroe is. And there was no way that my surrogate parents in California would take that twelve hour flight, simply to be approved of by a family in Japan. Immediately it was game over. Though I understood their concerns; not knowing anything about me, my background or my family, I cursed him in my mind.

"Do you know what the FUCK your daughter and I went through thirty days ago?"
"Do you have any clue?"
"It's not like you're some royal fucking family or some shit like that. It's not even like you got cash."
"I could totally understand if you had assets to protect, but you're fucking bankrupt, and I was even willing to share the burden of supporting your ass."

But showing great restraint, I contained my true feelings, displaying some tatemae for the duration of my visit and departed on respectful terms.

In my Western thinking I was not willing to appreciate the over-attachment to her family, especially in light of what she and I had endured just a month prior and particularly because I wasn't requesting the hand of an underage 16-year-old. She was almost 30. Such curtailment of freedom is anathema to me and having rebelled against the control of my own family since 15-years-old, I harbored no intention of bowing to someone else's. As I understood it, Fu and I were two adults planning our lives, two adults capable of deciding to abort our pregnancy so we could plan our lives together and do things right in the future.

But my understanding couldn't have been further from the truth. She misled me, though I think unintentionally, into believing that there was autonomy between her and her family, when the fact was that she, of her two sisters, bore the full burden of her parents' welfare. The way I saw it, I had three choices; continue dating, ask her to oppose her family or end the relationship. Had we continued dating for a year, my apartment would not have ceased being the most illuminant red light district in Kobe, of which I was already becoming quite bored, though it was not until some 2 years later that I drastically curtailed my whoring.

Requesting opposition to her family was out of the question. If she rebelled on her own, yeh, that would have been great. But I respected her and her family too much to make such a request. I have no family, so I do not intend to drive wedges through the families of others, especially that of my future wife. Since she did not see the need to object to what I interpreted as her parents' over-control, then I wasn't going to introduce the idea, least because I was fully aware of my advantage in finding a partner in this market and appreciated that such extensive parental control was an example of cultural differences to which I couldn't be party.

Korean family ties are much more indelible than those of Japanese families, so it was either I accepted the situation as is or leave. Not one to subscribe to the whole nonsense of soul mates, I knew that given the advantages of my erotic capital in Japan, finding a wife would be easy, though I had to accept the glaring fact that finding a wife with her level of intellect, spunk, maturity and confidence would be selfsame as trying to find a grain of sugar among the sands of Negril. In Japan, aka Disneyland, eye candy is ubiquitous but brain candy is frustratingly sparse. In my stable of women, she had no competition except in the aesthetics arena. Surely there were other women who were much prettier, but none with her wisdom, maturity and confidence. None laughed as heartily as she, none with as powerful a stride and none as intellectually stimulating.

Before departing from my first and only meeting with my ex-future-parents-in-law, angry and hurt I decided that love asphyxiation would be my choice if Fu did not oppose her parents, which I knew she wouldn't. We continued for another thirty days with regular discussions, but her overnight stays were reduced to one or two nights a week even though her job was only 30 minutes from my place, as opposed to an hour and a half from her parents' home.

"I can't do this anymore," trying to be as honest and direct as possible. In fact I even entertained the thought of informing her of my tryst with her co-worker just the semester before, to further illuminate the extent of my sickness and the disadvantage to her of our not living together. But upon reconsidering, I thought sleeping dogs should lie, as that would have been too much information.

"So because of your ego, you're going to leave?"

"Yeh, I prefer freedom over love. Your parents can control you. That's ok, they're YOUR parents. But by controlling you, they are controlling me too, and I don't like that."

"But they just want us to date one more year before we get married, they didn't say we couldn't get married?"

"I know this is a cultural difference, I know. But I don't want parents telling me when to marry their almost thirty-year-old daughter, especially after she and I just aborted our pregnancy."

Fu understood my anger and I understood her cultural obligations, but the twain could not be reconciled. Neither could she oppose her parents nor could I overcome my venom, so one night in late August was our last together. I ebbed and flowed insider her as tears streamed down the sides of her face.

"I never thought we'd have a last time."

"We can still meet sometimes," I comforted.

In the crevices of my mind I was hoping that some time later she'd oppose her parents, and perhaps she too harbored hopes that I would change my values, but neither materialized. The next morning, rising from a futon drenched in tears, sweat and other body fluids, Fu disappeared from sight as I watched her from my third floor balcony. Returning to bed, I crawled beneath my duvet in unspeakable gloom. It's one thing to break up, but it's an entirely different kettle of fish to initiate a separation from someone you love. We remained in contact deeply connected, even visiting love hotels in condomless passion once or twice a month, until it became emotionally impossible for both of us. Having stopped the love ho visits, we continued to see each other platonically, which over the years was reduced to occasional phone calls and then sparse e-mails.

NAO

On the last train home from Sannomiya in March of 2003, packed with boisterous, inebriated passengers, Nao was returning home from her hostess job as my friends and I conducted a booty survey. Like all hostesses in Japan, she was immaculately clad and well put together. Hers was a posterior of the highest standard, round and distending from her garments. Twenty-eight year-old mother of a three-year-old son, Nao was married to a salaryman who like most, preferred the company of his co-workers to that of his beautiful wife. My friends and I gave her a flirtatious thumbs-up.

"Thank you. Where are you from?" She blurted.

After a quick evaluation I concluded that she may well be a *chocolate lover*, one of those none Negroe women who are into Negroe men.

"*With an ass like that, she gats to have chocolate eyes.* She seemed like the R&B species as opposed to the Dancehall type.

"I'm from California and these guys are from Texas."

"Ii naaaa!" (That's great!)

On our first meeting thereafter, she took me to an Italian restaurant in Tachibana, but I wanted to be spared the formalities and just get straight to the point. At the restaurant her chocolate eyes affliction was validated when she revealed how much she loved hip hop and R&B and that she was having an affair with a sax player, a brother from San Diego who visits Japan every six months. Those three strikes; chocolate lover, English speaker and hostess told me that our relationship would be very short-lived and though since I began to acquire the language, I vowed to refrain from all *charity* encounters, as she was quite attractive, I continued to listen to her and inquired about her relationship with her husband.

"We had dekichatta kekkon. (Shotgun Wedding) I don't know how to say that in English."

"We haven't had sex in a year, we are more like roommates. I don't even want to touch him and I don't want him touching me. But he's a good provider."

"So what are you gonna do, just continue like that?"

"Shoganai. (It can't be helped) There's nothing I can do," another mantra of the Japanese. Even the most correctable problem in Japan is met with "shoganai." Nao's plight followed the pattern of so many married Japanese women and it didn't require the mind of a rocket scientist to know where her mouth would soon be.

After our meal she dropped me home for what to me was uneventful penetration, but orgasmic for her, and after our third time some three weeks later, when she placed her spent sanitary napkin in my transparent trash bag, which Fu had discovered, she was gradually released.

CHIKA AT BIGOT

Seven minutes walk from my apartment, Chika was sitting by herself at Bigot patisserie, enjoying some pastry while looking for a job in "Town Work" magazine. Beautiful with short cropped hair, she did look as though she could speak English. In fact, judging from her fashion she looked as though she might have been fluent, as hers was not the attire of the typical Japanese young woman. No multiple layers and mismatched colors with clashing stripes and polka dots. Possessing a Western flair to her, she was well coordinated and simple in her dress, appearing grounded and comfortable with herself. "Looking for a job," I interrupted. "Yes, I just came back from Australia three weeks ago," with a slight Aussie accent, crap brown teeth disrupting her otherwise rapturous face. And what a disappointment that was. "How'd you know I speak English? That's pretty strange, you just spoke to me in English, how'd you know?" Chika had spent the last two years in Sydney after a painful five-year marriage, and was now in culture shock upon her return home. She quickly saw me, a Westerner, as a symbol of the freedom she had tasted in Australia but unbeknownst to her, she would just be one of my many subjects.

In a week's time I invited her to *dinner* and after a round of fairly uneventful sex, we ventured on to the subject of her ex-husband. Though she was an extremely beautiful woman, our less than stellar first sex, her history of orgasmic dysfunction and ironing board anterior were precursors for the early mortality of our sexual relationship. I know I stated earlier that I'm not really keen on breasts, but that by no means should be interpreted as my possessing an ability to be aroused by the absence of mammary glands, which was the case with Chika. For though she had a sexy bottom half with a very acceptable waist to hip ratio, her chest was negative.

In fact mine could have easily been twice hers. Her intellect and analytical personality filled our sexual void and Chika was one of the few Japanese women with whom I could discuss any subject. "Do you know borderline personality disorder? My husband was borderline." A diagnosis made by her sister who was a psychotherapist.
"I am a borderline expert," I assured her, especially after discovering

Marsha Linehan's writings some seven years ago, during my ordeal with Anne. Back in the days of my own litany of personality disorders, the only women I sought for romance were borderlines and upon arriving here, I initially thought that Japan was a hotbed for culturally sanctioned borderline personalities.

According to Linehan theory, borderlines are born with an innate biological propensity for a more intense response to lower levels of stress than others and to take longer to return to baseline. Their emotional peaks are much higher on far less provocation and take longer to calm down. In addition, they were raised in traumatic and abusive environments in which their beliefs about themselves and their environments were continually devalued and invalidated. Perfect descriptions of Karin. These factors combine to create adults who are uncertain of the truth of their own feelings. Such invalidating, devalued, traumatic and abusive environments may well describe the typical Japanese family and the society in general, where negative reinforcement is the norm. Compliments are completely anathema to the way of Bushido, which teaches that one must endure unnecessary hardships for self-conditioning. Junior high school students must remain in track and field even if they hate it and would excel at, say tennis. One must *gaman* (endure) in a despised dead end job as opposed to pursuing a job one really enjoys. Praising is uncommon in Japanese society, as it is thought that compliments would bring about over-confidence and that berating is more effective in getting one to master a skill.

Generally overindulging, Japanese parenting techniques place little or no emphasis on building and nurturing children's self-esteem. Instead, children must gaman through an onslaught of perpetual borderline inducing processes. Obsessed with face saving, many like Karin's parents simply want to show off their children, while chastising them for anything less than stellar performance. Children in Japan are saddled with the burden of preserving family honor, as parents constantly engage in performance comparisons among each other's kids. Most kids survive though not unscathed, even becoming contributors to society, while others become hikikomoris, a phenomenon unique to Japan. As mentioned previously, it is conservatively estimated that a hikkikomori is present in over 400,000 families nationwide, a direct result of overindulgent Japanese parents enabling this maladaptive behavior by taking their children their meals in their rooms. It is categorically inconceivable that I could have dictated to my single mother that I was going to isolate myself in my locked room and not attend school, even if there were bullies at school waiting to behead and castrate me, which there were. Her response would have been something along the lines of, "bwaii, don't mek mi chauge fi murda in ya tiddeh!" (don't cause me to be charged for murder today!) Besides, we shared a single *roomette* anyway, so staying locked up in my room would have been physically impossible.

Still many poison, roast, bludgeon, behead or slash their parents or a parent to death in Japan, while others engage in random public slashings and or heinous public acts such as: pushing strangers from platforms in the path of oncoming trains, or resorting to massacres. Most perpetrators of these acts, parricide included, cite as their motive, parental pressure to perform academically. Still others even opt for exiting. Two thousand three National Police Agency data confirm that suicide by elementary and middle school students is a grave social problem, which saw an increase over 2002, by a whopping 57.6%, representing a total of 93 lost lives, 34 more than in 2002. Among high school students 225 opted out of life, a sharp increase of 29.3% over the previous year. The number of college students exiting also increased in 2003, which produced a 22% rise among those 19 or younger committing suicide. And in 2005, seven elementary school students decided to rid themselves of their lives. Most people can't fathom the idea of elementary school students committing suicide, but as one who harbored suicidal ideations since the tender age of four, it is all too familiar to me. It is my belief that such children are genetically predisposed to a lower threshold of stress, possessing an acute and gifted early awareness of and sensitivity to their surroundings.

According to psychiatric authorities, two to three times more women than men are diagnosed as borderline and in some reports, 75-80% of those afflicted with the illness are females. This could possibly be attributable to genetic or hormonal influences, but an overwhelming contributing factor is the greater frequency with which women, as children, experience incestuous relations and sexual abuse, a major determinant for BPD. Some statistics state that girls are ten times more likely than boys, to experience sexual abuse and other data conclude that a quarter of all women have been sexually victimized. Recently I came across data purporting that, as high as 60% of girls and 30% of boys are sexually violated and that the figures for BPD in the general US population are as high as 14%. Given Japan's misogynistic patriarchy, its militarily structured society, masochistic and invalidating parent child relations, and according to the government, a crisis in teachers sexually abusing girls in schools, it stands to reason that those numbers may well be double in Nippon.

In the dawn of my *whoring* in Japan, it did not occur to me that I was conducting some kind of social experiment, hence I did not inquire of my subjects about childhood sexual molestation until the twilight of my addiction. Simply put, I was just too strung out to see the potential for a book and the possible high frequency of sexual molestation among the women I bedded in Japan. When I finally began to inquire about such personal details, of 32 women, five had been sexually violated or had experienced inappropriate touching as children; Yukari was *devirginised* and for two years, repeatedly sexually assaulted by her high school basketball coach, who later committed suicide. Shoko was molested in a parking lot at eight, by two high schoolboys, and was groped by her junior high school drama club teacher, who also attempted to neck her. Kaori was fondled at age seven by two teenage boys in the stairwell of her apartment building, Anita was fondled by her father, beginning at age eight, followed by penetration from age12, Makiko was fondled and abused by her father at ten and experienced an attempted rape at 19 and was a virgin until 33-years-old when we met.

At six years old the show jumper, who I will later introduce, was grabbed by an old man, who took her to a secluded area to fondle her. Had I thought to investigate this matter from the beginning of my sexual escapades, the numbers may have doubled. It is my unscientific opinion that the ubiquitous incidences of mothers brutally slaying theirs and other children in Japan, is strongly related to the possible frequency of borderline personality disorder. Again, this is unscientific and only my opinion, as I am but a mere high school dropout, but I can only surmise that borderline personality disorder impairs the secretion of oxytocin from the pituitary gland, inhibiting or retarding the process of bonding between mother and child.

Chika had other traumatic aspects to her history. At 12 years old her father had committed suicide and a year later, one night returning from the supermarket, her mother accidentally plunged in a river several meters to her demise while on her bicycle.

"See this railing? They put this up after my mother died," she pointed out one day as we stood at the scene of her mother's demise.

It was surreal. I could almost see her mother with the evening groceries in the front of her bicycle as she rode over the river bank, and for a moment I was consumed by overwhelming sadness, tears welling, imagining the sheer and profound pain endured by a 13-year-old girl after losing both her parents. Having experienced such adversity, she became a rock of a woman and unbelievably optimistic. She took crap from no one and was direct and outspoken, often hated, she said by other Japanese who thought she was a disgrace to Japanese people. Over four months we bonded emotionally, but sexually it was a desert. We often went to the gym together and lamented her dismal prospects as a divorced, 28-year-old, uneducated, flat-chested returnee to Japan. Even she herself found humor in her absence of breasts. Odds were stacked against her and she eventually settled for a temporary *Office Lady* position, like one third of working women in Japan.

On our last date together at a sayonara party for Paul, a Polish American, who had replaced me a year earlier at the school in the countryside, present and also from the small rice paddy town was Miho, a stacked 5'10", Zena Warrior princess built, whiplash inducer. She had high upwardly slanting cheekbones, which matched the angle of her big Betty Boop eyes. Equine came to mind when observing her walk from behind in her stilettos, strutting as if on a catwalk. Her phenotype was atypically Japanese. In fact I would have thought she was Southeast Asian, perhaps Thai. But she was a striking, healthy Japanese country girl, a cross between a mermaid and a mare. Toward the end of the gathering Paul pulled me aside.

"Look, you have to call that girl, she loves foreigners and she's fucking crazy. Get this, she's into fisting."
"WHAAAAT?!"
"No bullshit, she likes it when your whole hand is insider her."
But I wasn't into any of that. I'm just a straight addict, so all those extra-curricular sex acts; fisting, bondage, S&M, homie wasn't interested. And just as I had passed on one of my students to my friend in Kobe the year before, Paul had passed on Miho to me.

"Don't worry dude, I'll take care of her, trust me on that one. I'm all over that." "Here's her number, I told her you're gonna call."
Before the engagement was over, Miho engaged in light and cautious conversation with Chika and me, as she naturally assumed we were an item. The urge to abandon Chika and viciously attack Miho was strong, but I restrained myself as Chika and I bade our good-byes.

A few weeks later, to my relief, Chika initiated separation, after I nonchalantly and irresponsibly fired off inside her during an unprotected episode.
"DID YOU COME INSIDE ME," she screamed.

"Yeh, if you get pregnant, well, we'll just get married."

"How the fuck do you know that's what I want. You have no respect for women!" "Do you think you can just get me pregnant and I should marry you even if I don't want to. I don't like that, you're just as sick as my fucking ex-husband." And with that she got up, got dressed, disappeared from my life and changed her phone number. But I admired that, she was an empowered woman. Her strong character was exactly what I sought in a partner, but unfortunately, our sexual compatibility was minus zero.

KARIN: THE ADVENTURE ENDS

Several months earlier with Chika's help, I had overcome my obsession with Karin and regained self-control. Having been whipped, reduced to stalking her, waiting in the cold only for her to return home to slam her lobby door in my face, my new found confidence was most welcomed. Such was my miraculous recovery that after sex, I was able to leave her apartment without begging like a wuss, or even inquiring about our next encounter and In fact, soon began telling her of my pending marriage to Fu. Observing my new found strength and learning that she no longer could pull strings to my emotions, she made a whopping, night and day about face, a metamorphosis tantamount to Lucifer becoming Gabriel. Suddenly, this callous, frigid woman who frequently blocked my telephone calls and e-mails and regularly exploded in threats to call police and immigration, was now showering me with affection and professing her newly found love, tears – long crocodile tears – streaming down her face. "I made a big mistake." She would sob. "I didn't realize how important you were to me and now you're marrying someone else."
"*Yeh yeh yeh, classic borderline drama,*" I thought to myself.
"You're gonna marry her, aren't you?"
"In a couple months."

Over the next few weeks, though not divulging the details of my pending separation from Fu, Karin begged, pleaded and beseeched me to marry her instead, and knowing full well that she was indeed unstable, I made a decision for the second time to leave the functional for the dysfunctional. However, this time sinister motives were included: I wanted revenge. It had been my childhood fantasy to have the tide turn in my experiences of unrequited love. Of course our earth shattering sex was perhaps the main motivating factor to reconcile, followed by my desire to produce children with her, but my need for revenge was undeniable.

Having been madly in love with her in the past, I was sure those sentiments could have been rekindled, but before agreeing to marriage, she was placed on probation and we would marry three months later in December only after my conditions were met. First, she would accompany me to the gym five days a week, two hours a day for a complete body sculpting regimen. She would also start taking birth control pills until we actively decided to have children, even though back in the drama days I was actively trying to impregnate her, but failed to on account of some secret illness, for which she was taking some mystery medicine. There would also be no more hysterical behavior, no more threats to call the police, no more kicking me out of her apartment in the wee hours of the morning during our arguments. In other words, there would be no more drama. Instead, we would endeavour to resolve our arguments through communication and never go to bed angry at each other. To the average Westerner these requirements would seem quite normal but to her, the bar was exceptionally high, most difficult being the gym. Exercise was anathema to her and I was sure she could've fulfilled every condition except the gym. But I remained reticent in my demands, determined for her to reclaim her once athletic figure.

Less than a month after our decision Karin announced the news to her parents and arranged for us to meet, all the while diligently enduring my physical training. In fact this rigorous program bordering physical abuse, caused her on one occasion to faint at Okamoto station after a session in my absence. But after the transformation in her physique, reducing her body fat percentage from 29 to 21, ridding her of the Jaja Binks slouch, generating more frequent stalking from strangers and continuous compliments from her friends who requested to join us at the gym, she eagerly continued. This new found Karin was a complete make over from the person of old. Inundating me with daily phone calls and e-mails, solicitude replaced her usually arctic personality, while public displays of resentment were now supplanted by displays of affection. No longer concerned with the chance meeting of our coworkers, she initiated hand holding and even began kissing in public. However, she still hated to be inconvenienced by leaving the comfort of her apartment to spend the night at mine. Considering her dramatic change for the better, this was a minor problem, though it required the compromise of sharing her Lilliputian bed.

Karin Hirota morphed into a whole new person from the one I had met earlier, to someone I hadn't known before, a woman reborn.
"I finally got over my ex-boyfriend in America," she reasoned.

But though I relished in this new found woman, the woman I had wished she was upon first meeting her, a part of me simmered in angst and resentment. "*How dare she rip out my heart, hack it to pieces with a chain saw, whip it in an Osterizer then feed it to me, only to act as though nothing had happened? How dare she think she could just change, as though she had done nothing and expect no consequences? No way! She must pay and pay dearly,"* I monologued. Love and passion battled with the strong desire for vengeance and appeared to be winning, though not very deep in my subconscious revenge hovered waiting for justifiable moments to raise its head.

Among the many reasons Karin hated going to my apartment was the omnipresent strands of hair. Too much to remove, Shoko unintentionally left her long strands of straight jet-black locks throughout my apartment and all over my bed.

"When are you going to stop seeing her?" Karin complained. "When are you gonna stop seeing all these women?"

"When I get over all the pain you caused me for six months, that's when."

"I know, you're getting back at me. Wakateru. I know. You'll never forgive me for that."

"I'm sure I will," I responded in false assurance.

"Maiya!" (Whatever) One of her most common expressions especially after her metamorphosis. It might have been possible to change my philandering ways, but would have been difficult to give up Shoko, a young, bewitching and curvaceous fair maiden to whom I had given a partial introduction to the dark side during the tail end of my relationship with Fu. Moreover, in just two short months, a turn of events would ensure no change in my whore mongering.

A month after reuniting and two before our planned December broom jumping and Jamaican honeymoon, I met my future In-laws at an upscale Chinese restaurant in Osaka. Exactly as she had briefed me, they treated me with utmost respect and genuinely welcomed me into the family. Her mother, typical Japanese obaachan (grandmother figure), shared a striking resemblance and similar reptilian disposition, looking like someone who had experienced more than a few nervous breakdowns, which she had, as Karin later revealed. She appeared likeable and nurturing, regardless of the image I had conjured of her based on Karin's regular complaints about their masochistic relations, a perpetual futile quest to please her mother. In truth, so oppressive were her familial relations that it resulted in her younger brother's complete estrangement from the family for the previous ten years. Her father or more accurately, mostly absent father was the Japanese ojeechan (grandfather) archetype. Though chauvinistic and stoic, as to be expected of a high profile corporate lawyer in Japan, I thoroughly enjoyed his omniscience, as we conversed in my primitive Japanese and his near non-existent English, on an array of topics from my alma mater to Cleopatra. Meanwhile Karin and her mom gabbed away in Japanese, displaying no evidence of the chasm between them. Undoubtedly, her parents, especially her mother, were elated to meet me. It was evident in her smiles and the way she glanced at her daughter after looking at me that finally their worries were over, as their slightly off-kiltered daughter had found someone off-centred enough to marry her.

Meeting Karin's parents was a surprisingly, enjoyable experience, which overpowered me with guilt for planning catastrophic vengeance on their offspring. And it was then that I endeavoured to change, bury the hatchet so to speak and move forward. One month before our planned wedding, one of my live rounds hit the target and Karin was carrying our child. Though she, like most Japanese women had rejected the pill, we were not actively trying to avoid a pregnancy, other than her half-hearted requests to withdraw before launching. A request which I always ignored as in my thinking we were getting married and that's what married couples do: start families.

In a decision which would drive a stake in our new treaty Karin decided, against my pleas, to terminate the pregnancy, for reasons incomprehensible to the Westerner's – and certainly mine - mind: she was attending her friend's December wedding in Hawaii and wanted to be able to fit in her dress. Serious as colon cancer, that was her explanation. She saw nothing out of the ordinary with the reason for her decision, but upon voicing my dissent with its absurdity, she found a new explanation to terminate.

"My parents would be disappointed that I got pregnant before marriage," she rebutted, digging herself deeper in a hole. Two weeks later, she added my many women to her reasons for wanting a termination, but what struck me as incongruous was her desire to continue with our planned wedding after the operation. For in my reasoning, if my 'many women' drove her to such strong feelings as to wanting to abort our pregnancy, then it stands to reason that she would also seek to terminate our relationship.

Having known Karin for a year, nothing she uttered was a surprise. After all, this was a woman who adamantly stated that if we had a son, she would never want him to be as confident as I. Yielding to her insanity, I contributed my half of the termination cost, accompanying her to the hospital near Sannomiya on November 7th. Whereas a month earlier I was planning complete behavior modification, including plans to let

Shoko down easy, today I was hell bent on a phlegmatic, torturous end to our relationship. I would wage on her an all out emotional jihad until we separated or, she hurled herself in front of the special rapid train.

Unexpectedly, the following six months were relishable more often than not, as we traveled to Jamaica and throughout Japan, most times forgetting about the inevitable end. Returning from Jamaica where we bickered almost daily, agreeing to separate once and for all, I arrived in my freezing, dark apartment. Having forgotten to pay the bill before our trip, the electricity was disconnected, to which my solution was to share Karin's kid's size bed. A week later, both in mourning we sought counseling, as Karin, post abortion was a train wreck and I, a volcanic mountain of rage. Chisato Yamamoto who had spent some seven years studying in the UK was the most inept counselor I had seen second only to the one I saw in London over 20 years prior. Immediately after departing from her office, both in unspeakable pain, we decided to go our separate ways, a decision which lasted a whopping five days.

As our relationship hobbled to its demise, I had grown considerably attached to Shoko, whom, after eight months of frustration, I had finally fully introduced to the dark side while Karin was away at her friend's wedding. Furthermore, new on the scene was Azusa, a stupefyingly beauteous 21-year-old, whose name I had called repeatedly in slumber with Karin.

"Who's Azusa?" She queried one morning. "Is she new? You must really like her because you were calling her name in your sleep two nights in a row."

In a last ditch effort to save our rotting, dying relationship, Karin agreed to move into my apartment, but refused to give up her own one-room flat. Things came to a head one night when she suffered hour-long hallucinations, crying, cowering and screaming hysterically at my women whose faces were pouring from the light fixture in the ceiling, much like the hands she saw emerging from walls and rivers as a child.

"Can't you see them?" she screamed pointing to the light. "They're coming to attack me, many of them."
"What'r their names?" I inquired.
"I don't know. There are many of them."
"Maybe that abortion was a good thing," I thought and after a month of having her unpacked boxes in my bedroom, we arrived at the penultimate

decision that she would vacate the premises after our break up trip to Takachiho, Kyushu on June 25th 2004. In the end Karin apologized and extended profuse thanks.

"I know I can't be with anyone," she said, tears streaming down her florid cheeks. I'm not well, I always knew it and you are the first person to tell me, the first person who cared enough to try after what I did to you. I can't marry anyone." I had been vindicated.

According to her possibly manipulative report, after being utterly disappointed by our failure to marry in December 2004 as announced, her mother suffered a heart attack and was admitted to the hospital upon hearing the news of our separation.

HISAKO

In June of 2002 the then manager of my apartment building collected me at Shukugawa station to look at prospective apartments. As I sat next to her, immediately I became fixated on her short, thick, shapely legs imprinted through her thin, draping, floral summer dress and when she exited the car, standing at about 5'5," I beheld her low and narrow waistline with a proper rump calling out to me. The yellow Asian woman's low waist has driven me crazy since my childhood and as I walked behind her up the steps, with her sizeable buttocks, small waist and adequately spread hips swaying to and fro, her panty lines mesmerized me, causing me to place my hands in my pockets to hide the effects of her powers. Having lived in Boston for some years, Hisako, 35, divorced with a 6-year-old son, was a near native speaker with an amiable personality and average face. Not exactly the kind of face to which I was overly attracted, but her body rocked.

Coincidentally, I chose an apartment on the top floor of the building where she worked, with only marginal intentions of pursuing her as I thought, after seeing the constant inflow of my harem, there was no way she would want to be among them.
"It's just too close to home." But this was when I was still somewhat naïve about the sexual dynamics of Japanese women. Over the course of a year we became very friendly and I gradually understood that like most untouchables in Japan - divorced with a child – she too was getting no action, existing in quiet sexless and *affectionless* desperation. She made the monthly trip downstairs to pay my rent, one of hardened arousal as I always anticipated lusting after her hourglass curves. Like many Japanese women endowed with her glutes, they had been a source of a major complex since her childhood. Hence most of the time, to my disappointment she wore loose fitting clothes.

"My butt is not like a normal Japanese butt," she complained.
"Don't worry, it's perfect," I assured her, turning her around to get a good view.
"You like it?"

"Oh yes. Ass is very important to us black men."

"So desu ne? (That's right isn't it?) When I was in Boston, so many black men would approach me and my sister always told me it was because of my butt.

"Your sister is right, it's nice."

During our conversations, we sometimes talked about my whoring.

"So who's the new girl?" She regularly enquired.

And sometimes they accompanied me downstairs to pay the rent, where I would introduce them to her, thinking that there was no way she'd even let me near her given her full awareness of my blatant, in her face philandering. But finally I popped the question during one of our flirtatious episodes.

"So when are you gonna invite me to see where you live?"

"I have to see when my sister can keep my son."

Two Fridays later, after one of those volcanic events with Karin, where she as usual, threatened to call the police and immigration, Hisako instructed me to walk down the street and around the corner about 500 meters, where she would meet me after work. Understandably, her concern was her boss and our neighbors, at least the immediate ones. She didn't want them to see me leaving with her in her company car after work. Instead it would have been better if I appeared to have been walking on my own, when she showed up coincidentally and offered me a ride.

"Hey, where are you going?" pulling up beside me.

"I'm just going down to the station. Gonna give me a ride?"

And just like I did at Shukugawa station a year earlier, I hopped in beside her, only this time I immediately hoisted her dress to fondle her legs and caress her heat.

"Dame dame dame!" Slapping away my hand.

"Abunai kara, (It's dangerous) I can't concentrate to drive."

But I persisted, to which she responded by forcefully moving my right hand with her left.

"Hai, wakatta," (I get it) I complied.

"I'll wait 'til we get to your apartment."

Immediately after arriving, I pulled up her dress to palm her cakes while gently stroking her tongue with mine, picked her up, mouths still intertwined and carried her to her bare dining table where without any further foreplay I removed her knickers and sank my year-old crystallized desire deep inside her.

"Remember when you were walking up the steps in front of me to show me that apartment?" Tipping on my toes, slowly gyrating inside her.

"This is what I wanted to do to you."

"Really?" Barely getting out her speech as though I was touching her tonsils.

"Chotto itai." (It hurts a little)

"Motto yukuri," (more slowly)

It seems Hisako too had a year of pent up desire, as in no time she was clenching the edge of the table, pressing her eyes shut in shivers.

"Ikkkkkkkku," sounding guttural and barely able to speak.

After her arrival I turn her around arcing her over the table. The instant I slow dived from behind, bulbous cream cakes in view, I had to rapidly repel so as not to release litres of life sauce inside her. Thereafter, paying my rent would even be a more anticipated experience, as I would sometimes take her to the back quarters of the office where I'd remove her underwear and pleasure us on any available furniture.

Our adventures came to a halt after Hisako became involved with a newly hired assistant some ten years her junior, which lead to another unplanned pregnancy, leading to her second dekichatta kekkon. After she quit, he forbade her from contacting me, but two years later during a surprise encounter, she confided in me that she was currently distraught, facing her second divorce.

ANITA RETURNS

Early spring of 2003 gave me the shock of my life, when one day on my way to the Jamaican restaurant in Sannomiya, lo and behold, in front of my very eyes was Anita McKenzie, in the exact place I had met her a year before. I had sent her several e-mails to no avail and having written her off, seeing her again was even more of a shock. We hugged in greeting and she appeared genuinely elated to see me, screaming and smiling from east to west.

"Oh my God! In the same place, this must be a sign."

"How come you didn't respond to my e-mails?" I queried.

"I am so so so sorry, things were so hectic and I was going through a lot."

I didn't buy it for a second.

"Yeh, yeh, yeh. You just didn't wanna communicate with me, I understand. I'm a big boy, I can handle the rejection, its ok."

"No, trust me, it's not like that."

Shortly after, like a déjà vu, her same sour faced friend appeared, but before they disappeared, she released the digits.

"We can talk, I'm back for good."

We met twice a week on average, and I easily gained her trust, by showing no interest in intimacy, instead listening a lot and at most hugging her. In fact, though she had the perfect face and physique, in my extreme yellow preference, she aroused me only marginally, as she was only half-yellow. I derived more pleasure from admiring her stunning beauty and being in public with her was a gas for my ego. But a large part of me wanted desperately to be attracted to her more. Her beauty was show stopping. But sensing drama, I kept my emotional distance. Sometimes her days without make up revealed infrequent acne, but even then, her beauty was unspeakable and her blemishes just seemed like a constellation of beauty spots.

As I got to know Anita, it struck me as odd how a young woman 20 years old with such bullet train stopping beauty, a more beautiful Angelina Jolie meets a more beautiful Gina Davis – if that's imaginable – a native speaker of English and Japanese, could be so insecure, floundering directionless and aimless in life, battling depression and existing well below her potential. This re-affirmed my conclusion from a year prior that there had to be much trauma. *Unspeakable trauma,* I thought. Especially having spent half her life in the West, where women are far more confident than their counterparts in Japan, she should have been operating at full throttle. Something just wasn't right. Yes I understood very well her identity crisis, being a *double* and having spent equal time in Japan and Canada. Her concern of not knowing whether she belonged here or in Canada made sense to me and I empathized and advised as best as I could. However, in the absence of trauma, a woman in her shoes with such potential, completely aware that there are infinitely more opportunities for women in Canada than in Japan, would have chosen the West. Anita struggled through various menial retail and hostess jobs in the ensuing months, completely unaware of her super-star potential.

Eventually I gained her trust and she began to initiate affection with lots of cuddling, touching and hugging, transforming from the cold heartless person I had met a year prior. On a park bench one evening in Settsu Mottoyama, not far from Sannomiya, with her in my arms, sitting on my lap like a child, in my most compassionate and caring voice I investigated, "when you were little, what happened to you?"
"How'd you know anything happened?"
"That's the thing, I don't know."
"Did anything happen?"
And in the most matter of fact voice, as though she had relayed this event countless times,
"My father started to fondle me when I was eight, then he began penetrating me at 12, gave me my first orgasm at 14."
"*I knew it!*"

Immediately I became flushed with anger and nausea at this fucking anal sphincter who could do this to his own child. But strangely enough, it was somewhat arousing at the same time, kin to the paradoxical emotions rape evokes in me. On one hand I would love to castrate all rapists, but on the other hand, I am especially aroused by rape scenes in films. My conflicting feelings were followed by a strange desire to immediately reject her, perhaps because I knew from experience and from information I'd read and studied, that the victims of sexual abuse whose perpetrators were primary care givers – fathers or mothers – are especially incurable, plagued with high drama and are rendered permanently damaged. But I resisted the urge and held her tighter, as she continued to confide in me how, as the Canadian authorities were moving in on her father, her mother, in her typical Japanese thinking, abruptly relocated the entire family to Japan to protect her husband.

"I hate that bitch!" I hate my dad too, but I hate that bitch more, because she knew and didn't do shit."

I hated the bitch too and continued showing my support for several months to come, meeting almost daily and sometimes traveling domestically. Soon thereafter we became a pseudo-couple, with my advising her on her life choices, almost similar to how an uncle would advise a niece. But I became frustrated with the direction of the relationship: it was going nowhere, as she was only twenty and I was almost twice her age. The only hope was to make a full commitment to her and return with her to the West, preferably to California, where she would be able to pursue her passion in entertainment. However, she was just too young with lots of growing to do, and though for egotistical reasons I wanted her to carry my progeny, I couldn't bring myself to committing the selfish act of impregnating her after she had gained my trust. So I settled for satisfying my ego by using her as eye candy, sporting her at every chance. Part of me desperately wanted to help her, but in the end, like the scorpion which stung the frog as it carried him across the river, my nature overpowered me and I invited Anita over for dinner.

Upon removing her clothes, Anita revealed a perfect, flawless and unblemished body which would cause water to flow uphill. Flawless that is, except for unsightly feet disfigured from many hours of dance lessons and performances since childhood. Her chocolate-chip-nippled, latte-colored breasts were exquisitely shaped, as if sculpted by a master breast maker. With a small waist to hip ratio which made me want to fill her with semen to make my own football team, I began to gently massage her 36Bs as I lowered her to my futon. Disturbingly, though before me was a woman whose physicality was the embodiment of perfection, the missile rose only half mast. The reality was I had no burning desire for intimacy with her, just some juvenile drive to conquer, especially given her ego bruising snub a year earlier. In addition, if ever it was unclear before, my half limp phallus demonstrated the virulence of my yellow fever. The missile is specialized and can only be launched at the sight of 100% yellow.

For upon paying Karin a visit the next day, though far from Anita's perfection, the rod sprung to full attention for the usual wax-a-thon.

Fortunately, my semi erect war head was enough to do the job with Anita. So after going south and staying there for a while, I slowly inserted and began to grow to somewhat full proportions. Initially there was apprehension all over her face, as though she wanted to say, "*should we be doing this?*" But shortly thereafter she began to gyrate and fondle her clitoris as I fed it to her and in no time she was touching down trembling spastically. After her arrival, not trusting myself to withdraw in time, I eased out and had her stand over me as I relieved myself manually. Temptation was too great to at least try to impregnate her, so I unloaded in the air, all over my hands and the futon. After both our arrivals I held her in silence for what seemed like an eternity, as we lay there starkly aware that we had done the wrong thing.

"Is that the only way you can come, touching yourself?" I asked, breaking the silence.
"Yeh, my dad used to touch me like that when he was inside me."

The next morning it would have taken a chain saw to cut through the deafening silence as she got dressed.

"I gotta go to work, see you later ne," Anita and I were never the same, we were not like we used to be after that night together. She frequently made excuses to avoid me and the only times we met thereafter were during random encounters in the streets of Sannomiya, where she stared in my eyes in silent pain.
"*Why, why did you do that?*" She appeared to be querying. Knowing full well that I had violated her, after gaining her trust, just like her father did, I made several futile attempts at apologizing and rekindling our friendship.

IRIE (Y- RI-EH)

Shortly after my surprise encounter with Anita that spring, after leaving a junior high school in Akashi where I was teaching, I met Irie on a bus on the way to JR Akashi station. Irie, a former hostess during her University years at 19, was fly and I damn near stripped her visually of every garment, as we rode the bus together. I didn't want to know her name or anything about her for that matter. I just wanted to throw her on the floor, rip her Kobe fly girl clothes off and defile her, right there on the floor of the bus. We constantly made eye contact and smiled with each other, while I made my predacious motives perfectly clear, sending her overt but discreet messages that I wanted her for my next meal. Like Tomoko before her, Irie was petite, not more than five feet and accurately proportioned. She had the appearance of a doll and all I could imagine was curling her onto me. Ever since my childhood, I had always had a penchant for petite women, as so much more can be done with them and spooning with them is heavenly.

As probability would have it, upon our arrival at JR Akashi station we were both headed toward Osaka and noticing her on the same platform, I discreetly strolled over in her direction and stood by her. "Konichiwa," I opened.
"Wa! Nihongo shaberu!?" (Wow! You speak Japanese!?") "Doko kara kimashitaka?"
"Jamaica desu."
"Haaaaaay! Hunto?! Reggae dai suki." (Really!? I love reggae.")

Our second meeting was two weeks later at Harbour Land in Kobe, to which she wore the tightest jeans making public her member petrifying curves and derriere. It is said that amazing things come in small packages and Irie, like Tomoko, validated that saying. With her ten a day habit, she was among the rising 16 % of women who smoke in Japan, but as a testament to her enormous rod hardening sex appeal, I waived my disdain for cigarettes along with the accompanying breath and decided to endure the pounding headaches that would result in kissing her. Considering her half a pack a day habit, her grill was in acceptable shape, scarcely miscoloured with only a left upper canine malocclusion.

Within forty minutes I was hugging her and after the first kiss, I had to break it to her that, homie just could not handle kissing Jody Camel.
"Ja, tabako wa, yameta hoga ii yo," (I think you should quit smoking.)
"Aaa," she shrieked self-consciously. "Kusaii?" (Does it smell bad?)
"Aji mo." (It tastes bad too.)
"Gome, gome, gome. Yameru, zetai yameru. Gome." ("I'm sorry, sorry. I'm gonna stop, I'm definitely gonna stop.")
"Tabako to Kanachan no kao wa awanai, Kanachan wa kireii kara awanai." ("Cigarettes don't match your face because you're beautiful.")
"Yameru, yameru, zetai yameru. Taskete" ("Help me.")
And I assured her of my support, after which she began chewing some gum. After an hour of sitting and talking by the ocean, I convinced her to accompany me to my apartment citing our difficulties in communicating. She spoke no English and though my Japanese was adequate I pretended the opposite and sold her on the need for a dictionary, which I of course had at my apartment.

Irie, or Irichan wore absolutely no signs of trauma about her, just radiant smiles even when she was exhausted, as she usually was. A 23-year-old psychology graduate, like so many Japanese women she was overworked and overstressed, slaving away in retail some 14 hours a day, with only two or three days off per month. Twice a month she traveled to Korea on buying trips for the boutique, or more accurately, the plantation where she slaved. Immediately upon entering the freak pad, I stooped down to remove her brown knee-high boots then picked her up, all 45 kilograms of her, placed her back against the wall and proceeded to devour her breast in her clothes. "Chotto matte," (Hold on a second) I said.

"Ha migakishite," (Brush your teeth) gently lowering her. As she brushed her teeth, I began to pry her out of her skin tight jeans, lowering them to her thighs so I could wade through her bush from behind. As expected, from what was trying to burst out, the roundest glutes invited me to bend her over my bathroom sink. But as I waded through the woods, she lost all motor coordination and was unable to continue brushing her teeth.
"Matte, matte, hamigaki deki nai yo." (Wait, wait, I can't brush my teeth.)

After laying the naked miniature guitar on my futon, I began to wrap my mouth around her bulbous perfectly proportioned breasts, but to my surprise, she had no interest in foreplay, it was taking too long.
"Irette, irette, hoshi." ("Put it in, put it in, I want it.") And when I tried

to roll on the mag 5,
"Sono mama irette, kondomu kirai." ("Put it in without the condom, I hate condoms.)

Spreading her firm short legs to occupy her, I slowly slid in as she wailed, never before experiencing such full and complete occupancy. She was short and so was her heaven, hence a full third of me was out in the cold, as my corona, foreskin retracting with every advance, seemed to pound against a wall. I thought she would have needed an airlift to the emergency room, but instead she kept yelling,

"motto, motto, iku." ("more, more, I'm coming.") My leftward crooked girth monopolized her den as she screamed breathlessly, riddled with ecstasy as the levies broke. After she came, I picked her up again and began curling her like a dumb bell, sliding her up and down the axle until her flood gates opened again at which time I abruptly withdrew, microseconds before gushing inside her.

Irie damn near lost her mind, flooding my tatami. It was then that I suggested to her to get on the pill, since neither of us liked condoms. But my suggestion was met with skepticism and resistance.
"Daijobu, pill ga karada ni warukunaru kara." (It's ok. The pill is not good for your body anyway.)

Thereafter, Irie and I were never seen in public again, she came over only for servicing. Other than drinking, our fortnightly meetings were her only release from her *uberstressful* existence and she anticipated them like a child waiting for the ice cream truck. We continued for four months until Karin decided that she finally wanted us to be together, after which I abruptly ceased all contact with Irie, ignoring all her calls and e-mails. It took two months before she got the hint and stopped calling. In September of 2004, a year and three months after Karin and I permanently separated, I rang Irie and it was as though she had been sitting by her phone, life on hold, waiting for my phone call. Not once did she inquire as to why I had ignored her and failed to be in contact. Instead, by the end of our brief conversation, she had agreed to come over in three days.

We quickly continued where we had left off and on the first night of our reunion, as usual, she wanted me to go in unstrapped. Having not seen her coca cola bottle shape in so long, upon mounting and planting the nozzle, I quickly lost control and like an aircraft dumping excess fuel over the ocean, I emptied my vas deferens deep inside her. Surely I had dumped enough fuel in her ocean to impregnate her even if her ovulation period was two months away.

"It was just too late to withdraw, the horse had already gone through the gate so might as well enjoy it to the last drop," I thought.

Irie and I continued on her subsequent days off, taking x rated pictures and making our own porn videos, until some months later she stopped returning my calls and ceased all responses to my e-mails. When she finally did, she visited me on her earliest day off and produced a sonogram from the Kubo Mizuki ladies clinic.

"Kore wa nani?" I inquired. (What's this?)

"Watashi tashi no akachan." (Our baby)

"Nan gatsu?" (How many months?")

"Chuzetsushita." (I had an abortion)

Engulfed by inscrutable saturninity, we sat on my Le France bed in silence, before I held her petite body in my arms.

Even after the operation she was still resistant to the idea of the pill and we continued as before. Our only changes were,

"Naka ni dasanaide ne." (Don't come inside me, OK?)

Within a few months I was off to Jamaica where she e-mailed me after three months.

"Kaetara, mo awanai. Chuzetsushitakunai." (I don't want to meet anymore when you return to Japan, because I don't want anymore abortions.)

Seeking desperately to reduce inventory and concentrate on my two marriage candidates, her decision was welcomed music to my ears.

Three years past and after discovering her number on an old cellphone in March '08, within 48 hours of contact, two months before my final departure from Japan Irie was again on the scene.

MIHO

Two weeks after we met I made the journey to my Japanese hometown to visit Miho. After meeting me at the station in her lowered, *yankified* Honda T-max, she took me to a bar, proudly displaying me to her friends. Overpowered by the smoky environment, I urged her to leave, though I had no idea where we would go, or where I would be staying for the night. Wasting no more time, she drove us directly to a love hotel where she stripped of everything but her knee-high boots, following my request. Hers was a faultless body, from curves to protrusions, which sent my anatomy into shock. I begged her to stand to the side, to drool at the sight of her statuesque physique. Her English was sparse and once at the hotel she cared little for conversation, so we simply got down to business. Foreplay was brief and as she spread her long legs upon reception, the soles of her boots appeared to touch the ceiling. Momentarily I stopped to control my arrival, to give her first priority and after her quick climax I lost all logic. Overpowered by the primal instinct to breed, I emancipated an avalanche, which according to her, flowed from her for days.

Given her tendencies toward extreme possessiveness, Miho's presence on the list was short lived, prompted by her insistence on exclusivity almost immediately after our first encounter. She wanted to move in with me in Kobe, where she'd find a job. No doubt, having discovered that I was planning a long term stay in Japan, she sought to place me under lockdown. But as fine as she was and especially since her father was a member of the infamous yakuza, homie was just not going to venture in to that arena. So after only two months, she faded into oblivion.

KAZUMI

Working as a receptionist at the school which dispatched me to various junior high schools, 21-year-old Kazumi was another mini encounter. In fact, our short lived relationship was simply because she was one of the few well adjusted young women I had met in Japan, who terminated contact with me. Since the start of my employment at this company, I had been admiring her from a distance in the office, being careful to curtail my drooling and conceal my desire when conversing with her. As long as she was always at her post in the office, there would have been no way to step to her. But one day my luck changed. As I entered the building she was ascending the stairs, on her way back to the office. Stepping up the pace I quickly approached her from behind.
"Your boyfriend is a very lucky guy."
"You think so? But I don't have one."
"I'll find you one, so give me your phone number and I'll call you when I find him."
Before rounding the bend to the office, she reeled off the digits as I dialed them on my cell phone for storage.

Kazu was among the few women who, wearing no detectable trace of trauma, boasted of a loving, caring and supportive relationship with her parents, in particular her father.
"I love love love my father. He is the kindest man in the world."
"My father is the only man my mother knew, he taught her everything and made her the successful business person she is today. They are so happy with each other. That's the kind of relationship that I want."

From my experiences in Japan, those were indeed rare words about Japanese parents, especially coming from a woman about her father. In early May 2003, the night of May 5th to be exact, after my second date with Shoko, Kazu and I met in Sumiyoshi where an annual festival was being held. After hanging out for an hour, she accepted my invitation to my apartment, initiating her briefly into the satellite club. Upon arriving at my apartment there was no dinner as I had prepared for the others, just getting straight to the point of physical enjoyment.

Kazu was the only Japanese woman who insisted on my strapping up, prepared even to hold out and flat out refuse had I not don a condom. Encircling her dark nipples with my mouth immediately revealed the source of her adamancy: she was still lactating from a recently aborted pregnancy.

"Was he a foreigner?" I queried.
"No, Japanese."
But that did not deter her from multiple climaxes. A testament to her well adjusted personality - a rarity among the numerous Japanese women with whom I had been - after two months she abruptly halted our trysts.

"I don't want to go to your apartment anymore," she declared. "I was just curious about you since you were so popular among the junior high school students and teachers. The last thing I need is someone like you." And right she was.

"I know about foreigners like you," she continued. "You just come here and take advantage of Japanese girls because Japanese girls are easy."

Again, her statement was correct. Though I had known nothing of Japanese women before landing on the island, upon becoming familiar with the terrain, I most certainly took full advantage. As attractive as she was, her decision was most welcomed, as in Japan, given the high erotic capital of Western men, infrequent rejection was a source of regular, well needed attrition. Sparing herself a great deal of pain, unbeknownst to her, she had also granted me a favour.

AKIYO

Stepping off the Hankyu train one day in the late spring of 2003, I observed a pair of inviting cakes clad in tight black pants. Quickening my pace I moved in to evaluate her face, which in retrospect was a waste of time as I had already decided that, even with the face of a bull terrier, with such a round and protruding posterior, I wanted her on my futon. Akiyo's acne scarred, 33-year-old face showed signs of extensive trauma and her missing upper right bicuspid told me she wasn't exactly wealthy. With a body like hers; thick, curvaceous with big legs extending beneath a round rump, had she not been a lover of chocolate, she without question would have been a prime candidate. Her English was near native, having returned from four years in Canada, where she had endured years of torturous matrimony to a physically abusive coked out Jamaican. Nonetheless, her face was a little above average and in fact in the West, she would have been well sought after.

"So where are you from?"
"Jamaica"
"Oh GOD!" Rolling her eyes in *disgulief* (disgust and disbelief).
"But you don't sound Jamaican. I used to be married to a Jamaican."
"I left when I was a kid, lived in America and England," I amended, sensing a traumatic experience with one of my countrymen, given our penchant for causing pain.
"He was pretty bad, huh?
"Jesus! I can't even begin to tell you. He was drama 24/7."
"Yep, that's us. Not me though, I left that kinda drama a long time ago. But yo, Jamaicans aren't the only ones who are crazy. I got a crazy Japanese girlfriend."

Akiyo was one of those seeking to escape the oppression of her family and the choking restriction of Japanese society, by marrying a Jamaican who was on a professional basketball team in Japan. But escaping the frying pan, she landed head first into an inferno of daily whoop ass, baby mama drama and drug addiction, after which she escaped, found the Lord and returned to the frying pan. Now at 33 and back in the pot on the stove, she was saddled with a curfew, working for her father's container repair company and in her words, "worshipping the Lord."

Yes, trauma always takes people to the Lord, but I can give you what the Lord can't, thinking to myself. During the short walk from the station, we exchanged numbers and in two weeks she was at my apartment where we engaged in stimulating, sometimes heated conversation about everything, from the similarities of Japanese and Jamaican society to her inviting me to church. But all the while, I was just imagining her against the wall naked. Once during our conversation, I began to stare at her with laser eyes burning off her clothes.

"Why you lookin' at me like that?"
"I'm imagining what you look like out of those jeans," gently pulling her next to me and touching her lips to mine.

"You got a gir..." And before she could get the rest of the word out, our tongues were locked and I was hastily undoing her pants. Her rosy cheeks peered from black bikinis and I dug my hand into her forest. Like a junior high schoolboy taking advantage of a girl whose parents weren't home, I hastily unhooked her bra to liberate her perfectly shaped breasts and pulled both top and bra over her head. Standing her naked against my wall, I removed the limb from my pants and began to relieve myself as I stared at her. She was a thick *African* woman with a Japanese face.

"Why the hell are you Jamaicans all like that? My husband used to do the same thing."
"Good, so you're used to it," as I continued to stroke the trunk.
"What are you doing?"
"Chushite." (Kiss it), I requested.
And she knelt as if to pray but instead wrapped her lips around me.
What ever happened to all that talk about getting to know a man and wanting him to respect you before you have sex? Thinking to myself. Akiyo like so many other born again women whom I had known biblically, was in a constant tug-o-war with normal, natural human desire for sex and adhering to the absurd tenets of their religion. And as with all the other Christian women with whom I came in biblical contact, the flesh was victorious.

Moments later with my corona hitting her pallet, I desecrated her oral cavity with protein as I held the back of her head in detonating rapture. Since exposure to fellatio, I had not been a fan. Perhaps because I'm uncircumcised, it's usually uncomfortable and irritating, but Akiyo was amazing and one of the few women who could bring me to climax during that act. Living within ten minute's walk from each other, there were frequent booty calls at odd hours of the night, but eventually she became more demanding.

"How come you never take me out? I'm always coming over here in the middle of the night and you have never taken me out. I wanna be treated with respect, I'm not coming over here again," which seemed to be her mantra. But there were to be no sightings of us together outside, that was just not going to happen. Having lived in the West, she had the right idea, but she had it all backward expecting respect and to be taken out, after giving it up with no such prerequisites.
"Why would I take you out when I am getting what I want without doing so?"

Despite her bitter protests, she continued to come over on call, even bringing over candles and other decorative items, apparent territory markers. Periodically she would stop visiting.
"I have a boyfriend now, I can't come over anymore."
And I would be genuinely happy for her. But those moments were short lived and her midnight trips would be reinstated until I left Japan for a six month moratorium in Jamaica some two years later.

A year later, before my Jamaica hiatus, Azusa and I met Akiyo on the train, where I introduced the two.
"This is my fiancé Azusa."
"Azusa, this is Akiyo."
"Wow she's cute. What the hell is she doing with you?"
"What can I say? I think she's blind," sensing some venom.

Speaking in Japanese, they exchanged information about each other's family names, domiciles and the possibility of hanging out together.
"Is your apartment still messy?" she asked turning to me.

Immediately I knew what that question was all about: to create drama, to let Azusa know that she, Akiyo and I were intimate at one point. Azusa detected it too, but fortunately before introducing them to each other, I had preemptively told Azusa about her upon first spotting her on the train. Given Akiyo's acerbity, she was the prime suspect regarding a spooky, anonymous letter received by Azusa's parents, stating that the sender is a friend of mine and Azusa's. The sender continued to express concern that, since Azusa and I were getting married, Azusa's parents may want to know that I had been spotted on the train with a foreign woman - who turned out to be Janelle, half Dutch and half Japanese – bad mouthing Azusa while trying to get Janelle to accompany me home.

After several futile internet encounters, Akiyo met some brother from California, who within a few months arrived in Japan for them to cohabitate. However, from my observation and from my friends' accounts, such arrangement has a high probability of failure. Many Japanese women, who *import* Western white or black men, or who return to Japan with the men they met in the West, are fully aware of the demand for these men in Japan. As a result, they can be extremely possessive and sometimes obsessively restricting, prohibiting the men from socializing. They are quite aware of the high probability that, within a month or so these men would begin spending their new found erotic currency.

JANELLE

Returning home on the same train where I had met Akiyo some months earlier, I spotted a Caucasian woman, or what I thought was a Caucasian woman, thumbing away at supersonic speed on her cell phone. More shocking was her blasting away in Japanese.

"Wow, your Japanese is pretty good," I interrupted.
"I'm Japanese," she responded defensively as though offended.

Her curt response immediately clued me in to HER source of trauma, displayed in her jowls, like many other Japanese in my daily observation on the trains. Though Janelle had a Japanese father and was born and raised in Japan for some 24 years, her phenotype was like that of her Dutch mother. There was simply no hint of Japanese blood in her except for maybe her stature of five feet.
"Ever since I was a child, I've been trying to convince people that I'm Japanese."

"Hello, in this society where you were born, you're not Japanese, you can't be Japanese, your mother is from Holland and you don't look Japanese, you look like a foreigner, you look like a white woman, that's the reality. So, until you stop fighting that reality, you are gonna have to live with your identity crisis."

Aside from her sad countenance, she was fairly attractive and quite shapely. But as I suffered from yellow fever, fortunately for her, she would not have been a target of my pursuit, at least not immediately. But having nothing else to do I accompanied her on her twenty minute walk home from the station.
"Jesus, you walk up these hills everyday? Why don't you just get a scooter or something?"
"It's good exercise."
A few meters before arriving at her home, we stopped at a park overlooking Kobe, where she divulged the news of her virginity at the adult age of 24. Straightaway she became more attractive to me and my interest in her

increased. I wanted to be her first for none other than egotistical reasons. But I was in no hurry, my plate was already full.

During my teenage years it was a big ego boost to introduce a maiden to the world of sex, a notch on the belt so to speak. However, as I got older and my addiction became more pronounced, I began to despise them and developed a policy requiring women to come to the table – or the bed - with their tools, ready to do work, as opposed to arriving with books ready to learn. I grew tired of teaching. Recently I was reacquainted with an extra-ordinarily beautiful Norwegian lady whom I had met some seven years ago in 1999 at a club in Los Angeles. Almost immediately after our conversation started, she began to remind me of my brutal rejection because she was a virgin. Barely recalling my actions at the time, I was awestruck by my dismissal of such a perfectly, breathtakingly attractive 20-year-old woman, on account of her virginity. But all that changed after touching Nippon soil.

The virgin, that nearly extinct *species* in the West, especially after the teenage years, is a dime a dozen in Japan. In the West, especially in the US and Jamaica where most of my life experiences lay – pardon the pun – adult virgin women combined with the possibility of having experienced some trauma, are usually Christians adhering to the strict doctrines of their religion. However, in Japan adult virgin women are simply the result of a social dynamic which breeds a profound inability for the two sexes to communicate effectively.

Male female relations here are based on archaic Confucian ideologies and while this ancient Chinese way of thinking may have some virtues, healthy relations between the sexes are by no means among them. If in absence of Confucian thought in the West, men are from Mars and women are from Venus, then in Japan men are Marsian fish and women are lemurs from Venus. Confucianism, from which a significant part of Japanese ideology is derived, holds women in contempt and maintains that the socialization of the sexes should be separate and unequal.
"The woman with no talent is the one who has merit."
"Woman's greatest duty is to produce a son."
"We should not be too familiar with the lower orders or with women."
These are but a random few of the many Confucian tenets regarding women and to which contemporary Japan clings.

Ironically, China, the origin of this thinking, has loosened somewhat its Confucian choke hold on women, but Japan still clutches it as an integral part of its existence, as it does to outdated laws borrowed from old Europe. The Europeans have since modified those laws many times over, but Japan still maintains and adheres to many of them, outdated and useless in their original form. The Chinese are an overwhelming majority at schools where I've taken Japanese language classes and upon questioning them, the women all spoke of awe after observing the dismal plight of Japanese women.

"I couldn't believe it when I first came here. The women have to do everything for their husbands, even make their bath. They are like, like, I don't know in English, dorei." (slave)

"When I cook dinner," another chimed in, "my (Japanese) husband has to wash the dishes. For example, today is his day off, so he stays with the baby while I come to Japanese class."

Those words could hardly hail from the mouth of the average Japanese woman. This oppressive social arrangement is in and of itself traumatic to women en masse in Japan and is even perpetuated by their own fathers, who themselves are torchbearers and gatekeepers of the danson jyohi shakai. (male-chauvinist society). These men who are generally inept in communicating, are especially so with their daughters. If father daughter relations are strained in the West, then the tendency is several times greater in Japan.

A few blocks from my apartment near the Kansu supermarket, there is a toddlers' park where I frequently observe parents interacting with their children. Though overall there have been massive improvements since 2001 when I first arrived, observing Japanese fathers interact with their children is still a painfully awkward sight and even more cringe inducing when interacting with their daughters. Distant and non-interactive, they seem to no sooner enjoy electrolysis on their testicles than interacting with their children. Their behavior is akin to those of people in the West who take their dogs to a dog park, just standing back and letting the dogs run around. In fact, from my observation, the Japanese male is far more interactive and tactile with his dog than he is with his children, at least in public. Interacting with his daughter is even more of a teeth extracting activity. While he is likely to touch and sometimes hug his sons, daughters pine for their fathers' touch to no avail.

"Why don't you touch your daughters?" I asked some fathers, including some of my students.

"So desu ne." (That's a good question), inhaling through their teeth, lamenting the answer to my apparently mind boggling question.

"Seku hara," (Sexual harassment) one student responded. "

How bizarre," I thought, failing to see the connection between sexual harassment and affectionately touching one's child. But my student's response hinted at the intractable and deep seated discomfort Japanese men harbor in interacting with members of the opposite sex, even if it's their own baby girl.

Add to the aforementioned schism the trauma of overt and salient abuse, such as molestation, a common experience among women - both here and the world over, though generally unaddressed here - and the result is women with strong aversions to men or more accurately, Japanese men. My conclusion of some five years ago was validated in a June 2006 article, where Mr. Kunio Kitamura of the Japan Family Planning Association stated, "generally speaking, in Japan the ability of men and women to communicate smoothly is very low," a condition which works very well to the advantage of male Westerners, socialized in an environment free of Confucian chains.

The article also included the results of a study conducted in May of the same year titled, Male and Female Life and Awareness, which made public the reality that over 10% of Japanese men between the ages of 40 and 45 are still virgins. And in another report 30% of unmarried men in their 40s had never had sex. While the *Forty-Year-Old Virgin* was only a film in the West, here it's a reality for a great many who passionately participate in air sex competitions. In other data compiled from a 2002 survey by Shigesato Takahashi, chief demographer for the National Institute of Population and Social Security Research, over half of all unmarried men between 18 and 34 have had no sexual, friendly or casual relationships with a woman. And among unmarried women of the same age group, 40% reported that they have had no casual or intimate relations with men. In other words, still virgins. Moreover, 30% of men between the ages of 25 and 29 and 35% of Japanese women in that same age group have never had sex.

Among my four virgins was an *Office Lady*, company class student of mine, who still had her calcified annular hymen firmly in tact. At 36- years-old Wakako, my oldest virgin, hemorrhaged litres all over my tatami. To the average newcomer to Japan, an attractive, curvaceous, 156 centimeter 36-year-old virgin woman would have been incredulous. But having resided here for six years, I had anticipated her stories of severe trauma, stories of double parental loss in her youth and a frightening attempt at sex at twenty. Further securing her *purity* until nearly 40 years old, was her attendance at an all-girls high school and university, depriving her of badly needed interpersonal skills necessary to communicate with members of the opposite sex. Wakako reported that after graduation from university, she simply buried herself in work in order to cope with the loss of her parents.

After two months of cell phone e-mails, Janelle was scheduled to visit my apartment, where I gave her the usual treatment; cooked her dinner, showed her some affection, and introduced her to the world of orgasms. She insisted on a no entry policy, as I was not prepared to commit to her and I respected that. In fact, it was quite a relief, as I harbored no further intentions had she not approved drilling rights. On the day of her debut visit, she waited outside my apartment for an hour as I overstayed my visit with Fu. After providing her with her first climax ever, I taught her how to pleasure herself, advising her,

"You don't have to give up your virginity if you don't want to, but I'm gonna teach you how to make yourself happy when you're at home." Returning home, she e-mailed me with a glee that radiated from my telephone screen. "I just did it three more times, thanks for teaching me."

Like most of the others, Janelle and I never dated. Being spotted in public together was only during our accidental meetings on the train, at which time I would spontaneously invite her over for her *orgas-ma-fest*. Usually she was helpless against my invitations. Many times she made attempts at reception, but would quickly give up on account of the pain, which usually prompted her to reassert her no boyfriend or love, no entry policy.

Janelle, like many others, existed within the confines of a miserable family headed by a cold, unaffectionate, non-communicative Japanese father.
"I don't even remember my last conversation with him."
Her mother, a former stalwart from the Netherlands, had been reduced to a pusillanimous maid, lonely in her marriage, and her two other sisters left home at the earliest opportunity, fleeing to Europe. However Janelle remained, I surmised for reasons of diffidence. A year later during one of our many outdoor encounters at a nearby lake, with my hand in her underwear, Jan looked up at me.
"You wanna have sex with me, right?"
"Yeh, of course I do."
"Then why can't you tell me you love me?"
"Because I don't."
"But you could lie. Why can't you lie?"

"Such desperation at such a young age, how very sad."

Perhaps because I was now older, wiser and more considerate, but having devirginised Shoko just a few months back I had become sentimental and started to appreciate the sacredness of a woman's virginity. Subsequently, though that was my original motive a year earlier, I had no intentions of deceiving Janelle in order to be her first.

Gradually our rendezvous were reduced to even less frequent chance brushes on the train, when I would invite her to my apartment for pleasure from my digits and futile entry attempts. This continued for a year and a half until a January e-mail from her with a change of tone.

"My parents are on holiday in Amsterdam," it read.

"Can you come over?"

"I can't be there until the 20th."

"Ok, I will meet you at the station after work at nine."

Finally acquiescing to the reality that there would be no love or exclusivity agreement, after holding out for over a year, she was ready.

Her parents' house in the hills overlooking Kobe, was a sprawling institute of grey concrete, with the warmth and comfort of a medieval dungeon. Just being there partly explained the reason for her droopy face. Most county jail cells in which I had spent countless weekends in California were more appealing. I am utterly convinced the Japanese would be so much happier with central heating in their homes. For a moment I thought I had stepped into a frigid classroom at one of the junior high schools in Osaka or Akashi where I taught, but this was the supposed castle of an extremely wealthy trading company owner in the Beverly Hills of Japan. Bracing against the elements, we prepared to take a hot bath together in her tenement looking bathroom, one which replicated the shower area at Santa Clarita minimum security facilities in California.

Too preoccupied with the after bath, the bitter cold which awaited me upon setting foot outside the tub, I was unable to fully enjoy the experience and after rising from the tub I quickly abandoned her, sprinting faster than Usain Bolt to her room. It had taken Janelle over a year to psych herself up for the occasion, and indeed she was a trooper even as her flesh slowly gave way, transforming her sheets into a Matador's cloth.

Two months later I went to Jamaica and upon re-entry from my six month absence, we continued where we left off until our encounters returned to chance meetings on the train. After some three years she finally came to her senses and found the strength to resist my invitations when our paths crossed arbitrarily.

"I made the worse mistake of my life. I wanted to give my virginity to someone who loved me. You are such a terrible person."

"Well, at least I didn't lie to you," I rebutted. "You would have felt much worse had you found out that I had lied to you just to get you into bed." The fact of the matter was, I had changed. No longer did I possess the desire to persuade her to join me in my apartment. I was making the transition out of the game, settling down, actively dating and preparing to marry two women.

In 2007 Janelle finally heeded my preaching and moved to Europe where she would further her education and put her multi-lingual skills to good use.

SHOKO

On April 15th 2003 about two months after meeting Chika, I beheld a young breathtakingly beautiful, doll faced queen as I descended the escalator at Sannomiya station. Exuding elegance, she was attired in a sweater and a plaid, pleated burgundy and ash Burberry miniskirt. Though scandalously short, it was classy, exposing her delicious, vanilla porcelain thighs. With earphones firmly planted in her ears, her demeanor screamed, "*don't even think about talking to me.*" To the average person her trauma might not have been visible, however with my traumadar (trauma radar), my keen awareness of the pervasive state of depression which haunts many Japanese, I interpreted her countenance as a cry for help, beckoning to me in a quest for human affection. In any event, with that pulchritudinous face and resplendent attire, had she been wearing subwoofers and 15 inch Cerwin Vegas over her ears, homie still would have been severe about stepping to her. After seeing her for only a few seconds as we passed each other on the escalators, I rushed down to board the upward bound escalator in full pursuit, praying that my prey looked half as good from behind as she did from in front. Boarding the ascending escalator and taking in the view leapt my nature out of control, as not only was she orbiculate, but her micro-mini revealed the firmament and all its heavenly bodies, sun, moon and many stars. Hastily I hiked up the moving steps to catch up with her.

"Do you speak English?" invading her personal space and interrupting her isolative countenance.
"No I don't," slowly waving her hand in front of her face. But like so many other Japanese, her command of English exceeded her confidence. After some ten minutes of butchering each other's language, it was time to close the deal, otherwise I would have been late for work, or more accurately, more tardy for work.
"You should give me your e-mail, I'll write to you so you can practice your English and I can practice my Japanese."
Whipping out her cellular to show me her e-mail address, surprisingly revealed none other than the singer Maxwell on her wallpaper. This was a sign both good and bad: Bad if she had chocolate eyes and had been

exploring the chocolate community, but good if she simply had an interest but not yet initiated. Fortunately, the latter was the case. Besides, with a rump like hers it was only natural that she would attract chocolate.

In contrast to her parents,' especially her mother's loathe for foreigners, Shoko had been a closeted admirer of foreign culture since her junior high school days, but like most Japanese, diffidence far superseded her interests. Al Green, a singer I despised in my childhood but began appreciating in my late twenties, was among her favourites, which made me quite embarrassed for despising the reverend for all those years. For here was a typical Japanese woman of 23 years old who, as I later discovered, knew all of Al Green's songs and even sparked my interest in Maxwell. Never could I have imagined that this royal looking dame, with such repellant beauty would be into rhythm and blues. From her elementary school days, Shoko's parents had been drilling in her psyche, their abhorrence for foreigners and strictly forbade her from even thinking about dating one.

"You would really disappoint us if you ever dated a foreigner," her mother constantly reprimanded. Obviously they had never heard of psychological reactance theory. Shoko reminded me of my favourite flowers: Gerber daisies. Except that she, like many of her peers, was wilted and trampled by depression. By no means was she alone in her suffering. Based on a 2002 survey, some 60% of female employees and 50% of males in small and medium sized companies suffered from depression, while 16% of females and 11% of males reported that they suffered moderate to severe depression. According to another survey, doubling the rate recorded in 1993, some 64,000 people per day in Japan either consulted specialists or were hospitalized for mood disorders in 1999. Satoru Shima, professor of clinical psychology at Kyoto Bunkyo University, headed a survey commissioned in January 2007 by the Ministry of Health Labor and Welfare, which revealed that 2.2% of the workforce in small to medium sized companies in Tokyo's Ota and Chiyoda wards had attempted suicide in the past year. This was an alarming increase from the results of previous surveys, which showed that only 0.1% of employees had attempted suicide in the same period. In a 2007 white paper report, the number of people suffering from mental disorders in Japan hit a record high of 3.03 million in 2005, marking an increase of 450,000 from 2002. One third, the largest proportion, suffered emotional disorders such as bipolar disorder. The report continues that about 2.68 million people were out patients, an increase of 440,000 from 2002, while about 350,000 were institutionalized, marking an increase of 10,000 from three years prior and the highest amount of hospitalized mentally ill patients in the world. At 406 days,

Japan also has the longest average stay for the mentally ill.

A 2007 report from The Ministry of Education revealed that of the 7,655 teachers at public elementary, junior high and senior high schools who took sick leave in the 2006 academic year, 4,675, or 61% suffered mental illness including depression. The Ministry of Education, Culture, Sports, Science and Technology states that both figures are record highs, as the number of teachers taking days off due to mental illness, increased for the 14th consecutive year.

Japan's jaw dropping beauty runs counter to the collective unhappiness and dismally crippling emotional conditions of its populace. A global poll on values conducted by the Pew Foundation revealed that among wealthy nations, the Japanese are the most pessimistic. Only 9% of Japanese surveyed were satisfied with their society. In 2006, Researchers at England's University of Leicester, utilizing data compiled from 178 countries, created a happiness index on which Japan was 90th, the US 23rd, Canada and the Bahamas in the top ten and Denmark number one. And in the aforementioned June 2008 Durex Global Sexual Wellbeing survey of 26,000 people in 26 countries, in contrast to 50% of the British and 74% of the French, only 19% of the Japanese – the lowest in the world – are happy with their psychological health.

Children are by no means spared in Japan's masochistic society. Researchers at Hokkaido University discovered that one in four junior high school students is depressed, far more than their counterparts in the United States and Europe, and to which an increase in suicides among elementary and junior high students speaks volumes. Data from the World Health Organization estimates that with a population of 126 million, Japan is second only to the United States in the number of depressed individuals, though the American population at 300 million is more than double that of Japan's. Two thousand one was the year Paxil was introduced to Japan, which generated $96.5 million in sales in the first full year. Two years later sales skyrocketed to $298 million, almost matching the per capita sales of the drug in America. Adding misery to the crisis, according to the WHO, there are only ten thousand psychiatrists for the millions suffering depression in Japan, which along with demonstrating the primitive state of psychiatry in the country, also exposes general inadequacies in medical care.

Also in acute shortage are obstetricians and gynecologists, the very doctors necessary in the event Japan were to experience a remotely unlikely miraculous increase in its nose-diving fertility rate. Deterred by among other factors, the highest malpractice rates among medical professionals, med students avoid OB_GYN, like I avoid natto, that sticky, foul smelling delicacy of fermented beans. As a result, this aversion creates an inhumane workload for doctors currently in the field, which only deters more students from entering. "Why choose OB_GYN?" asked one of my students, an extremely bright but damaged 33 year-old surgeon, for whom I had utmost respect and admiration.

"The hours are long, the pay is relatively low and there's a high probability of getting sued, even jailed."

It pained me to hear of the unfathomable, repetitive rejection Tomoya had been experiencing from her childhood at the hands of her father, who had wanted a son but was *cursed* with two daughters of which she was the elder; one a surgeon and the other a baby mama Not in Education Employment or Training (NEET). During our first lesson in free conversation English, she embarked on a rant about her disdain for her medical researcher father who abandoned her in a Yokohama park at 6 years old, and returned home in Tokyo to her mother and sister. They had been out together collecting insects, but when she feared removing a cicada from a tree, he simply marched off angry and frustrated, leaving his six year old behind to fend for herself. And that was only the beginning of his neglect.

Much to her father's chagrin, she rejected research to become a gifted surgeon. But this talented doctor too, frustrated with the deficiencies of the medical field in Japan, has since abandoned her own shores for greener pastures in the United States.

Michael Moore's documentary SICKO may have illuminated the disturbing truth about health care in the United States. But should Mr. Moore be moved to produce a sequel to his 2007 exposé, SICKO II would do well to focus on the dismal plight of medicine in Japan, which like most dysfunctions here, maintains a problem-free facade. A July 2007 Organization for Economic Cooperation and Development (OECD) report divulged disturbing shortcomings in the medical system, particularly underscoring Japan's underdeveloped system of preventive medical care. In 2004, Japan's ratio of physicians to the population was an embarrassing 2/1000, meaning, for every 1,000 people there were only two physicians. This performance ranked Japan 27th among the 30 OECD industrial countries and below the OECD average of three doctors per thousand.

These states of affairs result in doctors compelled to see more patients than do their counterparts in other developed countries. At 8,400 patients per year, doctors in Japan see 3.5 times the OECD's annual average of 2,200 patients. Under the harsh working conditions common in Japanese hospitals, it is common for doctors to work uninterrupted 36 hour shifts. In the words of Hyogo Brain and Heart Center director Teishi Kajiya, "It's become the norm for doctors to work 36 hours straight, which is emotionally and physically exhausting. We never know when one of us might collapse."

Japan's plummeting birthrate has decreased the number of possible doctors and patients for which they would care. Since many if not most hospitals are privatized, lack of patients translates to slashes in revenue, mounting prefectural debt, hospital closures and a freeze in doctors' salaries. Stagnant salaries serve as a repellent to potential medical students, which results in a shortage, hence *normalizing* the 36-hour shifts for current doctors. Naturally, observing these dynamics, students are choosing less stressful and taxing careers, while some doctors, especially women like Tomoya the transplant surgeon, Akari, a new doctor in internal medicine, and Nozomi, my cardiologist at a Kobe hospital, have chosen to abandon their homeland.

On an NHK program telecasted in early 2008, Koseikai Kurihashi Hospital's Vice President Dr. Hiroshi Honda grieved, "Because the number of doctors is not enough, one doctor should play multiple roles as surgeon, chemo-therapist, palliative therapist, emergency doctor and others. This causes serious negative effects on the quality and safety of medical services."

Resultantly, cognizant of litigation threats, doctors are hesitant to assist the sick in disciplines in which they possess little training, and have embarked upon an onslaught of rejection of incoming emergency patients.

Among the countless rejections, in 2007 an 89-year-old Osaka woman died on December 26 after her ambulance was refused admission at 30 hospitals. In August of the same year, nine hospitals refused a woman who later miscarried after the ambulance crashed. In August 2006 a pregnant woman died after rejection from 20 hospitals. The Fire and Disaster Management Agency reported that, in 2006 a total of 667 expectant mothers transported by ambulance, were rejected by at least 3 hospitals

Adding fuel to the fire is the high frequency with which the Japanese visit the doctor. At 13.8 times, the number of visits per capita was the highest among 28 OECD countries, which makes such data available. In its horse backward policies, Japan places greater emphasis on treatment than it does on prevention. The report concluded by bringing to light Japan's below average ranking in health spending per capita in 2004. During the same year, the OECD's health spending average was $2,759, while Japan's was $2,358, 19th among the 30 OECD countries and the lowest among G7 countries.

JAPANESE DEPRESSION MIRRORING MY OWN

As a former victim of severe and chronic debilitating depression since 4 years old, detecting depression among the Japanese is something at which I excel. The face, gait and posture of depression are all blatantly obvious to me. Growing up in a masochistic mother son environment similar to the hell through which Japanese parents put their children, I too was tightly clenched in the jaws of depression. One of my most vivid memories is at four, informing my mother of my desire to roll off the bed and die. The succeeding chastisement on my posterior, in an effort to "chase the devil out of me" is also indelibly etched in my psyche. Though now a devout atheist, it was in fact the fear of my mother's God's wrath which kept me from taking my life as a child. According to the tenets of her fundamentalist Christian dogma, hell would certainly have been my destination had I done so. And others in the community believed that I would reincarnate as the same person to undergo the same perils and trials, after committing this *sin*. So I suffered in silence, daydreaming at every chance and incessantly engaging in para-suicidal behavior, frequently darting out in front of moving traffic, but only being struck once by a motorcycle at ten years old. In retrospect, the teachings of heaven and hell might have been a load of rubbish, but in deed they were the main deterrent to suicide in my childhood.

As an adult I discovered that both my mother's parents had at least visited the Bellevue Hospital in their youth and my grandmother had suffered dissociative episodes. This revelation resolved my long-standing curiosity as to why my mother's immediate family, many of whose members were nothing short of geniuses, were so wrought, marred and mired in colossal underachievement in America the land of endless opportunities. My father's immediate family on the other hand, was obsessed with success, especially in the medical field.

Emigrating to the United States at fifteen brought about some reduction in my suicidal ideations but the darkness persisted, even forcing me to set firm departure dates on occasions. June 16th 1982 was one such date, but fear and diffidence kept me alive. Since my childhood until my early twenties, had breathing not been an automatic body function, I would not have had the confidence to perform even such a basic act. Para-suicidal behavior escalated after obtaining my drivers license at fifteen and my first car a year later. Armed with an automobile, a hundred miles an hour, especially on narrow roads was my permanent speed limit and regular major accidents along with routine suspensions of my driving privileges, were no deterrent to my wreckless goal. One such accident on my 18th birthday, where I was broadsided by a delivery truck as I blasted through a red signal, coincided with my mother's visit to Denver from Jamaica. Beholding the white, mangled Z twisted debris from which I escaped with only a massive headache, she fell to her knees and wept in prayer to her God.

"A mi prayas a keep yu," (It's my prayers that are keeping you.) she charged, wagging her index finger in my face.
"If mi nevva goo dung pan mi knee every maunin noon an' night, yu woulda dead arready." (Had I not been getting on my knees every morning noon and night, you would have already been dead.)

From age 15 to 22 there were seven major accidents, including one rollover and another where my head formed an intimate relationship with the windscreen, but thaumaturgicly I always walked away unscathed. Buckle up, seatbelts do work. Later in my adult life, I discovered that anti-freeze, an agent with which I was in almost daily contact throughout my teenage years, could have easily done the job. Most recently as of April 2008, the new suicidal trend in Japan utilizes hydrogen sulfide, which can be produced by simply mixing household detergents and bath lotions to create a concoction emitting deadly fumes. Had I been aware of these methods back then, you the reader would be spending your precious time more constructively.

There's a saying in Jamaica, "cats and dogs don't have the same luck," and if I were a cat, then my cousin Andrew was a dog. For though we had similar driving habits, his young life was snuffed from him just days before his 18th birthday and only a few years after arriving in America from Jamaica. Influenced by my hazardous driving he lost control at 80 mph on oak-lined Monoco Boulevard, a 30mph zone, resulting in his car launching some six feet into a tree. The tree sustained minor damage but after assuring his mother that there was no hope, Doctors switched off his life support system.

Moving to England at 21 took me face to face with suicidal attempts. For six months, it took unexplainable will not to hurl myself in front of the Gatwick express from the platform at Clapham Junction station. In fact, I had traveled to the station three times for exactly that purpose but could not muster the balls to follow through, opting instead to seek therapy for the first time. The therapist, an inept, graying white man in his sixties, told me I was just fine.

"You'll be alright," he quipped flippantly, completely discounting my distress.

"I think you'll get over it."

Back in 1985 psychotherapy in the UK, likewise dental hygiene was in a markedly more primitive stage than they are contemporarily, so in retrospect his incompetence is understandable.

Paris Syndrome, an affliction limited to some Japanese visiting Paris, bears a stark resemblance to my own *London* syndrome on my first trip to Britain at 21. First detailed in 2004 in the French Psychiatric Journal *Nurvure*, Paris Syndrome is a condition in which Japanese tourists find themselves, after discovering the disparity between the real Paris and their romanticized expectations of the city. According to an October 2006 article in the International Herald Tribune, about 12 Japanese tourists annually are in need of psychological treatment after visiting Paris, the result of shattered expectations. A third of the patients recover, another third relapses and the rest experience full blown psychoses, said Yousef Mahmoudia a psychologist at the Hotel-Dieu Hospital, next to Notre Dame Cathedral.

"For us, Paris is a dream city," stated a Japanese woman. "All the French are beautiful and elegant. And then, when they arrive, the Japanese find the French character opposite to their own."

It may well be that the prevalence of depression in Japan, increases the probability that many Japanese traveling abroad would be depressed before arriving at their destination. In other words, simply put, there is a high possibility that they had arrived in Paris already emotionally disturbed. Add to that their general naiveté, underdeveloped emotions, their Eifel tower expectations of Paris and the stress of being in an unfamiliar environment, and viola, Psych ward here we come. Like the Japanese's adoration of and great expectations of Paris, growing up in a former British colony, I aggrandized the *motherland* as a place where all my problems would have been solved. England beckoned with a massive electromagnetic force, a must see place. And just as it's likely that those Japanese traveling to their perceived *motherland* were suffering from depression, I too was under the spell of crippling depression, hoping to escape my plight and find happiness in England. But nothing could have been further from the truth. Arriving in London in November 1985 was followed by my first plan to attempt suicide and just like those Japanese suffering from Paris syndrome, I too had to seek psychological counseling.

Returning to the United States after unspeakable darkness in the United Kingdom, I continued therapy at the community college where I had begun studying. However, soon thereafter at 23 years old I became a father, a role for which I was completely and utterly unprepared on all fronts. For the first time since returning to the States, I began to firmly plan not only my own certain demise, but emulating an almost weekly occurrence in Japan: suicide preceded by the murder of my then infant daughter.

As the fog eerily tumbled across the Golden Gate, I drove with an unwitting infant only months old, safely strapped in her car seat, during what were the most aphotic moments in my life. No one would have suspected my intentions. On this surreal afternoon, I would have been just some anonymous Negroe strolling reposefully on the bridge with an innocent life in his hands. However, as I reached toward the back seat to free her, she, one of the most beautiful babies I had ever beheld, greeted me with the most angelic smile of bare gums, sabotaging my macabre scheme. Earlier in an anthropology class, I had learned that the reason babies of mammals are so cute and cuddly, was to generate nurturing feelings from both parents and strangers. On that fateful Saturday that theory was tested and proven.

Therapy continued and gradually progress was made, including my ability to display an overly extrovert personality in public, which lead to positive responses among my peers and the Vice Presidency and Presidency of Student Government at my community college. By then it would have been a major dent in my pride posthumously to commit suicide, as I had entangled myself in a web of deceptive extroversion thus gaining the admiration of many. Disappointing my peers by initiating my own exit, became a major concern, especially since they all saw me as this person on a mission with dreams and vision, when in truth my existence was purposeless. After all, who but Stefhen Bryan would regularly take his year and a half old baby daughter to class and senate meetings with him?

My peers' acceptance of my fatherhood dramatically reduced my anxiety and that which I thought initially shameful -I, an ill-equipped father showing up at college with my baby in arms - turned out to be as rewarding with women as driving a *Ferrari*. But after five years at community college, my first mini vacation from reality occurred almost immediate after transferring to UCLA, which landed me on the psychiatrist's couch, joining the millions of Americans on the wonder drug Prozac. Unfortunately in my case, the depression worsened and the thoughts of suicide returned with a vengeance. With the meds withdrawn after a month, again I suffered in silence, collecting countless letters of academic probation, but finally managing to scrape through and graduate in 1994. The entire ordeal from College of San Mateo to UCLA had spanned eight years, with the three at the latter institution pushing me to a nervous breakdown. Four years later while living parasitically off my then Thai-American girlfriend, with the advent of new drugs I made a second visit to a psychiatrist, where a cocktail of pills was prescribed with similar results as before; increased depression and suicidal thoughts, nausea, headaches, but sparing me the diminished libido.

"*This is just fucking hopeless*," I thought, by then 34 years old.

It was then that I hashed out a final plan to disappear to Asia in order to engage in a *dramaless* exit, once and for all in anonymity. It was my conviction that an unprepared trip to Asia, a most unfamiliar environment, would result in immeasurable anguish, similar to the trauma I suffered during my unprepared maiden trip to England. Only this time, a full-fledged atheist, I was confident there was no hell fire or even an afterlife awaiting me. I had arrived at the unwavering conclusion that life, in and of itself, is absolutely meaningless and that the only meaning therein, are those which we are socialized to attached to it, which in my case was naught but darkness and despair. The secret of life was finally revealed: it was simply a perpetual game of self-delusions, which I had been unable to master, whether for clinical or social reasons and now I was finally free to leave. But just as emigration had intervened at 15 years old, an unwitting face saving act would fling a wrench in my plans.

Saga Boy was the quintessential alpha male. Muscular, ex-military man with some 70 kills under his belt in Angola, he was an intellectual ladies man whom I had met at an audition, for my first paying gig on television: a villain on "America's Most Wanted." A graduate from the American Conservatory Theatre in San Francisco, his thespian skills made me look like a kindergarten performer, the kind often appearing on Japanese television. Saga was seeking a workout partner, and in the interest of upholding the hard ragamuffin image of my Jamaican ethnicity, I agreed to accompany him to the gym. Up until then I had shunned that hyper-masculine, testosterone infested place, like I had shunned getting my eyebrows plucked. Teeth extractions were far more appealing. But with the prospects of drooling at skimpily clad women and possibly meeting some of them, I gave in and ventured into a 24hr nautilus in West Los Angeles.

What followed was an ironman regiment fit for any Olympiad, a regiment which consisted of 30 minutes of cardiovascular training, an hour and a half of weights, then 15 minutes more cardio, five days a weeks. Death had been an entertained desire since the tender age of 4 and it seemed, after 31 years my dream was finally materializing. But instead the hitherto unimaginable occurred: after just one month of this rigorous Kamikaze training, the world changed to Technicolor, the doors to the penitentiary which had detained me for 31 years flung wide open, eructating me into life from my straight jacket, like a fighter pilot being ejected from a doomed aircraft. This gave birth to my second addiction, which fed my first, as more exercise resulted in higher testosterone levels, which increased my already insatiable appetite for sex.

Now at the age of 42, I have only two regrets; that in my diffidence I didn't learn to fly at 17 when I could have for only a thousand dollars. And two, that I did not heed the advice of all my psychologists - especially the psychiatrists - to start a regular exercise routine. They all marveled at the fact that I had never tried to opiate my condition with alcohol or illicit drugs, which they thought anomalous, as most people in my condition would be mired in alcohol and or drug addition. Instead I simply *gamaned*, I simply endured, daydreaming as much as possible, well into adulthood and of course using sex as my drug of choice.

Two years later after my introduction to the gym, Japan became my home where in the first year a long time acquaintance from Los Angeles, an accomplished and successful screenwriter/producer, paid me a visit in my Kobe apartment. Immediately upon seeing my sparse and simple abode, he launched into a tirade about my minimalist lifestyle. "Yo, what kinda life you livin,' man? You came all the way to Japan to live like this? I'm buying a Hummer when I get back to LA," he bragged. "And you over here livin' like a monk."
Little did he know it had only been two short years since I had actually begun living, period, and was quite content, in fact ecstatic just to be alive without the desire to die.

TRAUMATISED WOMEN

My intimate relations with Japanese women – 40 in the first three years and twenty after my *retirement* from playing the field – clearly revealed that trauma from all major social institutions; family, education, employment, inescapable trauma, was a common denominator among all but a few. Though understated, the results of a recent survey indubitably validated my own observations. The Health, Labor and Welfare Ministry found that fully 15% of Japanese women, one in seven between ages 20 and 24 - a demographic with which I had frequent biblical interactions – inflicted injuries to themselves, such as cutting their wrists. In the euphemistic words of Kunio Kitamura, head of the survey and the Japan Family Planning Association Clinic, "We cannot deny the possibility that pessimism has become a prevalent mood among young women particularly and that bitter feelings about society have caused them to harm themselves," However, what he had neglected to acknowledge was that, this self-mutilation was a sure fire sign of Borderline Personality Disorder, which is sharply increasing among women in Japan.

Conducted in November of 2006, the survey included some 1400 men and women between 16 and 49 years old, which revealed that of the total respondents, 6% of women inflicted injuries on themselves, in comparison to only 2% of men. Among women, 20 to 24 twenty-five percent reported that they had entertained thoughts of self-injury, while 11% stated they had inflicted injuries on themselves repeatedly. In my five years of teaching in junior high and high schools in Japan, self-mutilating girls were quite salient, but even more disturbing was the ignorance of the teachers. No teacher knew the causes of the scars decorating the girls' arms. "She said she had an accident with some glass," some teachers responded, oblivious to the underlying emotional disturbance.

Paternal absenteeism, again similar to, but better than that of the African-American and Jamaican Diaspora, is the norm in Japan. Here the father lives at home and provides financially for his family, but there is often no emotional connection, or physical bonding. In that way, he is an absentee father.

According to government studies conducted in 2006 and reported in The Yomiuri Shinbun in November 2008, among fathers with children aged 9-14 years old, 23.3% had no contact or interaction with their children on weekdays. Fifteen minutes of daily weekday contact was made by 14.7% of fathers, 21.9% had 30 minutes and 24.1% had about an hour. No weekend contact was mentioned in the survey, but given the plantation-like work conditions in Japan, fathers spending their entire weekends in slumber, is by no means a stretch of the imagination.

At least in the West, children experiencing abuse in families can find respite in school, and educational institutions along with the police can be relied upon for intervention. Anecdotally speaking, school was my only safe haven from social and familial trauma, but not so in Japan, where school can be a motivating factor for taking one's life and where the very teachers promote abuses.

For a period of six weeks from October 6th 2006, Japan experienced a rash of bullying induced teen suicides, where some 14 teenagers took their own lives. In one such case in Chikuzen, Fukuoka Prefecture, the school's principal stated that a junior high schoolteacher was the chief fire starter in bullying, tormenting the 13-year-old victim to the point of hanging himself. The boy's main teacher had labeled him a liar and revealed personal information about him which led to a nickname the boy had hated. Upon questioning, the teacher responded that he bullied the boy so relentlessly because "he was easy to make fun of,"

Though most teachers are normally adjusted, dedicated professionals, a growing number of unprofessional behavior by some points to a widespread problem. In December 2006, a 33-year-old elementary schoolteacher with unusual extra-curricular activities was arrested when his *Club Kids* site was discovered on the web, where he specialized in photos of dead children, some unclad. What is more, it was also discovered that several of his professional colleagues, shared his perversion. Having fondled several of his girl students, he was quoted as saying, "I just wanted them to feel closer and more comfortable with me. January 2007, a 44-year-old junior high schoolteacher was alleged to have fondled three male students, after which he paid them 500-2000 yen to keep it a secret. The next month in Ishikawa Prefecture, Education Board officials revealed that an elementary school principal in his 50s had molested three female students by inserting his hand in their underwear while playing sumo and tag with them. Fortunately the students were bold enough to report it to a teacher, who reported it to the Vice Principal, which resulted in the Principal's suspension five days later. Curiously, the Board of Education, not the police, is pending a decision on his punishment.

One conscientious, perverted former elementary schoolteacher, now an erotic novelist, could only be interviewed anonymously. "I've always," he says, "had a taste for very young girls. But as a teacher I couldn't do anything. I mean, these were my own students. It was terrible. I had to constantly suppress my desires. That's why I quit teaching." A paedophile with a conscience. Parents can breathe a sigh of relief that Mr. "M" was able to control his urges and changed jobs, but that is definitely an exception as opposed to the rule, as evidenced by informal surveys by Spa! Magazine and Weekly Playboy, whose reporters in early 2007, set out to interview elementary and junior high schoolgirls nationwide, regarding how they felt about their teachers. Based on their findings, the dysfunctional teachers constituted three main categories; those lacking in common sense, the unruly ones and the erotic, or ero-teachers, among them a former porn actor.

In the article, according to *Yukiko*, a third-year junior high school student in Chiba, "in health class he (the former porn star) passed out pornographic books to all of us and said, 'this, children is how babies are born.' Once he called me into the teachers' lounge. When I went, he called up erotic images on his computer and whispered in my ear, 'You'll be my own girl, won't you, Yukiko?'"

"When I was in grade five," states *Minako*, now a third year junior high school student, "the gym teacher would make only the girls run. Many of us weren't even wearing bras yet, and the teacher would be openly staring at our breasts. And he'd make the girls with bigger breasts run the most."

Unlike students in the US who go to the locker room to change for gym, students in Japan do so right there in the class room. Sixth grader *Manami* recalls, "Once when I was in second grade I was late for class, the teacher was angry. Later, when we were getting ready for gym, he said to me, 'You can change by yourself on the verandah.' I thought, 'What?' But I did -- and saw him looking at me through a window, grinning. I was terrified."

"It was during art class in elementary school," says Maiko, currently a first year senior high school student, "I went to the teacher's desk to get some clay. I opened the drawer and found it full of pornography -- books with pictures of girls no older than we were."

"My 4th grade teacher was arrested," said 6th grader Satomi. "He was caught paying a junior high schoolgirl for sex. The Principal called an assembly and said, 'Just forget that teacher was ever here.'"

Speaking in anonymity, a 57-year-old junior high school principal admits the problem. Mirroring the constabulary's dilemma, "the quality of teachers is declining," he lamented. "Teachers are being hired en masse to replace the retiring baby boomers. The result is that we are seeing more teachers who lack dedication and a sense of responsibility."

Working as an Assistant Language Teacher (ALT) for four years, positioned me in front row view of extensive physical abuse of students by teachers. In one case a hated English teacher, living at home with his parents and perhaps still a virgin at 37 years old, flung a female student to the ground then apologized to me. In another memorable incident, in my presence along with that of the principal, the same teacher had his hand firmly planted around a student's neck, to which the principal responded, "Take that in my office, there's a foreigner here." One teacher asked if I had thought a second year student was sexy, a question which, coming from the West, put me at extreme unease. If questioned, many Assistant Language Teachers, even those on the Japan Exchange Teachers (JET) program, will have similar stories of such sightings. In the incidences of sexual abuse, concealing teachers' sexual misconduct is not an anomaly in Japan. "The teacher has a family to feed and shouldn't be reprimanded," justified one principal.   And in far too many cases, protecting the image of the school out weighs the rights of the students.

Being typical Japanese, Shoko's experience was no different. Having been violated at eight years old by high schoolboys, who inserted their hands in her underwear and fondled her in a car park, followed at 13 years old by a junior high schoolteacher who groped her breasts while trying to shove his tongue down her throat, at 23 she was a card carrying man hater, or more accurately, a hater of Japanese men. All this she internalized until meeting me. Masochistic relations with her parents especially her cantankerous mother - typical of contemporary Japanese parent child relations - fueled her depression.

Thankfully, unlike many of her peers she resisted the urge to bludgeon, roast, hack, poison or behead her mother, a phenomenon which saw a boom in 2006.

PARRICIDE IN JAPAN

National Police Agency (NPA) statistics illustrates a marked increase in children offing their parents or making attempts to do so. According to the NPA, in 2005 there were 10 such cases followed by 17 in 2006 with two case recorded in August and September. Previously there had been only 3 – 10 in any given year since police began compiling such data. In April 2006, a 12-year-old boy in Yamamoto, Kanagawa Prefecture slashed his mother's throat, after being stressed out because, "I was told to study and clean up my room." His mother's haranguing had escalated after he had begun junior high school, he reported to the police.

Two months later in Nara a 16-year-old first year senior high school student transformed his family's home into an inferno, extinguishing his step-mother, young half-brother and his half-sister. The son of a medical doctor, the boy was on the receiving end of severe and unrelenting pressure from his father, to "study hard," in order to gain entrance to a prestigious medical school. The NPA has further reported that in the overwhelming majority of these cases, the impetus was parents deluging their children with pressure to perform academically. In the Nara incident, the student set his house ablaze on the very day his school was to inform parents on midterm grades. Having not lived up to his father's lofty and perhaps unrealistic expectations, he resorted to drastic preemptive actions.

Two thousand seven began very colorfully with a 53-year-old man in Tokyo, murdering his 83-year-old mother. Minoru Tsukumo got angry, shoved socks down his mother's throat then strangled her with his bare hands, all because she told him to - brace yourselves for this one – "get a job." "I got mad when my mother told me I had no job and that I am just wasting my time doing nothing," he reportedly told the police. But the mother of all parricides is the unspeakably gruesome and disturbing matricide which occurred on May 15, 2007, when a 17-year-old high school senior in Fukushima turned up at the Aizuwakamatsu police station with a bag whose sole content was his mother's head.

The teen was described as cheerful and well mannered during his junior high school years, and had been a perfectly adjusted well above average student, excelling both academically and athletically, especially in ski jumping. But all that transmogrified when his parents, most likely his mother, embarked on the grand idea of ripping him from the family, in the interest of attending a prestigious high school. The family rented an apartment where the boy was made to stay, some fifty kilometers away from their home, but close to their targeted supposedly prestigious high school.

In this *gakureki shakai* (a society where educational background is most important) where affection, nurture and human relations in general, take a distant back seat to entering the right kindergarten, elementary, junior high, high school and university, in order to get that elusive and limited right job, the teenager's parents resorted to what amounted to neglect. Suddenly, this child was torn asunder from his happy environment, cast in isolation from his family, limited to weekend visits by his mother to do his laundry. What's more, along with isolation from the family, adding to his stress, he was also thrust in the role of caregiver, responsible for his younger brother with whom he shared the apartment.

Suddenly neglected and cast aside, the teenager began to develop psychological problems and sawed off his mother's head and arm on her 47th birthday, painting her amputated arm white and planting it in a flower pot. The Japanese lamented this sheer grotesque and macabre scenery, unable to fathom its occurrence, but as one who harbored matricidal ideations, I could most certainly relate.

Parricide offenders, usually adolescents, hail from severely abusive parents. A small minority is extremely mentally ill, or disturbingly antisocial. However the vast majority, over 90% of those who kill a parent, experienced what they perceived as intolerable abuse by said parent. It is unfathomable to the Japanese that their education obsessed parenting constitutes profound psychological abuse. And in deed, most would concur that, it was in the child's best interest to abandon him in the name of education. After all, parricides are not the norm, so most interpret them as the actions of evil children, when in fact for every parricidal child there are millions of children who suffer their parents' abuse in helpless and hopeless desperation usually making it to adulthood, most likely perpetuating abuse to their own children.

It would be easy to conclude that the Fukushima teenager was among the extremely low frequency mentally ill parricide offenders. But observing the fact that he had been a perfectly adjusted boy in his junior high years, it is clear the psychopathological impetus was his parent's pressure and neglect. It is shuddery to imagine that Korean society is even more educationally obsessed.

Like Japan's high suicide rate, matricide is a phenomenon with which I am also very intimate. At nine years old, I didn't just threaten to take out my own mother, I promised her, as serious as cancer, kitchen (bitch) knife in hand, that I would cut her into little pieces as soon as I turned twelve. And I meant it. At nine years old, twelve was a distant age, a magical age where I thought I would have had enough meat and muscle on my bones to overpower her. Like many Japanese mothers, mine was immeasurably oppressive and overbearing. But unlike Japanese mothers, her concern was not my academic performance, or more accurately, lack thereof. For not once was I ever scolded about my dismally low marks, especially after starting high school at 11 years old. Mom's obsession was with church, as far back as I can recall until I began to stand firm in my opposition at thirteen. There was absolutely positively nothing of greater import, than the "Lord and his mercies." Our one-compartment squalor was literally above the church and attendance three times a day on Sundays, once Mondays, Tuesdays, Wednesdays and Thursday nights, was mandatory since babyhood. Friday nights and Saturday nights were reserved for cleaning the entire church, only to repeat the torture on Sunday mornings.

This hell continued until I was thirteen, at which point I decided to take violent nightly floggings instead of participation in the despised church activities. In my calculation, she could not have continued the beltings indefinitely, and I was right. Three weeks later broken by my resistance, she grew tired, acquiesced and "left me in the hands of the Lord." All that multiple daily prayer, twice daily drawing the Lord's *promises*, – small flash cards of scriptures from the bible – from the promise box and her dedicating my life to *the Lord* since I was born, went up in smoke. In her fanaticism, secular music was strictly forbidden and any minor infraction, even perceived ones, would be met with severe physical abuse, justified by the book of proverb's "spare not the rod and spoil the child." So I understand all too well the spate of matricides sweeping Japan, I too was socialized in a Japan of a different sort. However, unlike Japanese children oppressed by their parents, I had intervention, the chance to flee, thanks to my own absent father.

SHOKO CONTINUED

Shoko, the beautiful and younger of two girls, existed in the shadows of her over-achieving sister, the apple of her parents' eye. Constant sibling feuding, fueled by her sister's envy of her stark beauty - a result of some kind of genetic throw back - and Shoko's envy of her sister's academic prowess and parental approval, began early and included an incident where her sister at six years old, attacked her with a knife when she was three. Shoko is grateful for her parents' intervention, otherwise the incident might have been fatal. From the beginning it was clear that she would require some *work*, this was simply just not going to be another *dinner* guest.

"But that's OK," I thought, she possessed the perfect combination of features I worshipped, natural pheromones which attracted me and a *Viagral* waist-to-hip ratio on her 156 cm, 108 pound frame. With glutes so protrusive, the hem of her micro-mini violently whipped to and fro, in a synchronized dance to her struts. There were organic elements to my attraction. Her damaged state made her cautious and skittish, and some three years later she disclosed to me that my dark hue and arrogant Jamaican swagger, commented on by adults even in my childhood, instilled so much fear in her that on our first date to see the film "Chicago," anxious and terrified, she alerted her sister of her whereabouts "just in case." During the film I gently took her hand just to test the waters and though she didn't expose it at the time, years later she told me how shocked she was of my *bold* move which sent her heart racing.

"No Japanese man would have done that."

To my wonderment, this nubile hyper-beaut had never been touched biblically or otherwise, having had only a few pseudo-boyfriends with whom she had ventured to love hotels a few times, but nothing went beyond first base. Moreover, as she was a highly sought after young woman, in insecure male bravado these men, sometimes her co-workers, would frequently lie about their conquest, causing her great embarrassment and deepening her contempt for men. Her reported history of boyfriends who were already otherwise attached, hinted at promiscuous expectations of men. All the better for me, as that meant my other women would pose no problem. Unlike Western women, most Japanese women with whom I had intimate relations did not demand exclusivity and if they did, soon acquiesced. Not that I had tried to hide my philandering from any of them, for if I didn't make my behavior verbally clear, it would be blatantly obvious from the plethora of feminine objects, sometimes even underwear strewn about my apartment to greet each of them. However, several months later Shoko's only request was that I rid my apartment of such evidence before her arrival, to which I happily complied.

Though my physical ideal, Shoko's juvenile - sometimes infantile - behavior was a source of endless frustration. But fortunately our meetings were restricted to once a week, which itself was also a source of massive frustration. On one hand, I was in a constant state of arousal. I wanted to meet her daily, but her childlike manner and strict 9pm curfew were intolerable. Other women in the collection helped to diffuse my frustration, but it was never entirely eliminated, as my cravings for her mounted. This juvenile behavior was by no means limited to just her.

Immediately upon my arrival in Japan I could not help but notice the profound arrested emotional development pervasive throughout the society. My initial impression was that Japan was a society of 9-year-olds, only to read a year later where McArthur some 60 years back, stated that Japan was a society of 12-year-olds. Back in California my 23-year-old girlfriends were already professionals in decision making positions, enjoying their lives independent of their parents. One, a Southeast Asian-American was earning six figures as a Financial Analyst in a renowned investment banking firm. Another, an East Asian-American was a high performing IT Recruiter and yet another, a South Asian-American, already held a master's degree, stationed in South Asia working for the United Nations. After living in the United States, especially California for some 20 years, I began to take women's relatively high social status and ambitions for granted, until my discovery of the jolting reality of Japanese women's dismal social conditions.

COLLECTIVE ARRESTED EMOTIONAL DEVELOPMENT

My observations and numerous conversations disclosed that many Western white men, especially American men, insecure and unable to cope with the empowered *Oprahfied*, American woman, are bated by the demure, feeble and unempowered Japanese woman, perilously oblivious to the detriments of said females' emotional retardation, until upon divorce she absconds with their children, never to be heard from again. This is but only one of the many manifestations of low emotional quotient of Japanese society. In the West it is common knowledge that a divorce is especially taxing on children and that every action should be taken to ensure they encounter as little trauma as possible. While an amicable divorce is still traumatic, it is likely to be less so, if even only marginally, than a knock down dragged out divorce where the parents are emotional retards, ignoring their children's needs. Acknowledged in the West as the actions of immature adults, harmful to children and society, such *baby mama drama*, are socially and culturally normative in infantile Japan. The status quo here is that after divorce the mother will be granted custody and there will be no further contact between the children and their father, all because the adults are feuding. Arrangements for parental visitation are unfathomable to the Japanese, because their inadequate socialization is void of effective communication, critical thinking and conflict resolution skills. Instead, an over-reliance on emotions, underdeveloped as they are, is very frequently the means of resolving conflict.

Before arriving in Japan, after having evolved, thanks to numerous years of therapy including anger management therapy, I was finally able to appreciate the destructive impact on my child, of the perpetual warmongering between her parents and was ready to make peace. Initiating mediation, I entertained hopes of civility with her mother, in the interest of our then 14-year-old daughter's emotional health. We began the session with my thanking her for participating. "I hate you," I continued. "And you hate me more." And I hate you even more than that, and your hate for me is infinitely more than mine for you." In fact, our hate, disdain, animosity and abhorrence for each other were sempiternal.

"Nonetheless, the reason why I requested your presence today is so we can lay down our arms and begin the process of erasing or coming to terms with the hatred between us, as this is in the best interest of our child."

My plea was met with resounding objection.

"I don't care for whose benefit," she responded. "I am not interested in making peace with you." To which the mediator, a salt and pepper haired African-American intellectual in her early fifties pensively responded, "wo, then mediation, which requires two people, simply cannot continue."

What originally was a scheduled one-hour session came to an abrupt halt in 15 minutes. After mediation, in her continued anger and hate, she imposed a personal injunction barring our child from visiting me or any of my relatives, - my mother and grandmother included - who were the only relatives my daughter had in the States. That in my view was an example of emotionally retarded behavior, for our daughter suffered needlessly and continues to, some six years later. These dynamics common in the West, tend to be more prevalent among the poor, less educated and communicatively inept, often exacerbated by the presence of personality disorders and are definitely not the social norm.

However, *baby mama and daddy* drama, where feuding adults systematically ignore children's needs, is the way in folk society Japan. Six years here and conversations with at least 200 divorced women have yielded only two who attested to having an emotionally mature relationship with their ex-husbands. In the words of one of the women, "we are very civil to each other and are better friends now that we are divorced and the kids spend weekends and holidays with him." This was the complete opposite of the norm whereby children have zero contact with their fathers after divorce, and shared custody is as common as a shark in a tuxedo. In contrast, in the United States some separating couples battle for shared custody of even the family dog.

For the most part, traits of arrested emotional development are blatantly obvious in this Never-Never land, whose inhabitants suffer from a form of Michael Jackson Syndrome (MJS). Here in this California sized amusement park, it's the norm to hear 'it's a small world after all' blaring in supermarkets and stores. At Akashi station, an electronic version of "I've been working on the railroad," warns of approaching freight trains. The Japanese in general, clutching their transitional objects akin to babies and their blankies, are obsessed with infant-like cuteness and hold deep reverence for puerility and dependence. These transitional objects - mostly stuffed animals, figurines and effigies of cartoon characters - suspend ubiquitously from cell phones, handbags, rear view mirros and are owned by males, females young and old alike, many with multiple effigies.

Toddler friendly graphics in advertising is preponderant, created for maximum appeal to the tyke-like mind. Television commercials, though of the utmost in production value are usually revoltingly puerile and even signs invoking social obedience are often juvenile in format, featuring cartoon characters and or caricatures of animals. Tom & Jerry implore us to relinquish the designated seats on public transportation to the elderly, handicapped, or to those with children, or to be mindful of our earphone volume. Near my apartment building there are two signs reminding us to clean up after our dogs. The sign in Japanese features triangular personifications of dog excrements, arms flailing in the air, appealing to be picked up, as they emerge from a dog's anus. The English version requesting compliance has no graphics. It simply reads, "Clean up after your dog. It's the law," with the ordinance code stated at the bottom of the sign.

In the United States, the only place I saw the Aflac duck was in television or print ads. However since May 2003 Chibi-duck – as it's affectionately known in Japan – has been among the many dangling transitional accoutrements on daily display. Veritably speaking, in this Peter Pan society, these cute corporate characters work wonders for a company's bottom line. Food flavorings maker Ajinomoto, the inventor of monosodium glutamate (MSG) and whose amino acid beverages were made available in the United States as of late 2006, has enjoyed a 2.7 times rise in sales since painting its Ajipanda character on its 75gram seasoning bottles. Even American household products giant Procter & Gamble's jumped on the bandwagon, creating Pampa the baby elephant especially for the Japanese market. Many of these *cute* corporate cartoon characters become icons, such as NTT DoCoMo Inc's ghastly mushroom character, the now defunct Nova Language Schools' rabbit character and Daikin Industries Ltd's Pichon-kun, which is a droplet of water with a super skinny body, legs and arms.

Hiroyuki Aihara, head of toy maker Bandai Co.'s Character Research Institute, claims that experts still hotly debate the reason for the Japanese's glorification of cartoon characters. The reason for the *hot debate* escapes me. Aihara made the answer crystal clear in his euphemism theorizing that compared to the West, Japanese society draws a less distinct line between adults and children, a gross understatement for a disturbingly low emotional quotient country where adulthood is postponed indefinitely. If knowledge is power in the West, cute is power in Japan.

The police, a symbol of authority in most countries is represented to the public through a mascot, a cartoon of a big bird with an oversize beak. On the evening of September 29th 1999, 42-year-old Yasuaki Uwabe drove a rented car in Shimonoseki station in Yamaguchi Prefecture, mowing down pedestrians on the sidewalk and inside the station. He then emerged from the car, kitchen knife in hand and embarked upon a stabbing spree, leaving five dead and ten injured. One police officer tossed his helmet in his direction, but refused to shoot him. By no means am I advocating LAPD style policing where in the same year for example, a 72-year-old woman brandishing a screwdriver was felled by police bullets. But this is a clear case where at least one round maiming the psychopath would have been justified, possibly saving a life.

In the summer of 2004, a man in Saitama after being pursued by a raging gang, did what any citizen in any normal country would have done: took refuge in a police station. His pursuers entered the Koban and proceeded to beat him as three police officers on duty cowered in fear, after which the assailants then dragged the man outside and continued to properly whoop his butt. In defense of gross neglect of their civic duties, the police argued that the matter was between gang members and that they were afraid.

In January of 2007, an 18-year-old officer crashed his car through a railway pedestrian crossing then fled the scene. And in another disturbing incident, an Akita Prefecture officer was caught spending his entire shifts, gambling at pachinko parlors. "I just don't have the confidence to go to work," his colleagues quoted him as saying. Indeed, reports of incompetence among members of the police force have been on the increase and these are but only two cases of police committing the very crimes against which they are meant to protect. Kanazawa Prefecture, May 2007 Tomoyuki Mukaide, a 44-year-old police inspector, inflicted stab wounds to his abdomen because, he "couldn't bear the thought of going to work." Mukaide had initially told investigators he had been stabbed upon opening his door in response to the doorbell, but later recanted and admitted to injuring himself to avoid work.

March 2008 was the month of an epic display of unparalleled police ineptitude, when a dragnet of 8 police officers was posted without radios, in and around JR Arakawaoki station in Ibaraki Prefecture. The eight plainclothes officers were on the lookout for murder suspect Masahiro Kanagawa, who went on a fatal stabbing spree in the station, literally beneath their noses. Having no radios, the constabulary members were unable to coordinate their actions even as one of their men was critically stabbed. A civilian phone call provided initial information of the attacks to the Prefectural Police, who then informed 4 of the 8 officers via their cell phones. The suspect had contacted police earlier to tell them of his planned whereabouts, after which a total of 170 officers were mobilized to the area.

Many experts agree that the status of the nation' constabulary force is in grave inevitable decline, as today's police officers are often lazy, greedy and incompetent. As Japan's agedness shifts into overdrive, baby boomer cops hemorrhage from the force in retirement, leaving a disappearing pool of young people from which to recruit. Inversely, as the crime rate rises, so does the rate of recruiting, which means that recruiters must diminish their standards to hitherto unacceptable levels. According to Noboru Iigawa, editor of Juken Journal, a publication specializing in civil service recruitment, in fiscal 2005, about 142,000 applicants sat the Police qualifying exam, but only 15,700 were successful, a 1:9 ratio. However, for fiscal 2006 the pass rate was about one in four or five. Can anything better be expected from a constabulary force, in essence mail carriers with guns, representing itself to the public as an oversized chicken?

Like the Japanese constabulary, Japan's Self-Defense Forces employ a cartoon character as its representative to the world. In official Defense Ministry literature, Prince Pickles, a cute perky cartoon character with round oversized eyes, miniature boot clad feet and big dimples, rappels from helicopters, poses in front of tanks and shakes hands with Iraqis. In the words of Ministry of Defense official Shotaro Yanagi, "Prince Pickles is our image character because he's endearing, which is what Japan's military stands for," hoping to soften, or more accurately further tenderize the SDF's already spineless image overseas. But critics like Rika Kayama, author and psychiatrist, doubt that childish cartoon characters will prove effective in the adult world outside Japan which is defined by its obsession with infantile innocence, even among grown-ups. Echoing my sentiments exactly, "this could only happen in a country that is so open to immaturity," she stated euphemistically. Further adding that, "authorities here feel it's easier and less threatening to use characters to get the public to accept them, rather than explain the facts," which meant that even authorities are fully aware of the juvenile state of the masses.

Doraemon is the ubiquitous main character in a weekly TV animation series and an annual feature film among the most popular in Japan. Traveling backward through time from the 22nd century, this earless cat assists a schoolboy with gadgets such as an *anywhere door,* allowing anyone to travel to any imagineable destination. However, as of March 2008, thanks to the Foreign Ministry, this toddler friendly feline became a new Ambassador from Japan. At a March 19th ceremony the character or at least someone dressed as the earless blue and white cat with a propeller protruding from the top of its head, is scheduled to receive its official assignement letter. "By appointing Doraemon, we hope people in other countries will understand Japanese anime better and deepen their interest in Japanese culture," said Yuko Hotta, a foreign ministry official.

Japan the land of the eternal *bye-bye,* is a nation where farewell wishers wag their hands violently until they fall off or, the train carrying their loved ones is out of sight. At Kansai International Airport's Sky Café, adults wave bye-bye to departing airplanes until they have completely vanished. That was among my favourite pastimes at the Norman Manley International Airport when I was 8. Among the few enjoyable moments of my childhood, were the bitter sweet trips to the airport to see a family member off to some unimaginably far away land. Sweet because it meant leaving the hood and going for a drive, bitter because, well, I was bidding good-bye to a loved one, usually my jet setting grandmother to whom I was quite attached. As the aircraft ascended I, in fine Japanese style, would flail my arm vigorously, gradually slowing as the craft disappeared in the distance. However, that behavior came to a halt by the time I was ten.

This societal childishness manifests itself even in big business and international affairs. Those in power though geriatric for the most part, whine and throw temper tantrums whenever they perceive themselves as victims, but like egocentric children, when the tide is turned and they themselves are the victimizers, are usually oblivious to their violations and are pedomorphically lacking in continuity.

In 2001 a stock trader in the Tokyo office of the Swiss bank UBS erroneously typed a sale order, an error which cost UBS as much as $100 million. But both the Tokyo Stock Exchange and Japanese regulators were unsympathetic, forcing UBS to eat the loss. In a similar incident on December 8th 2005, Mizuho Securities, the brokerage arm of Japan's then second largest bank, mistakenly placed a sell order for 610,000 shares of J-Com - a small Japanese job placement company – for one yen, less than a cent each. The transaction was meant to be a sell order of one share at 600,000 yen or $5,242. Unable to abort the botched transaction owing to the Tokyo Stock Exchange's antique trading systems, Mizuho Securities suffered a los of 40.5 billion yen or $347 million.

Foreign companies were the largest beneficiaries of Mizuho's error, with UBS leading the pack earning 11.8 billion yen, almost as much as the 16.2 billion yen it had lost in a similar error four years earlier. But what succeeded was an onslaught of indignance which could have been generated only by toddlers in the *terrible twos* stage. Politicians and the media embarked on a demonizing campaign to shame the banks into returning the millions they rightfully made on Mizuho's blunder. In blatantly implike naiveté, the nation of adult children was whipped into an astronomical frenzy, feeling slighted that foreign companies had profited from a Japanese company's misfortune. "It's not a pretty thing to hear that they knowingly exploited the mistake to acquire the shares for their own accounts," Financial Services Minister, Kaoru Yosano was quoted as saying, conveniently forgetting that Japanese companies benefited handsomely just four years earlier, from a similar mistake made by UBS.

The fiasco calls to mind similar incidences of naïve discontent during my prepubescent years in my maladaptive childhood. Though I loved marbles, it was by no means a game at which I excelled. In fact, I sucked. While other boys won their marbles fair and square, I on the other hand was forced to purchase mine, which meant an annual acquisition of a mere three or four, as my mother and I existed in abject poverty. Most of my marble collection consisted of chipped, old marbles which I had found, which no opponent wanted me to use during our games. On my precious few victorious occasions, after collecting my spoils, I pranced and danced in great exuberance. However, when the shoe was on the other foot and I lost my marbles – pun intended – which constituted the majority of the time, I railed in protest, citing previous imaginary fouls by my opponent.

Ironically, 2005 was a year when foreigners were the most aggressive purchasers of Japanese stock, pushing the Nikkei 225 stock average to an almost 40% gain by December that year. Yet still, the Japanese authorities saw it fit to scapegoat foreign companies for a goof which was clearly the result of prehistoric hardware at the TSE and like a parent yielding to an obstreperous child, UBS agreed to relinquish its share of the profits.

Regarding North Korea's abduction of Japanese nationals, Japan educes sympathy and empathy from the international community, as is quite normal. We should all be concerned and sympathetic to the abducted. But on the flipside of the coin, again in infantine amnesia, authorities in the land of the rising sun, turn a deaf ear to the umpteen Western parents in their pleas to be reunited with their children abducted and taken to Japan by their Japanese national ex-spouses. The Hague Convention Treaty on the Civil Aspects of International Parental Abduction stipulates that children must be returned to the countries in which they were living when kidnapped. However Japan is the only G8 nation which refuses to ratify this treaty. In fact, Japan and only one other country, Mozambique, refuse to sign the agreement. Over the last 16 years, North Korea abducted 30 Japanese nationals, but hundreds of foreign children are stolen by Japanese nationals annually.

Existing perpetually in social infantilism, Japan will never be able to grasp the similarity between North Koreans abducting Japanese nationals and Japanese nationals abducting foreign children, as that would require some ability to engage in deductive reasoning, a rare concept in Japan. In their eyes it's better to rely on childlike emotions, as deductive reasoning is much too cold. Having not signed the treaty in the Hague Nippon is a haven for child abduction, even in the face of arrest warrants for the abducting parents by INTERPOL. Aiding and abetting the perpetrators, Japanese police simply ignores the International Police Agency.

The pre-kindergarten mentality populous is a contributing factor to the rapid increase in child abuse in Japan, as depressed, emotionally unprepared adult children themselves beget children. At 23 years old back in 1987, I too was one such father, with urges, strong urges, gale force urges to hurl my infant daughter to the ground at the sound of her angelic cries. But therapy helped me to manage those compulsions, until they disappeared. Most child abusers in Japan aren't that lucky, as counseling is simply not readily accessible. Jun Saimura from the Child and Family Research Institute stated that there were only a thousand reported cases of child abuse per year in 1990 when the government began compiling statistics. In 2002 he added, the number had soared to 24,000 and climbed to 35,000 by 2006. However, he readily admitted that 35,000 is probably an understatement. Based on statistics by the Japanese Ministry of Health, Labor and Welfare, after the enactment of the *toothless* child abuse prevention law in 2000, child abuse continued to escalate. Three years after enactment, saw the death of 127 children from abuse and in 2004, according to the National Police Agency, a further 51 children were abused to death and a total of 251 have been massacred between 2000 and 2005.

"The baby just wouldn't stop crying," is a common mantra for abusers when questioned about their murderous deeds. Shuddery acts, in the absence of illicit drugs so common in the West, are clearly the result of some kind of psychosis, personality disorder or, emotion regulation problem, characteristic among children. No one knows that more than I, who have walked through that inferno, not being psychotic but definitely personality disordered and with infantile emotion regulation ineptitude at the time of my daughter's birth.

Senseless, unfathomable child murders are voluminous in Japan and they all leave one awestruck, *gob smacked* with jaws touching the ground. Westerners unfamiliar with Japan's dysfunctional social dynamics would ask the question, "How could that be in *safety* Japan?" One particular murder is indelible. In late 1999, a 35-year-old mother of two murdered her neighbor's 2-year-old daughter, who had gained entrance to a prestigious kindergarten, to which her own daughter had been denied. Affiliated to prestigious universities in Tokyo, this coveted kindergarten all but guarantees entrance to the right elementary, junior high and high school, which are prerequisites to entering the few dream universities with which the kindergarten was associated. Mitsuko Yamada, a former nurse denied that jealousy was the motive for the killing but instead blamed the ostracizing and snobbish behaviour of the child's mother toward her. "By killing Haruna, I would no longer have to socialize with her mother again," the killer argued. Overkill, this massive disparity between the problem and the chosen solution and or misdirected aggressions are consistent among a great many murderers in Japan and at least speaks to childish, under-developed problem solving skills, and at most some kind of psychopathy.

In 2004 a man engulfed by wrath, drowned his flat mate's three children. Though both in their 20s, the original tenant of the apartment was the other's junior by a year in junior high school and also his junior in a motorcycle gang to which they both belonged. The junior member obliged his senior and three children to stay with him temporarily, but the senior soon began abusing his status in the hierarchy – as is common in Japan - hogging the only air-conditioned room in the apartment, not contributing to the rent and eating the junior out of house and land. Unable to confront his senior, or perhaps having done so in vain, the junior took matters a bit too far and hauled the senior's three kids to a nearby river and drowned them. His chosen solution to the comparatively minor problem will never cease to amaze me. Had that been in the West, perhaps there would've been some kind of exchange along the lines of,

"Hey yo, I can't do this no more dude. You and bebe's kids gatta go. Forget this." To which the parasite would respond, "Who kids you callin' bebe kids? Motha fff." Fists would become airborne, worse case scenario killing each other, but sparing the innocent children. Misdirected aggression though unjustified is conceivable, but misplacing aggression to children 2 – 7 years old is indicative of at the very least, acute arrested emotional development.

On February 17 2006 a woman in Nagahama fatally stabbed two 5-year-old friends of her daughter's, who were entrusted to her for transportation to their kindergarten. After pulling the car over, she unleashed 20 stab wounds on each child, right in front of her own daughter's eyes. Reports have it that as a Chinese immigrant, she was having language difficulties and problems associating with the other mothers at the Kindergarten.

As previously cited, no sooner had the sun risen on the year of the boar – January 3rd to be exact - did 53-year-old Minoru Tsukumo kill his 83-year-old mom because she told him to get a job. Teenage matricide is morbid but understandable, if for no other reason but the crude nature of the brain at that stage. However, here was a 53 year old man who couldn't control his emotions of anger toward his octogenarian mother. Again in Tokyo the next day on January 4, 2007, twenty-one year old Yuki Muto bludgeoned his 20-year-old sister with a sword handle, dragged her to the bathroom and mutilated her corpse in 15 pieces. His motive? She accused him of "having no dream." Muto San, whose parents and grandfather were all dentists had sat the dental school exam thrice unsuccessfully and was in preparation to resit it in April. No doubt Mr. Muto was among those elementary schoolboys forced to wear balls-high shorts in the dead of winter, in order to *toughen* him up. But in its misguided focus, his society neglected to nurture healthy development of his emotions. To further illustrate his embryonic problem solving skills, after placing the dismembered cadaver in 4 plastic bags, he then put them in a closet beneath an empty fish tank, after which he forewarned his father that there may be a foul smell, as a shark which he had received from a friend had died.

Four days later in Yokohama on the eighth, a 70-year-old man bludgeoned his 68-year-old wife. And what was HIS motive? "I thought she had changed my bank account without my consent." Turned out he had been mistaken.

SHOKO'S DINNER

Shoko's invitation to *dinner* was preceded by a few dates and frequent brief meetings outside where everyone, men, women, foreigners and Japanese alike, exalted her astounding beauty and I, usually behind her, walked in a perpetual state of fortified arousal. On several occasions, upon meeting her as planned at JR Sannomiya station, even after knowing her for over a year, I was forced to retreat to the men's room to relieve myself before setting out on the date. The attention, though thrilling was mostly uncomfortable, especially given our sixteen-year age difference. Recently emigrating from the West, I still felt uneasy with this age gap, but eventually adjusted to the fact that the disparity between our ages is nothing to balk at in this society.

In male chauvinistic Japan, a historically polygamous society where women are relatively powerless, such wide age differences are not an issue. Shoko was a graduate in law, who had been slaving away at her part-time job at a patisserie, while studying diligently for exams required to become a civil servant. Unlike her sister, having failed the Japanese BAR exam much to her parents' discomfiture, Shoko had settled for her second choice: to spend the remainder of her life uneventfully in acquiescent civil service. "It's not what I want to do, but it's a good job forever and it's safe," she reasoned in self-sacrificing defeat. But to her good fortune failure was also the fate of her government job exam, which required some $3,000 in preparation courses and six months of arduous studying. In industrialized countries like the United States, life as a civil servant requires a simple high school diploma, but here in Japan it is necessary to have passed an exam almost tantamount in difficulty to the Japanese BAR.

Unable to endure her torture, I invited her to *dinner*, where instead of waning, my torture and frustration escalated to new peaks. After the usual culinary concoction with which she was most impressed, stripping the fruit of my desire, to my disenchantment, our first kissed affirmed a greenness not seen since my prepubescent days trying it on with prepubescent girls. She simply left her mouth open, clueless about what to do with her lips and tongue.

"My kiss is terrible, please teach me," she admitted sheepishly. But that was the first sign of a young innocent Gerber daisy willing to learn everything. Disembarrassing her of her garments, including the girdle she donned in a futile attempt to flatten her *Africoid* posterior, I began her kissing lessons, to which she was quite receptive. "Dou? Am I getting better?" she constantly queried. "You're a good student," I encouraged so as not to get her disheartened, when in fact she was dreadful. It was more a battle of the teeth than kissing, as my arousal hardened in mounting frustration.

Like many Japanese women with her body type; curvaceous with a bulbous posterior, Shoko harbored mammoth insecurities about her physique. Unlike her straight, rail thin, unattractive sister, she was convinced she saw obesity in the mirror and since her childhood could not understand from whence she received her *unJapanese* rump, which she constantly tried to compress with a girdle. Hence she was in complete awe and disbelief at my hypnosis by her body. "EEEEE! No way," she resisted, trying to cover her nudity with my duvet. "Iya Iya, zetai Iya.!" (No way, No way, definitely no way) She responded when I tried to unwrap the comforter from around her, wooden frustration hitting the ceiling. After much coaxing and convincing her of my deep admiration and appreciation for her physique, including her champagne glass sized breasts, she gave up, stood against the wall in my tatami room, just to let me gawk at her.

A rarity among Japanese women, Shoko was well manicured and I wasted no time before engaging in a southward plunge head first. Delirious in ecstasy, she rained a small pond as I caressed her baby mounds and feasted on her until it was just too much to bear. "Itai itai itai stop stop stop stop stoooop!" she shouted, reeling in pain. "Hajimete?" (Is this your first time?) "Yes," she replied apologetically. Shoko was constantly apologizing. Profuse were her apologies, even for matters and events completely out of her control, a cultural characteristic which added fuel to my elephantine frustration. Judging from her trembling fear and excruciating pain, she would be an extended term project, I thought, or I would have to abandon her as my frustration became immeasurable.

One of her fears was that she would fall uncontrollably in love with me after sex. And judging from her profile of trauma and pronounced distrust of and animosity toward men, once I gained her trust to let me in, it was clear that like a newly hatched bird beholding its first object, I would be *imprinted* in her psyche. But speaking with the little head, I discounted her concerns. "That can never happen," lying through my teeth. "You're 23 years old, you're an adult. That only happens to teenagers." Given her undefiled state, I was prompted to undergo a complete battery of venereal disease screening, including my first AIDS test in Japan. Back in the States my AIDS tests were as frequent as twice a year but not longer than once every two years, with my last test being on the month I left three years prior.

Main vein bursting, I begged her just to stand in place as I explored her globular buttocks and manually brought myself joy. Again she apologized for being unable to satisfy me and causing me to resort to such an abominable act. It may well have been that, having felt inadequate, Shoko tried to make up for her short comings by allowing me to take pictures and videos of her and indulging me in my voyeurism and erotic role play games outside. She found pleasure in allowing me to glare up her micro-minis as she climbed the stairs at the station, sometimes even reminding me. "I'm going upstairs now. Don't you want to watch?" My favourite, my absolute favourite was our role play games on the trains. Before boarding, we pretended to be strangers always sitting directly opposite each other, where I'd be able to see between her legs. Then I would e-mail her, instructing her to discreetly open her legs, as I proceeded to take pictures. This launched the rocket and mystified the surrounding passengers, but being Japanese, they were always frozen in unreactionary shock. Upon arriving at my apartment we'd embark upon a foreplay frenzy, which for the first 8 months ended with futile attempts at entrance and my reacquaintance with Miss Palmer.

As if my frustrations were not enough, Shoko was not just your ordinary maiden, but at 23 years old, having never even as much as ridden a bicycle, her hymen, which might as well had been a steel fortress, was still firmly intact. It took some four months of regular unendurably agonizing attempts just to breach it, but one fateful day, with only minimum penetration, she endured, teeth gritting, eyes clenched shut, screaming, trying to follow my instructions to breathe, as her flesh ruptured sending a hematic stream on my futon. "Stop stop stop!" She yelled, pushing me off her, tears streaming down the sides of her face. "Shin no hudo no keiken." (That was a near death experience.)

This unwelcomed sexual delay resulted in my getting to know Shoko, which revealed that, though directionless, she was uniquely socially aware among Japanese women and possessed enormous ambition with an aversion to the male dominant status quo in her society. Prepared from an early age to forego marriage and children over marrying a chauvinistic Japanese man, she was adamant about finding a career as opposed to becoming a housewife. Though her fashion was elegantly conservative, unlike her peers there was no obsession with name brands, no Prada handbags or Fendi umbrellas.

Having failed the BAR once and watching her alternative dissipate before her eyes, aimless and distressed, she was prepared to do what most Japanese in her predicament would: repeat the BAR exam well into her 30s or until she had succeeded. In consequence, out of sheer annoyance by her whiney juvenile character coupled with her distress, I began to administer sincere, sound advice, but in a harsh, coarse, impatient military styled delivery, aimed somewhat at repelling her. "Look, I know you're Japanese and you know only one way to do things, but think! Kangaete! Instead of wasting your youth and energy trying to pass the Japanese BAR, you should put that effort into going to the United States, studying English as a second language at Community College, taking an LSAT preparation course, attending law school, and then pass the American BAR."

At the time she sat the exam in 2003, the pass rate for the Japanese BAR stood at a whopping thousand per year, less than 3%, in comparison to the 80% or higher in the US, depending on the state. Thus, as a fan of probability, I thought spending her time studying law in the States would maximize her benefits, as opposed to doing things the inefficient, head bashing, shugyou way of the samurai. For the same amount of energy she would be assured the greater reward of being an International Lawyer, plus unlike many Japanese, she'd gain fluency in English. Even after Japanese jurisprudence education was modified adding 68 American style law schools in 2004, the pass rate for the new BAR introduced in 2006 was only 45-50%, well below their targeted 75-80%.

For encouragement, I told her of my cousin in Jamaica who had obtained a scholarship to study medicine in the former Soviet Union though he knew no Russian. Upon arriving in Kiev, he was given intensive Russian studies for one year only, after which the entire med school curriculum was in Russian. After seven years he graduated top of his class. "You already speak English," I chided. "And law is much less taxing than medicine." "That's a good idea but I don't have confidence to do that," she lamented. A typical feature of the average Japanese woman. "Well stay in Japan wearing that stupid brown uniform at Henri Charpentier, or become an Office Lady. It's your choice." As frustration from Shoko was a regular experience when we met, so was my mantra to her about her plague of diffidence.

Shoko's part-time job, curfew and studies limited her visits to my apartment to three times a month, but we met regularly at the JR station nearest her home, if only for a few minutes. Three months after our sanguine breakthrough, at the pinnacle of my frustration, I decided it was time for full and complete entry. Seven months had elapsed, when on November 30, while Karin was in Hawaii for her friend's wedding, the same wedding for which she had aborted our child in order to fit in the dress she had planned to wear to the wedding, Shoko paid me a visit.

Welcoming her with hardened enthusiasm, slowly I began defrocking her in preparation for a long, hot, relaxing bath together. Hitherto, I had shunned baths in Japan, but for the sake of getting her completely relaxed, I endured the conditions of the infant sized tub. Her kisses had improved greatly since her first lesson and we embarked on an hour of oral and tactile exploration as she loosened and moistened. Emerging from the bath, with water from her milky, porcelain body dripping onto my bathroom floor, I wrapped her in a towel before taking her to my tatami room to enjoy her southern cuisine.   And after generous sensuous applications - to myself and her - of heavy-duty, industrial strength Astroglide, I eased in gently, determined to make her a woman. Screaming in the throes of my occupation, with eyes wide open, she tried to catch her breath, inching up my futon, "zembu haita?" (is it all in?) "Madda, atto mo chotto." (Not yet, just a little left.) "Zembu irete," (Put it all in) as she endured an agony close to that of child birth. And with complete occupation I exploded deep inside her, the day after the lady in red had returned home.

For an entire month, Shoko's ambulatory skills were impaired and for the next year, every time it would seem as though she was a virgin all over again. As presaged, almost immediately thereafter, the prey had developed a deep and fathomless attachment to her predator, but what was not predicted was the lion's incurable attachment to the dove. In a sentimental transformation, for the first time I had interpreted some kind of sacredness in a woman's virginity. But then again, that was the first time I had spent so much time with a woman, getting to know her before defiling her of her innocence. Before it was always a condition which I had resented, seeking only to rid the woman of it, so I could get down to the business of enjoying sex. However, this time was much different. The young daisy I had come to know over the previous seven months was one of the most selfless, self-sacrificing, maternal and giving women I had ever met, extending emotional support even during Karin's termination. Plans to abandon and discard her like day old newspaper, would have been a cardinal crime against humanity and rejection would have most certainly solidified her despise for men, especially Negroe men.

In no time it was obvious that she had become irrevocably attached to me, as though she had literally come from my loins, even enduring my "be all that you can be" army style boot camp. Though she appeared meek and passive, in her personal time, she may well have been pondering my harsh words to her about her dismal future as a young woman in Japan, if she didn't cultivate the confidence required to take life in her own hands and pursue that which brought her happiness. But all of that was mostly out of hoping that she would develop, spread her wings, move on to bigger and better things, leaving me to my vices.

However, her love, the kind about which songwriters and poets muse, the kind so heavy, not as in burdensome but that which could be felt in all her actions, voice and e-mails, just kept mounting. By her 24th birthday, Shoko had blossomed into an adult still not quite knowing how she was going to achieve her goals but, possessing much greater confidence than she had the year prior. So much so, she obtained a passport and took her first trip overseas to Thailand. Though the majority of our rendezvous were brief, sometimes just going for a walk at nearby shrines or by the beach, they were all special and I anticipated them like a child waiting for the return of his parents. Desecrating her parent's car outside her house was among our favourite pastime. Soon, out of all the women whom I had been seeing, including my girlfriend Karin, my preference was to spend time in Shoko's arms and presence.

In fact, a year after meeting Shoko, Karin for the umpteenth time - in one of her many episodes of crockery hurling - asked when I would finally stop seeing Shoko. Reflecting on the previous two years, which included six months of pure torture from her and most recently her aborting our child a month before our planned wedding, I told her "I can't," leaving her and all her craziness behind. I finally decided to give up drama for drama-free. "I wanna stop seeing you."

A year after meeting Shoko, I had met and began actively dating Azusa, a hyper-beautiful 21-year-old. Precisely as I had prophesied to myself some months back, meeting Azusa hurled a wrench in my relationship with Shoko, for whom I had left Karin and it wasn't long before I had to acknowledge to myself and to them that somehow I had found myself in the midst of a love triangle, a stressful situation, though the envy of many a men. Though my love and attachment to Shoko was unmovable, within a few short months Azusa and I had spent more time together than Shoko and I did all year. On average, excluding over night stays, Azusa visited me some six times a month in comparison to Shoko, who was able to come by only once or twice a month. While Shoko and I had multiple mini-visits, Azusa frequently had multiple overnight stays, eventually spending more time at my apartment than with her parents.

Initially, Azusa knew of Shoko, but Shoko had no awareness of Azusa's existence. As far as Shoko was concerned, she was my new girlfriend. And she was. But thanks to the freedom of Azusa's family, she was so available that the frequency with which we saw each other created an attachment almost as strong as my bond with Shoko. In deed, the unintentional early meeting of Azusa's parents immediately resulted in the same respect and gradual attachment as the unintentional delay in sex with Shoko. In concern for her feelings, I decided to reveal the state of affairs to Shoko in a special meeting, but little did I know she too had some news to break to me.

Sitting cuddled on a bench by the Daimaru department store in Mottomachi, I began to lay it all out on the table. Though partly out of respect for Shoko, another reason for unveiling Azusa's presence on the scene was simply to avoid the stress of concealing the relationship. "Buyer beware" is my mantra and besides, so complete was Shoko's attachment that in my calculation she would never have left.

"I feel so stupid, I thought you left Karin for me," tears streaming down her watermelon coloured cheeks.
"We can't meet because of your parents, but Azusa and I meet everyday," I said, escalating her disdain for her autocratic parents. They had been the topic of many emotional conversations, during which I had made my sentiments perfectly clear regarding parents like hers, which frequently ended with her weeping, wishing she had different parents. Having been constantly rejected by parents of Asian and European-American women I had dated in the States, no longer was I inclined to beg the acceptance of anyone's parents, especially since I was now a grown 40-year-old man. I assured her that given her parents' prejudice, she and I would have had no future together, as I by no means wanted her to have to choose between me and them.

"Yeh, Karin might have been crazy, but her parents loved me," I reminded her.
"And so far since I've been in Japan, in my experience, parents like yours are in the minority. Understanding her vulnerabilities, citing her parents'

rejection was also my trump card to quell any possible protest against my maniac philandering and more immediately against Azusa's presence. Pain flowing down her cheeks, she understood.

"Shoganai," (It can't be avoided) she must have thought, the common Japanese response to almost everything, and agreed for us to continue seeing each other whenever we could.

After extended silence, hurt still coursing down her cheeks, Shoko began to tell of the tardy lady in red: the crimson goddess, previously as punctual as Japan Railways, was now twelve days late. Immediately I was drenched in a cold sweat.

"Not this sweet innocent young dame, who by happenstance was simply just walking up an escalator, minding her own business a year prior," I thought guiltily. Only six months earlier, Shoko had waited to meet me outside the hospital where Karin was undergoing her termination. I had accompanied her to the hospital but after she disappeared for the procedure, I left to join Shoko, who insisted on being supportive through the ordeal. Such an abomination was Karin to me I could have hardly waited to flee the hospital to join Shoko, whom I vowed never to put through that hell. I had developed a hitherto unknown respect for and attachment to Shochan, but not enough to take effective contraceptive action, and thoughts of her in the abortion chamber, pulled at my heart. She wanted to get married, an idea which I found unsettling. After all I was still not quite emotionally healthy enough to be marriage material and she was still somewhat, though less so, annoyingly immature. However, even more unsettling was the thought of this innocent young woman, who had only recently lost her virginity, undergoing an abortion.

"Why couldn't you marry me?" She queried.
"Because I'm crazy and I would make a terrible husband and father," I thought to myself.

Three days later in an SMS text message, Shoko informed me of the arrival of the red baroness and a colossal burden was lifted from both our shoulders, though unbeknownst to her, I had decided to step up to the plate and marry her had she been pregnant. Immediately I advised her to join the whopping 2% of Japanese women who used oral contraceptives, and post haste she complied. In fact, Shoko was the only woman in Japan, who without hesitation took my advice regarding birth control pills.

AZUSA

On the night of Monday May 10th 2004, after finishing my class at the very large electronics manufacturer, I sat at the end of a seat on a JR Todai train from Kyobashi to Nishi Akashi, where directly across from me sat a woman who was no less than a heavenly body. Azusa was angel meets mermaid, some kind of being from a fairytale. Svelte at a mere 49 kilos and 161cm, she was the type I frequently saw on the arms of white men in the States and wished to whom I could be gestaltly and comfortably attracted, beyond just being enamored by their stupefying beauty and wanting them to bear my progeny. She was the type of beauty who, once on Western soil would be scooped up by men who would swarm her like flies, the second she deplaned. But in Japan, she was ignored, as public acknowledgement of a woman's beauty is taboo.

Since childhood my attraction had been compartmentalized and like many men, the women who aroused me the most sexually were not necessarily the women with whom I wanted to procreate or marry. And likewise, women with whom I wanted to procreate aroused me only marginally. These divisions almost always have been mutually exclusive and the dilemma was, finding a compromise if ever I were to marry, otherwise I would find myself in the Hugh Grant syndrome. Most people, especially women are unable to grasp why Hugh, though dating the stunning Elizabeth Hurley at the time, had to seek out Brown's Divine services on Sunset Boulevard. But I understand it all too well. The trouble with those model types is that they lack the primal visual cues, the nubility to which I respond with heightened sexual arousal. That hip-to-waist ratio just isn't there. Instead, perhaps by social conditioning, they are seen as status symbols, ideal for creating beautiful progeny, which to me is of utmost importance. Long ago I had decided to give up pursuing extremely beautiful women to whom I wasn't completely attracted and instead be comfortable with my tastes and accept the fact that, long chopstick legs, that tall waif look, though quite an ego boost, do very little for me sexually. The boost in ego was always fleeting and inside I tired of the need to show the world that I too could have a hyper-beaut on my arms, while suffering through painfully uneventful sex in private. This I refer to as Hugh Grant Syndrome.

Azusa fell dead smack in the *procreate* compartment. Immediately upon laying eyes on her I wanted her eggs, wanted to impregnate her right there on the train, I wanted my genes combined with hers, I wanted her to be the bearer of my progeny, though sex with her was furthest from my mind. I knew she would have been only marginally arousing. As I sat there awestruck by her face, trying not to make my hypnosis blaringly obvious, for the second time since arriving in Japan, my Jamaican confidence was temporarily misplaced, thinking,

"Naw, she's too fine, I'm 40, maybe twice her age. Aw hell naw! No way she'd go for me."

Then to my relief and disappointment, but more to my relief, she rose to disembark at Amagasaki station. My dilemma had been resolved, a burden lifted from my shoulders because now, I didn't have a chance to mack, given my complete awareness of a hopeless future with her. But on the other hand, she was hella fine, in the words of my boy JP upon meeting her, "stoopid fine" and I wanted to at least get rejected by her.

"Yeh, I scared her," I thought.

"FUCK! Maybe I shoulda been more subtle. Gaddaaam she's FOINE."

The thought crossed my mind to escape from the train in pursuit but, I simply let it go and accepted the situation as it was. After all, I was quite happy with the prospects of finally separating from Karin, to settle permanently with Shoko. And moreover, as an ADHD adult, I would have soon forgotten about the Tozai line beauty.

"She would've thrown a spanner in the works with me and Shoko," I pacified myself.

In a sudden change of events the angel returned to the train, but in a different car where she sat by the dividing glass doors, legs and umbrella extended.

"Oh, I definitely scared her, she's not interested."

Gradually rising from my seat I moved toward the dividing doors to discreetly monitor her feet and Fendi umbrella for any signs of disembarkment. Her navy pumps with thin red and white trimmings at the top are still vividly etched in my memory.

"Where ever those pumps goeth, there goeth I, even if it's at the end of the line some two hours away and even if there is no train back and it meant spending the night outdoors."

As the train approached Kobe station, I observed some movement before she rose to her feet, gait exuding cocksure confidence as she engaged in a most stately stride toward the door. As it turned out, though she was slim, her proportions were at the absolute borderline for my liking. Any taller and or slimmer, even with her gobsmacking face, it would have been mission aborted. By then regaining my confidence in her absence, I exited the train to intercept her atop the escalator at Kobe station.

"You were on that train?" Fronting surprise and presuming she spoke English.
"I thought you got off at Amagasaki."
"I wanted to get on the super express but the platform was too far."
"Do you live in Kobe?"
"Yes, my mother is picking me up at the station. Where in Kobe do you live?"
"Who me, I don't live in Kobe. Au, I'm just, visiting a friend in, I forgot the name of his place. Near Harbour Land."
After more small talk we exchanged numbers, with my inputting her information with the memo "AZUSA MOST BEAUTIFUL!"
"My mom is there waiting."
And on that note I bade her good-night and waved to her mother. Immediately after returning to the train, I shot off an e-mail to her telling her how wonderful it was to have met her, but embarrassingly, my mail was sent out with the heading "AZUSA MOST BEAUTIFUL!" which was meant only for my own personal files. However, to my shocking delight her response arrived with the heading "MOST HANDSOME STEFHEN."
"Houston, the eagle has landed."

As it turned out, we were mutual admirers of each other on the train and like me, she worried about overstaring, as she thought her admiration would anger me. Azusa did not possess the milk skin which I fetishized but, hers were upturned eyes like the ones I worshipped. She later revealed to me her operation at 19 to remove her epicanthic fold to make her eyes more Western, but as earlier stated the procedure was somewhat of a failure, as they still looked very archetypically East Asian. Coming from the West, especially having lived in Los Angeles, where women like her were profoundly aware of their aesthetic currency, it was unfathomable that she could be an easy lay, so I prepared myself for hard work. On our first date on May 31 we attended an annual beach party in Osaka. Donning her Christian Dior one piece, she was a hit as I fielded inquiries after inquiries about her.

"Yo, who da FUCK is she?"
"I just met her on the train two weeks ago."
"GADDAAAM!."

In fact, for the first eight months or so, it was most uncomfortable being with her in public, due mostly to my own insecurities, unable to fathom what some super fine 21-year-old woman would want with a broke ass 40-year-old man. But this was Japan where the erotic capital of black and white men alike is off the charts. It is this high erotic capital coupled with the low empowerment and self worth of Japanese women which afford men like my aforementioned neighbor, the balding, unattractive, pot bellied, white male of 54 years, the privilege of sporting a 26-year-old wife, the likes of Azusa. Having met her when she, like Azusa was 21, in his own words, he "knocked her up ASAP to remove her from the market."

"*What a dick,*" I thought. Back in his native Canada he wouldn't even have been able to pay a dog to urinate on his ankle.

Of the forty Japanese women in three years, Azusa was the first to bring out the venom in Japanese men when we paraded out together. They looked at her with scorn and at me with anger and envy.

On one occasion during conversation, one guy whipped out his cell phone to showcase his beautiful wife.

"Anata no kanajo wa?" (What about YOUR girlfriend?)

But when I fired back with a cell picture of Azusa, he responded in rage. "Nande anata no kanojo no hoga kirei? Boku wa nihonjin da kedo, konna ni kirei na koibito ima made deki nai." (Why is your girlfriend more beautiful? I'm Japanese but I have never been able to find a girlfriend this beautiful.)

"*That's just it,*" I thought. "*I'm not Japanese.*"

Azusa told me of her possessive, 21-year-old boyfriend, with whom she constantly feuded for her freedom and who kicked her in the chest upon reading one of my e-mails on her phone. I empathized with his insecurities, as I too was of such possessive character at his age, lacking in confidence especially when dating women like her, who were constantly driven away by my behaviour. Reciprocating, I told her of Karin, who had recently moved into my apartment after my begging for two years. However, after well over a month she still had not unpacked her numerous boxes in my bedroom.

"We are gonna break up soon," which actually occurred after our separation trip to Kyushu six weeks after meeting Azusa. After a month and a half of regular meetings, I had arrived at the same point with Azusa, which took several months with Anita: the point where I had finally accepted that there was no future between us, so I should just get a piece and move on. Our eighteen-year age difference was unsettling to me, as I was fully aware of the dismally low level of maturity among Japanese women in general, but especially among those in their early twenties. I had suffered such frustrations a year earlier after meeting Shoko who was then 23, but who was less emotionally and intellectually mature than my daughter at 14.

"*Yeh, she fine,*" I thought, "*but I don't wanna do anymore babysitting.*"
And that's when I just broke it down to her.
"Let's go to a love hotel," I suggested on the phone.
"Love hotel? Iya! I don't want to go to a love hotel."
"Ok, come over to my apartment and I'll cook you dinner."
And to that she agreed. By then it must have been obvious to her that I was not inviting her over to hang wallpaper. Having invited her to a love hotel first, my objectives were perfectly clear and after dinner I pounced on her, like a cat on a mouse. Having to work that evening, time was of the essence. Gradually stripping her designer clothes revealed forty-nine kilos of an almost too slim but proportionately sexy, curvaceous body, adorned with perfect champagne glass sized breasts with long dark nipples on which I began to suckle. Gradually rising to the occasion, I grew not to my max, but enough to leave her breathless upon my unprotected entrance to her liquid, forest covered cave.

Picking her up, I began to curl her on my somewhat aroused anatomy. Then, with my Toshiba washing machine in spin cycle, I mounted her on top and emptied myself inside, fantasies of impregnating her swirling around in my head. Just as I had anticipated, the encounter was most uneventful and it was crystal clear that there was no hope between us, especially since at 21, she was even more infantile than Shoko at 23. After *raising* Shoko, I was not prepared to repeat that tooth and nail extracting process. But Azusa's beauty could not have been ignored. Getting dressed for work, I began to feel guilty for my selfish performance. After all, I was her debut on foreign soil and was ashamed of my less than stellar execution.

"What do you like? What makes you come?" Fixing my tie in the mirror.
"I like top."
"*I can handle that,*" I thought.
She aroused me enough, so I'd be able to just lay there as she did all the work.
"Wagamama hechi gomen ne, (Sorry for my selfish sex) next time I'll pleasure you."

In a few days she returned to display her advanced fellatio and equestrian skills, and given her slightly protruding Venus mound, her proclivity to abundant, hyper-frequent arrivals. Exactly as I had foreseen, her svelte physique, was anathema to my propensity for more nubile women. She was the greater beneficiary of our intimacy, as my arousal was a little above marginal. Had there been one woman with whom I could not have been monogamous, Azusa would have been her. But her beauty was other worldly. Fully aware of my sentiments toward her, especially my far less than uncontrollable sexual urge toward her, I decided to be her pleasure toy, while using her as eye candy until she outgrew me and left. But an especially unforeseen event directed things in a completely different path.

Atypically Japanese, Azusa's parents were the most permissive I had met in Japan, condoning her frequent visits and overnight sojourns in my bed. At 21 and a senior at one of Japan's most prestigious Universities, she had no curfew and was allowed unprecedented freedom by her family. Before meeting her, the progressive idea of Japanese parents allowing their 17-year-old daughter to have sex in their house, to me was unfathomable. After our debut, Azusa and I saw each other with effortless frequency, with her sometimes attending class in the mornings from my apartment. On the eve of her fifth visit to my apartment, she was scheduled to meet her parents at the Sogo department store in Sannomiya, for which she was late, of course owing to her new found hobby as a jockey. Already she had been an hour late having not even left my apartment.
"Do you want to meet my parents?" She asked half joking.

I had met her mom, a kind, soft-spoken woman of average beauty, on the many occasions on which I escorted Azusa to the Kobe station, where mother waited patiently to collect her daughter at the end of our almost daily courting. However, I had no interest in meeting her dad and especially didn't want to meet her parents together. As a predator, meeting the parents, especially the dad is by no means something I wished to do, as doing so would humanize my prey, and result in unspoken pressure to respect her. Moreover, coming from the West, it was inconceivable that I, 40-year-old international slacker, would be well received by the parents, again especially the father, of some uber-beautiful 21-year-old babe. Let's face it, if I had a stunningly beautiful 21-year-old daughter who introduced me to a middle-aged pauper as someone with whom she was having intimate affairs, he would be promptly introduced to my shotgun, had I one. And had I not been in possession of one, he would most certainly be incentive to take a trip to Bill's gun shop. But a part of me wanted to meet these uniquely open minded and permissive parents, an anomaly among the Japanese.

"If you don't want to meet them its ok," with a grin of subtle disappointment.

"No, I do want to meet them, it's just that, we just had sex," trying to hide the fact that I really didn't wish to meet them.

"So what?" She retorted. "I used to have sex with my ex-boyfriend in their house. They even walked in on us once."

Arriving in Sannomiya together, nervously anticipating rejection, I presented a package of Blue Mountain coffee beans which I had brought from my trip to Jamaica with Karin six months earlier. It was a hit. Throughout our meeting, I kept anticipating the emergence of the shotgun as after all, I was only six years her mother's junior and ten years her father's. But at no time did Mr. and Mrs. Ogawa show any resentment. In fact, they too were nervous, as she blushed to shrimp red and he, strapping judo master and police detective awkwardly accepted my offering, hands trembling slightly. Even with the heavy bags beneath his eyes from slaving away on sometimes 72 hour shifts, Azusa's father was a dashingly handsome and gentle man. It was he who was the source of her faint-inducing beauty and her mother, still svelte at 46 years old, provided the gene for her slenderness.

After this unexpected but refreshing meeting of the parents, they frequently requested my presence for dinner at their home and at restaurants. No longer could I view Azusa as some random yellow cab of which I had planned to take advantage. Instead, developing the desire to protect, direct and cherish her, I began to exercise patience and tolerance with her childish behaviour, all the while reminding myself, that once she matures into adulthood she would be a powerhouse of a woman. Allowing her access to the psyche of dissocial personality disordered men like me, I began to reveal my dark side to her, alerting her of the need to protect herself, as I had advised my own daughter.

"You can't just make yourself sexually available to men you have just met and allow them to have sex with you, especially without a condom," I advised, the manner in which her father should have. "Apart from possibly contracting STDs, you, not men, are vulnerable to pregnancy, you must protect yourself."

Upon informing her that I had emptied myself in her during our initial and second encounter, tears welled up in her eyes.

"Hidoii," (You're terrible) she responded.

"Oh yes, I am. I already know that, that's why I'm qualified to warn you, especially since I know your family. You're hearing it straight from Mr. Terrible."

It must have hurt, but she was getting it straight from the horse's mouth. For whom better to tell her of such matters than I, the very man against whom I was warning her? What's more, in the West where I was encouraging her to go on a working holiday, there are many such men, so it's best that she was prepared.

"In the West, men - even sex addicts like me - don't respect women who make themselves so readily available sexually, but I started respecting you after meeting your parents." "Besides," I added, "you are an abnormally attractive woman. You shouldn't be giving it up that easily." Both here in Japan and in the West men will fall over themselves just to be in your presence, but you will lose credibility and respect if you just open your legs to them immediately after meeting them."

Azusa explained that she had been quite attracted to me and my love hotel proposal hurt and disappointed her. "But I didn't want to lose you, that's why I decided to have sex with you," she justified.

Though possessing off the charts beauty, like most Japanese women I had met, she was oblivious to her self-worth. She had agreed to come to my apartment instead of a love ho, as sex at my apartment made her feel less cheap, given that I had made my intentions perfectly clear, by proposing a hotel initially.

My having met Azusa's father illuminates the dire necessity for all men with daughters of dating age, to insist on meeting the men with whom their daughters are intimate. Contrary to the common practice of fathers flying off the handle in rage, when their young daughters begin dating, meeting the boys, or men, is far more effective. Meeting fathers can even dissuade the likes of me, a walking text book dissocial personality disorder, from mistreating their daughters. Far less important was the fact that her father was a detective in the Japanese Constabulary, but more impacting was that I had met him; we made contact, shook hands and looked into each others' eyes. Suddenly, his daughter was now a human with feelings, as opposed to just the day's catch. Conversely, meeting mothers is devoid of such impact, as unlike fathers, they are usually perceived as sex objects.

My words to Azusa may have been common sense to young women in the West, but in Japan where women are collectively naïve, still equating sex with love, kept unempowered on a short social, political and economic leash, such Western ideology is an alien concept. All this was news to her. Never before had she heard this subject matter directed at her so bluntly and directly. After all, in Japan, communication, especially on this topic, if at all mentioned, is usually indirect and fathers never hold these kinds of discussions with their daughters.

Separate from her child-like behavior, Azusa possessed almost all of the qualities I sought in a partner, qualities starkly absent in most Japanese women. First and foremost, she was *trauma-free*, with confidence percolating from every pore. With amazing drive and ambition, she sought empowerment and wanted to escape the confines of Japan. At such a young age, she possessed none of the inhibitions which crippled her peers and according to her parents, since her childhood, she had always strived for independence and sought to find her own path, doing things her way, even in the face of ridicule. Like me, she had been obsessed with thought since her childhood.

"I always wanted a boyfriend like you," she'd say. "Someone strong but kind who can advise me."
But like most Japanese women, her relationship with her work-aholic father would ensure her search for a father figure.

The elder of two children, Azusa told me of her brother - a hikkikomori three years her junior - who had hardly left his room in six years. In a population of 126 million, according to Ministry of Education data in August 2005, Akihiro was among the 2% of those enrolled in high school, but permanently absent from class. Like most other hikkikomoris, he was also the victim of bullying. In elementary school his extreme handsomeness and intelligence, elicited the envy of other students. Indeed the inability to conform to Japan's one size fit all society is a common feature observed among hikkikomoris I have met. Akihiro, a strikingly beautiful young man was, like his sister, of movie star ilk. Upon hearing that his sister was involved with a foreigner, he warned her of the dangers and advised her to be careful. But little did he know that the very gaijin whom he had feared would be his life saver, first getting him out of the house and then some two years later into a gym and on to university.

Hunch backed and disfigured from years of slouching in front of his computer, his curiosity about me lured him from his room to karaoke, a favourite Japanese past time. Karaoke and manga were among his few pleasures and his stench, not unlike that of the cesspool in which I fell at 4 years old, permeated the small room as he sang with his mother, sister and me for some two hours. At 17 years old his tall, lanky Lurch-like posture was in complete disaccord with his Adonis face, whose mouth produced no more than five words throughout the entire time. Particularly rewarding to him was our mutual enthusiasm for the bands Spitz and Pornographiti, two groups introduced to me by Mayu in the countryside.

"We haven't seen him like that in a long time," Azusa told me a few days later. "He really likes you, you've changed him."

It then became the norm for him to accompany us when his family treated me to dinner and months later, after sporadic attendance he graduated from high school. One year later, in a grand display of genius, Akihiro studied by himself and was successful in his university entrance exams, though he had avoided school, for most of six years since 11 years old.

My influence on Akihiro served to further solidify my acceptance by the family. After futile years of attempts at sociability, his parents may well have thought I was his Messiah. My deeper acceptance in the family resulted in covert pressure to embrace and shield their precious daughter. All ill intentions to use and discard her had to be dashed, as my attachment to her increased in proportion to the love and support showered on me by her parents. Patience and mushrooming respect replaced intolerance, and soon I began to put her through the same empowerment boot camp - albeit with a different motivation - with which I had been torturing Shoko for over a year. My empowerment homilies to Shoko were partly out of repelling her.

As Shoko was the typical diffident Japanese, though never complaining, I was 100% sure she would have crumbled, deciding to leave under my constant hammering for her to pursue her dreams. Azusa on the other hand, was confident and had always been waiting for someone like me to motivate her hence she and her parents, especially her mother, welcomed my encouragement.

"You've found a good man," her mother told her. "Stay with him, he'll make you a success."

It was almost as though she understood her daughter's need for a father figure.

In December 2004 Azusa and I set out to Jamaica, on our first trip together overseas. As her mother drove us to Kansai airport, Azusa was still sniffling, tears streaming onto her lap, from my having hurt her feelings earlier, by admitting that Shoko, not she, was my first choice for companionship to the island. In deed, it was only after Shoko's shah-like parents' refusal to permit her departure, that I requested Azusa's company. Shoko understood, as she lacked the confidence, even at 23 years old to oppose her parents' wishes. After Azusa explained this to her mother, mom's advice was to "stop the crying," lest she chased me off with her immaturity.

"You should enjoy your trip to Jamaica."

For me this was further evidence of their, or at least her mother's unconditional acceptance, as I interpreted her parental advice as validation and support of my actively dating another woman along with her daughter. This came as a relief. After all, they had been treating me like their own son hence I was frequently consumed by guilt for actively dating Shoko also.

At The Seacliff Hotel in panoramic Montego Bay, Azusa and I frolicked and basked in three weeks of unspeakable bliss. One year earlier in the exact suite, Karin and I had engaged in fierce daily battles for almost 30 days, her continuous bleeding was a vivid reminder of her senseless abortion a month earlier. But diametrically opposite to what amounted to torturous camping with Karin, at no time did Azusa and I leave each other's arms. Sex on the beach was no longer just a cocktail, but an almost daily activity in the golden red sunset.

"I know you're gonna marry her," she said, coming to grips with my undying attachment to Shoko, "but I want to at least have your child." I liked what I heard, as I had strongly wanted her DNA to combine with mine. Furthermore, at that time I had not planned to marry two women, but given my dramatic background, a child with one while married to the other was quite feasible, providing they were both in agreement.

Azusa met my entire family at a Christmas gathering, which further complicated things as they spontaneously presumed there were wedding bells in the atmosphere. After all, I had taken her *home* for Christmas, which, though meaningless to me, meant a great deal to them. So we must have been getting married, they'd have thought. Beyond question, acceptance by her entire family and her complete acceptance by mine, brought about indubitable unspoken pressure to tie the knot, or jump the broom, giving her yet another advantage over Shoko, who had circumstantial factors stacked against her. While Shoko's parents were like prison guards, Azusa's were permissive. Shoko's parents were adamantly opposed to interracial or international unions, but Azusa's whole family embraced me categorically. While I had met both Azusa's parents, both sets of grandparents, uncles and aunts on both her mother and father's side, Shoko's sister was the only person I had met on a regular basis and only briefly did I meet her father. During my only visit to her home, her mother refused to meet me.

Returning to Japan in January 2005, Azusa's parents, over dinner in the presence of my future brother-in-law, thanked me profusely for traveling with and ensuring the safety of their daughter.

RAPUNZEL & YEAR THREE IN JAPAN

Year three in Japan brought about clear signs of over-ejaculation; photosensitive vision with floaters flying around in my field of view, semi flaccid erections, no semen upon ejaculation and even impotence, especially at the sight of a condom, which became a regular occurrence. Other than being a strung-out, yellow-fevered sex junkie, condom erectile dysfunction was another contributing factor to my practice of unprotected sex in Japan. First experienced at 29 years old during my senior year at university, sudden malfunction of the tool was a distressing jolt to the psyche.

Rapunzel was a heart-stomping nuclear meets atom bombshell whom I had met in Campbell Hall. Eighteen, from a Swedish father and German mother, Norma Jean would aspire to be her in her next life. With authentic mane of gold streaming down to her *nubianesque* aerobics-carved posterior, she bounced and bubbled, flashing her flawless, auroral smile, sex appeal dripping from every pore even shabbily clad in sweat pants and a t-shirt. On our first date she proclaimed to me that her first orgasm was at the tender age of eight, in a manner that only she could have thought of. At that age, she confessed, she applied peanut butter to her pleasure zone only to have her cat remove it with his rough tongue.

"How clever for an 8-year-old," I thought, genuinely impressed and happy to hear of our early childhood feline experiences in common. Rapunzel, was the desire of men black, white, young, old, rich and poor, but evident from her vernacular, Little Miss Golidie Locks was a die-hard *chocoholic,* blacker than BET. Possessing a supreme combination of the four Bs; beauty, booty, bust and brain, she was my indefectible fantasy girl in the flesh. To date, no other woman I have met has held so paradisiacally and owned that amalgam with such confidence or air thereof.

"No one could be that cocksure, she must have some kind of emotional Achilles' heel," I reassured myself, trying hard not to make her see me sweat. Former head of her cheer leading squad and high school Valedictorian, fantasy girl chose UCLA over Ivy League universities because, "I didn't wanna leave

my mom," who raised her and two brothers in the absence of their fathers. The chance to analyze her never availed itself, as soon we were whipped up in a passionate tornado, desperately holding on for our lives trying to catch our breath. Her exhibitionism held me captive, especially when she wore my favourite skin-toned crocheted dress, minus undies. With pink nipples and immaculately manicured blond botany trying to catch air, the silhouette of her defect free bust and the slightly visible breach of her circular protruding derriere, she was greeted by honking cars as spectators heads turned in whiplash.

Man eater extraordinaire, she was regularly showered with gifts from jewelry to big ticket items, from men just wanting to be in her presence. In one case when she was 15, a staff member at her high school, after buying her a new sports car, divorced his wife of twenty years, under the misguided impression that they were going be together. For years she strung him on, jerking him around like a rag doll, even while we were together.

Starving senior year student, I too was plummeting in this abyss, or ascending in the frenzy of passion, but she would accompany me on my journey. At her mother's apartment on our first night together, after an extended hedonistic shower followed by hours of foreplay until three in the morning, I grew to dimensions never before seen. But reaching for the Trojans, it was as though magician David Copperfield had performed one of his tricks and my scud was reduced to a strand of overcooked spaghetti. Manhood dismembered, shredded and obliterated, ego massacred, my immediate response was to activate damage control by pretending, "*I didn't wanna be with her anyway,*" or come clean and confess my condition.

An awful panic set in. For there I was 29 years old, "welcome to Jamaican, enjoy your stay" in bold typeface emblazoned on the equipment, but soon I would be on Oprah. "Meet Stefhen Bryan a young Jamaican in his twenties, who, is, impotent." Images flashed through my mind of Bob Dole's public service announcement on erectile dysfunction. A disgrace to my race and nationality, from that moment on, I thought, I would take offense to the casual greeting, "how's it hanging?" I imagined her ridicule. After all Rapunzel was pretty much a white Li'l Kim, who had mastered African-American mannerisms, speech and attitudes. Though white on the outside, to the chagrin of her KKK wannabe father, Rapunzel was all black within. Sexual underperformance among Jamaican and African-American men is brutally ridiculed by women of the same nationality and ethnicity. Hence, Rapunzel being *African-American*, I could almost hear her conversation with her friends. "Who? Dat nigga? His shit died!" Dreading the approach of dawn, I began to think of places to go into exile, where we would never be able lay eyes on each other again, because, unlike Japanese men I and a great many Negroe men, derived a significant part of our manhood from the sexual pleasure we are able to provide women.

Recalling Richard Prior's openness and frankness about the human condition,
"I don't know what happened, but my dick just died," were my exact words. And what emerged from her lips was the shock of many reincarnations.
"Is it me? Is it something I did?"
And it was then that I discovered that like all humans, my fantasy girl also has insecurities. For why else would the most arousing woman with whom I'd been to date, inquire about her possible deficiencies? Not knowing how to proceed from there, I rang my roommate and best friend Sebastian and explained the situation.

"It's 4 o'clock in the bleedin' morning!" was his response. In my attempts to cope with this new crisis, as if chronic depression weren't crippling enough, I decided to tell everyone, strangers included. In fact transforming my tragedy with a comedic twist I began using it when initiating conversation with beautiful women on campus.
"Excuse me. Can I ask you a question? I would interrupt. When you look at me, what do you see?" I opened. To which they'd respond with a list of adjectives.
"You don't see IMPOTENCE, now do you? Which got them exploding in laughter.
"It's true, you may think its funny, but I think it's tragic."
Then I assured them that's it was perfectly fine to give up the digits, as given my state, they could be sure that I wouldn't just be after sex.

Interestingly, all of my female friends to whom I lamented about my condition reassured me that I was indeed more than my phallus, and that I should "get over it already." But all my male friends extended their support by offering to drive me to the Golden Gate bridge.

The following day I visited the doctor on campus, who tried to reassure me that such events were normal and I may well have been over aroused. After a terrifying 48 hours, normalcy was regained and Rapunzel and I were hurled in a rapturous, Mack truck of a relationship, only seen in films. Instead of *9 ½ Weeks*, our movie would have been *9 ½ Months, One Miscarriage and Two Abortions* – Coming soon to theatres near you.

For almost one year, nowhere was spared, not the garage at our apartment complex where I'd hoist her crocheted dress and bend her over the bonnette of her RX7, to the playground of the elementary school on campus, to the Catholic House where I stayed for a few months. A fine of a thousand dollars each would have been levied had we been caught. For days at a time it was impossible to pry ourselves from each other's arms, except to relieve ourselves. And even then the process was in tandem, as I had mastered the act of urinating between her legs while she sat. Academic probation letters mounted in our mailboxes, as we blew off several midterms and final exams. Shortly thereafter, I was relieved of my-on campus job. Terror smitten but electrified by the emotional avalanches of raw, primitive lust, love, need and lecherous cupidity, neither of us could fathom an existence within more than an inch of each other. Her entire mouth was like food, with her lips, lower section of her upper lip slightly elevated in the middle, being dessert. Like the cat in her childhood, head firmly planted between her thighs, I often feasted on her for hours, swelling her *lips* and bringing her to multiple orgasms.

Completely out of control, on the third pregnancy in nine months, just weeks after the second was terminated, in an attempt at responsible behavior, and accepting our perfervid emotions for each other, we decided to marry. Things were out of hand and two pregnancies in eight weeks? That was too crazy. However, fear got the better of us and we opted to abort, which put a stop to our marriage plans. Finding no other viable means of wresting control from this drug, immediately after graduation I fled, not just the state, but the entire North American continent. And it is to this day that *Little Blonde Riding Hood* is the zenith of my sexual experience.

The tendency to lose my erection at the sight of a condom, resurfaced only after being strung out in Japan and upon finally acknowledging my condition, a break from the crack house was the only prescription. Again as with my months with Rapunzel, things got well out of hand. However, instead of just one sex partner, there were up to 17 at one time. My childhood fantasy had materialized, bringing with it stress which bordered that of my university life. My apartment in this upper-middle class, Palo Alto-esque Kobe suburb was a revolving door of pleasure mates, from 18 to 46, single, married, divorced, single mother, house wives, virgins, medical resident, office ladies and women whose names I didn't even know. Among the nameless and faceless, was a woman I took home 30 minutes after meeting her at a nearby Family Mart convenience store. With the lady in red deterring us from getting busy that night, she apologized profusely for the inconvenience, gave me fellatio, thanked me for the opportunity and guaranteed me she'd return after the lady's departure. Four days later she reappeared at my door. Another was a 27-year-old professor of English whom I had met at the JR Nishinomiya Station, who after two sexual encounters threatened to call the department of immigration if I didn't marry her. Recognizing the futility of her threats, she solicited the help of a male friend who telephoned me with news of her alleged suicide, since I had refused to make her my bride.

From the looks of things I by no means was alone in the crackhouse, many African-Americans, especially those in music, were also struggling, overwhelmed with this sex on tap.

"I have to ask the Lord for help," one brother joked, dead serious.

On the other hand, not having a *Lord* to turn to, I had to take matters in my own hands, which drove me to a convenience store in pursuit of a porn magazine. In the West, it is quite common for men to purchase pornographic magazines in the absence of a sex partner, but here I was in Japan, consuming porn because I had too many sex partners and desperately sought attrition. In the mornings before setting out to work, I would pleasure myself to reduce my sex drive, so that on the train I would simply bury my head in my International Herald Tribune/Daily Yomiuri newspaper, not making eye contact with anyone. For a short while this proved effective, but the reality was, in an effort to detoxify, there was no choice but to flee the environment.

JAMAICA MARCH

Jamaica, where the women of my preference hardly existed, would be perfect for detoxification. Many of my friends thought I was jumping from the frying pan into the fire, but little did they know of my hyper-specialized attraction. By then it was virtually impossible to become aroused by any other than yellow women. Moreover, even if I could have overcome my Mongoloid flu, having lived in *soapland* where I fished with a large bowl in a bath tub, it would have been impossible to readjust to the patience required when fishing with a line in the real world. I had grown accustomed to sex on tap in Japan. In any event I was not going to Jamaica for sex, but to escape it. In addition, having been previously embroiled in baby mama drama, or almshouse business, as we Jamaicans refer to it, intimacy with the natives was out of the question. Attrition was also another benefit of escaping to Jamaica. In my mind, absence away from both my prospective wives would bound to cause one, or both to leave. For though I had given in to the reality that I was well on my way to bigamy, time away from them both would at least reveal who was completely committed and who would have defected. Or so I thought.

As it turned out, probability which had been working in my favour since my arrival in Japan, again was on my side when I was made redundant from my cushy junior high school job which I had secured when Henni stood me up in the rain some three years back. It had also availed me with the opportunity to begin a partnership shipping salvaged cars from Japan to Jamaica, even though it would be in a part of the island I had most despised since my childhood. Resultantly, in March 2005 I arrived in Santa Cruz, a small town in the very rural Parish of St. Elizabeth, where for five months I entertained and pleasured myself daily, many times twice a day, with a collection of pictures and videos of both wives to be and other women, on two cell phones I had taken with me.

While in Jamaica, Shoko, now best friends with her digital camera provided me daily enticement. She had become increasingly skilled at taking pornographic photos of herself in all manner of beckoning positions and angles, especially exposing her rump, which she knew was my deity. Demure, prissy and extraordinarily sentimental – much more so than Azusa - she sent me off on my trip with good luck charms and her usual heartbreaking, tear jerking letters of love and deathless, illimitable devotion, whose composition required endless hours of slaving with a dictionary.

"And anyone, anything will not able to stop me from loving you," she penned in her farewell card. As a compromise since I had been spending far more time with her, Azusa, in consideration for Shoko's feelings understood my request to be seen off by Shoko at Kansai Airport, especially since it was already established that she, Azusa would visit me in the summer. Fully aware of Azusa's advantage yet again, Shoko sent a daily barrage of photos, doing her best to ensure that she would be at the forefront of my thoughts.

In what was among the most under-developed parishes on the island, with frequent interruptions in water and electricity, having never seen me with a woman, hazardous rumors began spreading among the locals that there was a homosexual in their midst and on one occasion, a proposition was even extended. The danger of this gossip was by no means owing to any homophobia on my part, for having emigrated from the island 24 years prior, I had long since lost such primeval inscience.

After moving to San Francisco at 21 in 1985, I had still retained this primitivism from my socialization, though not strong enough to support gay killings, but enough to support them being beaten. The catalyst came while dating Marissa, an alarmingly beautiful woman of half Iranian, a quarter Italian and a quarter Irish decent, whose parents were adamantly opposed to our union. In fact, her step-father's father had been active in the Klu Klux Klan and was deeply disturbed by her choice, which also further strained relations between her and her Iranian father. "Vy nigger?" She joked, mimicking her father's disgust. Her mother's parents, Italian mother (Noni) and Irish father (Papa) were the only supporters, frequently validating us and advising us to ignore ignorance.
"You twos love each other, that's all that matters."

During one of our frequent stimulating discussions, Marissa inquired about my response to our hypothetically gay son.
"He wouldn't be my son, he would have to leave. No fucking way, I would disown him. He could never set foot in my house," I rebuked.
"Exactly how you would feel about our son being gay is exactly how my parents and the parents of other white women you've dated feel about you

now."

It was an epiphany, and after a few rebuttals of lame defensive denial, I was forced to acknowledge her truth and modify my thinking.

It may not have been known internationally but since my childhood I was fully aware that Jamaica, this barbaric land of my birth, is the most vehemently and religiously homophobic place on earth, where one can be hacked to death just on rumors of being gay. Losing my life was not among the reasons I had traveled there. In "Hated to Death," Rebecca Schleifer of the American-based Human Rights Watch confirms this in her biting and accurate report on the island's entrenched homophobia. In the year prior to my arrival, on June 5th 2004, Brian Williamson, a noted Jamaican gay rights activist, the island's Martin Luther King Jr. of gay rights, was slaughtered in the most barbarous fashion. Williamson, co-founder of the Jamaican Forum for Lesbians and Gays (J-FLAG), a man known for personally providing refuge for homosexuals on the island and actively tracking down gays who had suffered discrimination, was savaged by machete and suffered some seventy, as in 7-0 – not 17 – wounds to the neck and face. Though a crowd even celebrated over Williamson's mutilated body, Police downplayed the *solomassacre* as motivated by robbery as opposed to homophobia or hatred of Williamson's lifelong work.

Also in June of the same year, internationally known dancehall artist Buju Banton, along with some other hooligans, charged into a gay man's house, pummeled him and five others with kicks and blows with planks, relieving the targeted homosexual of an eye. Banton, whose most popular song "Boom by by," a call to arms to murder gays, was charged only after pressure from international human-rights groups, but in January of 2006 the case was dismissed for lack of evidence. "Boom by by," incidentally is an onomatopoeia for gun fire, which Banton implores us to direct at homosexuals' heads.

Continuing in 2004, a man after learning of his teenage son's sinful ways, invited a mob to lynch him at school and later that year, with the support and encouragement of the police, a reprobate mob stabbed and stoned a gay man to death in Montego Bay. Three months after my September departure from that year's per capita murder capital of the world, Lenford Harvey who ran Jamaica AIDS Support for Life, was gunned down on the eve of World AIDS Day. Harvey's organization provides support to gay men and sex workers and upon breaking into his home, gunmen confronted him and his two roommates regarding their sexuality. The roommates denied being gay and were only gagged and bounded, while Harvey having remained silent, was forced into his company vehicle and kidnapped, only to be found dead two hours later.

January 2006, Nokia Cowan was pursued by a bloodthirsty posse shouting "batty boy," the equivalent of 'faggot.' In a desperate attempt to flee from the beasts, Cowan leapt into Kingston Harbour unable to swim and perished in the vile waters thereof. In Cowan's case, it was only alleged that he was gay. Cowan's experience replicated scenes I had personally witnessed at 9 years old, in the slums of Dunkirk. Valentines Day 2007, a mob attacked two gay men in Half Way Tree, who luckily took refuge in a department store until Police arrived. Even whilst being escorted in police custody, barbarians were still hurling blows and attacking the Police for carrying out their duties. Twice in April 2007 in the rural town of Falmouth cave dwellers descended on two gays. On one occasion, the police intervened taking the victim to hospital, where the vicious mob was awaiting the victim's release, in order to resume the beatings. Such is the magnitude of homophobia in this alleged island paradise, many gays are forced to seek asylum abroad. In fact, it's reported that the first Jamaican man to win asylum based on sexual orientation did so in 1998 in New York.

Respite from my manual intercourse came with Azusa's visit three months later, whose arrival with her glamorous movie star looks, parading on my arms in hot pants or daisy dukes, quelled any rumors about my sexuality. Along with the pleasantries and hospitality of most Jamaicans, she, like all other women who had accompanied me to Jamaica, was often greeted by crass and lewd remarks in the island's vernacular, indiscernible to her.

"A weh mek fi har pussy suh fat?" in reference to her slightly protruding pubic mound, was a common remark among women.
"Fat pussy chinie gyal, beg yu a fuck nuh," bellowed some uncivilized men, which by no means surprised me. This uncouth behavior was the norm in my childhood and most embarrassing during visits to the island with other foreign women.

Enquiring minds wanted to know who Azusa was and I relished in their shock when I informed them that she was one of two marriage candidates, who were very aware of each other. Most men wanted to know where we met, how they could get to Japan, or if she had any friends to whom they could be introduced. Desperately seeking a way out, like I was as a child, many beseeched with her to intercede with her friends on their behalf, upon her return home. Azusa's month long visit was the only time the celibacy was broken and it was during that time we made plans to tie the knot, after reinforcing to her that it would be impossible to leave Shoko, since I had promised her marriage a year before Azusa and I had met. Initially uncomfortable with the idea when it was first proposed, in her liberal expansive thinking, - one of her many characteristics which I exalted – though recognizing the difficulty, she accepted this double marriage, especially since we spent more time together than Shoko and I.

"I can't leave either of you," I explained, just as I had done to Shoko. "I love both of you."

Earlier, friends had suggested leaving them both, but that too was indubitably out of the question.

"But if either or both of you are, or become, unhappy and want to leave, that would be completely understandable."

Leaving either of these women would be tantamount to severing one of my arms, for though I'm right handed, I am by no means willing to part with my left. In her open-mindedness she endeavored to make it work. Like Shoko, who was also initially uncomfortable with the plan, Azusa thought it better to share me than to be without me.

Among the bounteous memorable experiences of our month together in Jamaica, was our day pass at Hedonism III, a resort on the north coast of the island where anything goes. Those subscribing to the teachings of the bible, firmly believe that when their Lord returns to earth, he most certainly will make an appearance at this resort, not as a guest mind you, but to rain down fire and brimstone on the premises. It was here among the liberated others that Azusa and I frolicked along the beach, natural as the day we were born, baring her perfectly proportioned, naturally tanned physique to a naked audience. Unable to control my nature - the result of viewing all the activities - the muscle rose to full mast as we strolled together to take refuge on a pool side chair. On my back, timber pointing skyward, Azusa mounted and proceeded to ride as if her life depended on it. Moments later as her untamed mane thrashed to and fro, her otherwise dainty nostrils began to flair. Head flung backward, she released her usual high-pitched squeals followed by a protracted grunt. Gradually opening her eyes after her enraptured gallop, I signaled her to dismount, as I was dropping anchor. And tilting her head to the right, she smiled, bashful and self-conscious, upon realizing that we had applauding spectators, some of whom were masturbating to our performance.

"Man, that was awesome," shouted one voice.

"Yeah!" Exclaimed others.

A portly, balding man who had been our closest voyeur approached, hardened phallus in hand.

"I love the way your wife moves. Could we have a threesome?"

"We're not really into the threesome thing, we are just exhibitionists. But thanks anyway." I replied, as she drew closer to me, oblivious to his request.

"Nan te?" (What did he say?)

"San pi hoshikatta." (He wanted to have a threesome.)

Had he been significantly more appealing, I would have loved to watch them together.

"No problem," he replied. "Man, you guys were great," as we thanked our fans and bade our good-byes. That event lead to our decision to hold a nude wedding at Hedonism, but to our dismay they were discontinued on account of protests from the overwhelming religious conservatives on the island

Saddened by Azusa's departure and homesick for Japan, my stay took on a torturous complexion, leading me to redirect my energies to survey my native land for evidence of change as I waited to leave. Not only was this an attempt to occupy my time before departure but, at 40 I wanted to explore the environment in which I grew up and experience it as an adult. *"Was it really that bad?"* I wondered. Could it have caused me so much long suffering and enervating depression from such a young age? The answers were stark, as in the two and a half decades since my fifteenth birthday, there were only marginal improvements on the status quo from 1980.

Deplaning at the Montego Bay airport immediately launched me face to face with the stark increase in the probability of dieing. Perhaps it was because at forty, having in essence started to enjoy life only five years prior, and or because my country of reference was now the unspeakably safe Japan as opposed to the United States, the fifty mile journey to Santa Cruz was a heart stopping exercise of death taunting proportions, as the driver, one of my business partners showcased his aeronautic, acrobatic driving skills.

"Everyting cool brejrin, mi 'ave it aunda control," he reassured me in response to my prediction that "everyday the bucket goes to the well, one day the bottom will fall out, and I don't wish for it to fall out with me in it." But his words did not stop the constant images of my life flashing in front of me, which continued on a regular basis for the remaining six months.

Outside of the white-sand, blue water havens of the developed tourist areas and mansions of the affluent communities, death, from which most of the natives seemed habituated, hovered in the atmosphere. I too was among the acclimatized, but having left for so long and especially after a pleasure filled, trauma free life in Japan, bereavement in Jamaica was ubiquitous. It is with uncanny and prodigious accuracy that Junior Gong's hit of the same year "Welcome to Jamrock" described the state of the nation. Immediately upon arrival, unable to catch my breath in a town smoldering from massive forest fires, I soon developed life threatening respiratory problems requiring medical attention. No more than two weeks after my arrival, on a quiet stroll into town one Sunday afternoon, I was jolted by a woman screaming at the top of her lungs, carrying her discolored, lifeless toddler from a small private clinic.

"Him dead! Jesus Christ, mi baby dead! She hollered in hysteria, trailed by her shouting mother.

"A obeah dem obeah mi gran pickney." (Someone put a curse on my grandchild.)

Far from the killing fields of *Killsome*, as Kingston was referred to by the natives, my most frequent confrontation with the grim reaper was on the roads, in overcrowded route taxis from Santa Cruz to Mandeville in the adjacent parish of Manchester. Just two weeks earlier, my daily routine consisted of a relaxing fifteen minute bicycle ride to the train station, where I would board the tranquil special rapid, begin firing off e-mails on my 3G cell phone to my friends around the world, read the newspaper, chat up local women, or otherwise catch up on my sleep. But now here I was in sardine packed taxis - older toyota corollas, designed for five passengers but routinely carrying eight or nine - blazing down breathtakingly beautiful Spur Tree Hill – what may well be the most dangerous roads in Jamaica – at 120kph. Having walked away from countless major traffic accidents in my teenage years, it was most unnerving to sit passively participating in experiments taunting the hands of probability. Older and wiser, I knew it wasn't if, but a matter of when I would have been a helpless passenger in one of those mangled cars I frequently passed on Spur Tree.

There was a ubiquitous sentiment that life was cheap, as there was nothing for which to exist when subsisting in abject poverty, and having been there, having worn those same shoes, or no shoes at all, I could sympathize and empathize. Literally fearing for my life, I began to interview my prospective taxi drivers, about their driving habits and assured them that at anytime during the journey, if my life was threatened by their driving, I would request a stop and disembark without payment. Of course, this was not expressed in English, but in the Jamaican Patois, as English would have been far too pious a means of communication for these circumstances.

Upon approval of their driving, I would take their telephone numbers and contact them directly for their transportation services, often times waiting for their arrival. In my four months in Santa Cruz, there were at least four fatal accidents along the Mandeville to Santa Cruz route, one involving a driver with whom I had vowed never to travel again. Critically injured he survived, but a woman in the front passenger seat on her way to delivery at the Mandeville hospital, perished along with her unborn child, though her critically injured 5-year-old daughter in the rear seat somehow survived. Two months after my departure from the island, as I had predicted, the bottom of the bucket fell out when my former business partner wrote off his car but managed to escape with his life. But by the end of 2005 some three hundred people including former classmate and star footballer Peter Cargill, were not so lucky, succumbing to the high probability of road fatalities in Jamaica.

Had it been possible to overcome my anxiety over their driving habits, the murder rate would prove impossible to ignore. Jamaica with a population of 2.7million, in that year for at least the second time in my lifetime, reclaimed the world record for murders per capita. One thousand six hundred and seventy-one people were felled, an increase of 200 over the previous year. Over 100 children's lives were extinguished, including two girls ages seven and eight found in a cane field in the parish of my visit. But the most stunning of the child murders was that of a 6-year-old girl in Kingston, who had been raped by her condom wearing assailant prior to the murder. Immediately I saw arrant parallels between the gruesome child murders in Jamaica and those I had left in Japan, for though the two countries are diametric opposites in some sense, they are also alarmingly similar. Among the murdered that year, was a senior member of the Azan family and his Chinese son-in-law. Of Middle Eastern decent, the Azans are among Jamaica's richest and most influential families, the murder of whose senior prompted the Private Sector of Jamaica to initiate a nationwide closure of businesses, apparently in protest of the killing spree gripping the island. However, the achievements of such remonstrance was unclear other than reinforcing what impoverished Jamaicans of African descent had already suspected: that the lives of the influential non-African minority are far more important than those of the poverty stricken African masses. For had it not been so, a 6-year-old being raped and murdered would have caused an island wide shut down for decades. It is the height of irony that the nation with the highest murder rate per capita, also sports the most churches per square mile.

HOOKED ON THE CRUCIFIX

The writings of Maximilian Weber 1864 -1920, one of the founding fathers of modern sociology, provided definitive answers to this paradox and an explanation to why Jamaica possesses such an unquenchable penchant for permanent and steeped entrenchment in antidevelopment. In Weber's analysis, it was religion which was the incubator for economic development as Protestants broke away from the Catholic Church and deemed nothing sinful about earning profits and improving their economics. Weber identified two currents; one which favours the poor and the other which prefers the rich and successful. He labeled the former, (Roman Catholics) *Publican* and the latter (Protestants) *Pharisaic* and notes that any society where the Publican form is dominant, will be resistant to development, as the poor will see their plight as justified and the rich, even subconsciously, will view themselves as sinners.

But Weber's theory was turned on its head in Jamaica where over 60% are Protestants, only 4% Catholic, while more than 34% are of other sects including spiritualist cults. In Jamaica, it's the Protestants who take on Publican traits, handicapping the masses while Catholicism is the sect of the elite. In order to maintain full control over slaves, Protestant missionaries who transplanted Africans to Jamaica refrained from extolling the virtues of self-empowerment, erstwhile a cornerstone of the Protestant movement. In its stead they emphasized patience for rewards in the afterlife. With over 60% worshipping in oppressive Publican sects and more than 34% in superstitious cults, the minds of over 95% of Jamaicans are entangled in deity worship deleterious to economic development.

My mother a seamstress of the highest order and a devout member of the Church of God, possessing no more than a 9th grade education and no vocational training, in the absence of a pattern could replicate a Versace suit just from a magazine picture. However, instead of utilizing her talents for economic upliftment, she chose to remain in squalid deprivation, doing the *Lord's* work, making her church sisters' clothes free of charge.

"What does it profit a man to gain the whole world and lose his own soul?" "The meek shall inherit the earth" and, "It's easier for a camel to pass through the eye of a needle, than for a rich man to enter into the kingdom of heaven," she constantly chanted, upon listening to my many childish inquiries about her then asinine decisions.

In retrospect, she too may well have been suffering from debilitating depression which she opiated with the crucifix. By no means was she isolated in her crucifixion addiction, this was and still is one of the many, albeit less destructive opiates on the island, a legacy of days gone by when Protestant Christian missionaries introduced enslaved Africans to the island for economic gain. Those like me, lacking the ability of self-delusion – a skill necessary for proper mental health – perilously hurled themselves in the ocean. Generations later in contemporary Jamaica, the religion that tricks them into survival is the same religion which keeps them passively trapped in survival mode, awaiting their expiration, or for the return of their Lord to deliver them to the land of milk and honey.

Spending the first fifteen years of my life in a God-obsessed cesspool of an environment, my preparation to enter Uncle Sam's pearly gates or the real world in general, was at best inadequate. Though most of the cesspit years were spent opposing my defeatist socialization, some parts of it managed to seep through and many of those said handicapping ideologies were internalized. Among the rubbish I was taught as a child was that prayer was the only way to achieve and if one did not pray enough, or one's achievements were not the will of God, they will not materialize. Such learned handicap, coupled with disabling and endless severe depression contributed to the acute absence of successes in my life then. I hated prayer. I simply just did not believe. But I was brave enough to reject those doctrines and a great deal of my socialization, even in the face of no alternatives.

Landing on American soil and experiencing the epiphany of having to do things for myself was jarring beyond belief. Most discombobulating, decades before my introduction to Max Weber's writings, was the epiphanous discovery that the same God who frowned on financial wealth in Jamaica, promoted it in the United States. It was a massive shock to learn that the Billy Graham to whom my poverty stricken mother would donate money, at the expense of my going without lunch, was an extremely wealthy man. Also visible was a dynamic where Americans of European descent, the majority, were Pharisaic while those of African descent, similar to my Jamaican contemporaries, were Publican. At popular entertainment awards, upon accepting trophies or other objects of recognition presented to them, African-Americans usually first thank their God, while European-Americans thank their parents first.

INTERVENTION

Wednesday, February 2nd 1980 may well have been the most impacting date of my entire existence. Thanks to my then step-mother - who for 10 years pressured my absent father into sponsoring his son's green card - my escape from Jamaica at 15 years old has been to date the only gift from my father. My arrival in the States coincided with an era when African-Americans, before they referred to themselves as such, were painfully inhospitable to Africans from other parts of the Diaspora, or to their own African heritage. Bob Marley among other reggae entertainers frequently lamented the absence of African-American faces at his concerts. Ironically back then, the most afrocentric audience members throughout the United States were whites.

"All I always si is a sea a white people," I heard Bob once comment in an interview.

Except for the enlightened few, African-Americans then steeped in inferiority complexes sought to distance themselves from anything African. I too suffered those inferiority complexes so I'm able to identify them. However, having been born and raised in Jamaica, regardless of my own self-hate then, given the ubiquity of an Africa centered socialization and the back to Africa fantasy purported in reggae music and by the Rastafarians, I had no doubt that my ancestors were Africans.

Indeed it would not be until the mid to late eighties that African-Americans began to embrace their African ancestry en masse. First manifesting in the short lived fad of the leather African medallion in 1986, the movement gathered momentum after the marriage between reggae and hip hop, thanks to pioneering crossover artists the likes of Shabba Ranks and Shinehead. Further gratitude was due to a growing presence of Jamaican artists in mainstream hip hop, such as Heavy D and Busta Rhymes. Steely and Cleevy's "We Are the Champion" was a breakthrough in the reghop amalgamation. The end of the eighties saw many African-Americans scraping to claim some great great Jamaican grand parent in order to affirm some connection with the island. In just ten years I had gone from being asked by African-Americans, questions such as, "where's the bone in your nose?" Or, "How are you getting used to wearing clothes in America?" to being en vogue.

Adding insult to my dismay, African-Americans I had encountered initially were quite the opposite to those I had envied on the pages of Jet, Right On and Ebony magazines. A great many were poor, much poorer than whites. In fact, at that time over 50% or more of African-Americans were at or below the poverty level, a percentage which has seen dramatic improvement in 26 years. According to 2005 statistics, 25% are considered poor. Before emigrating to America, in my naiveté I simply thought that like Jamaica, Africans were the majority. Hence arriving in America and observing such widespread poverty among Negroes, all but confirmed that yes, the people of my race, this race to which I was attached for life, were doomed it seem internationally. Once again after examining my surroundings, I was left holding a bag of questions to which no one had answers.

Immediately upon my first day of high school, I was struck by an epiphany: things in America were either black or white, as were one's actions and behaviour. Activities which hitherto were colorless, were now color coded. Homework was white, truancy was black. A strong desire for international travel was white, hanging out at the *crib* getting high was black. Driving a new car was white, driving a rust bucket was black. Attending university after high school was white, while handling baggage, or working in the flight kitchen at Stapleton International airport - my first job at 16 - was black. Ever since seeing the intro of ABC's wild world of sports as a child, where as the voice-over states "and the agony of defeat," a skier tumbles down the slopes, I had harbored a deep rooted fantasy to ski. However, upon arrival in Colorado, I learned that skiing was white, a massive portable hi-fi at one's ear was black. At 15 in 1980, had it not been clear to other teenagers of African descent - again with no one to answer my questions - the message was explicit and lucent to me: Success was white, failure was black. I had no intentions of associating with failure, which given my self-hate at the time, on the surface justified my dissociation from African-Americans. But the fact of the matter was, *failure* had no intentions of associating with me, so I and other Africans from the Diaspora were outcasts, constantly referred to as Uncle Toms.

In December of 1980, a whopping 3 months after my 10th grade debut, I made the bold move to withdraw from high school to sit the equivalency exam after learning that the primary education system in Jamaica was two grades superior to that of the United States.' Though having repeated the

9th grade and placed 39th in a class of 40 students, TJ - white Boulderite, but more Jamaican than I - assured me I would have had no problems with the exams. "You come from Jamrock mon," in his excruciatingly bad Jamaican accent. "You will mash up dat test." He was right.

With no legal guardian at 16 years old, observing (white) Americans, bustling to and fro, well groomed, suited and armed with attaché cases in downtown Denver, I desperately sought answers. Mustering the courage to approach them at random, pretending to be on a school assignment, I inquired about their professions and how they got there. They were *Directors of Marketing, Investment Bankers, Reporters for the Denver Post,* and held other titles most of which I had never heard. Upon inquiring about the processes through which they obtained their positions, not one mentioned *the mercies of God*, or the *goodness of the Lord*. In fact, to my shock and awe, church, blessings, or Jesus were absent from all their responses. Instead, they all mentioned their pursuits after university and while their pursuits varied, university was constant among them all. This was in antipodal contrast with my indoctrination, where only God could determine one's success, if it were in HIS will. Observing this I was hell bent on becoming *white*. Along with wearing my seatbelt at sixteen long before it was even mandated by law, though knowing nothing about universities, I had to find the means of attending one, in order to emulate white Americans, even if it meant being buried in debt. For it was better I concluded, to be educated and in debt than to be debt free and uneducated.

JAMAICA CONTINUED

Skyscraping levels of sexual charge contribute to Jamaica's abundant afflictions. No doubt another opiate of the masses, sexual stimuli ooze from every crevice of the society. From lyrics in the music and the accompanying videos to the ever present batty rider (daisy dukes), to the infinite display of cleavage. Hot Fuck, simulating rough sex, is a popular dance craze on the island. The World Health Organization defines regular sexual relations as those lasting more than a year and in Jamaica, multiple regular sexual relations – the likes of which I practiced in Japan - are the norm, practiced by 54% of men and 30% of women. While women cited economic support for their families, as the primary reason for engaging in this practice, for men it was simply a matter of sexual adventure and variety, proving their virility, and gaining status in the community, particularly among their male peers. During my childhood, boys aspired to be *cocksmen*, collecting as many sex partners and baby mothers as possible.

We Jamaicans become sexualized very early in life. In one study, 69% of men and 48% of women had their first sexual experiences before 16 years old. High schoolteachers in Mandeville bemoaned to me, the frequency with which students were caught in unabashed copulation at school. But such social hyper-sexuality in a threesome with capacious exiguity and another infrequently addressed social scourge, make for terrible bed partners. Colossal would be a euphemism to describe the paternal abandonment rate of children in Jamaica. Over 50% of all children there are born to absent fathers. It may well be that nowhere near 50% of Jamaican fathers abandon their children, for I would very much like to think that most fathers on the island, especially in the rural areas, behave responsibly toward their offsprings. However, the high fertility rate of the minority of fathers, with their multiple *byaby madda*, perpetuate this despicable legacy of slavery.

Historically in West Africa, where most Jamaicans originated, a man's masculinity and status were elevated by high fertility. This model was perfectly compatible with the institution of slavery and its insatiable need for live bodies, as it illegitimized the role of father and husband among

273

slaves. Historians believe that over two-thirds of adult men who were fathers, did not cohabitate and often did not even live on the same farm with their partners and offsprings. Two hundred and fifty years after the beginning of slavery, enjoined from social status in general and denied their rights to their children and partners, in order to assert some semblance of male pride, men compensated by re-avowing the transplanted West African model of virility and high fertility.

Unsecured paternity is another negative externality of slavery, as Massa assumed responsibility to provide for the children of slaves while encouraging them to multiply the land as much as possible without responsibilities. During my childhood and to this day, it is a common tenet among men of the uneducated masses that real men don't take care of their children. That's for wimps. A real man's responsibility is to simply provide the sperm. Male pride is defined among many – formerly present company included – in terms of impregnation of women. Massa's double standard role model of sexual predator also shaped the thinking of his slaves. More recently, the elimination of racial barriers in popular athletics has resulted in the ascension of young African-American mega-star athletes, most hailing from disadvantaged backgrounds. The number of these larger than life characters may be microscopic in comparison to poverty stricken Africans in the Diaspora, but their influence as role models is planetary, reinforcing ideas of predatory sexuality and unsecured paternity.

A contemporary ingredient to the milieu is the unstoppable rise of hip hop culture, notably *gangsta rap*, bringing with it exalting glorification of sexual predation and paternal abandonment. It is common knowledge that America holds vast inescapable cultural influences over the world and in so doing, African-America along with its dominant influence in pop culture internationally, is especially emulated by Africans throughout the Diaspora. Hence, as hip hop and popular sports have normalized these destructive social models among poor inner-city African-American young men, seeking to emulate their brethrens overseas, ghetto youths in Jamaica so too have normalized the dysfunction.

MY CONTRIBUTION TO THE STATISTIC

Just as I had been conceived in this sexually predatory and paternally unsecured kinesics, in honoring the social model, so was my daughter. After reneging on wedding plans with Simone Chang, she had a nervous breakdown at 21 and I was engulfed in guilt. At 19 years old, high school dropout in the tentacles of depression, I had absolutely no idea what I wanted to pursue. In fact, I had no idea if I would have been alive from day to day, as I had set several dates for my exit, but lacked the courage to carry out the plans. Existing in a dark and dismal cocoon, though I had no idea what I wanted in life, except for death, it was perfectly clear what I did not want: to be stuck working in newspaper assembly, in essence factory work, married and saddled with the responsibilities of children. In my crystal ball then, I saw myself as a future mass murderer, solving my problems in Japanese fashion, offing my wife and children and then, most definitely myself. Recognizing this, I canceled our wedding plans by phone.

Back then in my naiveté I equated alleviation of guilt with spending large wads of cash and though our marriage would have been her only reason for emigrating to the States, I convinced her that emigrating would be in her best interest, even though there was no hope that we would marry. She adamantly objected.
"I don't want to go to America if we're not getting married," she grumbled. But already I had solicited the services of a friend, an American citizen who would travel to Jamaica, marry her and return with her to the States, all for a whopping $5000 in 1984, just so I could shed the guilt.

Immediately upon her arrival, it was clear that I had spent good money on an asinine idea. Her arrival coincided with the embryonic stages of my developing confidence and a positive self-image, thanks to the influence of an extremely extroverted cousin in Colorado. And I found her introverted, damaged, painfully shy personality excruciating and unbearable. In retrospect, Simone's characteristics bore strong similarities to those of the typical Japanese woman; frustratingly shy, demure, damaged by childhood sexual molestation and chronically socially inept, *the nice quiet girl* many Jamaican men in my childhood thought was the perfect catch and indeed the personality to which girls were instructed to aspire in Jamaica. Nonetheless, as I became enlightened and expanded beyond the limited Jamaican thinking, my preferences changed and I no longer found that weak, pusillanimous personality in women attractive. Good hair was no longer maintained as a standard of beauty.

Given their own inferiority complexes, African-American women rejected me in droves, even as other women - notably European-Americans - showered me with acceptance. This embrace by white women validated my rejection of African-American women, in my own inferiority complexes, and by 20 bestowed upon me a newfound confidence propelling me across the racial line, never to look back. But alas, I was still too diffident to pursue Asian or Latina women I saw in Denver, who made themselves far less available than European-Americans.

Unlike two women before her, Simone refused to abort, as she had nothing at stake. Tracy, my first abortion at 19 was a 17-year-old high school student who wanted to at least finish high school before having a baby. Twenty-one-year-old Noreen, a striking beauty from Trinidad, to whom I was engaged, had received a scholarship to attend Northwestern University before we discovered her pregnancy. Termination was a foregone solution and having been averse to relocating to the Midwest, our agonizing separation catapulted me into even deeper depression. Noreen's departure coincided with the arrival of Simone, with whom sex served as an opiate in times of darkness and or between girlfriends. Our frequent and careless unprotected sex was off the charts, leading to the inevitable two years later.

In love and desperately seeking love in return, Simone wanted a baby to fill the vacuous hole in her life. Akin to the dynamics commonly observed among pregnant teenagers, she wanted to be needed and even admitted that she had entertained the grossly misguided idea that I would have married her, given her pregnancy.

"That's ok, I'll raise the kid by myself, I'll just tell him that his father is dead," she stated in defiance, inciting rage and anger within me, of a magnitude never before experienced.
"Why would you want to have my child? Why would you want to have a child for someone who hates you? Can't you see that I was just fucking you? Don't you have any self-esteem?"

The despised fatherless dynamic I had observed among many Jamaican men and among countless other descendants of slaves, is the very social scourge to which I would then become a contributor, and I cursed her for dashing my dreams of being the father about which I had fantasized. Though it had become the normative dysfunction among Africans in the new world, I had always held in profound contempt and condescension the idea of single parenting and the entire *byaby madda, byaby fauda business*. A further source of umbrage was the possibility of repeating my father's abandonment.

Insecure and unprepared, having never had a father, I had no idea how to be one. And had I even a clue, I was much too emotionally unwell to be effective. All the father figures I had observed in my childhood were abusive alcoholics, if ever they were present. But I had dreamt of and planned on being a father like Mr. Ingles on "Little house on the Prairie," compassionate, supportive and kind, even if it meant several abortions until I was well. *Little House* and *Family,* two of my favourite TV series during my childhood, provided my only models of family as a child and comparing those two white TV families to the familial fragments in my reality, further reinforced my conclusion of hopelessness among my people. Four years after arriving in the States I met a family in California who adopted me at 19 and provided me a tangible working model of a functional, non-fictional family.

Consumed by repugnance for the mother of my child, which most definitely affected my interaction with my offspring, the war between my insecurities fueling by my paternal inadequacies, and the intellectual desire not to abandon my child, raged unabated in my head. For even if I didn't renounce my seed, it would have been impossible to reconcile my anathema for her mother, in order to interact positively with my child.

It was then that I embarked on the idea of intellectually motivated interaction, in other words, doing the *right thing* with positively no emotional attachment; faking it, deluding myself into thinking I was an uncle instead of a father. Less was required of uncles and they were more about fun and games, as opposed to the serious character development in which fathers are supposed to participate. This was the only alternative to complete abandonment and was actually quite effective. My daughter being a child could not detect that I had no genuine attachment to her. But though this process was quite effective, hate for the mother of my child proved more difficult to dilute, which resulted in my perpetual, physical, mental and emotional abuse.

Initially my anger was misplaced at Simone for wanting to keep the child, hence ensuring our eternal connection. This misdirected wrath resulted in many episodes where my fingers would spontaneously form an unbreakable bond with her neck, in several fits of rage, attempting to snuff out her life.

"Daddy, daddy, don't kill mommy," our then 8-year-old daughter screamed atop her lungs during one such episode.

On two occasions I was sojourn in county correctional facilities on account of my violent behavior, but fortunately with therapy I became more introspective and began to realize that my intertwined existence with her was the result of my own maladaptive coping mechanisms. After all, it was I who had actually paid money to get her to the United States, even as she protested. Furthermore, regardless of my addiction and depression, it was I who had been having sex with her, completely cognizant that she was someone with whom I would never have wanted to share progeny. Yes, it is true that I was once head over heels for her at 9 years old, but I had long since grown, gained confidence and changed my tastes and requirements in a partner. By the birth of the child I had started college, now confident enough to date hyper-beautiful women, completely ashamed of public appearances with my *byaby madda*.

Acknowledging my contribution to my own dilemma was one thing, but refraining from skapegoating her was an entirely different kettle of fish, which lead me to use more subtle long term psychological warfare, as opposed to physical abuse, to assuage my anger towards her and unleash vengeance undetectably.

"OK, you wanna have this child? You will pay with every ounce of your sanity."
And with that I set out to drive her completely over the edge with the only thing I knew: sex. Every orgasm I furnished, made her more attached and deluded her into thinking there was hope for us. Simone Chang was the only person with whom I have had sex out of hate and for seven years, like bonobus monkeys, we settled all our heated, sometimes physically violent exchanges with what to her was earth shattering sex, which eventually made me nauseous after the act. Seven years later, unable to cope with my post coitus nausea, I withdrew from this act and all manner of baby mama drama ensued.

MY JAMAICA

According to 2004 information from the detoxification unit, among 10-18-year-olds, 100% were smoking ganja and another 2/3 were abusing alcohol. In the 20-55 age range, 93% was using crack, 92% using alcohol and 90% smoking ganja. Can there be a semblance of anything but chaos in a drugged out hotbed for oppositional personality disorder? My motherland with the highest murder rate per capita the year of my visit, fueled by retarded conflict resolution skills, poverty, drugs, an incomprehensibly high paternal abandonment rate along with effortless accessibility to the gun, is also a state where the inhabitants harbour deep seated mistrust of each other.

We Jamaicans amuse ourselves with frequent banter and humor about our spontaneous untrustworthiness toward each other, but are usually oblivious to the fact that inter-personal trust is an indispensable criterion for economic development. The icing on the antidevelopment cake is Jamaica's place on Transparency International's Corruption Perception Index. Of the 145 countries surveyed in 2005, Jamaica placed 64th on the corruption scale, albeit a 10 point improvement over the previous year. A higher number on the scale indicates greater corruption.

Reacquaintance with the dark realities of my birthplace left me no choice but to re-affirm my childhood conclusion that, like so many other *Afritocracies*, Jamaica is a culture of failure. In fact during my six months there, not a day passed when the term *failed state* was not mentioned in the media, regarding the dire state of affairs on the island. Fortunately for the inhabitants, though engaging in passionate tango with and teetering on the edge of failure, it still manages to just stay afloat. Jamaica remains somewhat economically functional, a dreamland to many Haitians fleeing their failed state.

On another bright note, there is a light at the end of Jamaica's tunnel of decrepitude: the blinding light of creativity. Even in the face of, worse case scenario, all out failure or best case perpetual malaise, Jamaica the island of my birth, is a hotbed of creativity.

It is said that Japan is a *setsumeisho shakai*, an operation manual society where the inhabitants thereof cannot think spontaneously and are terrified of improvisation. As I've mentioned earlier, until recently it was impossible to obtain an extra packet of ketchup at Kentucky Fried Chicken in Japan, even if one offered to pay, because, that was the rule. But if Japan is a society where a manual is necessary, then Jamaica is one where the manual is completely discarded, thriving on ad hoc impulsivity. During my childhood it was quite common to hear the mantra, "yu haffi tun yu han and mek fashion," which translated to English means, one must always improvise, an absolute necessity for survival, in the absence of rudimentary resources. Japanese auto makers would be aghast to see what they would think was a *Mazda RX7*, being powered by the engine from a *Toyota Crown* and mated to the gearbox of a *Nissan*. Only in Jamaica can people of little or no formal education, in some cases illiterate, devise such imaginative solutions to all manner of problems encountered in daily life. Jamaica's bobsled team, epitomizes the *nothing can stop us* attitude of its people.

It is this fountain of creativity which puts Jamaica in the forefront of people's minds around the globe. Rap and hip hop, dominant genres in international pop culture, owe their existences to the tiny island. Marcus Mosiah Garvey opened the gates for the likes of Martin Luther King and Malcolm X. Colin Powell, formerly the most powerful mixed-race *black* man in the world and quite possibly the first person of color with a significant chance to become president of the United States, hails from Jamaican origin. This island roughly the size of Connecticut, produces Rhode's scholars like it produces bauxite: in abundance. Never in my decades of international wanderlust have I met someone who had not heard of the island. They might not have known its location exactly, but they had most certainly heard of it. The black, yellow and green X of the Jamaican flag is more recognizable around the world than those of some G8 countries and according to some reports, if Jamaica were a name brand, it would be the sixth most recognizable.

Unfortunately as much as this so called island paradise is awash in creativity, countering the mammoth cultural and social dynamics which keep it enmeshed in poverty has proven elusive. Creative individualism so embedded in the Jamaican psyche, is a deterrent to consensus, necessary to materialize basic beneficial interpersonal, social and economic schemes. In stark contrast to each other, the Japanese absolutely cannot function outside a group setting, which slows the decision making process to a grinding phlegmatic pace, whereas cooperating in a group, to Jamaicans may well be tantamount to pulling teeth. Unable to fully capitalize on its goodwill as a universal trade mark, the island fails to optimize revenues on its international image. Instead, Jamaica is a net exporter of creative minds, which developed countries are eager to utilize and properly compensate. It is this socialization forged by the determination to overcome, which all but ensures Jamaicans success in their chosen fields, upon emigrating to greener pastures such as the United States or Canada.

By then four months on the island, unable to engage in my first world rigorous gym routine, the depression of my childhood began steadily encroaching. Adding to the stew was the collapse of the venture I had begun with two other Jamaicans, which in retrospect was predictable. Impecunious and destitute, I was afforded much time to sit with my grandmother on her verandah and accompany her on her early morning walks down Mountain View Avenue, albeit not too far down, lest we were shot.

Ever since my arrival on the island, I had promised grandma that I would spend quality time with her, a debt I owed her having not attended my mother's funeral. In fact, my promises were not just hot air intent on pacifying the old lady, but genuine and anticipated plans, as I was older and had acquired the listening skills and patience, oh yes, patience, required to endure her sermons of pain and neglect. These were recitations of hurt and emotional abuse which I had been hearing since my childhood, but at 40 I was finally able to appreciate the sheer stalwart character which my grandmother possessed, having born nine children and married to my grandfather for nearly seven decades since 16 years old. Unlike the Japanese, Jamaicans are open and direct in their communication, and my grandmother could sink frigates with her direct speech. She was never one to mince words, regardless of how offensive they might be. Her stories of poverty and homelessness with nine children could coax enough tears to fill dams.

"I had to give away two of my own children like I was giving away puppies from a litter, all because of your grandfather squandering his money on women."

"Your fauda, dat no good wretch, rape my daughta," still seething with venom some 40 years later, and though I was the product of that violation, I too possessed an odd feeling of rage toward my father.

While grandma was on her first trip to Nassau as a domestic worker, my father, then unemployed seized the opportunity to overpower my mother in her absence. Eighty-year-old grandma, still livid about the incident which took place in 1964, broke the news to me in my thirties. In her words, after her return from the Bahamas my father approached her in repentance.

"Bwaii, Ms. D, mi du a bad ting while yu gaun a Nassau, y nuh." (Boy Ms. D, I did a terrible thing while you were in Nassau.)

Being from a deprived family of eleven, including her parents, living quarters were cramped and unaccommodating to my mother's new baby. So she bounced around, relying on the kindness of strangers until I was two, when she found refuge at my grandmother's church in Dunkirk. My parents had been dating, but she was holding out until they were married. However, seeing the kind of man my father was, she decided to cancel their wedding plans. Three months after my birth, upon taking me to my father's to show him his son, a second rape occurred, which lead to permanent severing of ties between the two. Traumatized, my mother relegated herself to a life of religious fanaticism and deplorable poverty, a poverty that made Mother Theresa look like Bill Gates, never even to date again. Mummy – she hated mamma, it was too braulin,' rawchaw and low class- was a startlingly beautiful woman.

In fact, during my adulthood, after overcoming my inferiority complexes, looking at photos of her at nineteen gave me butterflies, an unexplainable feeling of lust without sexual motivation. It was clear why my father or any man for that matter wanted her. She was an incredibly attractive woman. After kicking the complexes in early adulthood, the grandest epiphany occurred: I hail from a family of extremely aesthetically pleasing people, both on my mother's and father's side, but cannot comprehend how that gene had evaded me. One of my father's sisters even held the *Ms. Jamaica* title the year I was born.

An even larger eye opener followed, upon realizing that in general, there are some astoundingly beautiful Africans and people of African decent. Not the Halle Berry/Obama types, who benefit from the hybrid vigor phenomenon, but people of 100% Negroe decent, such as Kenyans and Ghanaians to cite two nationalities. However, nothing could top the grandiose and shocking discovery which came at 18 years old. While living in Colorado and England, like a wrecking ball it hit me that Europeans and people of European descent, whom I had held in God-like esteem, they too can be extremely unattractive.

Prior to those awakenings, I equated physical beauty with anything non-African and found it unfathomable that non-Negroes, especially white people, could be unattractive. Such are the complexes which plague many post colonized people of African descent and other post colonized people of color in general. Such are the complexes I have observed in Japan. Of course now, it is perfectly clear to me that all races are represented by the ugly and the beautiful alike, but it seems that a higher frequency of perceived dissonant phenotype is present among the so called racially pure, perhaps something to do with closeness of gene pool, British and Japanese royalty being perfect examples.

From as early as three years old, it was explicitly and unequivocally obvious to me that I had taken the wrong exit in birth, leading to the wrong fallopian tubes, down the wrong birth canal, which lead to an obsession until my thirties, with exiting life.

As earlier stated, my masochistic existence from babyhood in this prison mandated daily church service attendances, with pressure to participate in Wednesday night testimonials about the goodness of the Lord. And though I had absolutely nothing for which to thank their Lord I strongly wanted to mimic and please the adults. They all recited similar stories of traveling down this *crooked road*, stuck in a *miry claim* before being rescued by or having met Jesus. It wasn't long before it dawned on me that all these women, including my mother, had suffered some insurmountable loss, some great trauma, for which they had lacked the necessary adaptive skills to overcome.

A big break came at five years old, and I finally had something about which to testify after Brother Claire literally pulled me from a twenty-foot deep cesspool full to the brim of waste from everyone in the yard. The one and a half foot square shaped opening was just a few feet from my steps and that morning workmen had removed the cemented lid, replaced it with rusted corrugated zinc in anticipation of the cesspool emptier, a process undertaken every five years or so when the cesspool is full. If there was ever a time when being a skinny, scrawny and malnourished child came in handy, it was then. Had I weighed even an ounce more, I would have sunk to my death in that fecal grave.

Instead initially I sat in the semi-solid waste with my legs submerged from the knees, wailing and screaming at the top of my lungs, slowly sinking as I wiggled around.

"TEK MI OUT! OONU TEK MI OUT! SOMEBADY TEK MI OOOOOUT! Upon falling in, my unexpected presence disturbed a massive colony of cockroaches. Not just regular cockroaches, but drummer cockroaches. If a regular cockroach is a canoe, then a drummer is an aircraft carrier. I have only seen them in Jamaica, so they may well be the national insect. Twice the size of regular cockroaches, they make that reddish tone of their regular cousins appear to be exquisite works of art. Just the blitz of those monstrous creatures, ignoring the stench and the agony of slowly submerging in human excrement, was enough to give a 5-year-old a heart attack.

Looking up as I wailed and screamed, in full view was the square opening through which I fell. The sky was exceptionally blue, as dark hands extended to help me. But their attempts were futile, as our hands couldn't meet. Pandemonium appeared to be the order of the world outside as people scrambled around for solutions. After what seemed like hours, Brother Claire – the husband of a family who had housed my mother and I when I was 2 years old - arrived with pieces of cloth that he had tied together. Chest deep in filth, it seemed my wish to leave this earth after only a short five-year visit would really materialize.

"Stop di cryin!" he barked, laying on his belly. "Di more yu cry, is di more yu move, an' di more yu move is di more YU SINK! YU 'EAR MI?" And that was my first lesson in remaining calm and maintaining composure under immense pressure. Immediately I held it in, reduced my bawling to sobs and reached for the descending lifeline.

"OLE AUN TIGHT!" (HOLD ON TIGHTLY!) Were his next orders and I re-entered the outside world, embarrassed and covered in clumps of feces from the chest down, greeted by an unkind reception of scolding adults and jeering children.
"Yu si 'ow yu almos' dead?" (See how you almost died?) Said one woman. "If you a did fi mi pickney, a woulda buss yu aus." (Had you been my child, I would a whooped your ass.)

My mother had the same idea, because after hosing me down from a distance, with every disinfectant know to man, she opened up a can of whoop ass for A: disobeying her order not to go outside and B: for doing something to cause her worry. To this day I have a massive phobia for fecal matter and cockroaches. Confrontations with wild hungry lions and tigers would pose no problems, but the sight of a dead cockroach is enough to send me jumping out of a plane without a parachute. This early near death experience provided much desired fodder for my Wednesday night testimonials and for several weeks I stood on the church bench to testify how I too had been saved from the *doo du pit* by the Lord. However, that new found appreciation to the Lord soon faded under the weight of my depression and I began to think, had I not been so scared it would have been better to have died.

Just about the only source of happiness in my cripplingly depressing childhood was music, but unfortunately, secular music was strictly forbidden. Feet tapping to secular music reported by snitching children, was dealt with severely. Reggae, the music of hooligans and the devil, was definitely out of the question. In this tyrannical environment, forbidden to have friends for fear they would have *contaminated* my mind, I developed a most revolting hate for my mother,

After just one music class, unable to afford to continue lessons, my musical genius of a mother taught herself to read music and play the organ. As with my daughter and I, a firery passion for music burned in my mother. In fact, music and God may well have been her only passions. So much was her passion for music, that on a pittance of 15 Jamaican dollars per week, she saved for two years to buy a small hundred and fifty dollar pedal organ. By the arrival of this early stone-aged instrument, I had been introduced to Mozart by an aunt who took an LP to Jamaica from Colorado and I had begun to primitively attempt to recreate his music on the organ. At the same time, my mother began to administer music lessons, but after playing each piece once or twice, having relative pitch, I had easily committed them to memory. Like many music teachers she insisted on my reading and deprived me of perhaps what was my only predictably fun activity as a child. Soon thereafter, in spiteful rebellion - I ceased all playing and studying. This was a painful blow to her, but she continued teaching herself, eventually becoming the organist in her church.

Three years after my daughter's birth I recognized her father's, grandmother's and great grandmother's ardor for music and vowed not to repeat my mother's mistake. At three she loved nothing more than banging on her Casio keyboard which her mother had bought. She recognized dissonant and consonant chords and was able to do perfect pitch changes repeatedly. Her first piano teacher, like my mother, was a stickler for posture and finger exercises and all the other activities which deplete many children's zeal for music. My daughter complained after each lesson how boring it was, so her mother found her a new teacher who gave her the freedom to enjoy playing, made enjoyment her number one goal when playing music and insisted on her learning to read music only when she was ready. Before my mother died I explained this to her, and listening to the symphony that her multi-instrumentalist granddaughter was creating at eight years old, she understood clearly where she went wrong and apologized profusely, wishing to reverse the hands of time.

Church, a place where I honed my maladaptive, escapist daydreaming skills was a cacophony of scare mongering, an incessant barrage about brimstone and hell fire and how "dere was nutting down 'ere on eart' for us." And indeed, for the majority of the poverty infested in my community and Jamaicans at large, it appeared to me from childhood that there really was and still is nothing for which to live. Some Jamaicans cope through the *punaunie* fix, or the rum or weed fix, but most coped through the crucifix. And there are others who utilize all of the aforementioned.

During alter calls there was always much weeping and wailing and speaking in so called tongues. "Doola soola sooooooola maddoola," was Sister Diviney's staple utterances, along with some snake like hisses. These strange tongues were contagious among the congregation and they seemed to respond to and were egged on by each other, like animals calling in the wild. Violently tossing themselves around on the ground like rag dolls and fluttering like fishes on land they appeared to be in competition for the title of most absurd utterances. Missing the God gene, I was sure that they - every last one of them - were stark raving mad.

My mother was my grandmother's firstborn, dear to her heart. Mom had helped her raise the others in my grandfather's neglect, so it was only natural that she experienced bouts of disassociation for about a year after my mother's death. But she finally understood my absence from my mother's funeral. Given our masochistic relationship, I just could not have drummed up the motivation to take that 30 hour journey from Japan. However, I assured her with all sincerity that I would walk barefooted from the moon, on flaming shards of glass to attend her funeral.

Being penniless in Jamaica during my 6-month of *detox* afforded me the time to explore my childhood Dunkirk neighborhood to see how my perception had changed, particularly since my mother's death. Many warned that I would have been flooded with emotions, but they simply could not fathom the detachment I held for my mother.

"But maybe they are right," I thought. *"Bring on the Niagara of tears,"* I challenged myself. Arriving in my old neighborhood, the skyrocketing murder rate had brought on an eerie atmosphere of calm in the community, as this once vibrant though violent ghetto had become even more violent. So much so, it was now like a ghost town.

"Dem yout ya nowadays naw joke ynuh," (These young men nowadays don't play) warned Tyaila, a slim dark skinned man whom I had known since my days in nappies. His face badly disfigured having miraculously survived a vicious machete hacking by local hoodlums fifteen years earlier. No one could have imagined his survival.

"Dem yout ya nuh know yu, dem nuh know seh yu used to live ya suh. Yu madda dead now. Dem only si yu as farrinna, suh dough mek night ketch yu ya. (These young men don't know that you used to live here. Your mom's dead now. They see you only as a foreigner, so don't let the night catch you here.)

Tyaila explained that the violence had escalated to the point where people were reluctant to leave the relative safety of their yards to hang out on the streets, as they did when I was a child. Those who were not lucky enough to emigrate were dead and in fact, many of the ones lucky enough to touch American soil were also dead or incarcerated. 'Ugly,' whose face was decorated with ear to ear telephone slashes, along with others whose names I can't recall, were shot in police shoot outs. The Michael Manley market, pristine upon inauguration in 1973, was reduced to a dilapidated, decrepit piece of real estate infested by malnourished nomadic mongrel bitches with oversized extended teats.

Visiting my old neighborhood resulted not in an avalanche of darkness over my mom's death but further intensified my depression and brought about the same overpowering sense of hopelessness which I had felt as a child. Though not as desperate as others on Wild Street that day, the reality was that I was just as broke with no source of income and no funds in reserve anywhere. But unlike them, I was the possessor of a United States passport, if only I could find the cash for a plane fare out.

In the end, thirty minutes were all I could bare of my old neighborhood, which just two days later was featured on television news. In McIntyre

Villa, an infamous housing scheme built in the 70s, the very place where I was accosted at gunpoint as a child, a man and his pregnant girlfriend had been smoked in reprisal killings as they slept. Thirty years later, my childhood conclusion about the country of my birth, was all but confirmed.

On this hyper-sexual island paradise, poverty's intimate affair with rapacious sexuality results in daunting social consequences and oversubscription to oppressive religious sects espousing the mercies of God over the need for higher education, cripple the masses. And if those factors were insufficiently deleterious, both political parties are umbilically tethered to the *murder for votes barter*, the brainchild of the US Central Intelligence Agency in 1976. After observing and fearing the brotherly relations fostered by the late socialist Prime Minister Michael Manley and Fidel Castro, the CIA began supplying guns and anti-People's National Party propaganda to gangs affiliated with the conservative Jamaica Labour Party. The CIA's plot was most effective as the murder rate skyrocketed, Michael Manley's socialist party was blamed and they lost the next election to the Jamaica Labor Party. Three decades later the practice is still upheld my both parties on the island.

On September 7 2005, thanks to the generousity of Shoko, who wired me some 300,000 yen for my departure, once again I escaped Jamaica. Two days prior there had been a state of emergency in response to violence which had erupted over bus fare increases, and anxiety consumed me over the possibility of not being able to leave. The government had ordered citizens to remain indoors, especially along lower Mountain View Avenue, where gunmen engaged in reverse drive-bys – shooting at passing city buses. But as the engines roared and the nose of the aircraft pointed skyward, I exhaled a sigh of relief and fell into a deep slumber for the first time in six months.

BACK ON JAPAN SOIL

Upon my reacquaintance with Japanese soil, Shoko, the most reliable and dependable human being I have ever met, was there at Narita airport to greet me. Wearing my favourite pleated, plaid, burgundy and ash Burberry micro mini, she flung her arms around me as I swept her off the ground in rotation until we both were dizzy. One could never believe that this was the same woman, who two years prior could not as much as show affection privately, let alone in public. Since my departure from her six months back, having no reason to endure her unbearable parents in the Kansai region, she opted to stay with her sister Michiko and her husband in Tokyo, until my return. However, newlyweds of less than a year, they soon began experiencing marital problems, which carved a deeper gash in the relationship between the two sisters. Shoko, typically Japanese, was quick to accept blame and felt overtly responsible for her sister's premature marital demise. Numerous attempts to assure her that her contribution was marginal at most, were in vain.

A year before upon meeting the newly weds, it was starkly obvious to me that theirs was a marriage headed straight for the benki (toilette). Michiko and Yasuhiro were typical among many newly weds in contemporary Japan, where the decisions to marry are based not on love, but on meeting the requirements of family, educational background, financial status, earning potential and various other obligations. Contrary to historical tendencies, these are not omiaes, or arranged marriages, but are connubial arrangements where couples agree to wed, having met each other's requirements, assuming that love will follow. In essence, they are 21st century arranged marriages, exactly the type in which Shoko's sister was involved.

At 29 years old, Michiko in a rare feat had passed the BAR after sitting the exam once at 25 years old, and was under asphyxiating pressure from her zealous mother to marry. Yasuhiro, on the other hand, had only recently succeeded at the BAR, after his tenth try at 35. In lightning speed, just three months after meeting, they decided to exchange vows in a five million yen extravaganza. But through their film of simulated bliss, I had observed their stark, frigid interaction. A vapidity so painful to watch, I was sure that I had seen dogs and masters interact with far more affection. Michiko's face was always one of longing and envy upon watching her sister give and receive affection.

"Yusu could never do that," she sometimes expressed defeatedly.

Astonishingly curious was the fact that as newlyweds of only a few months, and in their early and mid thirties respectively, they slept in separate beds, in separate rooms, and had not been sexually active. I had come to understand this as a common practice among Japanese couples, but presumed that such arrangement was an eventuality arrived at after decades of marriage. Certainly, from my Western point of view, two months were just too early for a wedded couple to begin existing like flat mates.

"I give your sister's marriage one year," I predicted.

However, my crystal ball was off by thirty days, as they called it quits after 11 months. This meant that staying at Michiko's and Yasuhiro's apartment, subjecting her sister to our constant love bird behavior as we did on previous visits, was out of the question.

"That would be unfair to her," said Shoko, sympathetic and overcome by guilt.

Weeks before my arrival, she had rented a hotel room in Tebukuro for us to chill for a few days, before embarking on a week long trip to Mount Fuji, for which she had already paid. It had been six long and torturous months since we had last met and it was nothing short of heavenly being in her arms. Azusa's just didn't compare. In fact, I preferred her on my arms, but much preferred Shoko in them. Though she had furnished me daily with breathtaking and rock-hardening pictures of herself, I had forgotten how awe-inspiring and innocent her beauty was and how her extended, curved posterior thrashed to and fro hypnotizingly as she strode. Our travels around Mount Fuji, staying at a local Japanese style inn was nothing short of rapturous, though sometimes interrupted by thoughts of the reality of homelessness, unemployment and embarrassment awaiting me in Kobe. It would have been far easier to remain in Tokyo, a city with greater employment opportunities than Osaka or Kobe, but like New York City and Los Angeles, the grit and grime of Tokyo was much too intolerable for my delicate constitution. Even though Shoko and I would have been together, it would have been cripplingly depressing.

Shoko on the other hand, having discovered this new found freedom from her nagging parents, dreaded returning to Kobe, even if it would afford us more frequent visits to each other. Also jobs were much harder to come by in Kansai, as was proven during her months-long hunt for employment in law related companies before my departure for Jamaica. Shoko, like Azusa, was ambitious though with less drive and infinitely less confidence. In fact Shoko epitomized the typical Japanese woman: In cases where they are ambitious, they are simply too defeated and diffident to pursue their dreams. Azusa in contrast, was the antithesis of the standard Japanese woman. She proudly owned a fearless quest for achievement, which I deeply admired and wanted to further enable and support. Shoko, back against the wall facing further deteriorations in relations between her and her divorced sister, had become dissatisfied with her dead end customer service job, but was averse to the idea of returning to her Ayatollah parents. Shunning the status quo of becoming an Office Lady or house wife, tirelessly shuttling babies on a mama chari (bicycle used to shuttle kids), she finally faced the reality which I had been proselytizing: that young women, especially those with ambition face a hopeless future in Japan.

There are only four life paths for Japanese women; the career path, the path of the little princess, the desperate housewife path and that of the bad girl, all unfulfilling in their own right. The road to a career requires joyless toiling, to graduate from an elite university in order to secure an enviable post and climb the same 15 hour a day corporate ladder as men do. This more often than not, leaves them unhappily unmarried without any prospects at 30-years-old, in some cases even with their hymen still intact. The road of the little Princess requires no time wasted on studying, instead these women are engrossed in their girly femininity, obsessed with cute. Usually parasite singles living at home with their parents, holding large disposable incomes affording them the ability to splurge on everything Louis Vuitton. To them *CanCam* and *Classy* are not just fashion magazines, but sacred style bibles dictating their lives, while dreaming of marrying a rich man by 27. Such were many of Azusa's friends.

Desperate housewives perhaps constitute the path taken by the majority of Japanese women. Their average performance in grades and below average in style usually leads to technical school, marriage to any man who'd marry them before it was too late and or low paying part-time jobs, such as the loud and abrading announcers in sound cars during election campaigns. Finally, for bad girls - the category in which Minako and most other *GhettoJapulous*, chocolate eyed girls fell – studies were irrelevant, replaced by passion which usually lead to a pregnancy crisis and abandonment by the children's fathers. These women are usually well represented among employees in Japan's pleonastically ubiquitous hostess clubs. Shoko's acknowledgement of her bleak reality meant that my boot camp was finally bearing fruit, leading to her courageous procurement of a student visa to the US.

Truth be told, it was all in the master plan of having both women in my life. Whether I'd marry them both at the same time or engage in serial marriages, the initial phase was to get Shoko to the States. Remarkably, though nationalist to the hilt, paradoxically her dictator mother was most receptive to her plans to study abroad, albeit ironically, she regrets being the working mother role model during Shoko's childhood. In her reasoning, that caused her daughter to be too independent and career minded, unable to find a *good* Japanese husband. However, she appeared to understand the benefit of her daughter's pursuit of education overseas, despite the reality that most Japanese women who return from such endeavors, are still denigrated to tea making as part of their work duties, as companies fail to appreciate, value and utilize their experiences abroad. In essence they venture overseas to study rocket science, but return home to do gardening, or in the case of the poster child/woman for this scenario Princess Masako, a woman who attended both Harvard and Oxford - to have a nervous breakdown from adjustment personality disorder.

Shoko's mother agreed on the condition that she promised never to date a foreigner. In fact, a month after her arrival in the States, in typical asinine Japanese anti-logic, she demanded proof from Shoko that she had never dated and was not currently dating a foreigner, otherwise, "we won't send you anymore money." Shoko had been fully aware of my incalculable abhorrence for people with her mother's ideology and of the fact that her mother's ignorance had placed her, Shoko, at a gross disadvantage over Azusa, whose parents had elevated me to deity status. Since my days with Karin, Shoko seethed with hate for her own parents, hearing about how well Karin's parents accepted and accommodated me. Beseechingly she would attempt to convince me that if given the choice, she would most definitely choose me over her parents' wishes. However, I had not been keen on putting her in a position where such a decision would have been an option. Weeping and sobbing, she apologized profusely - which she had been doing ever since we met - for this their most recent bedlamite request.

But since her mother had actually agreed to support her studies abroad, I adjusted my perception of my future mother-in-law and assumed a more pragmatic perspective.

"It's OK," I said, consoling her. "She can be nationalists, racists, whatever. I don't care anymore."

And as long as she was forking out $120,000 for Shoko's tuition in the States, I honestly didn't care. She could have been the grand dragon or grand wizard of the Ku Klux Klan, burning crosses in front of my door, for all I cared. It was my insistence that both my future wives be empowered by furthering their education in the States, but Azusa's parents would not have been able to afford such undertaking, with the looming expense of her younger brother's education. Hence we would have had to shoulder the expenses. Shoko's parents' generosity was most welcomed, as unbeknownst to them they were doing the love triangle a favour. To pacify her mother, I advised her to take a picture with an East Asian student in any of her ESL classes, e-mail it to her parents informing them that he was her boyfriend.

"Maybe you could even pay him fifty bucks for his services," I advised. It worked and the funds continued to flow trans-pacific. The plan to marry both women was skeletal, but one thing was certain, I had already planned to convert to Islam if necessary. However, nothing could proceed before, not just getting my future wives to meet, but to meet and get along.

KANSAI REUNITED

Returning to Osaka, I was greeted at Kansai airport by my second wife to be, svelte and glamorous, as though she had just stepped from the pages of Vogue. Probability, which had by then become my best friend, had arranged it so that my apartment, the whore house which I had given up six months earlier was still vacant. However, arriving in September, as opposed to closer to April, there were few teaching jobs available. Loitering at the entrance of Garage Paradise, a once trendy nightclub in Sannomiya, I chatted up a stupendously alluring woman at the door, who was seeking a job as a hostess and or a singer. Though I had returned to Japan with the beast tamed, I could have easily slipped into my old predatory habits with Minako, that was until she alerted me of her status as single mother of three. Seeking to escape her pressure cooker society, Minako - or Minnie as she prefers to be called – fled for nowhere other than Jamaica at 17 years old, where naturally she was soon ensnared in drama, impregnated and abandoned twice by the same man.

Returning to Japan two children in tow, she hooked up with an Egyptian, had a third child and was thrice abandoned, fending with her children in project housing in Himeji. Napping at the wheel and crashing while driving home from her night club jobs seemed a favourite past time of hers, though luckily sustaining only minor injuries, even after writing off two cars. One such write off occurred just two weeks after we met on her return home from a night of partying together. After delivering me home, some fifteen miles out of her way, only one block from her apartment she was awakened by her deployed airbag, when the front of her car embraced a concrete utility pole. Minako burnt the candle at both ends and in the middle and, as I warned her, it was only a matter of time before probability would have been her enemy. The last thing she needed was intimate relations with the likes of me, which may well have resulted in another pregnancy, and the last thing I needed was her drama. Hence I opted for a platonic supportive relationship with her, leading her to foster the illusion that I was the nicest man on earth.

Moments after entering the club together, Minako and I were approached by a gentleman appearing to be in his early thirties assuming I was a singer. After all, I am a Negroe and in the eyes of the Japanese, all Negroes, especially Americans, are entertainers.

"Well, that depends," I responded. "What do you need?"

He explained that he urgently needed a singer for a wedding in Tokushima, an island approximately two hours by bus from Kobe, and wanted to know how much I would charge.

"Yeh, I can do that," knowing full well that the only singing I had done before was in my car on interstate 405 and more recently in the shower.

"You only need to do one song," in hopes of convincing me to consider the gig.
"One song?! Tokushima is far and I may have another wedding that day," I bluffed.

Then he informed me that travel expenses and accommodation would be compensated, implying that there would be an overnight stay.

"I can't do that for any less than 100,000 yen," I blurted, the equivalent of one thousand dollars.

Demand for the Western wedding, where fake pastors and gospel singers are hired, far outpaces that of traditional Japanese ceremonies. Pastors, white men supplementing their English teaching income, are required only to obtain a certificate, which can be easily downloaded. These fake Christian weddings adhere to rigid race roles where pastors are white and black gospel singers are a must. I too embarked on this weekend vocation, simply to rock the status quo boat and revel in the irony of an atheist conducting a Christian wedding ceremony. But the choice was short lived as it was immediately clear that I was fighting an unnecessary and most of all, futile battle. White pastors are required to do work for twenty minutes, for a mere $200 a wedding. All that laboring in Japanese for twenty minutes was tantamount to slavery, in comparison to the duties of the black *gospel singers*. A delivery of three cheesy songs would line homie's pockets with five Benjamins.

My first gig - a month before my departure to Jamaica - had earned me $300 for a few bars of the Rose and now this, my second gig, an even bigger joke: a grand plus hotel accommodations and transportation from

Kobe to Tokushima, all for a cheesy rendition of "All You Need is Love" in a vomit inducing recreation of a scene from the film "Love Actually.' Actually, it wasn't that bad really. The bride was moved to tears, which coaxed tears from my eyes, adding genuine sentimentality to what would have been a cheese ball performance. Being a country where mediocre replication of Western pop culture, music in particular, reigns king, their only concern was that I, the singer was black.

After the wedding, the gentleman asked if I would be available for another wedding a week later.

"I'd have to check my schedule, I think I am already booked for another wedding but I will let you know in two days." And so it was, thanks to my newfound irregular profession as a cheesy wedding singer, just on account of being a Negroe in Japan, the deposit on my old apartment was paid. Retrieving my scant belongings from my friends I re-entered the love shack where almost immediately Azusa and I commenced de facto cohabitation.

THE INEVITABLE COMPARISON

From the beginning it was impossible to avoid comparisons between my two loves, who in some cases were perfect complements to each other. Unlike Shoko, Azusa, aka Barbie, the first of two children, was the center of her family's universe, constantly doted on by her parents, grandparents, aunts and uncles, who over-indulged her in all her requests and desires. She had absolutely no domestic responsibilities and was free to do whatever she wanted to, whenever she wanted to. Shoko on the other hand, the younger, less academic and more attractive of two girls, was often assigned the responsibility of preparing the family meals, as her mother was burdened with the task of caring for her mother-in-law. Both women hailed from extended families, with an ailing grandparent; Shoko a cancer infirmed grandmother and Azusa a senile grandfather. However, unlike Azusa, Shoko was responsible for assisting her mother in caring for her grandmother, bodily functions included, which no doubt helped to instill Mother Theresa-like compassion in her character. Those who met or saw photos of Shoko spoke of warmth and nurturing along with her astonishing beauty. While Shoko referred to herself as a queen, Azusa thought herself a little princess.

In Azusa's family everyone, literally every member was of jaw dropping attractiveness, the men more so than the women. Her grandfather, a former World War II medical doctor, was still a dapper, handsome senior at 83 years old, likewise her 50-year-old father, from whom she inherited her face. Akihiro her 18-year-old brother was a Japanese Pierce Brosnan. In contrast, Shoko, among her parents, sister, aunts and uncles, was the only attractive member, appearing to be the beneficiary of some kind of genetic throwback: she bore a striking resemblance to her mother's father, whose photo hung above the butsudan (Buddhist altar) in her home. A few months after we met she had invited me over, not as a love interest mind you, but as a random foreigner to whom she was extending hospitality. During my visit, her typical Japanese parents were painfully shy, so much so her mother chose not to leave her room during my overnight visit.

Shoko was compact, nubile and curvaceous, while Azusa was slim and taller with less curves. My sexual arousal for Shoko was immeasurable, whereas Azusa hardly aroused me. While with Azusa watching the Pixar film "*The Incredibles*" at a cinema in Osaka, I found myself boiling in anger and frustration upon discovering that Mrs. Incredible, an animation character, could calcify the organ easier than could the woman who was my date. Shoko was selfless and giving to a fault, Azusa was a taker and annoyingly selfish. While Shoko would immediately attempt to organize and clean my apartment upon entrance, Azusa, who wasn't even responsible for cleaning her own room, would step out of her garments, leaving them strewn across my already slovenly apartment.

Though Shoko's attempts to disinfect and coordinate my hog pen were always met with resistance, I appreciated the gesture and would be moved to either help her in the process or clean my apartment in anticipation of her arrival. But Azusa's presumptuous addition to my litter, her impertinence of leaving her dirty drawers in my kitchen was infuriating. Azusa's major advantage was her family's unconditional acceptance. They welcomed me with adoration, while Shoko's family abhorred the idea of their daughter dating a foreigner. Azusa was glamorously and commercially beautiful, perhaps in the 5 percentile of beauty, where as Shoko was in the 15 or 20 percentile group, girl next door kind of beauty.

My first choice was Shoko, as I was always willing to compromise on extreme facial beauty given a physique with train stopping curves. The opposite arrangement: off the charts facial beauty on a marginally arousing body, satisfying only my progenitive, egotistical motivations and a need to be seen with eye candy, had always proven disastrous. However, the open acceptance of Azusa's family made the equation infinitely more complex.

In illustrating my dilemma, I will use the comparative analogy of the *Ferrari Modena* and the *Bentley Arnage*, both awe inspiring cars in their own right. If Shoko were the *Bentley*, then Azusa would be the *Ferrari*. My preference is the *Bentley*, as I have always, since my childhood despised sports cars in favour of four door saloons, clearly a result of my socialization. My earliest impressions of sports cars were that they were odd looking, sometimes ugly, requiring some getting used to, unlike the common four door sedan I had seen everyday. Perhaps this was the result of having not been brought up to appreciate the *finer* things in life. As a young adult, that preference was suppressed, and though they were uncomfortable, claustrophobic and impractical, I acquired sports cars and coupes, in the interest of impressing others.

So there I was with a Bentley, heaven on wheels, a car about which I was passionate, when along comes a Ferrari in my driveway. Though it gave me great driving pleasure, the Bentley came with a restriction of 10 miles a month, but the Ferrari, for me half as much fun to drive, offered unlimited driving. Twice while driving the Ferrari from behind, I had to view pictures of the Bentley on my cell phone, to maintain interest. Compensating for my driving displeasure, the service at the Ferrari dealership was unsurpassed. All repairs and maintenance were free of charge, with a coupon for dinner at my favourite restaurant. All that while the Bentley dealership hated me and provided me with no service, hence even if I could have driven the Bentley more frequently, I dared not do so too often, as that would have increased the probability of required service or repairs. Making matters worse, upon my return to Kobe, the Bentley was parked some 500 miles away in Tokyo, while the Ferrari was parked in my bed next to me. Circumstantially, I was then stuck with the Ferrari, longing for the Bentley, whose driving pleasure I could experience most frequently only through cyberspace. As a result, the inevitable occurred: my attachment to Azusa grew to near equal that of Shoko's.

Eight months earlier, back in March 2005, I in her father's stead, along with her mother, aunt and other family members, had attended Azusa's graduation which led to a job slaving away 14 hours a days, seven days a week administering facials and peddling skin care products. Only in Japan can a woman graduate from a prestigious university only to be hired in a job that high school dropouts perform in the United States. Shoko before her, though having graduated with a degree in law, was a clerk at a patisserie. In hindsight, it seemed that Shoko in the ultimate act of selflessness, had gotten me from Jamaica so Azusa, not she, could enjoy my company. In no time Azusa's belongings were at my apartment, though the more time spent with her, the more I yearned for Shoko, especially as she, Azusa, unveiled her obnoxiously selfish personality.

Unlike Shoko who slept ensconced with precision in my spooning embrace throughout most of the night Azusa dominated the bed, in the birthing position on her back, knees elevated with the soles of her feet flat on the bed, arms asunder. As if that weren't enough, the cacophony of her bruxism ensured hours of insomnia. Thrice nightly, I would awaken at the fringes of my own bed, only to wake her, each time more aggressively.

"Azusa! You're taking up the whole bed again! And stop grinding your teeth!"

Irate and subsequently sleepless in my own bed, I would stare at her, arrested by her indescribable beauty, sometimes taking pictures of her as she slept. It was impossible to remain angry. Her face paralyzed my vexation as she snored in slumber. Eventually I tired of waking her and resorted to simply gently heaving her over to the other side of the bed and rotating her to her side. However, gradually her self-centered hako iri musume (daughter in a box) personality grounded on my very last nerves, and even with her striking face and her parents' hospitality, I soon began to count down the days before her one year working holiday in Canada.

As with Shoko, I encouraged Azusa to travel and live abroad at least temporarily, as a prerequisite to our marriage and for her own enlightenment and maturity. Her first job post-university had been nothing short of insulting.

"You need to see the world and continue your education," I opined.

But unbeknownst to them, encouraging time in the West bore ulterior motives: a final test for attrition. Deeply emotionally attached to the Ferrari, though I had completely adjusted to my future as a bigamist - planning to marry Azusa at Hedonism III in December of 2006, then Shoko in California - I was still open to and expecting defection, in particular Azusa's departure. Life in the West would expose both beautiful and utterly desirable women to their full erotic potential never before experienced in Japan, as unlike men in Japan, Western men would most certainly pursue them in the same fashion which I did in Japan. Having romped with various men, exploring their sexuality and erotic power, if in fact they wanted to continue with the love triangle, then I would be assured of their sincerity. Shoko then 26, who was a virgin until we met three years prior, had formed an indefatigable appendage like attachment to me, whereas Azusa then 24, eighteen years my junior, had lost her virginity at 17. In my assessment, there was a far greater probability for Azusa to defect, as I anticipated her sexual exploration. After all, if I could pick her up on the train, then invite her to my apartment to mount her on my washing machine, I was not under the delusion that no other man could.

HENNI COMES TO PASS

Henni, whose son was now old enough to attend daycare, was the second woman I contacted upon returning to Kansai. Meeting at the same Starbucks without baby Saddam in tow, soon our tongues were doing the tango, under the watchful eyes of cameras in the stairwell of Sogo department store. Henni was and still is of astonishing pulchritude. Her exceptionally large grey eyes had lashes, real lashes so long you could paint with them. I began to hoist her miniskirt to grope her onion as shoppers passed by in the middle of the day.

"Camera aru yo!" (There are cameras here)
"You're right and besides, you're married. Why don't we just go to my apartment?"
"I have to go pick up our son. Next Thursday."
"Wear this same miniskirt for me."

The following Thursday, three years after our first encounter on the JR Sannomiya platform, Henni showed up at my door and before she could remove her boots, my tongue had returned to its familiar location from the week before.
"Today I have to pick up our son at noon."
I buried my head between her C cups as she grabbed my curved projectile bulging from my jeans.
"No marks," she sighed breathlessly. Then I pulled the crotch of her bikini aside to graze on her shaven fruit of my desire, rod bursting at attention as she wiggled in pleasure. Undoing her bra, I freed her breasts which barely showed signs of childbirth and I began to sup, sometime nibbling her tiny nipples, driving her mad. She hastily undid my jeans,   freeing the beast as I reached for some protection from under the bed.

"What is this are you putting in me?" In her usual sarcastic tone.
"Shinkansen?" (The bullet train?)
But she endured, mouth agape until I was docked deep inside. It was my intention to ride with a helmet on for the entire journey, since she was married and fairly newly wed. But great intentions pave the way to hell,

and after her first two orgasms, we both agreed to ride bareback to feel the full effect.

"Just don't come inside, please."
At the end of our session drenched in winter sweat, Henni was four times in orgasmic bliss, as I fed it to her and feasted on her in intervals.
"I can never have sex with my husband again."

I had waited three years and three months, but my predictions unfolded exactly as I thought they would have and now Henni was turned out, sprung. Finally in an attempt to recover from her dilemma of hopelessly economically *Siamesed* to her husband, she had begun studying cosmetology, in order to assert some financial independence from her spouse. But that would all become a pipe dream with a second child in June 2007.

"I gave up," sighing acquiescingly. "He still treats me the same, doesn't come home, and now I have two kids to take care of. What can I do? Shoganai."
The Henni today is browbeaten and diffident, the diametric opposite of the Henni I had met in September 2002.

LEAN TIMES IN JAPAN

Though it provided me with the funds to return to my old apartment, income from wedding singing was sporadic, at least because I was disgusted by renditions of cheesy songs from Disney animation films, which were staple requests. As my re-entry to Japan in October was most inopportune, the only teaching positions were at elementary schools, which until then, I had avoided like the plague. Not even the prospects of desperate, sex starved housewives – and there were loads – could entice me to endure such torture. With Japan a paedomorphic society, though I love and want many children, working with them on a daily basis, while living here would have been puerility overkill. But in the end, there was no choice, as the only employment opportunities which availed themselves then were at elementary schools. And so it was that I took a job teaching in four schools in the Sanda elementary school district.

Initially most disturbing were the ubiquitary micro-minis on little girls throughout the schools, but more unnerving was the faculties' condoning attitudes. The same scandalously short skirts which made my eyes pop upon arrival in Kobe three years back, were the same ones barely covering little 8-year-old girls. Public elementary schools can require uniforms at their discretion in Japan and the Sanda elementary school district was one district in which uniforms were not stipulated, consequently the miniskirt became the de facto uniform. Mass daily unmitigated crotch flashing by little girls was a disturbing aspect of my job to which I had to adjust.

In discussions with the principals of all four schools, I was told that nothing could be done to correct the problem, as parents are free to dress their children in whatever fashion they wished. Among developed countries, child sexualization is by no means limited to Japan, but at least in other nations such as the United States, there is discourse about the detriments of sexualizing an 8-year-old. Contrarily in Japan, such acts appear to be socially sanctioned.

Japan is a world leader in odd ball products and quirky ideas, at times downright revolting, with the latest in that category being the trend of preteens posing suggestively in slinky swim suits. The T back (G string in America, thong in Australia) Junior Idol craze began in 2005 - the year I first taught elementary school – when 12-year-old Asuka Izumi (not a pseudonym), then modeling for a DVD, donned a string bikini at the director's request. In the two years since her T back Junior Idol debut, she has appeared G string clad in four photo books and in countless DVDs, and in just the last year, 2006, over three million copies of those books have flown off shelves. Though containing no full nudity, be ye not mistaken that such publications are some teen magazine targeting teen and preteen girls. For T back Junior Idol photo books are positioned immediately adjacent to hardcore porn and feature sparsely attired children seductively photographed blowing a flute or licking an ice cream cone. Since Azuka began the trend, the girls' ages have plummeted. Introducing 9-year-old Rei Asamizu (also not a pseudonym), who appeared in April 2007's *Melty Pudding*, a photo book showcasing her wet, on a bed in a G string.

This begs the question, do these girls have parents? And yes they do, self-sexualized mothers oblivious to the dangers of sexualizing their children. In fact, sexualization is far from these parents interpretation, it's just kawaii (cute). Anecdotally, of my adult students in company classes only two out of twenty four, one woman and a man objected to their elementary school aged daughter wearing a miniskirt. A student in a class at a chemical company in Osaka, Yuzo's peers responded to him as though he had lost his mind when he told them he would never allow his little girl to wear a miniskirt.

"AAAAA!? Why, why why? They asked.
"Because she's a little girl, the miniskirt is for adults. My wife should wear a miniskirt, not my little daughter."
An earlier response by a 65-year-old doctor echoed the response of several adults to whom I had posed a question about miniskirts on children.
"Miniskirts on little girls are charming, but on adults they are offensive."

This I interpreted as the society's discomfort with that which is overtly sexually arousing. Their sentiments speak to the relationship of cognitive dissonance in which Japan is inundated with sexual cues and immodesty in a society where modesty is virtuous. Most are shocked to hear that the miniskirt is an adult garment made popular in the West in the 60s.
"AAAA! I thought they were for kids," was the common response.

Judeo-Christian societies' disgust for nudity and contemporary Japan's shame for the miniskirt on young adult women share some similarities.

The miniskirt and other sexy attire are for children, teenagers and women in their early twenties, but contrarily hardly a woman over thirty, especially in the Kansai region, and in particular, women who are mothers, would dare to bare their thighs to the public. In contemporary, paradoxically sexually repressed but liberated Japan, where women are self and socially sexualized and objectified, men's admiration and acknowledgement of a woman's beauty is taboo. Hence the miniskirt became acceptable children's wear, as technically, a little girl in such attire should not stir sexual arousal. In their naïveté, sexualizing a child in skimpy attire is considered innocent. Transferring their arousal discomfort onto children may on the surface ease the arousal anxiety experienced from the daily barrage of sexy adult women, but unbeknownst to them, sexualizing a 6 or 7-year-old, and in recent cases three year olds, creates an even greater conundrum for the child, men and society at large, a phenomenon which Japan as a society is incapable of grasping.

Ironically, though admiring a woman in public is anathema to Japanese men, it is perfectly admissible to consume hardcore pornography whilst sitting next to her on the train. Public arousal by a woman is unacceptable, while public arousal from pornography, while sitting next to a woman is perfectly admissible. Had Japanese men not been socialized in this inefficiency with such handicapped communication skills, they would have been more than capable of simply initiating conversation with the women next to them during their commute. After all, they are already, literally in physical contact.

"I don't have a problem with my daughter wearing a thong at her age," said Azuka's mother, a former model. She continued by naively describing her daughter's body as having a "neutral, sexless beauty" that only a premature girl can possess. Having discovered her daughter's photo books on display among hardcore porn in Tokyo's Kabukicho district, she was not the least perplexed.
"I feel that anyone who buys Asuka's work has the right to do whatever they want to do with it,"
Kotomi Izumi does not feel as though she's taking commercial advantage of her daughter, just simply helping the 14-year-old to be successful in what she wants to do.

According to Koji Maruta, author and lecturer in the international communications department at Okinawa University, "Unlike the West, Japan has tended to be more open about sex and sex culture and has slowly been implementing legal measures against child pornography, but the ambience, culture and religion of the country makes people less uncomfortable about such issues compared with Western societies." Though his assertions are valid, Maruta neglected a crucial contributing factor to Japan's irresponsible approach to child pornography.   As a society, Japan discourages intellectual thought and reasoning among its citizens, but instead spends far more energy on maintaining its child-like charm.   As a result, Japan may not possess the ability or will to fully comprehend the April 2007 American Psychological Association's report on the catastrophic interpersonal, intrapersonal and intrascocial effects of socializing little girls and women in general.   After all, women in this society are restricted to social pompons, pleasure givers or baby making machines, having internalized their status for hundreds of years, transferring sexual objectification onto their daughters in the interest of kawaii.

Meanwhile, back at one of the elementary schools, 33 year old Tomoya, married, sex deprived mother of two small boys had begun driving me to my apartment on a weekly basis.

JUST AS I HAD EXPECTED.

Saturday February 25th 2006, returning home on the Hanshin train, from a podcast recording session for madgruve.com, I had put my cell phone on silent mode, in adherence to proper cell phone etiquette on the train. In so doing I had not detected a call at 11:25pm and began to listen to what I presumed was a voice mail left by Azusa, whose phone had accidentally dialed mine. In fact, this had occurred twice before, as her new Sony Erickson was a recent replacement for a Mitsubishi slide phone which had fallen in a benki, a Japanese style toilet. Unlike most cell phones in Japan, the Sony Erickson 909i was of flip-less design, prone to inadvertently making random calls as it was jostled around in her Louis Vuitton handbags. On one occasion walking hand in hand in Sannomiya, Azusa's phone positioned in her back pocket, dialed mine.

"You're calling me again babe," opening my phone to accept the call. "I think you should figure out how to lock your keypad," I advised.

Listening to the voice-mail, it was immediately recognizable that the call was unintentional. Clearly the phone was positioned in her back pocket, as with every stride, the rhythmic abrasions of her jeans against the phone's microphone could be heard. Her pumps, the same navy high heels she wore when we first met, were audible along with her playful giggles.

"Do you wanna go to the same hotel as before?" Asked a white American sounding voice in the voice-mail.

"I don't mind, its close by, or we could try a different place. It's up to you," Azusa responded.

"It's pretty close," responded the California sounding voice.

For two minutes, the entire capacity of the voice mail recorder, the laughter and dialogue continued until the call was abruptly discontinued. *"What were the odds?" "What was the probability of her telephone mistakenly dialing mine at the very moment she was on her way to a hotel for a fling?"*

Repeatedly I savoured and reviled the voice-mail, blood percolating, phallus hardening in a jealous ecstatic rage as I imagined her in her favourite position, head flung back, draping mane, riding him, attempting to sever his member, uttering that high-pitched orgasmic squeal, as she did with me.

I fired off an e-mail to her from my cell phone.
"Is that your girlfriend at whose house you were going to spend the night?" I wrote. "And are you going to fuck him?"

My e-mail continued with detailed and graphic description of my intentions once she returned home. Azusa was prone to bladder infections, and it was with perfect surety that upon her return home, as hardened as I was in jealousy, after a copulatory marathon, several bladder infections would have been the least of her affliction. I would have agonized her into a coma.

As a voyeur, I have always entertained fantasies of watching my girlfriends with other men, but in particular having only been slightly above marginally sexually attracted to Azusa, I had always entertained fantasies of watching her with someone else. This was the only way my sexual attraction for her could match that for Shoko. Hence, catching her in the act, euphorically agonizing, rapturously torturous, threw me into a marathon of self-pleasure, anticipating her return home. Like a katana sweeping through my bowels during multiple orgasms, It hurt badly, but felt so damn good. Azusa didn't respond to my e-mail until the next morning, said she hadn't recognized it.
"Where did you see us?" she e-mailed.
After which I telephoned her.
"Never mind where I saw you. Did you fuck him?"
"Where did you see us? Where were you?
"DID YOU FUCK HIM?" I screamed into her ear on the phone.
"Yes."
"And was it good? Did he make you come?" Again imagining her in the throes of his ecstasy. Hesitant and nervously, she answered,
"Yes, he made me come."
"Well when you come home, I want you to show me exactly how you fucked him."

On Sunday night, 24 hours after hearing her voice mail, Azusa finally returned home. She simply continued with her plans to hang out with her friends throughout the day on Sunday, leaving me to seethe in jealousy, hard, in pleasurable pain for the entire day. This I interpreted as a definitive act of irreverence, angering me far more than her actual fling. For in my mind, had I been in her shoes, I would have sought to conduct some immediate damage control by returning home as soon as possible, at least bearing flowers. Prior to that incident, in fact since we had met two years prior, I had been anticipating our wedding with one eye, while with the other, expecting to capitalize on the chance for her attrition upon her arrival in Canada. But her derision would skew the battlefield in favour of attrition. I still planned to marry her, only if my efforts at attrition failed.

I had planned to engage in marathon rogering the minute she set foot through my doorway, but by the time I heard her turn the key, I had already masturbated some six times for the day and was completely spent, able to do nothing more than talk.

"Tell me about him, tell me everything," I demanded. "I know he's white and he's from the West coast."

"Yes, he's from Oregon."

"What else? What did you guys do? Tell me everything from the beginning. How'd you meet?"

"Why do you want to know? It's just gonna hurt you."

And right she was, but masochist that I was, I reveled in the pain.

Oregon San, as I called him, was a white American she had met at a night club two weeks earlier. Four days later, they made their debut at a love hotel in Sannomiya. By no means was I surprised, as I am of the belief that if a woman allows me to enter her effortlessly after first meeting her, then she is quite likely to behave in such a manner with any other man. The macho military man, he immediately began displaying his possessiveness fueled by his insecurities. Just as I burned imagining some white guy driving my Ferrari, Oregon San burned to know that the apple of his eye was loyal to a Negroe and in an immature effort to exalt himself and denigrate me, began to pass derogatory remarks, deriding her choice of allegiance.

"Why would you want half-black children?" he questioned. "Half-white, half-Japanese kids are much better looking."

"Your boyfriend looks gay," responding to my photo on her phone's wallpaper.

"He's pretty muscular. Black men have to be muscular because they come from violent neighborhoods, so they have to be able to fight."

"I will never go to Jamaica, they got AIDS."

According to Azusa, he had taken control of her phone and read the e-mail I had sent to her, graphically describing the many miles of my petrified member, which she would have received upon her return home. "If you were a white woman," he cautioned, "he wouldn't have sent you this kind of e-mail. He doesn't respect you."

How pitiful I thought. When will the macho types learn, that women, especially extremely beautiful women are not impressed by insecurity? During my club hopping youth, in San Francisco, London and Los Angeles, I had often been in his shoes, having *gotten lucky* with astonishingly beautiful women who where otherwise attached. But unlike Mr. Oregon, rather than deride, *dis* and *hate* on their boyfriends, quite the opposite was most effective. I showered their boyfriends with compliments and commended them on their choices.

"He's a very lucky guy," I often recited. "I wish I were he."

In fact, during their complaints of their partners' shortcomings, I defended the men.

"I'm sure he didn't mean to hurt you," I sympathized. "You should give him another chance."

Since I held no interest in committed relationships, in most cases my behavior resulted in extensive, long term affairs, unbeknownst to their boyfriends. However, Mr. Oregon, brainless jar head, could have never grasped such advanced psychology.

That night, Azusa came clean and revealed that Mr. Oregon was not her first, since we had been together. She was also *active* with her German *friend* whom she had frequently mentioned since we first met, and often informed me before hand of their plans to *hang out*. During my six months in Jamaica, there was also a man from San Mateo, California. Being atypically unpossessive, I had no reason to suspect her, and if I had, by no means would I have investigated. After all, though at the twilight of my philandering, there was no bigger whore than I, who truly believed that in this case, "what's good for the goose," is also "good for the gander." If I could play, then most certainly could she. More importantly, Azusa, driven, competitive, less emotional, more rational and a bit more masculine in thought than most women, was the first woman I had met who concurred that fidelity and monogamy were mutually exclusive. The German tried in futility to get her to abandon our relationship.

But she was the kind of woman who only a secure man could handle, one who possessive men wanted under lockdown. She wanted to experience men of different races and harbored the fantasy of having a child by a man of every race. Azusa was exactly the kind of woman I had wanted, holding the perfect level of masculine traits, which made her more logical and less emotional than many other women. Unfortunately, my sexual attraction to her was marginal. Had she not been so available for the past two years, had her parents not opened their hearts and home to me and had I not want to use her for an ego boost, she would not have lasted. Azusa enjoyed the freedom to do whatever she wanted, because at the end of the day or night, no matter how late or early in the morning, or even a day later, she always returned home. I relished and savoured the knowledge of men falling over themselves to be with her. And even if they had sex, I enjoyed the fantasy of watching them.

Did you give him head?
"Yes," nodding sheepishly. I knew she did, she excelled at fellatio.
"Show me, pretend I am Oregon San," role play on which I insisted every time there after that we had sex. I relished in the pain and angst of my jealousy, as I imagined him on top of her making the beast with two backs, which frequently sent me into a manic furor and her to the hospital for bladder infections.

Upon inquiring about her motive for her flings, as I predicted she attributed her behavior to Shoko's presence.
"Because of Shoko I felt inadequate, she justified. No matter how much time we spent together, she's still more important. You love me only because of my family, but you love her for her."
I understood her reasoning. For here was a breathtakingly beautiful woman, who had always been the center of attention, since her childhood, but now had found herself in an intimate relationship in which she was second place, feeling expendable.

In her youth and naiveté, Azusa did not quite understand the racial dynamic which was at play in Oregon San's comments and insisted on continuing their relationship. Again, even more than the actual act of her continuing an intimate relationship with him, her lack of understanding was a painful implication of disloyalty and it was then that I became more intellectually determined to find a way of terminating our relationship.

Two days later, while in bed together, she agreed to send him an e-mail terminating the relationship.
"That's cold," read his response. "You're just gonna end it like that?" Anyway, I hope I didn't get anything from you."
Though a graduate in English from a prestigious university, like many other such graduates in Japan, Azusa's command of the language was far from advanced, hence his statement, "hope I didn't get anything from

you," was incomprehensible to her.

"It means he hopes he didn't get any venereal diseases from you. Thought you said you used a condom?"

"It tore."

That's when it hit me like a bolt of lightening, that the triad was in utmost unfairness to Shoko, who had known only one sex partner. It was by no fault of hers that she had fallen hopelessly in love with a potentially disease ridden philanderer, who gallivanted unprotected throughout Japan. But from my calculation, though the incidences of AIDS are on the increase on the island, the probability of my contracting the virus was still quite low, especially having encountered so many virgins. In comparison to all other countries, the infection rates per capita in the 15-49 age range was less than 0.1% in 2006. This in comparison to Italy's 0.4% and the United States' 0.3%. If Azusa, I reasoned, were cavorting with men from areas with higher infection rates per capita than Japan, then that would increase the probability of my and Shoko's contraction of the virus.

As expected, cohabitating with Azusa encroached on and began to erode Shoko's advantage. In all honesty, it would have been only a matter of time before my attachment to Azusa would have eventually surpassed my super glue-like connection to Shoko. After all, Azusa was completely accepted by my family and I by hers, while Shoko was available only solo, an arrangement from which would have been easier to separate. Azusa was scheduled to spend a year in Canada, after which she'd return to Japan where we would have continued co-habitating. Shoko on the other hand had gotten a five-year visa to study in the States. Azusa and I were planning to wed in ten months. Shoko and I would have wedded much later, if ever.

So again, even though I had originally met and planned to marry Shoko first, she was yet again at a circumstantial disadvantage. However, the interception on that fateful Saturday night, placed in the forefront of my thoughts, the need to implement some kind of affirmative action on Shoko's behalf to reward her, to even the playing field, allotting her more points given her circumstantial handicap and my organic attraction to her. The incident reinforced the hard cold fact that my preference was the Bentley and that I had stuck with the Ferrari for the past two years, only because it was so readily available with unspeakably lavish dealership support. However the fact was, though inevitably I had grown attached to Azusa, there were elements about her character which were anathema to me, but elusive was the ability to wean myself from her show stopping beauty

Certainly, my catching her in the act was itself not a motive for separation. Though extremely gut wrenching, her sexual liberty was one of the many things I adored about her.   Moreover, she was young and I had been encouraging her to explore and discover her womanhood, as long as she was safe.   But as open minded as I thought I was, the February interception unleashed a fury and jealousy like never before.   Perhaps we men just can't handle the thought of our partners with other men. The possibility of a woman we are with, perpetuating another man's DNA, might just be more than we can handle.   For even though I was not fully attracted to her, the fact that she was such a hot commodity for every other man, made me more attached to the idea of being attracted to her. I had been there before.   For five years in my twenties, I had tormented myself and my then svelte model like girl friend, not really happy being with her, but unable to let her go.   In the end I had destroyed her self-esteem, criticizing her fashion model physique, transforming her into an angry man hater.

"Never will I repeat such actions with another woman," I vowed to myself, and endeavored not to date women simply because they're beautiful, even if I am not completely attracted to them. I had kept my promise to myself for several years until meeting Azusa.

After Azusa disclosed Mr. Oregon's condom failure, I began to focus on the issue of safe sex, not for myself, but for Shoko, who was otherwise naively sexually inactive.   Including myself in the equation regarding safe sex was ineffective.   In my whoring in Japan, I had never cared about the risks of diseases, I simply lived by the pleasure principle in the reservoir of available and attractive women.   It was at that point, contemplating the triangle's unfairness to Shoko, when I decided to devise a scheme to surgically amputate Azusa, from my life.   I would have to engage in the equivalent of parking the Ferrari at a busy intersection in New York City, with the engine running, knowing full well that it would soon be taken.

Discovery of Azusa's *extra-curricular* activities did not deter us from our wedding plans and shortly there after we invited my future ex-parents-in-law to formally announce the news.   Among the specialties on the menu, was Shoko's spoon licking cream of pumpkin soup, whose recipe she had given to Azusa during their initial contact by phone some weeks earlier. The time had finally arrived when I had convinced them, especially Shoko, that given that we are officially in a love triangle, not only would it have been best for the two women to meet, but also to be civil and get along. Azusa, the younger but less emotional of the two, did not require much coaxing, she understood clearly. Shoko on the other hand, agreed after weeks of pondering and concluded that resistance would put her at an even greater disadvantage. For two hours the women chatted, cackling in constant laughter like two long lost sisters.

"Maketa," (I lost) I overheard Shoko say toward the end of the conversation.
"Sonna koto nai yo," (that's not true) responded Azusa. "He loves you so much. Even though we spend all this time together, he still loves you more than he does me."
"You haven't lost," I recall reassuring Shoko in my head. *"I just need to devise a way to get rid of her,"* which in fact was intellectually true. Their conversation ended with arrangements to meet in Canada in the summer of 2006.

Dinner with my then future in laws was an emotional event, where it became impossible to restrain tears as I extended sincere appreciation for their unconditional acceptance. Soon it became a cry-a-thon, bringing even Azusa's strapping judo master father, to the brink of tears. He was especially relieved to hear of the change in plans where his daughter would be accommodated by my relatives in Toronto, as opposed to strangers in Vancouver. But little did they know that a significant reason for this new arrangement was to enable me to separate from their daughter once and for all.

Originally, Azusa had decided to travel to Vancouver. However, after the Oregon San incident, I suggested going to Toronto instead, where the hospitality of my relatives, I reasoned insincerely, would reduce her anxiety. Oblivious to my ulterior motives, she agreed. In order to leave Azusa, she would have had to engage in what I would have interpreted as gross, blatant, disrespectful and dishonorable behavior. Hence after *the incident*, taking advantage of her own voiced concerns about HIV and following her predeparture AIDS test, under the auspices of safety, I proposed that she require an AIDS test from potential sex partners in Canada. By no means was I opposed to her being sexually active during our separation as in fact, I had even suggested separating for the year so she could explore and gain various sexual experiences, free of guilt or obligation. But, this proposal was met with resistance.

"I don't want us to break up," she yelled constantly, sobbing on my bathroom floor.

"Well you gotta have them get an AIDS test, because you are responsible not just for yourself, but for me and Shoko."

"I definitely will, I don't want to get AIDS, she assured me.

I had purposely set the bar in the agreement exceptionally high, where knowing her as I did, she was bound to fail, at which point I would interpret it as gross disrespect. What's more by staying with my relatives, I had presaged that she would be sexually active during their hospitality, which I would also interpret as profound dishonor.

Two weeks after arriving in Toronto, my cousin reported that Azusa would sometimes burst in spontaneous weeping as they drove together.

"I had to take her to the doctor for a bladder infection," she reported during casual conversation. I knew what that meant. Besides, her e-mails had become curt in the short time since her arrival in Toronto.

"Where's the guy from?" I questioned during a conversation on skype.

"What guy?"

"The guy you slept with of course."

And after an extended silence followed by equally long wailing, Azusa revealed that after only one week in Canada, she had agreed to go to the apartment of a Ghanaian, who had picked her up on the streets of Toronto.

"Did he get an AIDS test?"

"No, but he's clean," sobbing and sniffling.

"How do you know?"

"He said so."

SEX IN HISTORICAL JAPAN

Defecting from the States to Japan in early 2001 brought about numerous queries from friends prowling the club scene from London to Los Angeles.
"What is the deal with Japanese girls?" Asked a friend from Hollywood. "There's just a greater chance of taking home a Japanese girl I meet at a club. What is the deal with them?" As if I should have the answer, by nature of residing here.

Indeed, had he not been familiar with the *easy* reputation of Japanese women, the Ghanaian may have been quite surprised to bed so effortlessly, a woman who appeared to have stepped from the set of a Hollywood film. After all, it was men in New York back in the eighties, who coined the term *yellow cab* upon observing the effortlessness required to bed Japanese women. I too was taken aback by this phenomenon and wanted to explore the origins of these dynamics, factors which are ignored in East Asian Studies on campuses in the West.

As I have suspected Japan and the West hold fundamentally, diametrically opposing views on sex, though in fine Japanese paradox, contemporary Japan is among the most sexually liberated but repressive societies. From the very origin of Japan, sex, like alcohol was sacred and associated with the Gods. It is believed in Judeo-Christian mythology that an asexual male god, from nothing, created all which we know.

"Let there be light," he is believed to have said, and there was light. In the beginning, according to Judeo-Christian myth, there was god. Not so in Japanese mythology, where in the beginning there was sex. Japan's many Gods did not create heaven and earth, but instead the sexual convergence of heaven and earth created the first gods, among them; Izanagi the male and Izanami the female, both who were inviting by nature. According to the eighth-century "Nihon Shoki (Chronicles of Japan)"

"Izanagi and Izanami stood on the floating bridge of Heaven, and held counsel together, saying: 'Is there not a country beneath?' Thereupon they thrust down the jewel-spear of Heaven, and, groping about, therewith found the ocean. The brine which dripped from the point of the spear coagulated and became an island which received the name Ono-goro-jima." This is the island we now know as Japan.

"The two deities," it continued, "thereupon descended and dwelt on this island. Accordingly they wished to become husband and wife together, and to produce countries." The God and Goddess courted, eventually shyly discovering each other's sex organs, after which Izanagi announced: "I wish to unite this source-place of my body to the source-place of thy body," which produced islands as their first offspring, then a plethora of Gods and Goddesses.   Prostitution – professional musical and sexual entertainers - has been embedded in Japanese history where in fact, these Shamans and their trade were highly revered.   This was in complete contrast to medieval Europe, where relations with prostitutes were unsanctioned by the church, which promoted monogamy in holy matrimony as the sole approved environment for sexual relations.

In the Heian Period (794-1185), patronage to sexual professionals by members of the aristocracy, was a natural extension of their polygamous marital arrangements, since marriage was not a rigidly defined institution ordained by God, as it was in the West.

According to Anne Goodwin, author of "Selling Songs and Smiles," "by the end of the 10th century, these women, spiritual descendants of the Dread Female of Heaven, had developed their distinctive practice of using small boats to stage entertainments for men at ports [near present-day Osaka] on the Yodo River . . . " -- a fresh twist to the modern Japanese sex-trade euphemism "water trade."

"Their voices halt the clouds and their tones drift with the wind blowing over the water. Passersby cannot help but forget their families," wrote the 12th-century courtier-poet Oe Masafusa.   In the late 10th century, Oe Yukitoki wrote of the Asobis or prostitutes, who had become a fixture in Japanese culture from centuries past. "The younger women melt men's hearts with rouge, powder, songs and smiles, while the older women give themselves the jobs of carrying the parasols and poling the boats. If there are husbands, they censure their wives because their lovers are too few. If there are parents, they wish only that their daughters were fortunate enough to be summoned by many customers. This has become the custom, although no human feeling is involved.   Ah! A tryst in a boat on the waves equals a lifetime of delightful encounters."

During the Kamakura Period (1192-1333), which followed the Heian Period (794-1185), the venue for sexual commerce was moved from boats to inns on land, where strict regulations of the trade were enforced by the government. Such punctilious governance was propelled in part by the homicidal indignations of cuckolded husbands, whose behavior was quite opposite to their Heian predecessors. Whereas in Heian times, slighted husbands would brood and weep in vexation, the Kamakura Period, which saw the introduction of foreign doctrines, transformed husbands' passivity. The introduction of Indian Buddhism and especially Chinese Confucianism, created a chasm between the Japanese and their native Gods, permanently obliterating the natural equality of men and women. Confucian hierarchy dictated that men were heavenly while women were lowly earth beings, who should obey their men. And according to a Buddhist Sutra, women were messengers from hell. It was during this period that sexual pleasure vanished from the marriage bed, into erotic *zones* licensed by the government, and it was also then that cuckolded husbands began to off their wives' clients, a potential disruption to the social order, prompting government regulation to the industry.

Toyotomi Hideyoshi, the ruling warlord of the period, in 1589 ordered the construction of the Shimabara in Kyoto, the first licensed red light district, which was the predecessor to the politically sanctioned institutional segregation of non-reproductive sex. During the Edo Period (1603-1867), The Tokugawa shoguns designated 24 such red light districts throughout the country, and though licensed prostitutes peaked at 54,049 in 1916, regulated prostitution was maintained in Japan until 1946. Love hotels, and *fuzokus*, the network of erotic host and hostess clubs, *imekuras*, image clubs, *terekuras,* telephone clubs, *kyabakuras*, cabaret clubs, *delivery health* call girl services, lovelands, soaplands, Internet virtual sex sites, Internet *deaikeis*, encounter sites, etcetera, etcetera etcetera, are all descendants of the Dread Female of heaven, adding some 2.3 trillion yen to the nations gross national product.

Simply put, the Judeo-Christian West idealizes virginity, as evidenced in the biblical myth about the Virgin Mary giving birth to Jesus, while in contrast, Japan idealizes sex. After all, how else could an island the size of California end up with 126,000,000 people, had they not been sex obsessed? In stark dissimilitude to Japan, Korea with its over 25% Christian population, like the West, idealizes virginity, hence the popularity of hymen replacement surgery before marriage. Making the copulatory grass exceptionally green for Western men in Japan is Japanese men's chauvinism. As sex, like most things in Japan, is for the satisfaction of men, Japanese men, uncomfortable with the intimacy aspect of sex, cannot fathom the concept of sex with the objective of pleasing women, and the art of pleasuring women, sexually or otherwise is alien to them. They are oblivious to the power of furnishing women with multiple orgasms.

On a more contemporary note, though I have not encountered any literature in support of this, from the dawn of my philandering I have observed a high correlation between easily bedded women and those with no or fractured relations with their fathers. Male chauvinist Japan ensured splintered or non-existent relations between fathers and daughters, while culturally and socially sanctioned, paternal absenteeism magnifies the chasm between the two. The father daughter relationship is the first relationship for a woman, whereby she experiences platonic love and affection from a member of the opposite sex. In my experiences and observations, schisms in this relationship contribute to the destruction of women's self-esteem, leaving them with a subconscious yearning for a father figure, propelling them to making themselves easily sexually available in order to gain men's approval.

END OF A DILEMMA

Sensing the end, Azusa wept and even proposed returning to Japan for damage control. But that wouldn't have been necessary, I assured her. "You should have thought about the consequences before hand." Initially terribly remorseful, she proposed a return to our original agreement when we had met two years earlier. "I know I was terrible, it's my fault, I'm selfish, my ex-boyfriend used to tell me that too, but don't leave." "It's ok," she continued. "You can marry Shoko as long as we can have a baby, just like we planned originally."

Though the events had unfolded exactly as presaged, albeit much earlier than I had imagined, it became increasingly clear that my bond to Azusa had been deeper than I had wanted to admit to myself. And rightfully so, since we had been spending some 90% of the past 730 days in each others arms, in some 80% bliss. Looking back, I cannot recall our discords, only our elations, even in her nightly bed hogging. It must be admitted that I was officially deeply in love with two women and Azusa's actions, though expected, less than 14 days after arriving in Canada, drove a jackhammer through my chest. For the first time I understood the emotions behind honor killings and though she pleaded to be spared, her action was a severe blow to the ego and my emotions, which could have been rectified through no other means but through surgical *honor* disunion.

One month later, her remorse changed to finger pointing. "It's your fault!" she'd scream on skype, which we were now utilizing with a camera. "You did this to me, I wasn't like this before I met you, I never did this before I met you." "Did what?" I enquired. "Have sex with people so easily. He reminded me of you. You don't understand the stress I felt when I first came here," rivers flowing from her eyes and nostrils. "Yeh, I understand, but I didn't say you shouldn't have sex with anyone, we had an agreement that your sex partners would get an AIDS test, at least to protect yourself." "If you didn't do this to me," she continued, "I would have been able to control myself." Though her accusation was quite flattering, I was by no means going to be responsible for her actions and would not have been able to live with myself had I not finally separated from her.

Breaking the news to my angelic parents-in-law in the making, provided the greatest challenge. For it was only a few short months prior, to their glee, that we had made an emotional announcement of our wedding plans. Moreover, since Azusa's departure, her mother and I had begun communicating by phone almost daily, and in the interest of bonding, I had begun giving my future parents English lessons at my apartment on the two Saturdays a month which were her father's days off. Next to Korean dramas, her mother said, English lessons were most exciting. Like most other Japanese women neglected by their husbands, Azusa's mother was an avid consumer of Korean dramas. They enraptured her in fantasy and escape from the self-sacrifice women endure in the typical Japanese marriage. "I like Korean dramas because the men have big hearts," she stated in the presence of her husband, who even with large carry-on luggage beneath his eyes, eagerly attended my lessons. Our fortnightly bond brought them in indirect contact with their daughter, and me with my future wife, who we had missed dearly.

English lessons were sometimes followed by a movie on DVD, but always by dinner at the nearby Kobeya Bakery restaurant. Long before Azusa's departure, I had developed recondite admiration and respect for her parents, propelling me to endeavor to do right by her and to protect her on their behalf. Sympathizing with the inhumane demands of the renowned inefficient labourforce, especially the police force in Japan, I thought the least I could do was to respect and protect a father's daughter. So deep was my respect, that invasive thoughts of sex with her mother, evoked shame instead of the usual arousal. My future father-in-law, who usually worked a 72 hour shift on the constabulary force, had begun making arrangements to secure time off for our wedding, which had been impossible even to attend his daughter's university graduation. Even my bond with my brother-in-law, the Japanese Pierce Brosnan, intensified as I began training him at the gym to combat his depression.

In November of 2006, Azusa returned to Japan to attend a friends wedding. Months earlier I had said my final words to her by skype, this time without the camera, which was followed days later by a final e-mail. Hence she had hoped that we could have talked in person during her two week visit. "That won't be necessary," I wrote in an e-mail, maintaining the surgical nature of our separation. "Just please tell your parents to return the key to my apartment and collect your belongings. Please don't accompany them, let's just move on."

Breaking the news in my Tatami room, the very room in which we had announced our wedding plans several months earlier, brought the strapping, black-belt kung fu master to near tears. Her mother, dainty and impeccably attired as usual, hung her head in silence as I tearfully and sincerely extended my gratitude for their kindness during the preceding two years. "Where is Azusa's stuff?" Her father interrupted frequently, as if wanting to get it over with as quickly as possible. But they understood. "She can be a little self-centered," her father said. "We have known that all along." And with that, dejected and deflated, the Ogawas walked through my doorway, along the balcony, down the steps and disappeared in their new Toyota Wish, for one last time.

In retrospect, Azusa like me, may well have sought intellectually, to end the relationship, which influenced her actions immediately upon arrival in Toronto. Had I been in my twenties, of the two women I would have most certainly chosen her, the more glamorous of the two. However, at 42 having developed the ability to be true to myself, I was able to engage in the gut wrenching act of giving up the Ferrari, even if it sent me into months, almost a year of melancholic abyss.

SHOKO CONCLUSION

Back in Tokyo, relations between the two sisters reaching Antarctic conditions, oblivious to the occurrences between me and her rival Shoko had begun preparing for departure to the States. Surprisingly, she had stepped to the plate, embracing the daunting challenge of attending community college in preparation for law school in America. Japanese students studying law in English speaking countries, are most likely to have attended an international university in their home country, where the curriculum is presented in English. But here was a woman, who three years prior was too diffident to apply for a passport, but now planning on studying law in the United States, though she would have to start from ESL classes. After a farewell visit to me and her parents, two months after Azusa's departure, Shoko began studying in the States in the summer of 2006.

ETSUKO

Among my neighbours in this upper middle class suburb, was Mr. Yamada, a gentleman in his mid-sixties with intermediate command of English, to whom I spoke usually in passing. Frequently our conversations were limited to his then 14-year-old 1992 BMW 325i with an astonishing 10,000 kilometers on the clock.

"I have a favour I want to ask," he intercepted me one day. And proceeded to tell me of a lady friend of his who sought to emigrate to Canada, but knew no one there.

"Do you know anyone in Canada?" She only needs a place with her daughter for about one month."

Though I had several friends and relatives in the greater Toronto area, I assured him I would have had to meet her before making any recommendations, so I gave him my cell phone e-mail address for him to send me her details. Arriving home I began to conjure unpleasant images of this woman and became anxious about the hassle of contacting her. My days of being the good samaritan were behind me and even the prospect of sex offered no enticement, least because she had a child and I had vowed, after Veronica in London back in '95, never to be involved with another woman with children, unless the relationship would lead to marriage.

Separating from a woman with children is exceptionally difficult, especially on the youngsters. Having recently surgically severed ties with Azusa, with whom I was still deeply in love, I fell deep in emotional darkness and wanted no new people in my life, as I focused my energies on Shoko. *"Besides, she was divorced with a 5-year-old who was perhaps obstreperous and undisciplined as many children are in Japan,"* I thought. And given my expert knowledge on Japanese women after five years here, *"she was bound to have been suffering some kind of trauma,"* I concluded. If not from her typical distressing Japanese familial dynamics, then most certainly from her divorce and the monumental stress of being a single parent anywhere, let alone in Japan.

After Mr. Yamada's e-mail, as probability would have it, our chance meetings increased in frequency.

"Did you call Etsuko?" Was always his greeting. "You should call her, she's a very good person, she's like my daughter. I really want to help her, but I don't know anyone in Canada. Call her," he beseeched.

After a few weeks of phone tag Etsuko and I finally made arrangements to meet, but unfortunately having forgotten her name, erased Mr. Yamada's e-mail and not properly filed her number in my phone, I was unable to contact her to inform her of my two-hour delay on our scheduled first meeting. But she rang me after an hour of my tardiness. Emerging from the JR Sumiyoshi station, I observed an attractive, polished and elegantly dressed woman in a conservatively long, flowing skirt, exiting a Family Mart convenience store across the street. Appearing to be in her twenties, holding a little girl's hand, her fashion sense was adult and foreign influenced, with coordinated colors.

"*She is a babe!*" I thought to myself, waiting to meet Etsuko, who would be meeting me by the clock in front of the station. As I dialed her number to ask where she was, the princess across the street walking to her car, reached into her handbag to answer her phone.

"I'm behind you, turn around," I instructed her, as I crossed the street.

Etsuko and her daughter were diametric opposites of what I had imagined. Well above average in attractiveness, but faintly melancholic, Etsuko's face was make-up free, a rare sign of confidence among Japanese women. A divorce during pregnancy at 22 and subsequent single motherhood, had thrust her into adulthood.
"I don't have time for make up," she later told me. "I do everything for my daughter alone."

During our introduction before we entered her car, her daughter interrupted us with what to me, was a shocking declaration.

"I speak English, my name is Shion, I'm five years old." And it was then and there, that an inexplicable father daughter chemistry immediately burst into ignition.

Shion's declaration was shocking not the least because of the content of her speech, but because of the language and the confidence she displayed in commanding it at such an early age. Never before in my then five years in Japan, had I met a Japanese child who voluntarily spoke in English. Apologizing incessantly for my inconsiderate tardiness, I decided that dinner would be on me, at a nearby Jolly Pasta, where I bonded more with my new daughter than with her mother. Shion's personality was a mirror image of my daughter's at that age and it was clear, having never had a father but needing one, she instantly detected paternal instincts in me, regardless of our differences in race, and attached her arms around me for the duration of our time at the restaurant. Bidding good-bye took a whole thirty minutes, as she pleaded with her mother for them to spend the night at my apartment or to have me at theirs, either of which was impossible. It was only after guaranteeing her a visit in two Fridays, that her tantrum subsided.

"Zettai kuru?" (Are you definitely coming?) In her heart melting 5-year-old voice.
"Zettai, Zettai, Zettai," I assured her.

This peculiar attachment dumbfounded Etsuko, who had never before witnessed this behaviour in her daughter.
"This is strange, she really likes you. She never did this before." And with tears streaming down her tiny cheeks, Shion wagged her hands bye-bye until I disappeared from sight.

SAYO

Five months prior back in April I had begun teaching at a hospital in Osaka, where shortly there after my Friday routine was, being accompanied home by Sayo, a nurse in the class. Of the five students, which included three women, white pants hugging her figure eight, a gleaming smile and porcelain skin, Sayo was the only one to catch my eye. Although of average beauty, her toned hour glass physique certainly did compensate. Harboring no intentions of pursuit relieved me of distractions, however on that very first day, as the students began to participate in an introduction game, where they delivered a two minute speech about themselves and of each other, they all began to point to her as the only single student in class.

"She's single, no boyfriend. You should go to date with her," they all insisted, thrusting innocent prey on the hunter's stake. Sayo had recently separated from her boyfriend of three years, a co-worker with whom she engaged in a secret relationship. A secret they managed to maintain even after the break up, continuing to work together. This I interpreted as a clear indication that she was open to a surreptitious relationship with her teacher and in less than a month, our tryst began. Like most Japanese women with whom I had been intimate, Sayo was painfully immature, stuck at 15 though 29 years old and obsessed with J-pop group Smap. An only child still living at home with her parents, to my annoyance her fingers were always in my ears and nostrils in attempts at humor and she giggled incessantly. Rarely did our mind numbing conversations venture beyond the subject of food, or house keeping. Occasionally, this Friday routine was interrupted by Yukari who usually made her appearances on Thursdays, but sometimes would request Fridays when her days off from work were changed.

YUKARI

Much has been written about the incalculable beauty of springtime in Japan and indeed, though profoundly sentimental I am not, the sheer beauty of the Japanese spring, leaves me in worship every year as cherry blossoms transform the banks of Shukugawa into botanical fireworks. Another kind of *cherry blossom*, which is hardly mentioned in literature about Japan, has pronounced impact on some men's mental health, present company included. Every spring as the hordes of candy shed their unnecessary wrappings, exposing delectable thighs in micro-minis, my friends and I concur that we literally go mad.

Spring 2003 was my first experience with this phenomenon after going to the cinema with Karin. Emerging from the theatre at Hep five, the cherry blossom sweets appeared to occupy every millimeter of space and I gradually became numb, questioning my existence, as I walked in a daze.

"Doshitan no?" (What's wrong?") She inquired concerned.
"Daijobu?" (Are you ok?)

After arriving home, still in a daze, I crashed on my futon where I awoke the next morning in a stupor staring at the ceiling for the entire day.

Spring of 2006 was exceptionally stupefying as the preceding winter had been unusually long and frigid, which resulted in a visibly nubile transformation among Japanese women. Similar to my observation in 1985, just in my fifth year of living in the United States when I began to notice white women growing larger and rounder posteriors, so it was in my fifth year of living in Japan, that winter rid the terrain of chopsticks and brought to the fore more healthy, adult looking women. And just when I thought I was out, they pulled me back in. Yukari was among those *brand nubilized* princesses.

Preparing to board the JR Tozai train at Kyobashi, where I had met Azusa two springs earlier, I spotted Yukari's luscious pichi pichi (young) porcelain skin, outlining her hazardous curves. Having only recently emerged from months of winter her egg white skin exuded youth and vibrancy as she toed the yellow line in black pointy-toed strapped pumps. By then my fifth year in *Disneyland* and now well over forty women, I had come to understand that trauma may well be the most prevalent personality and character shaping factor among Japanese women and in extension Japanese society. Triple dose trauma; sexual, familial, scholastic are common denominators among the women, who in most cases were unable to escape all three.

As my age increased, so did the age gap between me and my conquests in Japan. Yukari, only two years older than my daughter, was fully 20 years my junior. Though only 21, she was immaculately clad in unusually adult, stately, almost regal attire. Unlike her contemporaries, her coordination and accessories bore hints of Western influences. Pitch black locks starkly contrasted her resplendent, snow-white skin, the color of her perfectly aligned teeth. Before encroachment I circled my prey for a full physique assessment, especially of the rump which met with my approval and observed that her shoulders were feebly wider than her hips, but definitely not enough to abort pursuit. Below her attractive face, were erect mounds, larger than those of the average Japanese woman. "*What manner of trauma is she harboring,*" I pondered, checking out her rounder than usual, bashful, slightly sagari me (down turned eyes.) Though there is no causational relationship between trauma and down turned eyes, they do exude an air of melancholy, but hers was faint. My fetish is agari me (upturned cat eyes) and observing her timid eyes, my first reaction in disappointment was to readjust my focus and cancel all plans of approaching. However, she was well above average in beauty, an 8.5 out of ten, hence I continued with the original plan.

"You look like you speak English," moving in with my usual opener.
"No, no no no no, no no no no," she responded in machine gun succession, smiling and waving her hand side ways rapidly in front of her face, as if fanning off a foul smell.
"Daijyobu, fuanshinaide kudasai" (It's ok, please don't be anxious.) I said. "Boku no nihongo wa pera pera yo." (I'm fluent in Japanese). To which she exploded in contained laughter, covering her mouth. Yukari laughed easily, a positive sign which in most cases meant, mission already accomplished.

"Hidooooi!" (You are terrible!) continuing in laughter, hand over her mouth. Perhaps nothing makes the Japanese more anxious than a foreigner, especially a stranger, mind you, suddenly addressing them in English on the street. Boarding our train, we sat together where we continued our conversation and she continued laughing hysterically, at one point hitting my left upper arm in laughter. This tactile behaviour was extremely rare among Japanese women. Never before had I experienced a Japanese woman touching me in laughter, especially just five minutes after meeting.

As she cackled audibly on the otherwise *noiseless* train I tried to find her source of trauma, which I detected in her second rarity: her living on her own since nineteen, a move I suspected prompted by the trauma of overzealous and overbearing parents. However giving her the benefit of the doubt, I thought her environment could have been trauma free and she could have been exceptionally adult and exerted her independence at an early age. Ten minutes into our conversation, hints of her trauma were revealed. When Yukari told me of her apartment of eight stray cats, immediately I interpreted that as a first sign of impacting trauma. For, "*In the absence of pain, which 21-year-old woman would be living with 8 cats, had she not been grossly in need of some kind of affection?*" I reasoned. As time unfolded, my *traumadar* was correct.

"Rikon no ato wa okaasan to awanakatta," (I couldn't get along with my mother after my parents' divorce) which was after her fifth birthday. Months later in the comfort of my arms, she disclosed for the first time to anyone, her experiences at nine years old, when she was abducted by an old man who pulled her in the men's room at a park and attempted to fondle her. However, she was fortunate, as hearing approaching footsteps he released her. But in high school where her physical education teacher *de-virginised* and continued raping her for two years, she was not that lucky. According to her report, after her graduation his actions were discovered leading to his suicide a year before we met.

Yukari still dieing in laughter, we exchanged contact information in parting and vowed a trip to the cinema soon. A few days later, having inherited a home entertainment system from a friend who was returning to the States, I invited her over to watch some DVDs, only to be rejected on account of her discomfort with going to my apartment alone. But promising to make her lunch soon alleviated her fears and in less than two weeks she appeared at my door exquisitely attired with two video discs. After watching the first film, some unbearably horrible sumo comedy, we ventured for a stroll to the nearby supermarket for the ingredients for lunch, where before returning to my apartment we were holding hands. Retreating to the privacy of my apartment, I immediately began to devour her lips, peeling away her designer garments. Bashful and desperately attempting to conceal her rod petrifying physique, Yukari's trauma was severe.

Overly self-conscious, unable to even open her eyes, she tried corybanticly to cloak herself with anything in sight. But sinking my hand in her T back, to explore her over-sized, uniquely erect and protruding Venus button, instantly rendered her helpless, as she buckled on my bed. Yuchan's pink crayola-tip-sized clitoris assured her of multiple arrivals even before I unveiled her from my bed sheets. Gaining   confidence, she allowed me to gently unwrap her, which brought to light large, delicious, C cups, the likes of which I had not seen in ages and though I am more appreciative of women's posteriors that their anteriors, it was truly energizing to be facing her milk colored, larger than usual Japanese bosom. My attempts to partake down south, were met with strong protest, as though there was some trauma associated with the act. Weeks later she admitted it brought back memories of her teacher, who regularly partook before entrance. This made little sense as fortunately, she bore no signs of trauma regarding penetration. It may well had been that her larger than life Venus bump was overly sensitive to oral stimulation. Unable to resist, diving into her heavenly body was bitter sweet, as I lost myself deep inside her, only to detect almost immediately that something was wrong.

In just a few short months and well over a hundred arrivals or departures, far more than she had experience before her debut on the dark side, Yukari was a changed woman. Where she was once overly self-monitoring and plagued with appearance anxiety, she too had adjusted to her new role as porn star, strutting about my apartment in the nude and now even able to go to work make-up-free. Of such magnitude was her transformation that in two months she canceled her wedding, scheduled to take place the following March to a young salaryman who had been transferred to Kyushu, where they were to live together after marriage. However, after her new foreign epiphany, much to the fury and hatred of the ex-future-groom and his family, she called a meeting and broke the news to them.

"I'm glad I met you, I really didn't want to get married and move with him to Kyushu." But having very little confidence to pursue her dreams, she thought she had little choice. It wasn't long before in her naiveté she began expressing her desire to bare my progeny, though fully aware of my loyalties to Shoko.

"I raise the child by myself," she reasoned, desperately wanting to love and be loved.

"After you return from studying dance overseas, when you get older and more mature," I assuaged her, though tempted by the idea of unsecured and irresponsible paternity.

"Having a baby and having eight cats are totally different," I assured her.

"Mmm, so desu ne." (That's right, isn't it.)

Shortly thereafter, frustrated by my unbending loyalty to Shoko, Yukari thought it best to leave, but couldn't resist my invitations, even though she had begun sleeping with a Japanese salaryman my age. However, alerting her of the Chlamydia she had *bequeathed* me, which I had detected almost immediately after our maiden voyage, she felt ashamed and could no longer bring herself to face me

"Mo hazukashii. Why do still want to see me? I gave you sick."

"Wazato janakatta, de shou?" (It wasn't intentional, right?)

But I fully understood. Face saving is of utmost importance to the Japanese.

ETSUKO CONTINUED

Recalling the countless times I had disappointed my own daughter by failing to appear after promising her a visit, two weeks after meeting Etsuko I canceled my Friday night routine and promptly made my way to visit my new *daughter*. Arriving at her home, fifteen minutes from the hospital where I taught, Shion, energetic and androgynous, joyfully flung her arms around my neck as her mother stood by the door in amazement.

"This is so strange I have never seen her like this before. She doesn't stop talking about you."

My sole reason for visiting that night was to see Shion who brought to the fore my nurturing paternal drive, which I was able to reveal only partially to my own child. It was unexplainable. Suddenly from out of the blue it seemed, came an onslaught of confusing, protective, caring, fatherly sentiments.

"Am I becoming a paedophile?" I worried. After all, I had heard about a convicted child molesting uncle on my father's side. So could it have been genetic? Ever since my traumatic childhood, I had always suffered from extensive invasive thoughts. From spontaneous murder to suicide, sex with animals, children, men, you name it and it has flashed through my mind. For a great many years they had subsided, only to resurface in 2005 upon my return from the traumatic six months in Jamaica. This abrupt attachment to this 5-year-old girl demanded my deep introspective analysis. "*What exactly is going on?*" I interrogated myself. But the answer was simple.

Fatherhood was a frequent theme of my childhood daydreams. Along with the perpetual daydreams of living in the United States, I fantasized constantly about being a superior father to mine who fled when I was two, and since abandoning my passion of philandering, paternal instincts rose to the surface. I was becoming well and more than anything now wanted to be married, after which I would father, raise, nurture and empower my progeny, daughters especially. Sons were and still are of no interests to me, as my vision is to raise and empower strong daughters. Though I would most likely adjust, having initial socialization in a predominantly female environment and thus partial to women, a male offspring is one of my biggest fears. Shion symbolized the extroverted, intellectual, strong and curious daughter I had wanted and had, but when my own child was her age my youth, personality disorders, insecurities and angst hindered my savouring the experience.

Certainly I had undergone a metamorphosis as previously, there was no way I would have chosen to hang out with someone's small child over sex. Instantly she saw in me the father she had long desired and I in her, my own daughter with whom I could not relax and display complete affection, having been too inhibited and overly self-conscious when she was Shion's age.

Entering their apartment, I partook in a feast which Etsuko had painstakingly prepared and laid out on the dining table and in the image of a father returning home to his wife and child I ate with Shion's arms tightly coiled around my neck.
After eating she proceeded to show me her fashion designer drawings and played me a few songs on her keyboard.
"Tomaru.?" (Are you staying tonight?)
"Mmm, Sore wa, chotto…," (That's kinda impossible.) making eye contact with her mom.
"Onegai, onegai onegai, okaasan to ishyoni futon de neru yo." (Please, please, please. You can sleep on the futon with me and my mom.)

Again I looked at her mom, uncomfortable with the proposal, but not wanting to disappoint Shion. *"Even the babe in suckling hurleth her own mother in the jaws of the beast."*
"Ii yo, it's ok," her mother said, sensing my hesitation.
"If it's ok with you, you can stay."

My lack of interest in Shion's mother by no means meant she was undesirable, as on the contrary she was an appealing 29-year-old with all the features which I had desired in a partner. But even more enticing, she was truly an adult and quite marriageable. Hence it would be at least awkward and difficult, if not impossible to slumber platonically on the same futon. Besides, Mr. Yamada, who she later revealed was madly in love with her and wanted to abandon his wife for her, had forewarned her against any intimate involvement with me.

"He is playboy," she said he alerted her. And he would know. For the previous five years, frequently our meetings were during my ferrying the collection of women on the back of my mountain bike, as if they had been the day's catch from the nearby lake. Even if it were possible to sleep with her without *sleeping with her*, or even touching her, she may well have thought something the matter with me or perhaps more likely, with her. After all, as she was apprised, I am *playboy*, so she may have questioned the ability of this playboy to sleep on the same futon with her and not as much as touch her, had there not been something grossly unappealing about her person.

Etsuko and Sayo might have shared the same birth year, but their levels of maturity were light years apart. Silent and introspective, with a vaguely melancholic countenance, Etsuko was a student of the school of hard knocks, a single mother divorced even before her daughter's birth. But even before her doomed marriage, her upbringing in the typical distressing Japanese familial setting had sowed the seeds of darkness on her face. She spoke of a father who, during Japan's bubble era, was never home, always working or on golf trips.

"The only time I saw him was during Obon in August and our annual week long ski trips in December." Her elder sister by six years, a hikkikomori who stayed home from high school for three years, was hospitalized at twelve for anorexia and depression.

"My sister decided to stay home after some students began to shun her from their groups. But she studied for the university entrance test by herself and got in."

This shunning or *freezing out* is quite common in this society where group acceptance is an obsession and even among adult co-workers *freezing out* is frequently practiced, sometimes with fatal consequences. Now 35 years old, Etsuko's sister resides with her parents, overly attached, manga obsessed, boyfriendless and still a virgin.

As a child observing her unfavourable familial dynamics, Etsuko endevoured to leave the household at the earliest chance, which for her came at 18 years old. However, jumping from the frying pan, she found herself in the fire, married to a man addicted to gambling, who later sent them bankrupt, prompting a divorce. After spending some months with her child in the US and Australia, she accurately arrived at the conclusion that, as a single divorced mother, life in Japan would be hopeless for both her and her child and it would be impossible to find a life partner and pursue her dream of being an entrepreneur.

"Most men I meet don't like Shion. They want to be with me, but always they want me to leave her at my parents' house. Sore wa iiya. (That's unacceptable) I don't choose a man over my child," as do many abusive single mothers in Japan. The media is inundated with incidences of women abusing, even murdering, or abetting their boyfriends in murdering their own children to gain his approval.

Shion was delighted to be snuggled up next to her new father, as I read her bedtime stories in Japanese, with her frequently correcting my pronunciation. In no time she was in dreamland ensconced between her mother and me, from where I lifted her to the opposite side of her mother. Though Etsuko was clad in anti-Viagral sweat pants and a T-shirt, as predicted it was difficult laying with her without consequence, which soon saw blood vacate the upper head as I held her in the spoon position, fondling her supple round breasts. Having had no such tactile contact in a year, she gasped and squeezed my hand onto her chest, then turned around to allow me full oral access. As I slid my hand inside her panties, she grabbed my wrist, but already I had detected her reason for arresting my hand.
"Gome, (I'm sorry) it just started yesterday. Let's go to sleep," apologizing sheepishly.
But my condition defied sleep, forcing me to relieve myself in her bathroom, before resuming the spoon position in slumber.

Feeling guilty for having taken advantage of her, in the morning I apologized for being unable to resist the urge to fondle her the night before.
"It's ok," she said. "I'm not prudish. I didn't expect you to stay in the same futon and not touch me. You are a man, deshou? Anyway, I enjoyed it."
A week later saw the beginning of a new Friday routine. During my next visit, an hour after entering Etsuko's apartment and playing with her daughter, Shion made a starling request.
"Ishouni ofuro hairu?"
"She wants you to take a bath with her," Etsuko translated.

"What?!" Trying to conceal my shock.

In Japan, it's customary for families to take baths together sometimes even until the daughters are in their teens, thus appropriately, it may well have been that having heard her friends talk about their baths with their fathers, she simply wanted to experience such paternal bonding. But my Western socialization was anathema to her innocent request, as Western, Christian civilization and its prudish and shameful take on nudity, had made me uncomfortable. Moreover, in the West it would simply be unheard of for a woman to allow her 5-year-old daughter to bathe with a man whom she had met only a month earlier. On one hand, it spoke volumes to the kind of trust I evoke in people, of which I am quite proud, but on the other it demonstrated a wide spread naiveté and absence of critical thought, so common in *safety* Japan. Furthermore, this would be a true test of the motive for my attachment to this child. Already I had intellectualized the reason as a strong need to father, nurture and care for a child. "But what if I were wrong? What if I indeed had perverted paedophilic tendencies?" This would most definitely be my chance to confront them.

"Get over yourself!" I monologued. *"The kid just wants to have a bath with her dad, so just get over your Western, biblical culture, get over the shame associated with nudity, your obsessive invasive thoughts, get over your baggage, get over the whole thing, take your clothes off and take a bath with the kid, for Chrise sake!"* Already I had interpreted Etsuko's look as saying, *"Yeh, she wants to take a bath with you because you're her new father figure, and that's what fathers do, stupid! It means she really likes you."* And not wanting to alert her to my laughable, mostly culturally based discomfort with their proposal, I proceeded to strip and remove Shion's clothes, as if she were my own daughter. Once in the shower together, I began to acknowledge and embrace all my sentiments of discomfort, a process I had learned some ten years ago in Rick Edelstein's acting classes.

"Yes, I am very uncomfortable with this situation, because I come from a background where nudity is associated with sex. But here I am with a 5-year-old girl, who I could not and did not sexualize, and as I reconfirmed after repulsion from my then present, unwelcomed cogitations, my obsessive invasive thoughts since my childhood derived not from desire to commit said acts, but from the fact that the acts themselves were so grossly devious. For looking at Shion's tiny 5-year-old body generated no sexual feelings, as it should not have, but further solidified and reinforced my paternal attachment to her, becoming venomous at the thought that there are men who'd sexually molest this and other 5 year olds. I wanted to empower her, as I did my own child, against ubiquitous child predators and on my next visit, with her mother's help we gave her the exact talk I gave my real daughter at seven, about anyone touching her private area inappropriately and suggested that at six years old, it would be a good time to enroll her in a martial arts class.

Back in the shower having been liberated from the puritanical ideas about nudity, Shion and I got down to the business of bonding in a father daughter bath. Earlier upon removing my clothes, a shock consumed her face.

"Nande karada no zembu hiyakeshita no?" (Why is your whole body sunburnt?)

Previously she had thought only my face, hands and feet were dark and couldn't comprehend that the skin color on my entire body was different from hers. She frantically summoned her mother.

"OKAASAN, OTOSAN NO KARADA ZEMBU HIYAKESHITA. MITE! She screamed, (MOM, DAD'S ENTIRE BODY IS SUNBURNT. COME LOOK!)

as I lathered her tiny body, explaining to her that around the world there are different kinds of people with different color skin and different kinds of eyes, hair, nose and lips. The amazement on her face was a Kodak moment.

"So nan ya?" (really?) Brows raised with hands akimbo.

Shortly there after her mother decided to join us, to which I objected, advising her to wait until Shion had exited, as her presence would most definitely have caused changes to my anatomy. Changes which would have been inappropriate, I thought, for her daughter to behold.

With Shion asleep, Etsuko and I made our intimate debut that night, tears streaming down the sides of her face.

"Are you ok? Why are you crying?"

"Nothing, I'm just overwhelmed, that's all. It feels good."

Before falling asleep, I had strongly urged her to begin taking birth control pills, as that first time was most definitely not going to be our last.

"It's too expensive," she said.

Considering her financial status of single parent living in government housing and planning to emigrate shortly, I promised to foot the cost. But a week later she decided against it.

"My friend said it gave her headaches," she said.

No later than two months after we had met on my fifth visit to her apartment, one night at the dinner table with Shion on my lap swinging from my neck, I noticed ever so subtle changes in her mother's breasts, to which she responded,

"We have a problem."

Another failure of the withdrawal method: a nightmare come true. For here was a woman who was sent to me for help, who is now carrying my child, pregnancy number four in Japan.

From every angle, though we both wanted to keep the pregnancy, the logistics were impossible. She had plans to emigrate, I had plans to leave Japan and marry Shoko and to top it off, we both were in an impecunious state. But it was romantically appealing to give Shion a sibling and support both *my* children.

On the morning of Monday November 20, 2006 Etsuko waved good-bye at Senri Chuo station, on her way to the hospital where I was teaching, and I went to work in Tennoji.

"Don't worry about me," she said. "I'm strong."

"Yeh, but this could have easily been avoided." However, like most women in Japan, she had internalized her status as sacrificial lamb on the altar of the Japanese abortion industry. It made much more sense to her to undergo an abortion, than to take birth control pills. At day's end, Etsuko and I held each other in silence for what seemed like hours, as Shion entertained herself, sometimes inquiring what's wrong.

"Shhhh, okaasan ga choshi waruii." (Mom's not feeling well.)

Shortly after the termination, though Shion whined and begged for my presence, protecting her emotions, Etsuko abruptly severed all contact between us. "I have to protect myself," she wrote in a last e-mail before blocking my phone number and e-mail address. "Please understand."

AKARI

Just as I had concluded that there were no spontaneously intelligent young women in Japan, or at least in the Kansai region, in March of 2006 while browsing the Kinokunya bookstore at Hankyu Umeda, I spotted an exceptionally statuesque and womanly frame from behind. At 5'9" she towered over other women, and proudly owned her atypically Japanese, Carmela Soprano figure. There was nothing girly about her big-boned, curvaceous physique. She was all woman, the type despised by Japanese men. Approaching her slowly, savouring every arc and parabola of her body, her rondure derriere seemed trapped in tight black pants. Upon walking past her to discreetly examine her face, I observed that she was reading, or at least held open in her hands, a copy of Scientific America magazine. This along with her inflated lips and her avant-garde orange and green spectacles stopped me dead in my tracks.

"Wow, that's pretty impressive," I interrupted. "You are reading Scientific America."
"Of course, it's my favourite magazine."
"It's one of mine too."
Akari, Japanese Condoleeza Rice, possessed a unique attractiveness about her, the kind that one might expect of scientific *brainiac* women of her prodigy. In fact, there was nothing regular about her, which was obvious from her imposing stature and artsy glasses. At 26 years old, this devout Dave Matthews fan, multi-instrumentalist, former punk band drummer and triathlete had recently obtained her medical license and was in the process of beginning her residency at a hospital in Tokyo. Meeting her called to memory an Asian-American prodigy with whom I was involved in common law marriage in California, whose first job after college, landed her a six figure salary. For two years during our relationship, there was an unending feud between my veneration for her brain and my need for eye candy on my arm. In the end, though I was far more attracted to her intellect and personality than to her physicality, the need for beauty was victorious over my appreciation for grey matter.

Akari was of similar ilk; fairly attractive, captivatingly athletic and unspeakably intellectually fit. I wanted to copulate with her brain. In fact I wanted her to bear my children. Immediately upon meeting, we launched into stimulating conversation on a variety of subjects from medicine, society, politics, and education, until it was closing time at the bookstore. After which we exchanged contact information, with her promising that we would meet again on her next trip from her home in Kyushu to visit her parents in Osaka. After five years of being in Japan, finally meeting a woman like her was like finding an oasis in hell, and our stimulating and invigorating exchanges continued even in regular phone e-mails before our next meeting a month later.

Convincing her to show up at my apartment, as I was a bit under the weather, she arrived with cold medicine, vitamins and orange juice, greeted by my pictures of Azusa and me in my living room.
"Is this your girlfriend?"
"Yeh, we're getting married this year."
"She is so beautiful."
Pictures of Azusa had an intimidating effect on women who came to my apartment. On one hand they were jealous of her stunning beauty, but on the other, seeing her beauty made them feel inadequate and caused them to want me even more. Even though they too were beautiful, in their minds I couldn't possibly want sex from them, as I had such a beautiful fiancée. Additionally, perhaps they were delighted that though she was so beautiful, I still wanted them. It was discernible from Akari's expressions that those sentiments were floating through her mind, but unlike the other women, my attempts to get her to join me in bed were futile.

"I know about foreigners like you," she asserted. "You just think you can do whatever you want with Japanese girls because we are easy. And you live in Japan carefree without responsibilities, just having sex with many different girls. I know, I used to be one of those stupid yellow cabs. I came to your apartment because you were sick and you are interesting to talk to, but I'm not gonna have sex with you. So if that's why you invited me here, it's not going to happen and I won't come back. Next time we have to meet outside."

Gob smacked, I lay on my back with her sitting beside me on the bed. She was right, 100% right and there was nothing I could have said in response.
"Besides, I told you I have a boyfriend."
Indeed, she had informed me of her divorced, early forties, Irish-

American, single parent boyfriend. But her hints about his intimidation by her genius, led me to conclude that theirs was a relationship whose end draweth nigh, especially after her relocation to Tokyo for her residency. "I'm sorry, I didn't invite you over for sex," I lied.

Having held her in the highest regard and not wanting to jeopardize our friendship, I aborted the pursuit of intimate relations, choosing contentment with our cyber-contact. Besides, I was in retirement, content with plans to wed not one but two consenting and amazingly beautiful women, both with whom I was madly in love. After all, for what more could I have asked? And even so, still there were Henni and Sachiko, another of my Japanese language teachers from the same school where Karin taught. Thirty-four years old, I had devirginised her only a year prior, before setting off to Jamaica. So Akari and I continued our e-mail exchanges. Nevertheless, ever since she had left my apartment, I began to harbor the notion that when the stressors of residency hit her, she would call me for relief.

Seven months into her residency, after Azusa and Shoko had left for Canada and the States respectively, I received an e-mail from Akari. "What are you doing this weekend? Can I come and see you?" It read. "But I have to tell you, I'm on my period." "What does your period have to do with anything?" Pretending sincerity. "It would be good just to see you." Originally I had thought her main purpose for traveling to Kansai was to visit her parents, but she made it clear that she wanted to spend the entire weekend with me. Arriving at my apartment she tried in vain to explain her reason for adding the disclaimer about her period. "I thought that maybe you'd expect something to happen between us and I didn't want you to be disappointed." "I don't know what you're talking about. Why would I expect that?" Fronting cluelessness. "You said you didn't want us to be intimate and I respected that."

My notion of some months back was right on the mark, as Japanese women had become all too predictable. Making her debut in Neurology, isolated in a new environment as fighting escalated between her and her boyfriend, the stress of her first tour drove her to board the bullet train for the 3 hour journey to the refuge of my arms. For two days I waited on her, pampered her and nursed her back to life.

"I feel so relaxed with you," a mantra I had heard from all but a few of the women with whom I had been in Japan. Six weeks later she returned for a weekend of marathon arrivals, some even self-induced. The only Japanese woman I have met, liberated and uninhibited enough to possess the ability to bring herself to orgasm, superwoman Akari could achieve multiples internally or externally through manual or oral stimulation. She was the only Japanese woman who articulated exactly how she wanted to be pleasured.

"That's my spot, you're hitting my spot," She would scream, body and face in contortions, appearing to have out of planetary experiences.
In a testament to the general naïveté and unempowered status of Japanese women, or at least those in Kobe, at no point did this doctor - among Japan's finest minds - request the use of a condom, not even in concern about diseases. And what's more, when I suggested birth control pills to her, she protested, citing concern about having to see the doctors at the hospital of her employment.

"I don't want them to talk about me or know my business. I work at that hospital, so I don't want them to know about my private life and there are no other hospitals around. I can't get the pill anyway. Only if I had some kind of problem, would they give me the pill. We can have sex without a condom, but I won't take birth control pills."

"So what if you get pregnant?"
"I know my body, I won't get pregnant."
"Yes, but what if you do?" I insisted. To which she paused.
"I don't know. I guess I would have to get an operation."
"You mean an abortion?"
"Yes, but maybe. I don't know."
It was indecipherable to me that her words originated from the mouth of a medical doctor. This was a replay of the kind of strange logic and countless red herrings I had heard from Karin, some four years earlier. Trauma based reasoning I labeled it. And indeed, in the ensuing six months, this doctor would reveal to me even more absurd reasoning.

Upon meeting Akari, though impressed by her outward appearance of confidence, beneath her strong presence, given my knowledge of Japanese society, I expected trauma. The second of three *brainiac* daughters, her father was a renowned heart surgeon and her mother a nurse. Like most Japanese women, dad was absent throughout her childhood, but she held him in high esteem and appreciated the demands which kept him away from the family. However, unlike most Japanese women, her father did instill in her a sense of empowerment. It may well have been that having three daughters, he was feminized and had no choice but to empower his girls, since his third child was not the boy for whom he might have hoped. Three years earlier I had observed a similar dynamic in Fu's family. She too came from a family of three high achieving girls and I suspected in the absence of sons, otherwise chauvinistic fathers are compelled to empower their daughters.

Given the extreme pressure to conform in Japan, it would have been absolutely impossible for Akari, atypically Japanese in so many ways, to escape her society's hammering unscathed. She may have hailed from one of the rare supportive and nurturing families in Japan, but entering elementary school saw the beginning of suicidal thoughts. As I have stated earlier, trauma is inescapable in the Japanese socialization. Having been taller, bustier, and brainier than her peers, Akari spoke of perpetual, unmitigated bullying, continual self-hate and daily haunting by suicidal ideations since she was eight.

"I'm more confident about my abilities than most Japanese," she agreed. "But I hate my looks. I don't fit the Japanese standard of beauty, I'm too tall, my lips are too big. When I see all those Japanese girls, those idols in magazines, I am so envious of them. It just makes me depressed."

This, her profound inferiority complex and life long trauma, all came to the fore upon informing her of Etsuko's Chlamydia which I had transmitted to her, or so I had thought. To my shock she protested treatment, just as she had protested using birth control pills.

"It doesn't make any sense to get treated, I'm just gonna get it again," she blurted in sheer asininity.

"Am I hearing what I'm hearing? Are these the words of a doctor?" I pondered.

My almost two decades of therapy and near equal time as a John Bradshaw fan, consuming his books and seminars on Public Television, told me that within Akari, there was abject disparagement of self. But the bombshell was yet to come.

"Actually, I have been having symptoms," said Dr. Akari.

"What kind of symptoms?" I queried.

"You know, discharge, smell."

"For how long? Since we started having sex?"

"For about three years now," responding nonchalantly.

"Then why the FUCK didn't you get it checked?" I yelled in the microphone during our skype call, leading her to believe that she had transmitted the bacteria to me. Perhaps out of shame, she shifted from the camera.

"I CAN'T FUCKING SEE YOU! COME BACK IN FRONT OF THE CAMERA!" Screaming at the top of my lungs.

"AREN'T YOU A FUCKING DOCTOR? DON'T YOU KNOW WHAT UNTREATED CHLAMYDIA DOES TO YOUR REPRODUCTIVE ORGANS? DON'T YOU KNOW ECTOPIC PREGNANCIES CAN BE FUCKING FATAL?

Akari was the third woman I had met in Japan who was resistant to my advice to treat her Chlamydia. First there was 24-year-old Saori, my sexual debut, who traveled untreated to Australia for a year, eight months after I had alerted her of the disease. Five years later there was Etsuko 29, who objected to seeing a doctor, on account of not experiencing any symptoms, though I had informed her that 80% of women are asymptomatic. Indeed Chlamydia, the silent killer is epidemic in Japan. A 2004 study testing 3,190 students between the ages of 16 and 18 at 13 high schools, revealed an infection rate of 11.4%, with most students carrying the disease unaware of their condition, while those who were cognizant, like Doctor Akari and Etsuko, refrained from getting treatment.

In Europe and the United States, infection frequencies are 1 to 2% of the population, nothing compared to Japan, which has the highest infection rate among advanced countries. For this, the blame lies squarely on Japan's primitive and irresponsible reluctance to provide sex education in high school. In typical Japanese cart before the horse fashion, some semblance of sex education is taught in elementary school but absent in junior high and high school, as the educators themselves are children, too shy to speak about the adult subject of sex. Hence Chlamydia runs rampant among Japanese teens. In another survey in 2005, it was reported that 7% of women in the 20-24 age group, are carriers of the bacteria. However, an abortionist in Osaka, the brother of one of my subjects, suggests that percentage could be more than double.

"I didn't think it was important to see a doctor."
Clearly there must have been a reason, and a damn good one, why a doctor, a medical doctor fails for three years to be treated for symptoms of a venereal disease. First her resistance to the pill and permissive unprotected sex was curious, but now, an adult with above average intelligence, a medical

professional resisting treatment for a sexually transmitted disease, now that took the cake.

"Only in Japan," I thought.

It brought to mind my friend Sahara's visit to the doctor in order to quit smoking.
"You're OK," the doctor assured her. "You're smoking only five a day, so it's not that bad."
Determined to get to the root of Akari's behavior, I continued to delve into her psyche.

"Actually I don't care about my reproductive system. I know about the dangers of Chlamydia but I don't' care. I never cared, I want to have many children, but I want to adopt, I don't want to deliver my own."

Akari thought her look so repugnant and ugly, that she never wanted to have children, out of fear they would look like her. It all made perfect sense. My entire being reached out in empathy for her inner torture, as I too harbored those exact complexes, the Michael Jackson syndrome, in my youth, obsessing that I would never produce offsprings, hence they be cursed with my liver lips and skin of tar.

The Michael Jackson Complex afflicts a great many people of colour, especially we Negroes. However, Michael, the most salient victim of this disease, and for whom I have named the sickness, had enough cash to surgically modify his phenotype, even perhaps going to the extreme of fertilizing his wife's egg with sperm from a Caucasian man. I too contemplated lip reduction surgery in my twenties and in my native Jamaica, since my childhood, dark skinned men and women have been bleaching their skin. Had it not been for therapy, education and traveling, I would have most certainly gone under the knife. During my teenage years in the Park Hill neighborhood of Denver, Colorado, it was common to hear African-American teenage boys, declare,
"Ain't no way my kids go have no nappy ass hair." Something tells me that a certain United States Chief Justice, whose name I will not mention, is among public figures suffering from this affliction.
It is safe to conclude, that where there was the presence of white colonizers, or a philia for white European aesthetics, there will be Michael Jackson Syndrome, Japan being no exception.

Only after threatening to withdraw my respect and reverence for her, did Akari seek treatment, after which we continued regularly scheduled weekend *orgas-ma-thons* and video sessions until my last few days in Japan.

SURROGATE SEX IN JAPAN

In 2003, during the Karin era, while boarding the train at Sumiyoshi, I met a lanky and handsome 33-year-old from the Ivory Coast. Immediately our conversation turned to women in Japan.

"Oh god! It's just crazy," snow-white smile peering through midnight lips, as he began telling me of a childless, married 50-year-old business owner in his collection.

"She gives me a spending allowance of 200,000 yen per month, a clothing allowance of 100,000 yen a month, rent of another 100,000 yen a month, plus she even paid the deposit of 1,000,000 yen on my apartment. And we have sex only once or twice a month."

Initially, I was convinced he was spinning a tall tale, but even if it weren't true, it was plausible. Such arrangements can be found internationally, but his addition to the story hit me for six and threw me in a loop. Frequently, he said in his thick African accent,
"We all go out together. Me, she, her husband, and he knows about everysing."
My jaws hit the floor of the JR train. Living in Japan, I had heard and seen it all, but the idea of a husband being friendly with a man who was pleasuring his wife was enough to put me in cardiac arrest.

Another friend of mine on the Japan Exchange Teacher's program, a tall blond from Nevada, told me of yet another eye popping experience. After having dinner with an official and his wife at their home, the wife excused herself from the table.
"My wife wants to have sex with you," said the husband to Tyler, who tried his utmost to maintain his composure. "She's going to take a bath, you should go meet her." Tyler obliged, as in his words, "dude's wife was hot." Following their romp in the bath, the husband's only beef was that Tyler had tainted the bath water with his semen.

After returning from Jamaica, Natasha, a friend from Hungary who had been studying Buddhism in Japan, introduced me to her friend, a 38-year-old spouse of a Shinto Priest. She had been on the prowl for a substitute lover, as hers lived in Algeria and traveled to Japan infrequently. Hence in an attempt to obtain a local standby boyfriend, she sought to negotiate with me.

"Oh, my husband doesn't care," she assured me. "We haven't had sex for almost ten years, so he doesn't care about my boyfriends. He just wants me to be happy." Markedly below my attractiveness requirements, any liaison with her would have been a charity affair. During our conversation at a Turkish restaurant in Osaka, severe trauma seeped from every facial pore and after telling of my own childhood trauma, she was comfortable enough to reciprocate with stories of severe depression, and of a mother who had made several attempts at suicide.

Natasha's friend brought me closer to believing those anecdotes about husbands supporting, condoning, ignoring, even encouraging their wives' pleasure mates, but meeting Masako drove the point straight home. Late August 2006 at Kyobashi station, where I had met Yukari and Azusa five months and two and a half years earlier respectively, I was mesmerized by a pair of pockets dancing on a rounded derriere climbing some stairs. Though I was headed to the Tozai line, my state of hypnosis compelled me to give chase on the loop line. However, as though she felt my laser piercing stare, to my disappointment, she wrapped her sweater around her waist, prompting me to move in for a face check. Masako was a beautiful, regal, athletic 46-year-old. Her short layered haircut reeked of a non-Japanese kind of confidence. Clone she was not. Her individuality was as pronounced as her lime green patent leather shoes, which matched her glasses of the same color.

MASAKO

Masako brought to mind those upper middle class housewives in Lafayette or Hillsborough California, after whom I was perpetually concupiscent in my twenties.

"You look like you speak English," I interrupted in my tired but effective opener.

"Yes, a little, but I haven't used English in a long time, so I am not very good."

On her way to her wine tasting class just two stops away, meant that time was of the essence and inveigling her contact information had to be quick. But revealing her interest in show jumping, opened the chance to request her name card, and resolved my pondering about her wonderfully toned arms.

"I want to watch you ride," I assured her as she departed from the train.

Two weeks later, I traveled to Shiga for lunch with her and her husband. Immediately it was blatantly obvious they were a sexless couple. She was athletic, vibrant, effulgent and extroverted, diametrically opposite to his almost anorexic appearance. Eleven years her senior, his silver locks thinned and his laughter - like that of Jim Carey's character in "The Mask," - revealed a touch of Autistic Spectrum Disorder or perhaps Asperger's Syndrome. Nevertheless, I admired Takeshi, a successful business man, who had steered a 200-year-old family business to monumental national success. In fact, it was most refreshing to meet both Masako and Takeshi who were true individuals in the Western sense. They both despised the status quo and were the butt of jokes and gossip in their neighborhood, on account of their non-traditionally Japanese behavior.

"But we don't care," Takeshi chimed with his awkward Jim Carey laugh. Adding to his statement as though completing it, his wife interrupted, "we live life to the fullest, with passion, to be happy. People in our society have no passion, so they think we are strange."

Lunch was on Takeshi, from which we returned on foot to their massive abode, where Masako showed me their collection of twenty cars, then took me for a spin without her husband.   Masako was a kept woman, whose husband derived pleasure in fulfilling all her wants, including the freedom to find a surrogate to meet the needs he could not.

"This Dino is my favourite car," instructing me to get in. During our exhilarating drive up winding mountain roads, I began to stroke her upper arm before holding her hand whenever possible.   Shortly thereafter she stopped at the summit of our journey overlooking the city.

"Shall we kiss?" She inquired. To which I was only too happy to oblige, while keeping a sharp watch on the time so as not to be too late for my first outing with Manami back in Osaka.

Returning to their multi-car *warehouse*, we continued our consumption of each other's lips, when the shutter descended far enough so our actions could not be recognized.   Mouth still locked, we hurriedly unbuckled each other's jeans, like teenagers trying to get busy before being caught. Her jeans appeared to have been welded, form-fitted onto her curvy athletic body and after much effort I pried them and her panties from her and began curling her, 52 kilograms and 158 centimeters, onto my north pointing member.   It had been five years for her, so my invasion was the source of great pain.

"I have to cook my husband's dinner," she said, as I curled her up and down. "Already we've been gone too long.   Let's meet next weekend again and go to a hotel."

"How was the drive?" Takeshi catechized upon our return to their home. "Did you like the sightseeing?

"Yes, your wife is a first class driver."

MANAMI

Manami had been waiting at Osaka station for nearly 45 minutes and by then, the film we had planned to watch was already 30 minutes underway. Infuriated, she threatened to return home.

"You were on another date weren't you?"

"Why would you think that?" I lied. "Why would you start out our interaction by accusing me? This is not good, I don't appreciate that."

She was quite right, fully aware of the kind of man I was from the very start. Manami's baggage was highly visible; Samsonite, American Tourister and a Jansport backpack, none of which could fit through the square opening to determine if they were check-in or carry-on luggage. However, in her case, this baggage served her well, making her atypically aggressive for a Japanese woman and protective from predatory men like me.

"I'm sorry, you're right," she responded. "I shouldn't have said that. I've had some bad experiences."

"I can tell."

I had met Manami late summer '06 at Umeda's Bagel Cafe, as she stood in line immediately in front of me, owning a figure more striking and Junoesque than Akari. From the looks of her cello-like childbearing curvature, athletic steatopygia and statuesque 168 centimeters, I concluded that, probability was high she was single, as hers by no means was the elementary schoolgirl body favoured by Japanese men, but the thick, buxom, womanly hourglass preferred by Jamaicans and other *Diasporic* Africans. As Jamaicans would say, she was in full possession of the *agony,* causing me to stand behind her in erectile torture. At 60 kilograms, she was obese by Japanese standards, which I predicted would have been one source of her trauma.

"You look like you speak English," I interrupted, hoping her face would match the splendor of the rearview.

"Yes, I just came back after two years in Hawaii."

Though trauma was detectable in her cheeks and downturn eyes, she was indeed a beautiful woman. Not like Shoko or Azusa, but beauteous, in spite of her malocclusion. In fact, in Manami's case her slightly crooked teeth were charming.

"Hawaii! Why did you come back?"

"So desu ne," face and body lilting south. "I ran out of money, and it's so difficult to get a visa to live in America."

For many Japanese women, returning home after experiencing the freedom of the West can itself be a major source of suffrage and adjustment trauma. Making matters worse, nubile 35-year-olds like Manami, who would be shown daily appreciation in the West – as she reported – are plentiful in Japan, where they are routinely ignored. But my trauma radar, from her reserved speech pattern, and adult face which did not match the youth of her hands, detected severe damage. Assessing her physicality, it was immediately obvious, that mad addiction to her was inevitable. From my years of experience, the most dramatic, damaged women possessed the most luring sexuality which caused complete loss of self-control. Manami was one of those women, I knew it immediately. The longing look of loneliness in her eyes told me she had been played like a fiddle and hurt too many times and, that she'd go off on the next man who attempted to dog her. She would have to be lonely; after all, she was an untouchable in Japan. My guess was, though she didn't overtly appear to be *chocolate eyed*, or *a Cadillac chaser*, in Hawaii she perhaps discovered that she disproportionately attracted African-American men, who like me, were only interested in her agony. As it turned out, bingo, I was right.

After enduring five years of abuse and neglect in marriage, to overcome her pain, Manami fled to Hawaii where she dated a few African-Americans, including one whom she found on a date with another Japanese woman. Two years later, at 35 years old she returned home bankrupt, still uneducated with no choice but to reside with her parents in a dodgy part of Osaka, while temping as an *Office Lady*. I had seen Manami's profile before. Tomoko in 2002, also uneducated, had spent seven years in England only to return to Japan in her mid thirties, to live frustrated and hopeless with her parents. And like Manami, Hisako fled the country after her divorce, returning after two years in Australia. Parents having died, her father from suicide and mother accidentally, 28-year-old Hisako resided with her aunt, while working as another uneducated *Office Lady*.

Finally arriving at the cash register, observing our friendly interaction, the cashier presumed we were together and calculated our orders as such.

"Chigaimasu, betsu betsu desu. Kare wa shiranai hito desu," (That's not so, the bill is separate. He's a stranger.) protested Manami, to which the young woman behind the counter responded embarrassingly with profuse apologies. By then Manami had already paid the 700 yen for my salmon bagel with capers, as it would have been quite a hassle to correct the problem.

"Don't worry," I comforted her. "Next time, movie on me."

"Yeh, you're just saying that."

"Well, let's just rent a DVD and watch it at my apartment."

"I don't wanna go to your apartment," she protested. "I don't know you."

"I understand, but I will make it up to you by fixing you dinner."

After some negotiation, she agreed, and the rest unfolded predictably as usual. Exactly as I had presaged, hyper-orgasmic, highly addictive Manami had the agony like only a selected few before her; Tomoko, Karin, Anne and Rapunzel. Her possessive personality which she had revealed on our first date, rapidly escalated and brought to mind Karin, who on one occasion had covered my kitchen floor with kerosene and decorated it with broken crockery, all because I suspected her of invading my privacy, which she denied. In her explanation, attempting to find a piece of her garment, she ventured into one of my drawers where she found some condoms with several missing from the pack.

"I wasn't searching through your things," she defended herself. "I was just looking for some underwear I misplaced, and found your condoms. I can see you're still fucking around."

In my book, any breach of privacy calls for immediate separation, regardless of how she tried to justify her behavior. All too often, I have heard horror stories of my friends' significant others exploring their cell phones, discovering evidence of other women, a gross invasion of privacy for which I have zero tolerance. Nothing Karin could have said could've made me believe her. And while her defense could have been true, mentioning her discovery was in poor judgment. My disbelief sent her into one of her many rages, the worse thus far, and after ignoring her hour long, stalker-like phone calls from outside my apartment, she began kicking on the metal door until well past midnight, when my neighbor Jacque intervened.

"Excuse me miss," I heard him say. "Some of us have to go to work in the morning."

Manami had similar potential, but as I was older and wiser, I had learned to heed the bells and flashing red lights. Almost immediately, on arrival at my apartment, she began to position my photos with Shoko face down and in less than a fortnight, insisted on viewing my pictures and videos on my cell phone. She clearly new what time it was, what Westerners like me were up to in Japan and as I was not about to conceal my activities from her or any other woman, I gladly obliged. Buyer beware, is my ardent policy.

"Here you go, knock yourself out, enjoy," handing her my cell phone.
"Hentai!" (pervert) she gasped, mouth agape on the train.
"You are sick! I can't believe this," enthralled by the progressively graphic photos. But soon, explicit pictures of her too would be added to the collection. As she became more attached, Manami insisted on an exclusive relationship, even imploring me to abandon my plans to marry Shoko.
"I don't want to see her picture when I go to your apartment," she demanded. "That's disrespectful to me."

"Well then, don't visit my apartment anymore." But that was impossible. Like many women before her, regular multiple orgasms had caused her pituitary gland to release enough oxytocin, that she had become obsessively attached. However, two months later, Manami was surgically abandoned after playfully suggesting that she would bobbit me, as in sever my penis, if I didn't stop my philandering. It may have been in jest, but from the look in her eyes, she was at least 50% serious, and I had no interest in keeping her around to find out.

MASAKO CONTINUED

Two weeks after meeting Masako and her husband, we all met again at a Thai restaurant in Hikone. However, as an appetizer to lunch, she took me to a love hotel before joining her husband, who was waiting at the restaurant. It became a frequent occurrence, to either visit the love ho, before or after lunch or dinner with her and her husband, with her sometimes insisting on a room in a hotel a few blocks away from their house. She enjoyed the thrill of our affair right beneath her husband's nose. In fact before me, six years prior, she had been intimate with one of her husband's employee's, 10 years her junior, often frolicking in the car near their home. However, overpowered by guilt, the employee terminated the affair. For me, a hotel so close to their home was just too close for comfort.

"Next time you have to come to my apartment," I insisted, to which she complied.

After two months, like many married women reported by my friends, and like Natsuko before her, Masako began to request exclusivity.

"Masako, you're married. Think about what you're asking for. How can you want me to stop seeing other women, when you are married and being supported by your husband? What benefit do I get for being in an exclusive relationship with you? Can I ask you to divorce your husband?"

"Yes, you're right I'll just have to share you. It's better than nothing."

SEX OUTSOURCING

The idea of men outsourcing to other men, their sexual responsibilities to their wives, might be anathema to Western Judeo-Christian societies, but here in non-Christian Japan, many husbands, given the reality that they fall short in fulfilling their wives sexual needs, and that they may well be paying frequent patronage to the soaplands, turn a blind eye to their wives affairs. In meeting the demand for sexual surrogates, a service has popped up in Tokyo for women who find unbearable, their sexless existences in matrimony. According to Kim Myong-Gan, the operator of this suburban clinic, every year 200 women who have been sexless with their husbands, some for up to 20 years – like Ai's mother- solicit his services. One woman had been married for 15 years but had not consummated her relationship with her husband.

"The women who come to see me love their husbands and aren't looking for a divorce," he's quoted as saying. "The problem is that their husbands lose interest in sex or don't want sex from the start. Many men think of their wives as substitute mothers, not as women with emotional and sexual needs." The women are required to pay an initial counseling fee of 20,000 yen, after which they are shown photographs of predominantly professional men in their 40s, from which to choose for a date, paid for by both parties. Dates are followed by regular visits to a hotel, whose cost is also split between the men and women. Said Mr. Kim, "The men love their companies; they live for work. Men don't even think it is a problem if they don't have sex with their wives. They have pornography and the sex industry to take care of their needs, but their wives have nowhere to go. They just suffer in silence."

THE INESCAPABLE

In September '06, a year and nine months before my departure from Japan, that which I had been dreading for five years: teaching at a high school, came to pass, when my downstairs neighbor recommended me for a teaching position at a private high school from which he was resigning. As if a test of my will power, the students were not required to wear uniforms, but the girls united on a uniform of their own: that of video ho. At this international high school in East Osaka, beguiling, physically developed teenage girls showed up daily in hip huggers with exposed midriffs and G strings at the waist. Micro-mini dresses and skirts provided a calcifying display of crotch, as they perpetually adjusted their make-up and curled their hair during class. Addressing the principal with my concerns, he assured me that nothing could be done about the girls' attire. "We've already told them that they could wear whatever they wanted to." It wasn't abnormal for me to stand in front of class, attempting to conceal a certain affected part of my anatomy.

Chiaki's eyes sprung to attention the second I walked in class on my first day. Seventeen years old, make-up an inch thick with cart wheels dangling from her ears, *ghetto japulous* Chichan fit the under-achiever profile of a chocolate loving Cadillac chaser. Her father, whom she adored, was an over-indulging parent who allowed his daughter to live with her boyfriends, all of whom were in their 20s, since she was 15 years old. Her current boyfriend was 27 years old and among her friends was a 14-year-old who was already a *baby mama* and another her age who had a dekichatta kekkon (shotgun marriage). "I love 2PAC and Bob Marley," she declared, bending over in her micro-mini exposing her underwear, as she showed me her MySpace pictures on one of several laptops in the classroom. "*That figures*," I thought. "This is me with dreads, and this is me with braids. "Kawaii deshou?" (Am I not cute?)

Positively, on account of her obsession with hip hop and reggae, her command of English far exceeded that of her classmates and by the second day of class, she requested my e-mail address. Coming from the West, I was hesitant to give students access to my personal information, but to my surprise, this practice was condoned by the faculty. "Ok, let me get this straight," I questioned another foreign teacher. "First, the girls are dressed like they're on Santa Monica or Sunset Boulevard and second, we can exchange personal information with them?" "Only in Japan, perfectly allowed," assured Matt, who had been teaching there for two years and confided in me that another foreign teacher had been receiving regular fellatio in the men's room.

During my childhood, I frequently heard a saying from my beloved grandmother: If yu put butta pan pus mout, im wi lick it auf. (When butter is rubbed on a cat's mouth, he will most certainly lick it.) Shortly thereafter, Chiaki and I began exchanging e-mails by phone. "I'm 17 now, but my birthday will be in December," read one of her e-mails, accompanied by a photo of her in the bath. After her 18th birthday, by then planning to resign from my position, Chiaki and I increased contact. After all I reasoned, if the school's leaders were irresponsible enough to condone and encourage the sexualization of these physically ripe students, then predator that I was, that was an open invitation to pounce.

By January, escorting her home to Hana Zono, I was fondling my student to orgasm on the train. But by February I had resigned without inviting her to my apartment as promised, gradually ceasing all contact. My resignation or failure to make good on my promise to her was by no means attributable to some moral conscience which I had acquired. I simply hated the school and its underachieving students, who provided a torturous teaching experience. And thanks to my Adult Attention Deficit Hyperactive Disorder, my desire for Chiaki vanished at the end of my two 3-hour days at her school. Moreover, I was just done, I had had enough already.

As if being tested by the universe, a month after quitting Chiaki's school I secured a teaching position with handsome remunerations at yet another high school. This time at a private girls' school also in Osaka, where I was an instant hit. Once again the fox was handed a job in the chicken coop. But the difference with this chicken coop was the chickens were in uniforms below the knees, regulations with which most girls complied. A small percentage of the girls elevated their hemlines to allow daily crotch viewing in class, and were met with only superficial reprimand by faculty members. One fulltime faculty member took the matter of these unruly girls to the principal, who responded by instructing her to refrain from scolding them about their crotch baring skirts in class.

Recently, Japanese educators have been experimenting with the idea of individuality, but in their misdirected interpretation of this entirely alien concept, they fail to comprehend the need for boundaries. Moreover, it is possible that like most men on the faculty, the principal derived pleasure from the view of his students' barely clad legs. I most certainly did. And though I would have much preferred to feast my eyes on those young girls, much to their chagrin, I took it upon myself to establish inspections at the beginning of my classes. While standing to greet me good morning, my students were now fully aware that, for this gaijin sensei's classes, all skirts must be below their knees. My, how times have changed. The fox now actually protects the chickens. But such are the multiple paradoxes of Japan. It was in this childish society that I evolved into complete adulthood, it was in this conformist society where I learned to embrace my individuality. And it was in this environment of endless sexual availability that I shook my sexual demons.

JAPAN'S DASHED OPPORTUNITY

In 2006 former Prime Minister Junichiro Koizumi was presented a grand opportunity to transition women in Japan, at least symbolically to the 21st century, by modifying the Imperial House law. According to the archaic regulation established in 1947 only male heirs with emperors on their father's side can ascend the imperial throne. However, in surprising progressiveness, a government panel in 2005 recommended revisions to the law, in order to allow women's ascent to the throne, given that a boy had not been born to the world's oldest hereditary monarchy in 41 years. So averse was the monarchy to any change in the law, in November 2005, renowned alcoholic Prince Tomohito proposed that Naruhito, Crown Prince of Japan, should take on a concubine for the purpose of producing a son. Others advocated divorce between the Crown Princess and Prince, hence affording the Prince an opportunity to try for a son with another partner.

With a majority of the public's support, Koizumi San - the man with the butterfly hairdo - pursued legislative amendments which would bring the monarchy into contemporary times. But it all was too good to be true, when this monumental attempt to modernize the monarchy was abruptly halted by rumors of Princess Kiko's unexpected pregnancy. Suddenly, fanfare for the new proposal, shifted to despair among 173 lawmakers, for the *hasty* modifications to a tradition which deifies the male monarchy. The national momentum which had gathered behind the proposed change of law was reversed to a national wait and see event, as law makers and the public held their breath waiting to hear the sex of the fetus. It was a boy, whose birth drove a stake through any plans for female succession.

Incoming Prime Minister Shinzo Abe sealed the book shut on the matter, in actions which echoed the 16th century Scottish theologian John Knox's view on the status of women. "To promote a woman to bear rule, superiority, dominion or empire above any realm, nation, or city," he wrote in 1558, "is repugnant to nature, contumely to God and the subversion of good order." Unbeknownst to him, Knox may well have been a spokesman for the Liberal Democratic Party. By shelving the female ascension issue, the Liberal Democratic Party has all but secured Japanese women's position as village bicycles for Western men and baby making machines for Japanese men.

EPILOGUE

By June 2007 Shoko, diligent and determined, had completed her first year at community college in preparation for the mammoth undertaking of attending law school in the US. And by the same time, the novelty of *Disneyland* had long expired. I had been on all the rides, consumed all the cotton candy I could, and now it was time to leave. My arrival here had been nothing less than a monumental rebirth, the kind which people describe upon finding God. Landing on the serene shores of Japan provided me the omni-present beauty for which I had been yearning since my torturous childhood and especially a few years before my departure from the States, where I had been entangled in a litany of *byaby madda almshouse*. It had become somewhat of a routine to be interned in correctional facilities, where after my first visit I was rendered unemployable. One such internment was somewhat positive and fairly lucrative.

During my final quarter at UCLA in August of 1994, while napping in Kirchhoff Hall on a break from my studies, I was jarred from slumber and summoned outside by a UCLAPD officer.
"Let me see your ID!" he demanded.
"Huh?"
"Let me see your student ID."
"Why?"

The day before I had been visiting my daughter in San Francisco where I had literally bit the dust in a skateboarding accident down one of those treacherous San Francisco hills. Danika then 7 years old found it incurably hilarious to watch her dad eat pavement right before her eyes and would remind me of the incident for years, often times spread out on the floor in laughter. A gregarious and extroverted laugh-a-holic, she enjoyed nothing more than her piano, romping and hearty laughter and on at least one occasion my brush with death – at least that's what I thought on the way to that intimate encounter with the asphalt – made her laugh until she peed. As if run over by earth moving equipment, my entire outer right thigh was shredded and so were my plaid Levy's docker shorts and navy silk shirt. The following day, except for flip-flops I wore the same tattered outfit to school. In fact everyday for three weeks I donned the same mangled shorts, as they were the only garments which could air my wounds.

"Show me your student ID!" The officer demanded at the top of his voice attracting an audience.

"And just what is your probable cause and reasonable suspicion for randomly requesting to see my ID, when as far as I know I am still in the United States of America and not in South Africa?" I responded, hoping to PISS him off. Of course this was pre-George W, a long ago ere when Americans were actually entitled to civil rights. It worked, he took the bait. Immediately he slammed me against the wall on the steps outside Kirchhoff Hall and all I saw were dollar signs circling around in my head.

"That's it, you're going to jail for battery of a police officer."

After 40 hours in Los Angeles county jail all charges were dropped and I was abruptly released, after which I immediately procured the services of a less than competent attorney. The officer in question was a rogue African-American who had made it a career to terrorize students, especially those of African decent. From conversations with him on the way to Los Angeles county jail, it appeared as though he suffered inferiority complexes having not obtained a tertiary education and was envious of Negroes studying. In a few months UCLA settled out of court in an amount far south of 6 figures, but nonetheless a much appreciated graduation present. And incidentally, ten years later in 2004 I was contacted in Japan to testify on behalf of a student who had been shot by the same officer.

With child support payments in deep arrears, salaries from gainful employment were garnished well beyond the point of sustainability. But the proverbial straw occurred when the state of California raided my bank account, leaving me with a zero balance. Homeless, penniless, unemployed and unemployable in the land of opportunity, called for drastic measures. But not the types requiring a handgun, for since my childhood I had held a strong aversion to confinement.

Years earlier researching the process to teach English in Asia, it was perfectly clear that holding a Jamaican passport would be a hindrance not just to employment, but to travel in general. And it was then that I had begun the process of applying for United States citizenship so I could leave. Probability which heretofore had been an unrelenting enemy, transformed to a staunch ally when citizenship was finally granted two years after my application. Immediately after swearing in, on that very day I applied for a United States passport, calculating that the information gap between naturalization and obtaining a passport, would mask my ineligibility for a passport on account of the child support in arrears. I was right and once again my new best friend probability, shone upon me in the form of a telephone interview following my correspondence with only three Language Schools in Japan. Two weeks later the school sent me a one way ticket to Kansai. It must be known that on the eve of my departure to Japan, I was slaving away in a work furlough program, retrieving rubbish on Interstate 580.

Had I subscribed to the notion of a God, I would have interpreted this as divine intervention. I had wanted to be in the world but not of it, isolated yet integrated, and Japan was exactly what the proverbial doctor had ordered. Ironically Nippon also provided an opportunity to be a child again, yet mature into self-actualization. It was respite from perpetual drama, baby mama and law enforcement drama, not uncommon to the Negroe male in America. And having shaken my depression I had sought a fresh new start for the new millennium. Besides, having voted for Al Gore in the 2000 election I was more that happy to leave the United States after observing the post-election fiasco.

But never in my wildest dreams did I, or could I have imagined fulfilling my boyhood fantasies of unlimited, unfettered, unprotected, irresponsible hedonistic sex with women of my exclusive preference. While most men would live in dread of plummeting libido, especially at 40, I welcomed with fanfare, the liberation from my sexual obsession since I was seven. My sexual experiences in Japan brought to mind my childhood obsession with sweetened condensed milk, which I would frequently drink from my palms or straight from the can. This infuriated my mother, whose budget afforded her the purchase of only one or two cans a month. Around my 9th birthday, to my surprise, mother brought me a can of Nestle sweetened condensed milk, for my own personal consumption.

"It's yours," she said. "I bought it for you."

I thought she had lost the remainder of her mind. For how were we suddenly able to afford such decadence, when the price of one can dented her salary so severely? But little was I aware of my mother's secret plan. Eagerly I drank, and drank, and then drank some more until I was nauseous and even then, continued to drink. After consuming almost three quarters of the can, I hurled for what seemed like days, but was only minutes, never to touch sweetened condensed milk again. In similar fashion my addiction was cured in Japan, where after the first three years of sex on tap, it literally became cloying. But my departure would not be for another four years.

Judging from cell phone videos and photographs, among my friends, my hedonistic experiences in Japan were tame. The opportunity cost of documenting my thoughts observations and experiences, meant that my philandering had to be at least curtailed for a year and ten months. But in fact, the thrill was gone and it was no longer exciting to have this revolving army of women flowing to and from my apartment. I had simply outgrown the need, though not the urge, though it too had subsided to normal levels.

Throughout my nearly three decades of wanderlust and slacker existence, from Jamaica, to the US, then the UK, bumming around Europe, back to the US then to Japan and travels around Asia, the lessons have been many. But most profound, is the lesson that we are all entangled in this web called culture, from which most humans cannot escape. My international observation has taught me that all humans are products of nothing more than our DNA and socialization. And though I spent most of my life until recently in unspeakable misery, I overcame. Thanks initially to diffidence and fear, then later to naïve optimism, and finally to therapy, education and international exploration, I did not remove myself from life and now feel fortunate to have arrived in midlife self-actualized, ready for the next chapter.

After reading the posted MySpace excerpts of this book, Morgan Hines, a West Midlands Briton of Jamaican parents messaged me in January '08. He had been afflicted with the same preference as I. Upon hearing of my pending departure from Japan, Morgan wired me a deposit on my Kobe apartment and its contents, rented out his house in the UK and sold his belongings. Three months after our initial contact, I collected him at the Kansai International airport and almost immediately, beginning on the airport limousine en route to his new place of residence his avalanche had begun.

January '08 also marked a year and a half since Shoko's departure from Japan. And after exposure to the freedom of the West, like most Japanese women with similar experiences, returning to her native land was anathema to her. So after receiving the results of my second AIDS test in Japan, and at least my tenth internationally since 1987, I repatriated to the States on May 4, 2008 where we jumped the broom 19 days later.

BIBLIOGRAPHY

Books

The Enigma of Japanese Power (Karel Van Wolferensen)
Culture Matters (Lawrence E. Harrison & Samuel P. Huntington)
The Japanese Have A Word For It (Boye Lafeyette De Mente)
Shutting Out the Sun (Michael Zielenziger)
Selling Songs And Smiles (Anne Goodwin)

Newspapers

The International Herald Tribune/Asahi Shinbun
Depression spreads in a struggling populace. September 20, 2003
Xenophobic manga: A worrying fad. November 21, 2005
Foreign banks vilified after Japan stock error.
     December 17, 2005 (New York Times)
The blame game in Tokyo. December. 2005 (Bloomberg News)
The long and short of how the world works. December 28, 2005
Monstrous crimes have roots in sick society. January 18, 2006
Rallying cry: 173 lawmakers oppose the 'hasty' move to allow female
     monarchs. February, 2006
From ostracized class, a hero for Koreans. February 23, 2006
Stressed-out pets: Why your dog might turn on you. June, 2006
Boy, 16, admits arson that killed 3 in his family. June 23, 2006
Mother held in slaying of daughter's schoolmates. February, 2006
Corporate character goods harness power of 'cute.' February 17, 2006
'Good wife' said to be lonely, at times violent. February 27, 2006
Teen poisoner sent to juvenile institute. May 2, 2006
Teen arrested over fire that killed father. July 4, 2006
The big business of boy meets girl. August 18, 2006
School's a drag for 10% of Tokyo kids. 2006
Japan 'unsuitable' for child-rearing. 2006
Spiritual convention's fortunes on the rise. October 7, 2006
Mewling about kittens is slightly hypocritical. October 14, 2006
NPA: More cases of teens killing parents. October 16, 2006
Teacher incited bullying against boy. October 17, 2006

Cop stabbed himself to get out of work. May, 2007

Cheerful boy transforms into 'loner' suspect in mother's beheading. May 15, 2007.

Japan must take steps to tackle poverty. May 18, 2007

Worked up: Japan's dismal labor productivity. June, 2007

10% of workers thought of suicide. July 13, 2007

The Daily Yomiuri

3 mil. had mental disorders in '05. June 2007

The Japan Times

Chlamydia rate for 16-18 crowd seen topping 10%. December 3, 2004

Unwrapping the 'nonsense' of Valentine's Day. February 14, 2006

The case for a baby princess. February 14, 2006

"Paris syndrome" leaves Japanese tourists in shock. October 23, 2006 (Reuters)

Everyone neglecting problem: experts (article regarding bullying) November 24, 2006

No stopping preteens walking on wild side. November 26, 2006

Pervy teachers showing unhealthy interest in kids. December 17, 2006

Suspect tried to cover up dismemberment of sister's body, police say. January 5, 2007

The decline and fall of the Japanese cop. February 4, 2007

The growing idiocy of teachers. February 20, 2007

SDF deploys perky mascot to boast cuddly image. March 1, 2007

Japanese working women still serve the tea. (Washington Post Foreign Service) March 2, 2007

Rising child-abuse deaths draw national scrutiny. March 19, 2007

Japan's love affairs with sex. April 29, 2007

Photos of preteen girls in thongs now big business. May 3, 2007

Baby hatch gives rise to empty moralizing. May 27, 2007

Shocking tales of Japan's 'idiot parents.' September 9,2007

Japan faces hunger pains as poor slip through net. October 2, 2007

Japan's Keystone Cops lack the knack. September 16, 2007

The Jamaica Daily Gleaner

Social riddles rooted in cultural identity. May 15, 2005

Magazines

Time

The wasted asset: Japan's gender crisis. August 29, 2005

Asia's over-scheduled kids. March 27, 2006

The most homophobic place on earth? April 12, 2006

The Kansai Scene

No sex please, we're married. June, 2006

Medical Emergency. May, 2008

The Economist

Sexual equality. May 28, 2005

Internet

JapanToday.com

Child mortality rate in Japan 2nd highest in world. August 8, 2008

Cartoon guide to Foreign Ministry featuring 'Detective Conan' issued.
April 6, 2007

Gov't to drop plan to allow for female monarch. January 4, 2007

Man, 53, kills 83-year-old mother after being told to get a job.
January 5, 2007

Student held for killing sister cites college exam pressure.
January 6, 2007

Health minister Yanagisawa refers to women as 'birth-giving
machines.' January 28, 2007

Assemblyman calls Fukushima, other women 'rusted machines.'
Februray 27, 2007

Amnesty attacks Ibuki's human rights remarks. February 28, 2007

Fifteen percent of women aged 20-24 have self-inflicted injuries.
March 13, 2007

Tokyo teacher fired for uploading dead children's images.
March 20, 2007

Teen holding bag with severed head shows up at Fukushima police
station, saying he killed mother. May 15, 2007

Australia accuses Japan of 'dummy-spit' over whales. June 4, 2007

OECD report indicates serious physician shortage in Japan.
July 25, 2007

192 cases found where 5 or more hospitals rejected pregnant women.
September 28, 2007

By age 40, 1 in 10 Japanese men still virgin. June 1, 2006
Animal cruelty rife in Japan. November 15, 2006

New York Times
   Victims Say Japan Ignores Sex Crimes Committed by teachers.
   June 29, 2003

Mainichi Shinbun
   VD doctor openly sore over state of Japan's genital health.
   June 20, 2005

The Guardian
   Japan's virgin wives turn to sex volunteers. April 4, 2005
   Whole lotta love needed if Japan birthrate to grow. March 16, 2007

The American Psychological Association
   Report on the sexualization of girls and women. April 2007

PsychologyToday.com
   Why kids kill parents

World Health Organization

AsiaTimes.com
   Japan: Land of rising poverty. February 11, 2005

Legal Affairs Magazine:
   Land of the rising Lawyer? Article by Annie Murphy Paul

Japan Children's Rights Network crnjapan.com

ACKNOWLEDGEMENTS

Ena, DeShawn and Cenea Jones
Ena: thanks for accepting me in your home and being a mother in my troubled teenage years.

DeShawn
For being a brother and the greatest influence on my personality.

The Muzios
For adopting me at the ripe old age of twenty and showing me a working model of family.

Grandma
For planting the wanderlust bug at such an early age. At nine years old, beholding your US citizenship certificate and passport had a profound effect.

The College of San Mateo
The most impacting of all my educational experience, Thanks for planting the seed of self-confidence.

Tim Stringari
For initiating the path to recovery

Dr. Zelte Crawford
"You're Black," you once said to me. "You can't afford to go to no San Francisco State University, or Cal State Hayward. You gotta go to a Stanford, or a UC Berkeley, or a UCLA!"

Michael Pariser
An immeasurably gifted therapist.

Carolyn Ramsey & Kitty Brown
For your academic encouragement

Mr. and Mrs. T
For encouraging me to write about my observations in Japan

KT
For friendship and inspiration

Rick Edelstein
For showing me how to be completely at ease with being vulnerable.

Dr. Beraclauf
Not once were you judgemental during my frequent episodes of STDs

Irie Lammi
For your everlasting friendship and for your guidance on the first twenty-five pages.

Edited by Susette Burton and Nancy Rousseau

Cover design by Stefhen Bryan

Illustrated by Shuji Goshomura

Made in the USA